Reviews for Other Ghost Books by Troy Taylor

Historians and cavers alike will find a wealth of information contained in DOWN IN THE DARKNESS and Taylor, a caver himself, also recounts stories of lost treasure caves and disputed civilizations underground. There is nothing better than a good cave book when you just can't get underground. This book should help you through those desperate times. Put on your helmet, turn down the lights and enjoy a unique journey into the dark, ghost-infested underworld.
PAUL STEWARD - National Speological Society News

Troy Taylor has brought a new level of professionalism to the field with the GHOST HUNTER'S GUIDEBOOK, which stands as the best and most authoritative book written to date on ghost investigation. Both beginners and experienced investigators alike should make this book their bible... it gives the straight savvy... the material is grounded, practical and informative. It comes as no surprise that Taylor's book has received international praise!
ROSEMARY ELLEN GUILEY, author of ENCYCLOPEDIA OF GHOSTS & SPIRITS

SEASON OF THE WITCH is the best documented and most definitive work of the Bell Witch to date! Mr. Taylor has outdone himself in researching and collecting the material necessary to thoroughly examined and address this most mysterious tale ... I highly recommend this book to anyone interested in the full story of the Bell Witch!
DALE KACZMAREK, author of WINDY CITY GHOSTS

THE GHOST HUNTER'S GUIDEBOOK offers a wealth of modern and really valuable information regarding sophisticated detection equipment, investigation procedures and methods... should be essential reading for anyone in the field of paranormal research, whatever their level of interest or knowledge in the subject.
ANDREW GREEN, author of 500 BRITISH GHOSTS & HAUNTINGS

GHOST BOOKS BY TROY TAYLOR

HAUNTED DECATUR (1995)
MORE HAUNTED DECATUR (1996)
GHOSTS OF MILLIKIN (1996 / 2001)
WHERE THE DEAD WALK (1997 / 2002)
DARK HARVEST (1997)
HAUNTED DECATUR REVISITED (2000)
FLICKERING IMAGES (2001)

GHOSTS OF SPRINGFIELD (1997)
THE GHOST HUNTER'S HANDBOOK (1997)
THE NEW GHOST HUNTER'S HANDBOOK (1998)
GHOSTS OF LITTLE EGYPT (1998)

HAUNTED ILLINOIS (1999 / 2001)
SPIRITS OF THE CIVIL WAR (1999)
THE GHOST HUNTER'S GUIDEBOOK (1999 / 2001)
SEASON OF THE WITCH (1999/ 2002)
HAUNTED ALTON (2000 / 2003)
HAUNTED NEW ORLEANS (2000)
BEYOND THE GRAVE (2001)
NO REST FOR THE WICKED (2001)
THE HAUNTING OF AMERICA (2001)
HAUNTED ST. LOUIS (2002)
INTO THE SHADOWS (2002)
CONFESSIONS OF A GHOST HUNTER (2002)
HAUNTED CHICAGO (2003)
DOWN IN THE DARKNESS (2003)
FIELD GUIDE TO HAUNTED GRAVEYARDS (2003)

GHOST TOURS
HAUNTED DECATUR, ILLINOIS TOURS (1994 – 2003)
HISTORY & HAUNTINGS TOURS OF GRAFTON, ILLINOIS (FROM 1999)
HISTORY & HAUNTINGS TOURS OF ST. CHARLES, MISSOURI (FROM 2000)
HISTORY & HAUNTINGS TOURS OF ST. LOUIS, MISSOURI (FROM 2002)
HISTORY & HAUNTINGS TOURS OF ALTON, ILLINOIS (FROM 1998)

FIELD GUIDE TO HAUNTED GRAVEYARDS

A Research Guide to Investigating America's Haunted Cemeteries

BY TROY TAYLOR

- A Whitechapel Productions Press Publication -

This book (as with all of the others) is dedicated to Amy, my light and inspiration. She has spent more time traipsing around cemeteries with me -- haunted and otherwise -- than she would likely care to remember. Thanks for all that you do because none of this would be possible without you!

Original Cover Artwork Designed by
Michael Schwab, M & S Graphics & Troy Taylor
Visit M & S Graphics at www.msgrfx.com

THIS BOOK IS PUBLISHED BY
- Whitechapel Productions Press -
A Division of the History & Hauntings Book Co.
515 East Third Street - Alton, Illinois -62002
(618) 465-1086 / 1-888-GHOSTLY
Visit us on the Internet at www.historyandhauntings.com

First Edition - December 2003
ISBN: 1-892523-34-5

Printed in the United States of America

THE HAUNTED FIELD GUIDE SERIES

Welcome to the new book in a continuing series from
Whitechapel Productions Press that will be dedicated to
providing the readers with "field guides" to not only haunted
places, but to ghost research as well. In the books to come, we
will continue to take you beyond the edge of the unknown and
provide detailed listings, maps and directions to haunted
places all over the Midwest and America, plus additional books
on ghost research and more!

We hope that you continue to enjoy the series and that you will
journey with us in the future as we take you past the limits of
hauntings in America and beyond the furthest reaches of your
imagination!

Happy Hauntings!

- Table of Contents -

Introduction

A few years ago, I wrote a book that dealt with what I felt were the darkest elements of ghostly tales -- those stories that delved into haunted cemeteries. As I said then, and still believe, there is not a single person among us who has not contemplated the mystery of death. For most people, it is the greatest fear that we will ever have to deal with. For this reason, we have devised not only rituals and practices to try and understand death but we also immortalized it with cemeteries, grave markers and with our most frightening haunts, legends and lore.

This book is about all of those things. But it is not only about the tales of ghosts and spooks but also about how to find and research the places where such tales -- and hopefully the ghosts and spooks -- can be found. With all of the books and how-to guides that I have written in the past, I have never delved as deeply into finding out the reason behind the haunting as I have within these pages. I hope to not only send you to the haunted graveyards but also hope to equip you with the knowledge that you'll need for a complete investigation when you arrive there.

But why this book? And especially in light of the fact that so many people have disregarded cemetery ghost research in the past? It is a common belief among most ghost hunters that cemeteries are not usually the best places to find ghosts. While most would fancy a misty, abandoned graveyard to be the perfect setting for a ghost story, such stories are not as common as you might believe. Almost all of us would agree that a place becomes haunted after a traumatic event or unexpected death occurs at that location. History is filled with stories of houses that have become haunted after a murder has taken place there, or after some horrible event occurs that echoes over the decades as a haunting.

Let's be honest though, does anything like this ever really occur in a cemetery? I think we can say that murders and horrific events do sometimes take place in resting places for the dead but no one spends enough time in a graveyard during their life to linger there after death. Most spirits remain in this world because of some sort of unfinished business, so this seems to leave out a cemetery as a place where such business might remain undone. Ghosts who haunt graveyards seem to be a different sort than those you might find in a haunted house. Most of these ghosts seem to be connected to the cemetery in some way that excludes events that occurred during their lifetime. The events that tie them to these places usually occurred after death, rather than before. In other cases, the ghosts seem to be seeking eternal rest that eludes them at the spot where their physical bodies are currently found. Cemeteries gain a reputation for being haunted for reasons that include the desecration of the dead and grave robbery, unmarked or forgotten burials, natural disasters that disturb resting places, or sometimes even because the deceased was not properly buried at all!

I have long been intrigued with cemeteries and with the ghosts who are said to haunt them. However, looking for ghosts in a cemetery can often cause a dilemma and it is here where we find ourselves straddling the fine line between "ghost hunting" and "ghost research".

The reason that we run into problems investigating in locations like cemeteries (or perhaps I should say *especially* in cemeteries) is the way that such investigations are often conducted. Conducting paranormal research in cemeteries really shouldn't be that much different than conducting an investigation in someone's home or in a building. Every investigation has to be organized and there has to be a point to it, otherwise we can't legitimately call it "research" or even an "investigation". To be able to conduct an actual investigation, we have to have rules and criteria to go by. The ghost hunter should have his own checklist of items to be studied at the site because while wandering around in a cemetery taking pictures is fun, it does not constitute an actual investigation.

The first thing to do when preparing for a vigil is to choose the site. This should not be done by simply picking a cemetery at random. Despite what some people apparently believe, not every cemetery is haunted. However, there are hundreds of sites where strange stories have been told, dark history has taken place and where people have encountered things that cannot be explained.

Once you do find a place that seems promising, start looking into the history of it so that you can decide if it is a location for legitimate research. You can make your decision based on the information learned by answering the following questions:

1. What is the history of this location?
2. What events have taken place here to lead you to believe that it might have become haunted?
3. What paranormal events have been reported in the past?

If the answers to these questions lead you to suspect that something ghostly may be taking place at the location, then you should consider organizing an investigation. Later in the book, we'll take a closer look at how such investigations can be done so that authentic evidence might be collected.

One of the biggest problems that you will run into when investigating a cemetery though is the "ghost lore" of the place. This is the one thing that will have almost any investigator chasing false leads and looking for history that does not exist. "Ghost lore" is the practice that society has of trying to explain strange events by attaching a legend to them. In many cases, stories of a "lady in white" or a "headless railroad brakeman" (and think about how many of those are out there!) have been invented to try and add understanding to sightings of ghostly white mists and mysterious glowing lights. Without these chilling stories, the weird locations might never be explained. To put it simply, people just have a need to try and explain things -- they crave a reason for everything, supernatural or not.

In many cases, these locations truly are what we would consider haunted. Unfortunately though, the true facts behind the haunting may not have anything to do with the legend that is associated with it. There may be another reason entirely for the strange phenomena reported but what often occurred was that, many years ago, local residents felt the need to attach an explanation to events they could not understand. A witness may have glimpsed some sort of pale apparition that looked like a flowing dress, and thus, the legend of a "lady in white" was born.

Cemeteries seem to be especially prone to this, as the mystery of death gives birth to legends of its own. By following the trail of the "ghost lore" to the local graveyard, we have to be careful about believing everything that we hear about the place. Many of the stories that make up the so-called "history" of the place are liable to be filled more with legend than anything else. Still though, even the folklore can be a place to start with many locations. Those tales had to get started for some reason, right?

My own investigations into cemetery ghosts have been many, but like most ghost hunters, many of them have been uneventful. I have chased stories and hauntings from vanishing hitchhikers to glowing tombstones and usually have come up with nothing. Thankfully though, I love a good story and as a writer, graveyards have given me years of tales, legends and eerie haunts. How many have been authentic cases of the paranormal? Not as many as I would have liked -- but of course, not all of them have been fruitless, which is why I decided to put this book together in the first place.

Within these pages, I have created what I feel is not only a helpful guide to the history of American cemeteries but also an unveiling of some of the practices, rituals and details behind funerals, graveyards and death that often cause such confusion to the researcher. From there, the reader will also find ways to research the histories of cemeteries, discover where to find death records and certificates, causes of death, what tombstones inscriptions mean and more. Then, the book will veer into the realm of the paranormal with an exploration of "portals" and "crossover points", a how-to guide on how to conduct cemetery investigations, an update on the best way to photograph cemetery ghosts, cases studies of some haunted graveyards and finally, a state-by state guide to America's most haunted cemeteries. I believe that you will find this to be the most complete book on cemetery ghost research ever compiled and a one of a kind addition to your library.

This is what the book contains but it still does not explain why I wanted to write it in the first place. The idea of if had come to me some time back, while contemplating an update on the *Ghost Hunter's Guidebook,* my sort-of all around research guide into ghosts. In an earlier edition of the book, I had really downplayed the importance of cemetery research because of the shoddy techniques that were being used to gather "evidence" -- mainly consisting of running around cemeteries with digital cameras in hand taking "ghost photos". But as my own research in the graveyard research field continued, I began to realize that there really was something to it and so, rather than criticize what was being done, I decided to toss out some suggestions about how to do it better. Even with these additions though, I still had not covered the subject to the extent that I wanted to.

However, nearly three years passed before I finally started on this book -- why? Well, I mentioned the idea of putting it together to an acquaintance of mine who is well-respected in the paranormal field and he literally rolled his eyes about it. Like so many others (myself included at one time) he discounted the idea of cemetery ghost research because of the antics of a few so-called "ghost hunters" who believe that digital cameras are the only tool you need to look for evidence of ghosts. I confess that his reaction did put me off the book for a time, but not for the reasons that you might think. I was not embarrassed to write it -- instead, I was all the more anxious to do it correctly.

You see, while I may have questioned the legitimacy of ghost research for a time, I have never questioned the legitimacy of graveyard ghosts themselves. My first introduction to this type of haunting came through the "ghost lore" of the cemetery -- the ghostly stories that involve those spirits who have risen from the grave for various reasons. I had always been fascinated with such tales, whether in books or in movies, but it would turn out to be in a cemetery that I would have my first encounter with something that I could not explain. I was in high school at the time and was already known for collecting tales of local hauntings and haunted houses. I began to hear eerie stories about a place not far from where I grew up in Central Illinois called Peck Cemetery. It was (and is) a remote and isolated place, enclosed by a rusted iron fence, and hidden from the road by thick woods. It was surrounded by heavy forest and trees loomed over the grounds. In addition, the graveyard was accessible only by way of a rutted dirt road and through a metal gate, which was usually kept locked. Trespassers were not welcome here and the reason for this was since the 1970's, Peck Cemetery had been a popular place for teenagers to go and have parties and attempt to scare themselves silly. If this were the end of it, that would not be a problem. Unfortunately, a small minority of these teenagers also felt the need to vandalize the cemetery. The burial ground was soon in deplorable condition as the majority of the stones had been toppled and broken.

Stories had already been told for a number of years before I heard about the place that suggested something lurked in this cemetery. Witnesses and late night visitors to the cemetery had come forward to claim a number of strange happenings and to recall many frightening events. Such stories included apparitions in the graveyard, inexplicable cries, whispers and voices, hooded figures, eerie lights, and even the sound of a woman's scream that seemed to come from nowhere.

After hearing such stories, I was determined to see this place, no matter how hard it apparently was to find. Because of its remote location, I needed to track down someone who had already been there and soon found a couple of acquaintances who had made the trip -- and returned alive. I was informed that it was a matter of bravery for visitors to the cemetery to go there late at night and to park their cars at the gates to the graveyard with their headlights pointed inside. As the gate was located at one corner of Peck Cemetery, they could angle the car so that the headlights would shine back to the farthest corner. The visitor's courage came into question when they left the car and walked all the way to this dark corner and then turned and walked back. It doesn't sound like much to the reader, I'm sure, but take my word for it -- it was not a pleasant prospect when you actually arrived at the place.

I arranged with some friends to go out to the cemetery the following Saturday night. Even then, I was more than a little bit of a skeptic when it came to other people's encounters but I figured that since there were so many stories told about this one location, at least a few of them had to be true, right?

A few nights later, we made the trip out to Peck Cemetery. It was (believe it or not) a dark and stormy night and as we turned off the hard road and onto the gravel lane that ran back to the woods and the cemetery, everyone in the car grew quiet. As we traveled along the rutted lane, we followed it as it dipped down into a low area that was filled with a spooky fog. After we reached the top of the hill on the other side, we turned the car sharply to the left so that the nose of it was up to the cemetery gates. The headlights stretched out in front of us and illuminated the jumble of broken stones and the glistening raindrops on the overhanging tree branches. Unfortunately, it was what the lights did not illuminate that had me bothered -- namely the far corner of the cemetery, which we planned to walk to in just a few moments.

My friend turned off the ignition of his vintage Camaro and we sat there for a moment with no one speaking. There was absolutely no sound but the drip of water on the roof of the automobile. I think that at this point, we had managed to spook ourselves so badly that if one of us had suggested that we leave and go home, we likely all would have agreed. As it was though, no one did and we quietly got out of the car. Once outside, I think that we finally realized how nervous we had been making ourselves and we started to relax. Joking and laughing, we started off across the cemetery, following the twin beams of light that pointed off into the darkness.

As we walked further and further away from the car, the laughter ended and we began to pick up the pace a little bit. I know that I simply wanted to get to the other side of the cemetery and then get back again. I can't really explain what made me feel this way (and I am sure my friends shared the feeling) but if you ever get the chance to visit Peck Cemetery, you will understand it. There is just a bad feeling here, a coldness that seeps into your bones and leaves you with an uncomfortable sensation that you just can't put your finger on.

Within a few minutes, we had reached the farthest corner of the graveyard and we turned to start back towards the car. Nothing had occurred on the trip over -- no lights, no ghosts and not even a single sound, save for the rain that was dripping off the trees. Feeling much bolder, we began walking back to the car, wandering to look at some of the vandalized tombstones as we made our way back. We were convinced by this time that nothing out of the ordinary was going to occur.

We were wrong.

We had reached the halfway point on our return trip when suddenly, the headlights on the car that we had left in the cemetery gates snapped out. The graveyard was plunged into darkness! Needless to say, we froze where we were standing. We now had a major predicament on our hands -- the question was whether to run back to the car, and possibly meet whatever had turned out the headlights, or to simply stay where we were, in a cemetery that we now had started to believe just might be haunted after all? We argued both points for a few moments, mostly concerned about the fact that the doors to the car had been locked. How had the lights been turned out?

We decided to compromise. We would return to the car, we agreed, but we would do so very, very cautiously. The four of us managed to get all of the way back across the cemetery and we crept up on the silent, and now darkened, automobile. After peering under the car and into the shadowy backseat, we determined that no one was hiding nearby. However, we had not solved the mystery of how the headlights had turned out? Could the battery have gone dead? Were we going to be stranded out here until someone came along to help us?

Concerned, the driver quickly unlocked the door and started to get inside. He was about halfway into the car when he stopped and his face turned white. His eyes were big when he looked over at me and he hurriedly climbed back out of the car again, stumbling a few feet away from the vehicle.

We asked him what was wrong and he simply told us that we needed to come and see how the lights had been turned out. Keep in mind, this was a 1960's era automobile and there were no fancy switches or time delays to control the headlights. The lights turned on and off by way of a knob that was fitted into the dash -- a knob that you pulled out to turn the lights on and pushed in to turn them off. My friend had left the knob pulled out when we had exited the car and started across the cemetery. Short of this knob, the only way that the headlights could have been turned out would have been to have the battery die during the few minutes when we were walking in the graveyard.

The battery was not dead. Somehow, through the locked doors and rolled tight windows, a hand had physically reached in and had punched the headlight knob to the "off" position.

And that was the end of the evening for us! I did not return again to Peck Cemetery for almost ten years. This occurrence remains fresh in my mind to this day and I have never forgotten it. Actually, I tend to get a fresh scattering of goose bumps whenever I re-tell it to anyone. It became my first experience with not only the unknown, but with graveyard ghosts as well. It would not be the last...

The first organized graveyard investigations that I got involved with concerned Greenwood Cemetery in Decatur, Illinois. If there is a single location in downstate Illinois that is more haunted than any other, it would undoubtedly be this cemetery. I had grown up in the area and had long heard the ghostly tales of this place. My interest later turned to the truth behind the stories and this is when I began researching the history and the real-life haunts of the place. I have since written an entire book on nothing but the ghosts of this old cemetery and as it stands, I am the only person who has ever thoroughly researched its history as well. Even genealogists and historians have used the book as the best record that has been compiled about the cemetery to date.

The beginnings of the place though are a mystery. There is no record to say when the first burials took place in the area of land that would someday be Greenwood. It was not the city's first official burial ground, but the Native Americans who lived here first did use it as a burial site, as did the early settlers. The only trace they left behind were the large numbers of unmarked graves, scattered about the present-day grounds. During the decade of the 1820's, it is believed that local settlers did use this area and legend has it that even a few runaway slaves who did not survive their quest for freedom were buried on the grounds under the cover of night.

In March 1857, the Greenwood Cemetery Association was organized and the cemetery was incorporated into the city of Decatur. By 1900, Greenwood had become the most fashionable place in Decatur in which to be buried. It had also become quite popular as a recreational park and it was not uncommon to see noontime visitors enjoying their lunch on the grassy hills. Unfortunately though, by the 1920's, the cemetery was broke and could no longer be maintained. It was allowed to revert back to nature and it wasn't long before the cemetery began to resemble a forgotten graveyard with overgrown brush, fallen branches and tipped and broken gravestones. Hundreds of graves were left unattended and allowed to fall into disrepair. The stories and legends that would "haunt" Greenwood for years to come had taken root in the desolate conditions that existed in the oldest section of the graveyard. Tales of wandering spirits and glowing apparitions began to be told about the cemetery and decay and decline came close to bringing about the destruction of the place. The cemetery became a forgotten spot in Decatur, remembered only as a spooky novelty.

At this point, the cemetery was nearly in ruins. The roads were now only partially covered mud and cinder tracks that were so deeply rutted that they were no longer passable. The oaks, which had added beauty to the cemetery, had now become its greatest curse. The falls of leaves, which had not been raked away in years, were knee-deep in some places. Fallen branches from the trees littered the grounds, which were overgrown and tangled with weeds and brush. Water, time and vandals had wreaked havoc on Greenwood's grave markers. Years of rain, harsh weather and a lack of care had caused many stones to fall at angles and many more were simply lost altogether. Others lay broken and damaged beyond repair, having given up the fight with the elements.

In 1957 though, ownership and operation of the cemetery was taken over by the city of Decatur and the township crews would now maintain it. Despite this, the place has not lost its eerie reputation and the stories of ghosts and the unexplained still mingle with fact and fiction, blending a strangeness that is unparalleled by any other location in the haunted heart of Illinois.

There are many stories that plague the history of Greenwood Cemetery, including that of a bride who committed suicide when her fiancée was murdered and now haunts a lonely hill within the cemetery; Confederate prisoners who perished aboard a train that was passing through the city and who were buried on a hillside, only to restlessly haunt the area; a phantom woman who appears on a staircase; and more.

However, the most enduring mystery of the cemetery is likely the oldest. And it's the one piece of local lore that drew me to the graveyard in the first place. The story involves the "ghost lights" that appear on the south side of the burial grounds. These small globes of light have been reported here for many decades and are still reported today. I saw these lights myself a few years back and while I have no logical explanation for what they are, or why they appear here, the lore of the cemetery tells a strange and tragic story.

The legend tells of a flood that occurred many years ago, most likely around 1900-1905, which wiped out a portion of the cemetery. The Sangamon River, located just south of the cemetery, had been dammed in the late 1800's and was often prone to floods. During one particularly wet spring, the river overflowed its banks and washed into the lower sections of the cemetery. Tombstones were knocked over and the surging water even managed to wash graves away and to force buried caskets to the surface. Many of them went careening downstream on the swollen river.

Once the water receded, it took many days to find the battered remains of the coffins that had been washed down the river and many were never found at all. For some time after, farmers and fishermen were startled to find caskets, and even corpses, washing up on river banks some miles away. There were many questions as to the identities of the bodies and so many of them were buried again in unmarked and common graves. These new graves were placed on higher ground, up on the southern hills of Greenwood.

Since that time, it has been said that the mysterious lights have appeared on these hills. The stories say that the lights are the spirits of those whose bodies washed away in the flood. Their wandering ghosts are now doomed to search forever for the place where their remains are now buried.

Dozens of trustworthy witnesses have claimed to see the "spook lights" on the hill, moving in and out among the old, weathered stones. The mystery of the lights has managed to elude all those who have attempted to solve it. Many have tried to pass them off as reflections from cars passing over the lake - but what of sightings that date back to before Lake Decatur ever existed? In those days, a covered bridge over the Sangamon River took travelers along the old county highway and for many years, not a single automobile crossed it, as motorcars had not yet come to Decatur.

Whether the cause is natural or supernatural, the lights can still be seen along the edge of the graveyard today. Want to see them for yourself? Seek out the south hills of Greenwood some night by finding the gravel parking lot that is located across the road from the cemetery fence. Here, you can sit and observe the hills. You have to have a lot of patience, and may even have to make more than one trip, but eventually, you will probably be lucky enough to see the "ghost lights".

My own patience paid off for the first time back in 1991. I had been told about the "ghost lights" for several years from people who came to me with their strange stories. In fact, I first heard about the lights from family members who, when they were teenagers (and this would have been in the early 1930's), used to park their cars along the road south of the cemetery in hopes that the lights would appear. I first starting seeking out the lights for myself in the late 1980's but it would take several years before my persistence paid off.

One night, a friend that I worked with and I drove down to the cemetery to try and look for the lights. We waited there, sitting on the hood of the car, for about two hours, quietly talking and watching the hills that stretched out in front of us. It was a cloudy night, but just enough of the moon seeped through the clouds to softly illuminate the stones of the cemetery in the distance. My friend, Larry, spotted the first light as it moved at a fairly quick rate of speed from the lower part of the hill to the top. There, it vanished in a second, almost as if it had been switched off. More lights followed and I began to see them too as they darted and zipped among the trees and the stones, some shooting upward and others speeding off into the darkness and fading away. The "light show" lasted for about 15 minutes and then no more of them were seen.

I have since seen them on other occasions but still have no idea how to explain what I have seen on these hills. The lights appeared to be about the size of softballs and are white in color and tinged with a faint blue. They have an electric sort of glare to them, as though they were light bulbs, surging with energy. What could have created them?

Obviously, it's very possible that these lights might have a natural explanation. I do believe that they are paranormal in origin, but only paranormal in the sense that we don't have an explanation for what causes them yet. Many researchers have cited the causes for "spook lights" as being railroad tracks, power lines or sources of water. Almost every "spook light" location has one (or more) of these things in common. In the case of the Greenwood lights, we have all three. The lights are seen on a hillside that is only a few yards away from the Illinois Central rail line. In addition, there are power lines running next to the tracks and both the railroad tracks and the power lines cross over the Sangamon River. Given all of that, I would say that it's possible, and perhaps even likely, that the Greenwood lights have an explanation that is of this world, rather than the next one. In other words, they are not likely the restless souls of the dead.

I will tell you though, as you are sitting out on the south side of the cemetery in the dark and happen to catch a glimpse of the famous Greenwood "ghost lights", it's easier to believe they are ghosts than anything that we can explain away as a glitch of nature. The most important thing about this sighting to me though was that it took place at all. And this was not so much because I was able to view the mysterious lights but more because it proved to me that they actually appeared. This meant that there really was an element of truth to the legends that surrounded the cemetery. If the story of the ghost lights were true (or at least partially so), that meant that other ghostly tales of the place might be true as well.

Which brings us back full circle to why this book needed to be written in the first place -- because so many of us are curious about the existence of graveyard ghosts. And also because graveyard research can be done in a legitimate and authentic manner. It does not have to mean that we run around cemeteries at night, looking for so-called "orbs". It can be done with the same degree of professionalism that so many of us try to bring to investigations of haunted buildings, homes and property.

Can we prove that these locations are really haunted? Perhaps no more than we can prove that a house is haunted, at least in scientific terms. In a field where no absolute answers exist, no one has yet to provide absolute scientific proof that ghosts are real, simply because the spirits refuse to perform on command. To be able to prove something scientifically, it has to be duplicated over and over again under strict conditions. As we all know, the supernatural does not work in such a way. However, I have long maintained that such "proof" of the existence of ghosts is possible, if we can prove a location is haunted historically.

Ghost researchers can provide historical evidence of hauntings by gathering witness testimony and details about a ghost that may be present in a location. We can then research that gathered information and match it to the alleged ghost when it was still a living person. Better yet, we can collect testimony of events that occurred in the house by residents in the past and then match that evidence to current events that are now taking place. Having independent witnesses, of different time periods, with matching experiences makes for some very convincing evidence. Technically, we have "historically proven" that the house is haunted and that ghosts exist.

Many researchers have come to accept this way of thinking and have adopted it for their own investigations. The problems with graveyard ghosts arise though when we try and provide historical proof of the ghosts in cemeteries. Few researchers have been able to gather the data needed to explain why a cemetery might be haunted, which is why many established researchers think so poorly of this type of investigation.

Hopefully, this book will provide you with the tools needed to do this and soon, the graveyards that you research and investigate will no longer be enigmas where strange phenomena occurs but no one seems to know why. Remember though, I do not claim to have the last word when it comes to cemetery research. There are no "experts" in this field and no one has all of the answers. As with my other guides, I simply wanted to pass along some information that you may not have had before and then encourage you to change it, adapt it and work with it until it suits you and your specific investigations. There is much that we can learn from each other in this strange and wonderful field and I wish you the best of luck with all of your adventures.

Happy Hauntings!
Troy Taylor
Fall 2003

1. The American Cemetery

Death is the final darkness at the end of life. It has been both feared and worshipped since the beginnings of history. For this reason, our civilization has dreamed up countless practices and rituals to deal with and perhaps understand it. We have even personified this great unknown with a semi-human figure, the "Grim Reaper", and have given him a menacing scythe to harvest human souls with. Yet, death remains a mystery.

Maybe because of this mystery, we have chosen to immortalize death with stones and markers that tell about the people who are buried beneath them. We take the bodies of those whose spirits have departed and place them in the ground, or in the enclosure of the tomb, and place a monument over these remains that speaks of the life once lived. This is not only out of respect for the dead because it also serves as a reminder for the living. It reminds us of the person who has died -- and it also reminds us that someday, it will be our bodies that lie moldering below the earth.

The stone monuments became cemeteries, or repositories of the dead, where the living could come and feel some small connection with the one that passed on. The earliest of the modern cemeteries, or what is referred to as a "garden" cemetery, began in Europe in the 1800's. Such cemeteries are common today, but in times past, graveyards were sometimes hellish and frightening places.

Before the beginning of the Garden cemetery, the dead were buried strictly in the churchyards of Europe. For the rich, burial within the church itself was preferred. Princes, clerics and rich benefactors of the church came to regard such entombment as a right rather than a privilege and soon the buildings began to fill. The Church tried hard to limit such burials but the abuse of the arrangements (usually after a large sum of money had changed hands) soon had the churches packed with the bodies of the dead. The accompanying health risks for the living forced officials to stop the practice. From that point on, only bishops, abbots and "laymen of the first distinction" could be entombed within the church building.

For those who could not be buried inside of the church, the churchyard became the next best thing. Even here, one's social status depended on the section of the ground where you were buried. The most favored sites were those to the east, as close as possible to the church. In such a location, the dead would be assured the best view of the rising sun on the Day of Judgment. People of lesser distinction were buried on the south side, while the north corner of the graveyard was considered the Devil's domain. It was reserved for stillborns, bastards and strangers unfortunate enough to die while passing through the local parish.

Suicides, if they were buried in consecrated ground at all, were usually deposited in the north end, although their corpses were not allowed to pass through the cemetery gates. They had to be passed over the top of the stone wall. During the late Middle Ages, the pressure of space finally "exorcized" the Devil from the north end of the churchyard to make way for more burials.

As expected, it soon became nearly impossible for the churchyards to hold the bodies of the dead. As towns and cities swelled in population during the 1700's, a chronic shortage of space began to develop. The first solution to the problem was simply to pack the coffins more closely together. Later on, coffins were stacked atop one another and the earth rose to the extent that some churchyards towered twenty feet or more above that of the church floor. Another solution was to grant only limited occupation of a grave site. However, it

The churchyards of the past were very overcrowded and soon posed a risk to public health.

actually got to the point that occupancy of a plot was measured in only days, or even hours, before the coffin was removed and another was put in its place.

Not surprisingly, with so many bodies crammed into the churchyards, a protest began to arise from the people who lived nearby. The decaying bodies and the vile stench coming from the graveyard were considered a great risk to local health and doctors began penning stern warnings about the unsanitary conditions. One solution to this was to begin "cycling" the bodies through the cemetery, whereby fresh corpses were deposited on top of coffins long since rotted away by natural decomposition. The burial cycle would begin and then ten or twenty-year gaps would take place between subsequent burials at the same site.

As the population continued to grow however, it became impossible for the churchyards to hold the dead. By the middle 1700's, the situation had reached crisis proportions in France. Dirt and stone walls had been added around the graveyards in an attempt to hold back the bodies but they often collapsed, leaving human remains scattered about the streets of Paris. The government was finally forced into taking action. All of the churchyards in Paris were closed down for at least five years and cemeteries were established outside of the city to serve the needs of the parishes within the city itself.

Closure of the city graveyards was still not enough though. In 1786, it was decided to move all of the bodies from the Cemetery of the Innocents and transport

..ombs that had been carved beneath the southern part of the city. It .ssive undertaking. On the night of April 7, a long procession of funeral ., carrying the bones of tens of thousands of people, made its way to the catacombs. The wagons were escorted by torchlight and buoyed by the chanting of priests. There was no was to identify the individual remains, so it was decided to arrange the bones into rows of skulls, femurs and so on. It has been estimated that the Paris catacombs contain the bodies of between 3 and 6 million people.

In addition to the catacombs, four cemeteries were built within the confines of the city. They were Montmartre, Vaugiard, Montparnasse and Pere-Lachaise, the latter of which has become known as the first of the "garden" cemeteries. It was named after the confessor priest of Louis XIV and is probably the most celebrated burial ground in the world. As it was, the cemetery began in debt and caused a great amount of concern for the investors who created it. If Napoleon had been buried there, as he originally planned, the businessmen would have rested much easier. As it was, they were forced to mount a huge publicity campaign to persuade Parisians to be buried on the grounds. They even dug up the bones of famous Frenchmen who had been buried elsewhere and moved them to Pere-Lachaise.

Ironically, it was the burial of people who never lived at all that gained the cemetery its popularity. The novelist Honore de Balzac began burying many of the fictional characters in his books in Pere-Lachaise. On Sunday afternoons, readers from all over Paris would come to the cemetery to see the tombs that Balzac described so eloquently in his novels. Today, the walls of this graveyard hold the bodies of the most illustrious people in France and a number of other celebrities as well. The dead include Balzac, Victor Hugo, Colette, Marcel Proust, Chopin, Oscar Wilde, Sarah Bernhardt and Jim Morrison of the Doors (if you believe he's dead, that is).

Pere-Lachaise became known around the world for its size and beauty. It covered hundreds of acres and was landscaped and fashioned with pathways for carriages. It reflected the new creative age where art and nature could combine to celebrate the lives of those buried there.

Paris set the standard and America followed, but London was slow to adopt the new ways. The risks to public health came not only from the dank odors of the churchyards but from the very water the people drank. In many cases, the springs for the drinking supply tracked right through the graveyards. Throughout the early 1800's, the citizens of London still continued to be buried in the overflowing churchyards or in privately owned burial grounds within the city limits. The call for the establishment of cemeteries away from the population center became louder.

In 1832, the London Cemetery Company opened the first public cemetery at Kensal Green. It was made up of 54 acres of open ground and was far from the press of the city. From the very beginning, it was a fashionable place to be buried and in fact, was so prestigious that it can still boast the greatest number of royal burials outside of Windsor and Westminster Abbey. The dead here also include novelists Wilkie Collins, James Makepeace Thackery and Anthony Trollope, among others.

But if Kensal Green is London's most fashionable cemetery, then Highgate is its most romantic-- and its most legendary. Over time, the cemetery has crumbled and has fallen into gothic disrepair but for many years, it was considered the "Victorian Valhalla".

Highgate did not start out as a cemetery. In fact, in the late 1600's, the grounds were part of an estate owned by Sir William Ashhurst, who had built his home on the outskirts of a small, isolated hilltop community called Highgate. By 1836, the mansion had been sold, demolished and then replaced by a church. The grounds themselves were turned into a cemetery that was consecrated in 1839. Perhaps the most famous person buried here is Karl Marx, but he does not rest here alone. Other notables include Sir Ralph Richardson, George Eliot and several members of the Charles Dickens and Dante Rossetti families.

For years, it was a fashionable and desirable place to be buried, but as the decades passed, hard times came to Highgate. The owners steadily lost money and the monuments, statues, crypts and markers soon became covered with undergrowth and began to fall into disrepair. By the end of World War II, which saw an occasional German bomb landing on the burial ground, the deterioration of the place was out of control.

If there was ever a location that was perfect for a Gothic thriller, Highgate was the place. Dark visions were created from the crumbling stone angels, lost graves and the tombs ravaged by both time and the elements. As the cemetery continued to fall, trees grew slowly through the graves, uprooting the headstones. Dense foliage and growth gave the place the look of a lost city. Although paths were eventually cleared, nature still maintained its hold on Highgate and in such a setting, occultists and thrill seekers began to appear.

In the early 1970's, the legendary Hammer Films company discovered Highgate's moody setting and used it as a location for several of their horror films. Other companies began using the setting as well, attracting public interest to a place that had been largely forgotten. Soon, stories of grave robbing and desecration began to appear in local news reports.

Not long after, rumors circulated that Highgate was a haven for real vampires, as many claimed to see a particular creature hovering over the graves. Scores of "vampire hunters" regularly converged on the graveyard in the dead of night. Tombs were broken open and bodies were mutilated with wooden stakes driven into their chests. These stolen corpses, turning up in strange places, continuously startled local residents. One horrified neighbor to the cemetery discovered a headless body propped behind the steering wheel of his car one morning!

Highgate Cemetery continues to hold a fascination for visitors, including for ghost hunters. There have been a number of spirit sightings here, including that of a skeletal figure seen lurking near the main entrance. There is also a white, shrouded figure that has been seen staring into the distance, seemingly oblivious to the surroundings. However, if anyone tries to approach it, it vanishes and reappears in a nearby spot. Witnesses also claim to have seen a tall, thin figure in a black, wide-brimmed hat. This phantom has been seen fading into the high wall that surrounds the grounds. Another, more elusive ghost, is said to be that of a madwoman who prowls among the graves searching for the resting places of the children she murdered.

In America, the churchyard remained the most common burial place through the end of the 1800's. While these spots are regarded as picturesque today, years ago, they varied little from their European counterparts. The colonists viewed them as foul-smelling, unattractive eyesores and in 1800, Timothy Dwight described the local burial ground as "an unkempt section of the town common where the graves and fallen markers were daily trampled upon by people and cattle". This view of the local churchyard intensified by the middle 1800's, when public health reformers began to regard graveyards as a source of disease. As a result, most burials were prohibited from taking place within city limits after the Civil War.

After the founding of the Pere-Lachaise Cemetery in Paris, the movement toward creating "garden" cemeteries spread to America. The first of these was Mount Auburn Cemetery in Cambridge, Massachusetts, which was consecrated in 1831. Proposed by Dr. Jacob Bigelow in 1825 and laid out by Henry A.S. Dearborn, it featured an Egyptian style gate and fence, a Norman tower and a granite chapel. It was planned as an "oasis" on the outskirts of the city and defined a new romantic kind of cemetery with winding paths and a forested setting. It was the opposite of the crowded churchyard and it became an immediate success, giving rise to many other similar burial grounds in cities across the country. In fact, they became so popular as not only burial grounds, but as public recreation areas as well. Here, people could enjoy the shaded walkways and even picnic on weekend afternoons. The Garden cemetery would go on to inspire the American Park movement and virtually create the field of landscape architecture.

The idea of the Garden cemetery spread across America and by the early 1900's was the perfect answer to the old, overcrowded burial grounds. Many of these early cemeteries had been established closer to the center of town and were soon in the way of urban growth. Small towns and large ones across the country were soon hurrying to move the graves of those buried in years past to the new cemeteries, which were always located outside of town.

There are several examples of wonderful Garden cemeteries scattered across America, but two of them are located virtually side-by-side in St. Louis, Missouri. Both cemeteries were created by the need to move a number of smaller burial grounds from out of the way of urban progress.

In March 1849, a banker and church leader named William McPherson and a lawyer and St. Louis Mayor named John Darby incorporated a new burial ground outside of the city. Together, they gathered a group of men, regardless of religious affiliation, and purchased 138 acres of land (which later grew to 327 acres) that became the "Rural Cemetery Association". That spring, the state of Missouri issued a charter to the men for the land along Bellefontaine Road and the graveyard later changed its name from "Rural" to "Bellefontaine". The cemetery today is largely the work of its first superintendent, Almerin Hotchkiss, a landscape architect and the former caretaker of famed Greenwood Cemetery in Brooklyn, New York. He remained at Bellefontaine for more than 46 years, creating a forested burial ground with over fourteen miles of roads.

The cemetery grew rapidly, mostly because of a terrible cholera epidemic that hit St. Louis later in June 1849. At the height of the epidemic, there were more than 30 burials each day. Thanks to a law that went into effect forcing all burial grounds to be located outside of the city for health reasons, Bellefontaine began to receive internments from most of the churches in St. Louis.

Today, Bellefontaine has become the resting place of governors, war heroes, writers and adventurers and noted residents include Thomas Hart Benton, General William Clark, Sara Teasdale, William S. Burroughs, the infamous Lemp Family and others. One notable monument here is that of the Adolphus Busch family of beer brewing fame. Their mausoleum has been designed to resemble a French cathedral, right down to the gargoyles. Another famous tomb belongs to the Wainwright family. It was designed by architect Louis Sullivan, who refused to put the family name on the exterior of the crypt. He wanted cemetery visitors to look inside out of curiosity. When they do, they discover a domed ceiling and walls that are completely covered with intricate mosaic tile designs.

Located on the other side of the roadway from Bellefontaine is Calvary Cemetery, another beautiful example of the classic Garden burial ground. Calvary was started in 1857 and also came about because of the epidemic of 1849. After the death of so many St. Louis citizens from cholera, most of the city's cemeteries, including all of the Catholic cemeteries were filled. In addition, many of these burial grounds stood in the way of new development. There was no question that St. Louis Catholics were in need of a larger burial ground, and thanks to the new law, one located outside of the city limits.

In 1853, Archbishop Peter Richard Kenrick purchased a 323-acre piece of land called "Old Orchard Farm" on the northwest side of the city. Kenrick established his own farm on half of the property and gave the other half for use as a cemetery. The ground had already been used for burials in the past, as a portion of the land had once been an ancient Indian burial site and as a burial ground for old Fort Bellefontaine. Kenrick lived in a mansion on the western edge of the grounds for many years, even after the Calvary Cemetery Association was incorporated in 1867. Archbishop Kenrick became its first president. Around this same time, many of the smaller Catholic cemeteries in the area were moved to Calvary, which now contains over 315,000 graves on 477 acres of ground.

Like Bellefontaine Cemetery, Calvary also takes advantage of the natural wooded setting and rolling hills. It also features amazing displays of cemetery artwork and the final resting places of many notable people like Dred Scott, William Tecumseh Sherman, Dr. Thomas A. Dooley, Tennessee Williams, Kate Chopin, and many others.

Strangely, while neither of these cemeteries boasts a single ghost story, there is a spirited tale connected to Calvary Drive, the road that runs between the two burial grounds, connecting Broadway and West Florissant Road.

The story is that of a classic "Vanishing Hitchhiker" tale about a girl who is sometimes picked up along the road but who then vanishes from the car. It started back in the 1940's when she was referred to as "Hitchhike Annie" and she limits her appearances to the time of day when the sun is setting and that she also sometimes appears on different roads in the same general vicinity. According to the accounts, motorists who passed along Calvary Drive (and sometimes other streets in the area) would be flagged down by a young girl in a white dress. She was usually described as being quite attractive with brown hair and pale skin. After climbing into the car, she would sometimes claim that she had been stranded or that her car had broken down. Either way, she would ask for a ride and direct the driver to take her down the street. In every case though, just as the automobile would near the entrance to Bellefontaine Cemetery, the girl would mysteriously vanish from the vehicle! The door would never open and no warning would come to say that she was getting out. Annie would simply be gone. The story of Annie persisted for many years, but by the middle 1980's seemed to die out.

In Chicago, Illinois, one burial ground actually created several Garden Cemeteries, although the most spectacular of them is undoubtedly Graceland Cemetery. Graceland and several others came about thanks to the closure of the old Chicago City Cemetery around 1870.

The City Cemetery was located exactly where Chicago's Lincoln Park is located today. Before its establishment, most of the early pioneers simply buried their dead out in the back yard, leading to many gruesome discoveries as the downtown was developed years later. Two cemeteries were later set aside for both Protestants and Catholics, but both of them were located along the lake shore, leading to the frequent unearthing of caskets whenever the water was high. Finally, the city set aside land at Clark Street and North Avenue for the Chicago City Cemetery. Soon, many of the bodies were moved from the other sites to this new location.

Within ten years of the opening of the cemetery, it became the subject of much criticism. Not only was it severely overcrowded from both population growth and cholera epidemics, but many also felt that poorly carried out burials here were creating health problems and contaminating the water supply. To make matters worse, both the city morgue and the local Pest House, a quarantine building for epidemic victims, were located on the cemetery grounds. Soon, local families and churches were moving their loved ones to burial grounds considered to be safer and the City Cemetery was closed down.

One cemetery that benefited from the closure of the graveyard was Graceland Cemetery, located on North Clark Street. When it was started in 1860 by real estate developer Thomas B. Bryan, it was located far away from the city and over the years, a number of different architects have worked to preserve the natural setting of its 120 acres. Two of the men largely responsible for the beauty of the place were architects William Le Baron Jenney and Ossian Cole Simonds, who became so fascinated with the site that he ended up turning his entire business to landscape design. In addition to the natural landscape, the cemetery boasts a number of wonderful monuments and buildings, including the cemetery chapel, which holds city's oldest crematorium, built in 1893.

There are a number of Chicago notables buried in Graceland and it is also home to several ghost stories as well. In 1880, a little girl named Inez Clarke died at the tender age of only six. Tradition has it that she was killed during a lightning storm while on a family picnic. Her parents, stunned by the tragic loss, commissioned a life-size statue of the girl to be placed on her grave. It was completed a year later, and like many Chicago area grave sculptures, was placed in a glass box to protect it from the elements. The image remains in nearly perfect condition today. Even in death, Inez still manages to charm cemetery visitors, who discover the little girl perched on a small stool. It is said that the likeness was cast so that Inez was wearing her favorite dress and carrying a tiny parasol. The perfectly formed face was created with just the hint of a smile. It is not uncommon to come to the cemetery and find gifts of flowers and toys at the foot of her grave. The site has become one of the most popular places in the cemetery, for graveyard buffs and curiosity seekers alike.

According to local legend, this site is haunted. Not only are their stories of strange sounds heard nearby, but some claim the statue of Inez actually moves under its own power. The most disconcerting stories may be those of the disembodied weeping that is heard nearby but the most famous tales are those of the statue itself. It is said that Inez will sometimes vanish from inside of the glass box. This is said to often take place during violent thunderstorms. Many years ago, a night watchman for the Pinkerton agency stated that he was making his rounds one night during a storm and discovered that the box that holds Inez was empty. He left the cemetery that night, never to return. Other guards have also reported it missing, only to find it back in place when they pass by again, or the following morning.

The cemeteries of America have taken a long strange trip in the course of their evolution and later on the book, our field guide to mysterious sites will visit all sorts of burials grounds from Garden Cemeteries to churchyards to rural cemeteries nestled deep in the woods. One thing remains certain with all of these various cemeteries though. It seems that no matter what different type of graveyard you mention, all of them seem to have one thing in common -- each of them has the potential to be haunted!

Grave Markers & Tombstones

The tombstone, or grave marker, underwent much the same type of transformation as the cemetery did. The graveyards changed from the crowded churchyards and charnel houses to the tranquil, park-like settings of the early 1900's. Tombstones also started out as crude items that were used more because of superstition than for remembrance of the dead.

The first grave markers were literally stones and boulders that were used to keep the dead from rising out of their graves. It was thought, in these primitive times, that if heavy rocks were placed on the grave sites of the deceased, they would not be able to climb out from underneath them. As time went on, a need came for the living to mark the graves of the dead with a reminder of about the person who was buried there. Many of the markers were made from wood, or rough stone, and did not last long when exposed to the elements.

Early monuments and grave stones in Europe and in old New England were crude and were carved with frightening motifs like winged skulls, skeletons and angels of death. The idea was to frighten the living with the very idea of death. In this way, they were apt to live a more righteous life after seeing the images of decay and horror on the markers of the dead. It would not be until the latter part of the 1800's that scenes of eternal peace would replace those of damnation.

Eventually, grave markers, monuments and tombs became a craft, as well as an art form. In those days, many brick layers and masons began to take up side jobs as gravestone carvers but soon demand became so great that companies formed to meet the needs of this new trade. Stone work companies formed all over the country, especially in Vermont, where a huge supply of granite was readily available. Many stones and monuments that were carved and cut in Vermont were done by Scottish and Italian immigrants. The most delicate carving was done by the Italians though. As children, many of them had trained in Milan, going to school at night to be carvers. Despite the thousands of statues and mausoleums that were created, only a few dozen carvers could handle the most intricate work.

The peak for the new funeral industry and for graveyard art and mausoleums came in the last part of the 1800's, the Victorian era. During these years, American cemeteries were packed with massive and beautiful statues and tombs. This was a time when maudlin excess and ornamentation was greatly in fashion. Funerals were extremely important to the Victorians, as were fashionable graves and mausoleums. The skull and crossbones tombstones had all but vanished by this time and now cemeteries had become very survivor-friendly and of course, heartbreakingly sad. Scantily dressed mourners carved from stone now guarded the doors of the tombs and angels draped themselves over monuments in agonizing despair.

The excessive ornamentation turned the graveyards into a showplace for the rich and the prestigious. Many of them became inundated with artwork and crowded with crypts as the society folk attempted to outdo one another. Gaudy and maudlin artwork like furniture, carved flowers and life-size (and larger) statues dominated the landscape. Realistic representations of the dead began to appear, as did novelty monuments like that of the Di Salvo family in Chicago's Mount Carmel Cemetery. This marker portrays the entire family on a round dais-- that spins 360 degrees.

The Di Salvo monument in Mount Carmel Cemetery. It spins all of the way around on its base.

There was nothing as elaborate in the Victorian cemetery as the mausoleum however. Tombs for the dead had been around already for thousands of years. The pyramids are the largest and most famous but even ancient man entombed their leaders and chieftains in subterranean and aboveground structures. Most of these were domed chambers created from circular mounds of earth, although some of the stone structures still exist today.

The word mausoleum comes from the name of Mausolus, who was the king of Halicarnassus, a great harbor city in Asia. When Mausolus died in 353 B.C., his grief-stricken wife, Artemisia (who also happened to be his sister), constructed a huge fortress to serve as his tomb. Inspiration for what would become the world's first mausoleum is believed to have come from the Nereid Temple, which boasted statues and friezes of battling warriors and female statues standing between Ionic columns.

The tomb at Halicarnassus was similar to the temple, but much larger, standing a full five stories and having hundreds of statues decorating all quarters. It was said to be surrounded by a colonnade of 36 columns and a pyramid-like structure that climbed 24 steps to the summit. Here was located a four-horse chariot, all made from marble.

Nothing remains of the tomb today save for a few stones from the foundation. It was most likely damaged during earthquakes and by the Knights of St. John of Jerusalem, who plundered the structure in the late fifteenth and early sixteenth centuries. They took the stones to strengthen their own castles and destroyed the underground tomb chambers. During its heyday though, the tomb attracted many sightseers, including Alexander the Great, who conquered Halicarnassus. The tomb is still considered one of the Seven Wonders of the Ancient World. The Greeks adopted the tomb of Mausolus as the new standard and began building their own "mausoleums" and coining the word. The Romans emulated the Greeks and influenced the modern styles of the nineteenth century, thanks to the fact that many great archaeological finds were uncovered during this period.

The Busch family mausoleum in St. Louis, which is in the design of a miniature French cathedral, is the epitome of Victorian era excess.

The rise of the American mausoleum came with the founding of Mount Auburn, the first Garden cemetery, near Boston. The arrival of this cemetery meant the end of the horrifying graveyards of the past and a new era for burial grounds. Although grave markers dominated the cemeteries, mausoleums experienced a Golden Age, starting in the mid-1800's and ending around the time of the Great Depression. They became the most desired burial spots in any cemetery and bankers, industrialists, robber barons, entrepreneurs and anyone else with plenty of money to spend committed their mortal remains to a mausoleum. They became like the pharaohs of Ancient Egypt, who if they were not remembered for their accomplishments, would be remembered for their tombs.

The best architects were hired and extravagant amounts of money were spent. Most mausoleums of the era were made from granite, marble and various types of stone and often the imaginations of the designers ran wild. They created everything from gothic cathedrals to classic temples to even Egyptian pyramids. One can find just about everything imaginable decorating the tombs of the period, from nude women to macabre animals and the sphinx. Not surprisingly, many of these bizarre structures have given birth to stories of ghosts and assorted strangeness.

Gravestones have proven to be just as fascinating to cemetery enthusiasts. As mentioned previously, the earliest American stones were copies of the old European ones with skulls, crossbones and death's heads decorating their surfaces. Later, carvings on the stone began to represent the grief of the family and began to make a statement about the life of the person buried beneath it. As time passed, even the plainest of illustrations began to take on a new significance.

A variety of different images were used to symbolize both death and life, like angels, who were seen as the emissaries between this world and the next. In some cases they appeared as mourners and on other graves, as an offer of comfort for those who are left behind.

Broken columns, inverted torches, spilled flower pots and funeral urns were meant as simple images of lives that were ended too soon. Some graves were marked with the image of an hour glass with wings that represented the fleeting passage of time or with ferns and anchors that were meant to give hope to grieving loved ones. Much the same can be said of clasped hands, bibles and pointing fingers. These symbols direct the mourners to look toward heaven and know that the worries of the world are now past.

Flowers, like roses or lilies, were common symbols that represented love and purity or that life is like a blooming flower, never meant to be permanent. There are other monuments where depictions of discarded clothing, opened books or forgotten tools have been etched or carved. Such items are meant to symbolize the fact that the dead have left behind the burdens of life. The depiction of wheat or a sickle would show the reaping of the soul and the gathering of the harvest to the next world.

Suns, moons, planets and stars have various meanings in the cemetery, from that of rising saints to that of glorified souls. They can also signify that heaven is the abode of the stars and the planets.

Trees, and most especially the famous "willow tree" motif, stood for human life and the fact that man, like a tree, must reach for the heavens. The willow itself often stood for mourning. Trees could also have other meanings, especially when the monuments were made to look like wood. Cemetery visitors can often find examples of chairs, centerpieces and even entire monuments that are designed to look like the rough wood of a tree. These markers symbolize the fact that the tree has died, its life has been taken away, just like the life of the person the stone honors.

Perhaps the most heartbreaking, and often most eerie, monuments mark the graves of children. These images include the images of disembodied hands from heaven reaching down to pluck flowers from the earth and small lambs, lost and alone. Cribs and beds are sometimes seen, holding the images of sleeping children, or are often empty, symbolizing that these little ones are gone forever. Most disconcerting of all are the life-size images of the children themselves. They stare out at the cemetery visitor with lifeless, and occasionally frightening, eyes.

Gravestones and markers have a myriad of meanings and symbolize both comfort and grief- and in some cases are not what they appear to be. Some of them (as the reader will discover later in the book) are actually haunted by the ghosts who are unable to rest within the bounds of the graveyard. In some cases, these tales are more frightening than the lore of the cemetery where the stones reside!

The American Way of Death

Death came on swift wings for our ancestors. There were so many ways to die in days gone by that it's almost amazing that any of the early settlers and pioneers lived to even a semblance of old age. There were deaths from disease and epidemics, accidents and childbirth. Early doctors, with their ignorance of medicine, likely claimed as many lives as they saved. Nature could be brutal as well and many lives were lost from fires, floods, natural disasters and sometimes from simply the hard way of life that could be found on the frontier. Few people could swim, especially children, and so many of them drowned in the lakes and rivers. Crime and violence took many lives, as did Indian massacres that once raged along the frontier. Wars raised the death toll dramatically, as did lynching, dueling and other violent acts. In those days, our ancestors produced as many children as possible because it was unlikely that all of them would live to see adulthood.

But even with all of that death around them, our ancestors never became tolerant of the Grim Reaper. They felt the loss of a friend or relative, and grieved for them, just as strongly as we do today. When an individual neared death, family and friends would gather to keep a continuous vigil by the ailing person's side. Known as the "death watch" or more commonly as "sitting up", loved ones would often travel for many miles to be near the dying in his or her final days. No one was left to face death alone.

In the days before doctors were common, family members were left to determine whether or not the moment of death had arrived. This was usually done in simple ways. A hand mirror was usually brought to the body and placed under the mouth and nose of the corpse for as long as an entire minute, checking for any fogging on the glass.

After that, a variety of rituals and superstitions were carried out, although mostly in rural areas. In town, a physician (whether present or not at the time of death) was required to notify the town clerk so that a burial permit could be issued. In many cases, bells would be rung to announce the death of someone in the community. The bells would be used to toll the age of the deceased and to spread the word that a resident had passed away -- and also to frighten away evil spirits and help the deceased to pass safely to the other side.

The rituals carried out in smaller communities and in rural areas were much more elaborate and strange. After death had been determined, mirrors and photographs in the house were turned to face the wall so that there was no chance that the departing spirit would see his or her reflection and decide to stay behind. All clocks were stopped in the house, both as a method of marking the time of death and also because when started again, it would mark a new period in the family's life. Shades and curtains were also drawn because it was believed that the next person to die would be the one that the sun shines on first.

Before undertakers took over the handling of the dead, it was the responsibility of family members and neighbors to prepare a body for burial. This was a detailed task that involved washing and dressing the corpse and then laying out for visitors to pay their respects. In the days before embalming was widely practiced, the typical time between death and burial in the summer would be no more than 24 hours. Cold winter weather and placing a body on ice made it possible for distant family members to arrive for a service but even then, most burials took place between three and four days of death.

Laying out the body was usually done by taking two chairs that faced one another and placing a "cooling board" on the seats between them. This long board was usually about the size of two table leaves. They body was then taken from the death bed and placed on this board, stripped, bathed and dressed for viewing. Some bodies were wrapped in shrouds but most of them time, they were put into their best clothes.

A pillow would be placed under the head, but not the same one that they were using when they died. The pillow would later be opened up and the feathers removed. There was a superstition that stated that if a person died in a state of grace, the feathers under his head would form a wreath. When this occurred (and no explanation exists as to how it happens) the wreaths were often framed and hung on the wall of the house as a remembrance of the deceased. Over the years, I have seen a number of these and I am puzzled by the eeriness of them.

When the wreath did not form however, and it was believed that the person had died in sin, this same superstition called for the presence of a "sin eater". A plate of food would be placed on the chest of the corpse and the sin eater would pull up a chair and eat the meal that was laid out for him. In so doing, he would also eat the sins of the deceased and cleanse their spirit. For doing this deed, he had to be paid in gold. If there were no gold coins around, jewelry or even a gold tooth would suffice.

Once the body was dressed and placed on the board, a quilt would be used to cover him from the waist downward. There were no shoes ever placed on the body. The hands were then folded across the chest, to make him appear as though sleeping, and the wrists tied with a ribbon or cord. A band of cloth was tied under the chin and over the head to keep the mouth from falling open. All of this had to be accomplished before rigor mortis set in or it would be impossible to get the body into the coffin. Silver coins were also placed on the eyelids and left until the body cooled. This way, the eyes would stay closed.

Four candles were then waxed to the chair posts and lighted. They would burn throughout the wake, both day and night, and would be replaced each time they burned down. Buckets of cold spring water would be brought in and placed nearby. Cloth was soaked in the water, wrung out and then placed on the face of the corpse. The reason for this was to keep the face from turning black in the days before embalming.

Over the next day or so, time would be spent in the house with relatives and loved ones. There would be eating, drinking and music and while not an altogether festive affair, it was not always a somber one either. It was a time for people to pay their respects and fondly remember the one who had been lost to them.

When the time came for the burial, the early Americans were wrapped in blankets or shrouds but by the middle 1800's, wooden coffins began to be used. Most of them were quite plain and were unfinished and unlined and usually made from poplar or pine. They were built by local carpenters and cabinetmakers and came with unhinged tops, rope handles and pre-drilled holes to tack the lid into place. When the coffin was delivered to the house, it was brought inside and placed near the cooling board and the corpse. These items were moved and the coffin was put in their place. Then a quilt, usually from the bed of the deceased, was placed in the coffin in a way that it provided a resting place for the body and served as a cover for the corpse to be carefully wrapped in. Then, the lid of the coffin would be hammered into place using a wooden mallet and clinch nails and then carried outside to the wagon that would be used to transport the deceased to the burial grounds.

Many old, rural cemeteries were equipped with what were called "lych gates". The gates were an opening in the cemetery wall or fence that was intended to allow only for the passage of the dead. The gate usually had four corner posts that encompassed an area about 10 x 10 feet. The corner posts also supported a roof and in the center of the enclosed area, running through the line of the fence, were three short posts with a wooden plank on top of them. This formed a long table where the coffin would be placed. A rope was strung across the entrance to the gate and had to be unhooked by the men who carried the coffin. The pallbearers who held the foot of the coffin (the dead always entered the cemetery feet first because it was believed

that if they came in head first, they would be able to beckon to someone to follow them to the grave) unhooked the rope and carried it with them into the gate. It would later be hung on the hooks at the outgoing end of the gate.

Draped across the plank in the center of the gate were the lowering ropes for the casket. The coffin would be placed on top of them and then the ropes would be threaded through the handles of the box. After this, the pallbearers walked back through the lych gate from the direction from which they had come and entered the cemetery through the main gates. They walked to the opposite side of the lych gate, removed the ropes and then passed it over the top of the coffin and hooked it again on the entrance. The men then carried the coffin by its lowering ropes into the cemetery and to the open grave that awaited it. In those days, pallbearers always wore gloves. It was not only for the practical purposes of handling the ropes and heavy wooden casket but also because it was believed that the spirit of the dead person could enter their bodies through bare hands. When the coffin reached the grave site, it was lowered and the ropes were pulled up and each person present tossed a single shovel of dirt into the hole. When this ritual was completed, the funeral service would be finished.

Much has changed since those days and aside from very remote areas, I would hazard a guess to say that there is no one in America today who prepares the body of his loved ones for burial or crafts a coffin from his own hands. Lych gates have long since vanished and "sin eaters" are a forgotten anomaly of a distant past. However, even in these days of impersonal funerals and sanitized mortuaries -- death remains as great a mystery as it was long ago.

Embalming & Preservation

The great changes began to the "American Way of Death" in the middle 1800's. It was a time when the American funeral industry was literally created. It would be in the years following the Civil War that American funeral customs would become a part of a huge industry that still prospers today. The local undertaker would no longer be a nearby cabinetmaker or carpenter and embalming would soon become an essential part of burial.

The art of embalming has been around in one fashion or another for centuries. The ancient Egyptians mummified the dead and began the first real rites of burial. The hot, dry climate of the region made it possible for the poor to be buried and preserved in the desert sands but rulers and persons of royal birth were given much more elaborate send-offs to the other side. Many methods of embalming were tried until a series of practices was established. The body would be purged and then soaked in chemicals for as long as 70 days. The bodies were also eviscerated and the brain and organs were placed in separate jars. The cavity would then be stuffed with spices and resins and then sewn up. The mummified remains were wrapped in yards of cotton or linen and then placed in a tomb for eternity.

As the years passed, the Romans and Greeks used their own methods of embalming, although normally only for persons of great personage to lay in state. The Romans also used wax masks to cover the faces of the dead, a practice that would be revived in later years and which is still in use today, although the wax has been replaced by heavy makeup to make the corpse appear life-like.

During the Middle Ages, important people were occasionally pickled or crudely embalmed. This method usually involved the boiling of the body in chemicals so that only the skin and bones would remain. In this way, the bodies could be easily transported. The Crusaders and the knights who traveled to fight on foreign shores always took their cauldrons along with them in case they might be killed.

Later, many attempts were made to preserve corpses for medical research and dissection and then in 1618, doctors discovered the circulation of blood. A century later, Dr. William Hunter devised a method for arterial embalming in which the blood is drained from the body through a vein and replaced with a formalin-based fluid through an artery. The only problem with this method was that the removal of the blood drained all of the color from the corpse and the bodies then had to be made up in order to be displayed.

Embalming became a common practice in America around the time of the Civil War. A number of embalmers appeared to prepare the dead soldiers for shipping home when relatives demanded it. They also began to fill the demand for more decorative coffins than plain wooden boxes as well and most would say that the American funeral industry was born during the war.

These were not the first embalmings to take place however. In 1886, an undertaker's journal called *The Casket* featured an article that recalled an early embalming. It stated that a young woman had hanged herself in a woodshed near Carlisle, Virginia in the spring of 1853. Her body was taken to an undertaker and he opened the abdomen, emptied the interior and then sewed the incision shut. Her body was then soaked in a solution of water, salt, zinc chloride and alum for four weeks. At the end of that time, the body had turned gray. She was then placed on a board to dry and small incisions were made to let all of the remaining fluids run out. After that, the body traveled across the United States several times on display and finally ended up in a vault in Peoria, Illinois, not in good condition and never very lifelike.

The first patent for embalming was granted in 1856. The process involved injecting the body with an arsenic-alcohol mixture, electrically charging it, then washing it with chemicals, covering it in oils and then sealing it in a coffin that was filled with alcohol. The body was probably not viewable after such a process but it did effectively preserve the corpse for transportation to far off parts of the country.

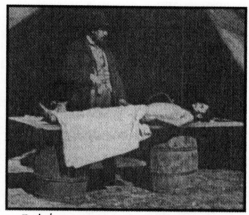
Embalming in America came into custom during the Civil War.

Most professional embalmers can trace their start back to Thomas H. Holmes, who (thanks to his passion for dissecting corpses and his ways of leaving them around in appropriate places) was expelled from New York University's Medical School before the Civil War. During the war, he received a commission in the Army Medical Corps and spent most of his time embalming soldiers who were killed in battle. He was said to have embalmed 4,028 cadavers in four years! He mostly embalmed officers (whose families were willing to pay for the service) and charged as much as $100 for each of them. Needless to say, he returned from the war a very rich man. He never revealed his formula for embalming solution but interestingly, he demanded that his own body not be embalmed when he died!

As mentioned before, embalming really came into its own during the war. It became popular thanks to the need for open caskets for war heroes so that their bodies could lie in state. Military authorities permitted civilian embalmers to work within military controlled areas and not until the last year of the war did the Army require them to be examined to prove their qualifications. It has been estimated that as many as 30,000 to 40,000 of the Civil War dead were embalmed.

In 1867, August Wilhelm von Hofman discovered a chemical called formaldehyde, the chemical basis for all modern embalming fluids. It would be several years before it came into common use but by 1885, embalming was commonplace and by the end of the century, was being used all over the country. In

1900, the Massachusetts College of Embalming was set up and undertakers began advertising in newspapers of their services. Today, embalming is commonplace in America and the most commonly used method of arterial embalming differs little from the early days. Funeral home operators inject three or four gallons of chemical into the large artery of the corpse, while simultaneously removing the blood from a large vein. They also undertake extensive preparations (and sometimes even reconstruction) to prepare the body for viewing and modern funeral directors do not have the worries of yesterday when it comes to bad smells or leaking fluids from the corpse.

Undertakers, Burials & Funerals

Although the role of an undertaker had been around for many years prior to the war, this period also marked the beginnings of the job being seen as an important position. The word "undertaker" was actually in use as far back as 1698 and it originally meant the one who "undertook" to make funeral arrangements and to keep the body safe. The duties of this person have changed many times through the years and in fact, the word "undertaker" is disliked by modern members of the industry. The term "funeral director" was first coined back in 1885, but it has taken well over a century for it to catch on. In the early 1900's, the word "mortician" was also devised, but it was never popular. The word "undertaker" persists but really should only be used to refer to early practitioners of the trade.

The undertaker's job began when the doctor's job ended. He performed tasks that, quite frankly, no one, especially the bereaved family, wanted to do. He cleaned and took care of the corpse and prepared it for burial. Early undertakers usually combined their funeral business with other trades. It was not uncommon for them to be cabinetmakers or furniture makers who made coffins as a sideline. They usually stressed the "furniture" part of undertaking (the coffin) in their advertising, as this was their major form of income. Businesses that combined furniture sales and funeral directing were common in America through the middle 1900's. In most cases though, undertakers in post-Civil War America began to rely on specialized coffin manufacturers.

The term "coffin" generally refers to the six-sided burial container, which was wide at the shoulders and narrow at the feet. A "casket" was rectangular-shaped and was first introduced in the 1840's and was in widespread use by the 1860's. For most guides (including this one), the terms are used interchangeably.

Caskets had originally been custom-made to fit the specifications of the corpse but by this began to be mass-produced. Metal coffins came into fashions and casket shops and warehouse opened at the same time. The family could choose a casket from an undertaker's catalog or display room and have it immediately available. Coffins have since been made from a variety of materials, including wood, cloth, aluminum, terra-cotta and even papier-mâché. The use of underground vaults as an protective receptacle for the coffin was not popular until the early 1900's. At that time, it was mostly just the wealthy who could afford them.

By the early 1900's, others had joined the ranks as undertakers. Many retired carpenters, grave diggers and the owners of horse carts saw undertaking as a good way to make a living. Owners of livery stables began to see increasing amounts of business with the rental of wagons, carriages and coaches that could be used for funerals.

Undertakers gradually began to incorporate embalming into the work, taking over the job from surgeons. The trade later organized as the Undertaker's Mutual Protection Association in Philadelphia in 1864 and by 1881 had organized in either other states as well. By 1900, it had become an acceptable career and by 1920, the National Funeral Director's Association had nearly 10,000 members.

For years, a social stigma surrounded the local undertaker. While active in the community, many of them were shunned and avoided. They filled a much-needed position and yet because of their constant contact with the dead, they were somehow seen as "unclean". This would begin to change as the Twentieth Century advanced and undertaking was seen as a true vocation. During this time, the practice of embalming and funeral directing also began to move from its early days into modern times. In the late 1800's and early 1900's, embalming was usually done in private residences with the embalmer bringing his own "cooling board" on which to prepare the corpse. The drainage from the body was be funneled right into the kitchen sink. At that time, most funerals took place at home as well. As times changed and funeral homes came into use, the job of funeral director began to be seen with more dignity and it came to be regarded as a true profession.

The customs surrounding funerals, and the days before them, have also changed much over the years. The tradition of sitting with and viewing the deceased is still known by various names like "the wake" or "visitation" and is still practiced today, although in a different way than in the past. Before funeral parlors, these events always took place in the homes of the dead. In the days before houses were equipped with screens, bugs and flying insects were unwelcome visitors at wakes, as were rats, dogs, cats and often small children. It was necessary for round-the-clock vigils to take place in order to protect the corpse from these intruders and also to maintain the body, as was described earlier.

This made the wake both a practical and a social ritual. The social aspects of the wake varied by culture and ethnic group. Perhaps the most festive wakes were held in Irish households, where there was always an indulgence of food and spirits. On some occasions, the deceased was propped up in the corner so that he could enjoy the party as well. Today, the visitation, as the practice has come to be known, does not require the family to "sit up" with the corpse. However, it does still allow for friends and family to gather in a setting where the body can be viewed and remembrances can be exchanged about the deceased. Most such gatherings are held at the local funeral home however, which tends to cut down on the more festive aspects of the old ritual.

Funerals themselves have changed as well. In early America, most funeral services were held after the burial because there was no way to adequately preserve the body. There may or may not have been a member of the clergy to preside over the service, especially for those living in rural areas. If a person died in the winter, when the ground was frozen, it's also possible that the funeral and burial could be delayed until the spring thaw. In this case, the body of the deceased would be stored in a temporary receiving vault or even in a barn or unheated room of a home.

Before the 1900's, most funerals were by invitation only. In cities, a man dressed in black (later, the undertaker) hand-delivered funeral notices and invitations. It was considered to be very rude to attend a funeral that you were not invited to. Funeral invitations were written on black-bordered stationary and placed in black envelopes so that the recipient would immediately know that someone had died. In the 1900's, when newspaper obituaries began to appear and telephones made it much simpler to spread the word about a loved one's death, written invitations to funerals fell out of fashion.

Funeral services, like wakes, were social occasions and were held in the home of the deceased and later in the church or the funeral parlor. The odor of the decomposing body could be ghastly during a funeral service and this created the custom of having floral arrangements surrounding the coffin. It added color and life to a grim setting but most importantly, it masked the smell of the corpse. Funeral wreaths were hung on the family's door to not only identify the house to visiting mourners but also to warn away unwanted visitors, like traveling salesmen.

After the service, a funeral assistant stayed behind to put the family's home back in order, while the mourners followed in a procession to the cemetery. The procession was led by the clergy, followed by the flower carriage, then the pallbearers, the hearse, the immediate family, the relatives and then finally, friends and acquaintances. Before the use of hearses became common, under bearers carried the coffin, while pallbearers (relatives or men of dignity) held the corners of the pall, a cloth that was laid over the coffin, to keep it from dragging on the ground. Palls were usually black, while children's coffins were draped in white, as were coffins of women who died in childbirth. If the distance to the cemetery was long, there would be a change in under bearers along the way, or they would be allowed to stop and rest. Over time, the tradition of the pall faded away and only one set of bearers remained.

In the late 1800's, when undertakers began taking over the management of death, they established "funeral parlors" or "funeral homes" to symbolize the parlor, or home-like quality, that people were used to. The undertaker handled the entire affair, from planning the funeral to contacting the clergy, arranging the music, selecting flowers and preparing the body and casket. He also secured a burial permit from the town or city and arranged to have the death certificate filed with the city clerk.

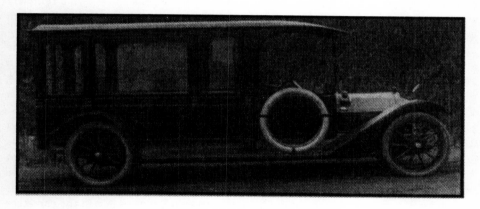

The undertaker's carriage transported the deceased with mourners following on foot and then later in carriages. Motorized hearses replaced horse-drawn carriages in the early 1900's and have gone through many changes over the years. Early on, the plume that was atop the horse-drawn hearse was actually used to indicate the status of the deceased. If there were no feathered plumes, the deceased was poor and if there were more than seven or eight of them, then it meant that the occupant was a wealthy one. All other areas of financial status fell in between.

At the cemetery, there would be a brief graveside service that focused on giving the body back to the earth (ashes to ashes, dust to dust) and the coffin would be placed on planks over the open grave. On occasion, the coffin would be opened one last time at the cemetery so that family and friends could place personal items inside with their loved one. In addition, if any precious jewelry was going to be removed from the body, this was also done at the graveside. The casket was then lowered into the ground and then handfuls of dirt, or sometimes flowers, were dropped onto the casket to symbolize the return to the earth.

The earliest burials were simple. The body would usually be wrapped in cloth and then placed on its back in the grave. Later, coffins, or caskets, came into common use, even though various types of enclosures for the body has been used for centuries. In early American though, the old adage of being buried "six feet under" was out of necessity. The odor of the decaying body had to be suppressed to keep animals from digging up the remains.

Before cemeteries were plotted and gravesites accurately recorded, gravediggers had to rely on someone's memory to make sure that they weren't about to dig a grave where someone else was already buried. If no one knew for sure, then a dowser would be brought in to determine where the graves were located. This method is searching for graves is still used today and is easily done. All that it requires is two straight pieces of wire that have a three-inch bend in them for handles. Holding a handle in each hand, the dowser can walk through the cemetery and when a grave is found, the wires will turn outward. If they cross, then underground water has been discovered.

Another method that was used in the past to search for graves was to hit the ground with a hammer or to stomp on it with heavy boots. A grave will have a hollow sound to it since the ground never settles back as solidly as it had been. A metal rod could also be plunged into the ground at regular intervals and where it slipped in the most easily, a grave could usually be found.

In many cemeteries, the graves were laid out on an east-west axis, with the feet to the east and the head to the west. In some cultures, this was done so that the deceased faced the rising sun. For Christians, it was done with the belief that on Judgment Day, Christ would return in the eastern sky and so the bodies would be positioned to rise in the proper direction. And while this was not set in stone, it was a considered a closely held tradition. With that in mind, if everyone in the cemetery is buried east-west and graves are found on a north-south axis, if might be worth checking local court records for the names of those buried in such a manner. It is possible that they may have committed murder, or some other crime, that might warrant their punishment extending beyond death. Likewise, those buried outside of consecrated ground may have committed suicide or some other sin that was deemed unpardonable.

Husbands and wives also have certain positions in the grave. Just as the bride stands to the groom's left during a wedding ceremony, she will also be buried to the left at the time of death. The custom came from the belief that Eve was created from the left side (rib) of Adam and is maintained both during the wedding and after death. You may find on some grave markers that the wife's name is to the north (on the east-west axis), which indicates that her position is to the left of the husband.

Women and their infants who died in childbirth, or shortly after, were often buried in the same grave. In this case, the custom comes from the belief that a mother's ghost will not rest if she doesn't know what happened to her child -- her spirit will be forever looking for her baby.

In America, the long traditions of simple burials continued to be held until the later 1800's, when a romantic period of excess dubbed the "Victorian Celebration of Death" began sweeping the country. For several decades, elaborate monuments and funerary art joined expensive mourning clothes, caskets and accoutrements in periods of extended grieving and protracted ritual. It became a time that would lead to huge amounts of money being spent on funerals and cemeteries all over America. The entire funeral industry would be transformed during these years and would never be the same again.

The Victorian Celebration of Death

Memorial customs and traditions varied widely in America but it was not until the late 1800's and early 1900's that funerals and death became a social event and an often morbid way of life. As mentioned previously, vast amounts of money were spent on funerals and on mausoleums and monuments. Most of the ornate and breathtaking artwork that can be found in cemeteries across America was designed and purchased during this era. Many regarded the massive tombs, the statuary and lavish designs as ridiculous . Author Ambrose Bierce called them the "folly of the rich" and pondered how the wealthy planned to enjoy such structures after death. Regardless, they became almost commonplace during this era, as did many customs and rituals. A large number of these formal and unusual customs have since faded into the past but many of them remain, with some variation, even today.

Wearing Black

While even the early settlers considered death and funerals a somber occasion, they did not have any typical style of clothing that was set aside for mourning. The custom of wearing black became popular in America during the Victorian period. Black was believed to make the living less visible to the spirits that hovered around the body of the deceased. Widows were always encouraged to a wear black dress (which became known as "widow's weeds") so that her husband's ghost would not come back to bother her. Most of the etiquette involving the wearing of black clothing pertained to women but men would often sport black armbands and were encouraged to wear dark and conservative suits and black ties.

Widows were expected to wear black dresses for the first two years after the deaths of their husbands. After a year and a half, a widow was allowed to add some trim to her clothing but only in colors of gray, lavender or white. The two-year period was considered a suitable mourning time and a second marriage during this time was severely looked upon. In fact, widows were expected not to attend any festive occasions during this time, such as weddings or parties.

If a woman was mourning the death of a parent or a child, she would wear black for one year. For the loss of a grandparent, sibling or close friend, a mourning dress was to be worn for six months and if an aunt, niece or nephew died, then three months was considered to be an appropriate length of time. Women who had large families (and especially those not blessed with longevity) could expect to be stuck wearing black dresses for a good part of every year!

Mourning Paper

And just as there were special rules for the wearing of black for a Victorian woman, there was also special stationary that she was supposed to use for letters during her period of mourning. Widows in their first year of mourning used stationary and envelopes with quarter-inch black borders. As the widow entered her second year of bereavement, the width of the black border decreased to one-eighth of an inch for the first six months of that period and then to one-sixteenth of an inch for the remainder of the time.

Household Decorations

When funeral services were held in the home, it was common for all of the mirrors in the house to be covered, for shades to be drawn and for clocks to be stopped at the time of death. These traditions gained strength during the Victorian era but actually hearkened back to an earlier time, when it was believed that the spirits of the dead could be distracted by their reflections in mirrors and picture frame glass and might remain behind the haunt the house.

During this period, it was common to hang a funeral wreath on the front door of the house but many families also covered the doorbell or the knocker in crepe paper. Various colors were used to designate who had died in the house: black for an adult, white for a child and black with a white rosette and ribbon for a young adult. In the 1880's, many families and funeral directors also began using a combination of purple, lavender and gray.

Mourning Gifts

During this period, it was also common for funeral gifts (almost like party favors) to be given to those who attended funerals and wakes. The most popular items that were given out were rings, broaches and scarves. Gloves were also a popular gift and were also sometimes given out as an invitation to a funeral. Even the poorest of funerals gave out some token to those who came to pay their respects.

During the Victorian era, rings, lockets and brooches were mass-produced and very popular among the middle class. These jewelry items might contain a miniature portrait of the deceased and perhaps even a lock of their hair. There were also chains, bracelets and necklaces that were braided from the hair of the deceased and sometimes whole wreathes of the dead person's hair were woven into elaborate designs and then framed. The jewelry items were made from black enamel, onyx and other materials and were decorated with symbols that were likely to be found in cemeteries, like weeping willows, broken columns and urns. Each of them were also usually inscribed with the name or initials of the deceased and their date of death.

Such macabre souvenirs remained popular for many years.

Memorial Pictures

Before photography was common, many mourners had paintings, lithographs or needlework memorials stitched in honor of their loved one. They were usually then hung in parlors or in bedrooms as a tribute to those who were lost. The portraits were mainly an upper society trend and most typically showed the deceased in bed, as if asleep. The middle class had their own posthumous portraits however and in most of these, the deceased was portrayed as being alive. The portraits were usually painted from the corpse or from a daguerreotype photograph.

Many such portraits contained hidden clues to show that the subject was deceased when the painting was commissioned. For instance, there may be clouds surrounding the person, a willow tree in the backgrounds or even a timepiece or a wilted flower in their hand. They remained popular through the middle 1800's but faded out of style when photography became popular in the Victorian era.

In addition to paintings, needlepoint portraits and memorials were popular as well. Patterns for mourning samplers appeared in women's magazines of the day and usually contained tombs, willows, urns and black-garbed people in mourning. For the most part, these samplers went out of style after the Civil War and were really never a part of the Victorian period.

Another oddity of the 1840's that is worthy of mention were the mass-produced Currier & Ives lithographs that came with a blank space for the deceased's name and dates of birth and death. They resembled a needlework pattern and usually had a stone or monument in the center that had an inscription that began "Sacred to the Memory of..." and then space where mourners could write in the name of the loved one. The lithographs faded out of fashion by the 1870's and were replaced by photographs and by memorial cards that families could send to relatives or save in a book.

Postmortem Photographs

Perhaps the strangest custom (at least to those of us in modern times) to come out of the Victorian era was the creation of postmortem photographs -- literally photos that were taken of the deceased in their finest clothing and then treasured by

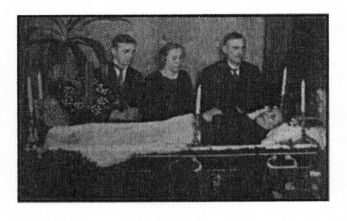

the family members after the burial.

During the wake and funeral services, families of all classes often had photographs taken of the deceased, especially when infants and children died. The resulting images were supposed to help the family through the grieving process and to remember their loved ones. It was not uncommon for the mourners to want to see the face of the deceased just one last time and with such a photograph, they could. These images also served as something to share with family and friends who lived far away and who could not be present for the funeral. Another reason for the popularity of these photos, especially those of children and babies, was that, thanks to the high mortality rate, many children did not live long enough to have their photographs taken otherwise.

Families of this era treated postmortem photographs the same as they did photographs of the living. They could be found hanging on the walls of homes, on living room mantels, in photograph albums and even attached to tombstones.

Photographing the dead dated back to the 1840's but reached its height of popularity in the late 1800's. Photographers routinely advertised in newspapers that

they were able to take photographs of the deceased with only an hour's notice. Since the wake, funeral and burial might all take place within a 24 hour period, the photographers had no time to waste, especially if they wanted to be there before rigor mortis set into the body. Most photos of this type were created in the home of the deceased and charges for the "sitting" ranged from $10 to $15.

Between the 1840's and 1880, the most common style of postmortem photograph was one that denied death. This was known as the "last sleep" and was intended to make the subject look as if he was merely sleeping and not dead. Most of them showed only the upper half of the body. The photographer and the family would place the corpse on a sofa or bed, or for children, in a cradle or a buggy. Often, flowers, a book or a Bible might be placed in their hands. Because the photograph tried to create the illusion that the subject was asleep, they were never posed in a coffin.

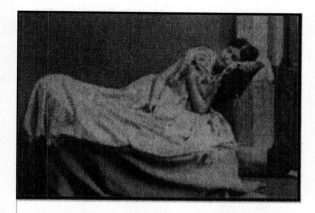

Starting in the 1880's and continuing on into the 1910's, it became more common to photograph the entire body of the deceased, often in a casket. This change coincided with changes in the funeral industry like the widespread use of embalming techniques, lined and lavish caskets and elaborate floral arrangements.

Another trend in the postmortem photographs of the time was to take pictures of the deceased with living family members. While this seems a little odd to us today, it was common to see photographs of mothers and fathers cradling dead infants or to see a husband or wife sitting next to a loved one that is stretched out on a bed. Funerals were not just a time to grieve for the departed but a social occasion as well, so it was not unusual to see an entire group clustered around a casket for a family (living

and dead members) portrait.

While photographs are still taken of the dead at funerals and visitations today, the custom of postmortem photographs died out in the early part of the last century. Those who still take such photos today often hide them away but are unknowingly carrying on a tradition practiced by their ancestors. Today, such a practice is thought of as "morbid" or "weird", simply because death is not as openly discussed in our society as it was a century ago. However, I have a friend who is a funeral director and he assures me that the tradition does quietly continue. He explained to me that many people have even come to him later and have told him how much they regret not taking one last photograph. I replied that I could understand this but did not share their regrets -- seeing a loved one stiffly made up in a coffin is the last way that I would want to remember them.

2. Beyond the Grave
Why Do Cemeteries Become Haunted?

At the beginning of this book, I mentioned man's fear of death. Does our fear of what awaits us on the other side extend to our fear of ghosts? The fear of death has its beginnings in our not too distant past, when life was short and death came calling much too soon. A mother in days gone by might give birth to six children in hopes that three of them might survive to be adults.

But today, things have changed. We live much longer and death has become remote and sanitized. In these modern times, few adults under forty have even seen a corpse. When death finally comes for us, it does so in the clinical setting of a hospital. We are protected and shielded from the horror of death -- or are we? In spite of all of the changes, death is just as mysterious now as it was two centuries ago. We may no longer die from exposure to the elements or from Indian attacks, but the result of the same. We are left with the questions of what happens when we die? And is there a life beyond this one?

And thus, our fear of ghosts is born.

What rational person wishes to return from the grave to wander the earth for eternity? Who would wish to spend their postmortem days and nights aimlessly pacing the corridors of the house where they once lived, doomed to loneliness, isolation and despair? Most importantly, what creature would desire to be trapped for all time among the crypts, monuments and tombs of a forgotten graveyard?

So, what causes ghosts to remain behind in our burial grounds? As mentioned earlier, the ghosts who haunt these spots seem to stay behind because of events that take place after their deaths. An indignity carried out on our body after we die is a fear that has remained with us since the days of the "body snatchers". Society endows on a lifeless corpse the capacity for feeling hurt and the expectation of respect. All forms of the defilement of the dead, especially thefts and the desecration of corpses, are regarded as not only distasteful but almost unholy.

And perhaps society is right about that, for the majority of graveyard ghost tales stem from terrible events that occur within the bounds of the cemetery, long after the hapless victims have died. Cemeteries gain a reputation for being haunted for reasons that include the desecration of corpses, grave robbery, unmarked graves, natural disasters that disturb resting places and more. Could such events literally create the ghosts of these haunted cemeteries?

I believe that they could and I am not alone in this. Many researchers have attempted to catalog the hauntings that occur in cemeteries across the country and aside from a few tales and accounts of lonesome ghosts and vanishing hitchhikers, most of the hauntings seem to have a root in desecration, premature burial, natural disasters and more. It seems that the disturbance of the dead is the single greatest reason why the ghosts of the past return to haunt the graveyards where their bodies can be found.

Interestingly, there are a couple of ways to look at this in order to find a solution to the mystery. Folklore would tell us that when the bodies and resting places of the dead are destroyed, moved or disturbed, the spirits of the dead return to wreak havoc on the living. Is this an example of "ghostlore" -- man's natural inclination to explain what is unexplainable? Could ghost-like phenomena have occurred after the disturbance of burial grounds in the past and then been blamed on ghosts, when the answer may not have been that simple? It's possible that the real answer to haunted cemeteries of this sort may actually lie in the disturbance of the site itself. Could the disturbance of the natural energy of the site be causing the strange reports that follow?

Science would tell us that the decomposition of a body will change the chemical makeup of the surrounding earth, especially in the case of older burials when liner vaults were not in use and the dead literally "returned to the earth". If that soil was then disturbed by digging or construction, this could perhaps release an energy that could be mistaken for ghostly activity. This might also be the case when the bodies themselves have been disturbed. A belief in ghosts is not required to consider the idea that energy stays in our remains after we die and since all matter is in constant motion (again, according to the rules of science) then eerie effects may occur if those remains are damaged or disturbed.

In other cases, cemeteries regarded as haunted have become that way after they have been desecrated and when the monuments and stones have been disturbed, rather than the bodies of the dead. Could a similar event happen here? Could the damage to the natural energy of the site be responsible for the strange reports that often follow? In this case, we have to look into the theories that surround the mysterious "portal" and "crossover" sites, which can often be found in graveyards. This may give some burial grounds an even greater opportunity for being "haunted".

In the pages ahead, we will delve into some of the traditional (and untraditional) reasons why cemeteries may become haunted, from the classic tales of body snatching in the dead of night to premature burials and the controversial ideas of portals.

Buried Alive

To be buried alive is, beyond question, the most terrific of these extremes which has ever fallen to the lot of mere mortality... the boundaries which divide Life from Death, are at best shadowy and vague. Who shall say when one ends and the other begins?

So wrote author Edgar Allan Poe in his macabre short story, "The Premature Burial". In his tale, Poe refers to being buried alive as a "certain theme" that is "too entirely horrible for the purposes of legitimate fiction". The narrator in Poe's story had reason to be afraid of such an end because he suffered from catalepsy, a neurological condition that could produce episodes of extreme paralysis, mimicking, and being mistaken for, death. Many believed that Poe himself suffered from this horrid disease, but this was not the case. His terror of being buried alive came from the dark recesses of his imagination, but he was not alone in this fear. It was a very common phobia during the 1800's and one that was justified given the state of medical technology at that time.

The fear of being buried alive is perhaps as old as the fear of death itself. Being taken from this world at the moment of death is bad enough, but the prospect of being mistakenly identified as dead and then waiting in suffocating horror-- well, it's too much for most of us to think about.

The obsession with premature burial reached its peak during the Victorian era but anecdotes of those unfortunate enough to be buried alive stretch back for centuries. Anxiety of premature burial still exists today, but thanks to advances in the medical world, it remains more of a private fear that one of public hysteria, as seen in years past. The terror reached its peak in the 1800's with well-known doctors and published accounts by authors like Poe making matters even more intriguing. Poe even wrote an article on what was believed to be a true account of a woman being entombed alive. It reportedly happened to the wife of an eminent official in the Baltimore area. She was seized by an unknown illness, and to all outward appearances, was dead. She was placed in the family vault and was left undisturbed for three years. At the end of that time, the tomb was opened for an interment and as the door was pulled open, the skeleton of the woman in her burial clothing tumbled out! Apparently, she had revived soon after her funeral and had succeeded in knocking her coffin from the ledge where it rested. It broke open and she was able to escape. She was not able to get through the door of the tomb however and she died there, her screams unheard by those passing outside.

While the medical profession was quick to disregard the claims of "rampant" premature burials, it was hard to ignore the accounts and evidence that came in response to public interest. One physician, Franz Hartmann, published a book called Premature Burial in 1895. He collected over 750 cases of people being buried alive and earned the almost universal condemnation of the book by other doctors. How could they not disagree? The public mania over premature burials highlighted the fact that doctors were merely human and sometimes made mistakes-- perhaps even mistakes that had people waking up from a trance and finding themselves entombed in a coffin.

The stories and alleged incidents of premature burial fueled the public's imagination and created both scandalous and spine-tingling reading. In 1849, a severe cholera epidemic killed 199 people. An old woman, who was in charge of the cholera wards, stated that as soon as patients died, they were placed into wooden coffins and the lids screwed down. They were then moved outside into a small shed so that they would be out of the way. "Sometimes", she coldly told authors William Tebb and Edward Vollum, "they'd come to afterwards and we did hear them kicking in their coffins, but we never unscrewed them, because we knew they had to die".

A particularly gruesome case was recounted in the *Undertaker's Journal and Funeral Directors' Review* for July 1889. A portion of the article recalled a New York case from 1854 in which a baker placed the coffin of his deceased daughter in a temporary vault in order for the girl's older sister to come to New York from St. Louis for the funeral. This was possible, testified the undertaker who performed the services, because the death occurred in the winter and the outdoor temperature prevented severe decomposition. When the rest of the family arrived, the vault was opened for the funeral. When the lid of the coffin was removed, they discovered that the girl had apparently been buried alive. Her grave clothes had been torn to shreds and according to the report, several of her fingers had literally been bitten off. She had supposedly eaten them in a vain attempt to prolong her life.

Another account, from *Eddowe's Journal* of August 1844, tells of a child who was accidentally buried alive. While the sexton was filling in the grave, he was startled to hear the boy calling for help. He quickly uncovered the coffin and the boy was rescued. He later made a full recovery and while this tale had a happy ending, the account ended with a somber postscript. "Not long ago, in making a grave in the same cemetery, a coffin was broken into, and it was found that the occupant had revived after burial, and had gnawed the flesh of both wrists before life was finally extinguished."

Today, it hard for us to guess just how fearful the Victorians needed to be about being buried alive. Certainly, there were many tales and stories of those who discovered bodies in a state that appeared as if they had been trying to escape from the grave. There were also plenty of "near-miss" experiences, told by those who fell into a stupor and were almost buried alive. In all honesty though, most of the fears probably came from the popular press. Such tales of death and gruesomeness played right into the public demand for ghosts and frightening stories. How much more frightening is a macabre event that can actually occur to you?

Premature burials did sometimes take place, but how did they occur? In the days of early medical science, tests for diseases and even the pronouncement of a person being dead were crude at best. It is commonly known today that we do not die all at once, but rather in bits and pieces. For example, our hair and our fingernails often continue to grow after death takes place. This is accepted today, but in years past, it was thought to be one of the supernatural signs of the living dead.

It was also accepted that true corpses feel no pain. This was often a fact that was used to decide if a person was dead or not. In the 1800's, a Dr. Josat invented a pair of sharp forceps that were used to viciously pinch the nipples of someone thought to be dead. Another idea was to thrust long needles under the finger and toe nails. (I would sincerely hope to be already dead if forced to undergo either of these tests!)

Doctors also used temperature to determine if a person was dead. Unfortunately, touching a cold corpse is not always accurate, as deeply comatose patients are also known for being quite cold. In the late 1800's, "necrometers" were used to check body temperatures and were calibrated to indicate if the patient was "alive", "probably dead" or "dead". Needless to say, they were not all that accurate and mistakes were sometimes made.

It has also long been a tradition to check for a person's breath in determining whether or not they are dead. Earlier in the book, I described using a mirror for people who died in their home to see if the glass fogged up or not. This method was used for years and was never totally reliable.

So, if we accept the fact that people could often be mistaken for being dead, what sort of ailments most commonly caused this to occur?

Catalepsy was probably the most common sickness to mimic death during the Victorian period. It has been characterized by the immobility of the muscles and was easily mistaken for death. During a trance state, a victim's limbs taken on a wax-like flexibility that causes them to be shaped into odd positions, where they can remain indefinitely. Catalepsy often occurred during moments of hysteria and was a common side effect to schizophrenia before drug treatments came into use. There were other diseases that could also mimic death like yellow fever and the comas caused by many of these ailments were often mistaken for death in the days of more primitive medical treatments. They tended to create a very deep, sleep-like state and often took a lengthy period for the victim to recover. The fate of the comatose patient in those days often depended on the patience and the vigilance of doctors and relatives and the legal time limits placed on the interval between death and burial.

As the horrific tales fed the public frenzy over premature burial, the Victorians soon began a search for ways to prevent such atrocities from taking place. In days past, the surest way to avoid being buried alive was to obtain the services of a doctor who could be trusted enough to actually view and examine the corpse. Many instances of premature burial occurred because of misdiagnosis by relatives or because of absentee doctors who, acting in perfect accordance with the law, were not required to actually see a body to pronounce the person dead. A certificate of death only needed to state that the doctor had been told they were dead. The obvious answer to this problem was for the relatives to be in no doubt about whether you were dead or not and if there was some question, for them to have explicit instructions about what to do to eliminate that lingering doubt.

During the height of the fear over premature burial, caskets were sold that actually had a "safety spring" inside that would cause the lid to open if the catch was triggered by the occupant.

The mystery writer Wilkie Collins always carried a letter with him detailing the elaborate precautions that his family should take in order to prevent his premature burial. Other people added to their wills that no one in the family would benefit until it was absolutely sure they were a corpse. They even went as far as to write friends into the will who would be given a substantial amount of money to sever their heads from their body or to pierce their veins.

The *Undertaker and Funeral Director's Journal* in 1889 told of a family in Virginia that had developed a curious custom and one it had kept for more than a century. Over 100 years before, a member of the family had been exhumed and was found to have been accidentally buried alive. From that time on, each member of the family who died was stabbed in the heart with a knife by the head of the household. They ended the custom around 1850 when a young woman in the house apparently died. The knife was plunged into her heart and she suddenly gave a terrible scream and died, awakened from the trance that she had been in. The incident broke her father's heart and he committed suicide a short time later.

There is no doubt that the worst possible experience of premature burial would be awakening while trapped inside of a coffin, below six feet of earth. No matter how loudly you screamed or clawed at the lid of the coffin, there was little chance for escape -- or was there?

In 1896, Count Karnice-Karnicki, chamberlain to the Tsar of Russia, invented an ingenious device to prevent premature burial. The count imagined the nightmare faced by anyone who might be buried underground. How could such a person summon help? The apparatus that he constructed was a tube that passed vertically from the lid of the coffin and then ended in an airtight box above the level of the ground. Resting on the chest of the deceased was a glass sphere that was attached to a spring running the entire length of the tube. It connected to a mechanism inside of the box. The slightest movement of the chest would move the sphere in a way that the spring would cause the lid of the box above to fly open and admit air and light. The spring also activated a flag, a light and a loud bell to attract the attention of anyone who might be in the cemetery. This device could be rented for a small amount of money and after a length of time went by (and there was no chance for revival) the tube could be pulled up and used in another coffin.

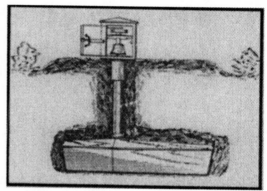

There were other devices invented too that allowed anyone who awoke in the grave to ring bells, sound alarms and wave flags. There is no record of what the success rate for these devices might have been but I can imagine that the inventions gave many Victorians no small amount of comfort.

A security coffin with a bell and air shaft. It was designed by August Linquist of Charlton, Iowa and patented in June 1893.

Others looked for a more direct solution to notify their families that they were alive. One man, John Wilmer, was actually buried in the back garden of his home. A switch that was placed in his hand at the time of his burial and was connected to an alarm in his house. If he awakened from any sort of trance, he could immediately summon help. For some reason though, apparently fearing a technical failure, he asked his relatives to be sure that they carried out an annual inspection of the wiring! The reader is bound to laugh at such a suggestion, wondering just how long Wilmer planned to remain alive in his grave? However, that laughter is bound to turn into a shudder after they read the strange account that follows.

Martin Sheets was a wealthy businessman who lived in Terre Haute, Indiana in the early 1900's. One of his greatest fears was that of a premature burial. He often dreamt of being awake, but unable to move, at the moment the doctor pronounced him dead and then regaining consciousness while trapped in a coffin below the ground. Sheets decided to fight his fears by investing some of his resources in the prevention of his being buried alive.

First of all, he had a casket custom-designed with latches fitted on the inside. In this way, should he be placed inside prematurely, he would be able to open the coffin and escape. He also began construction on a mausoleum so that when he died, or was thought to have died, he would not be imprisoned under six feet of dirt. The mausoleum was well built and attractive but Sheets realized that even if he did manage to escape from his casket, he would still be trapped inside of a stone prison.

The Sheets Mausoleum

He came up with another clever idea. He installed a telephone inside of the tomb with a direct line to the main office of the cemetery. In this way, he could summon help by simply lifting the receiver. The line was fitted with an automatic indicator light so that even if no words were spoken, the light would come on in the office and help would soon be on the way.

Death came for Martin Sheets in 1910 and he was entombed in the mausoleum. I would imagine that for several days afterward, cemetery staff workers kept a close eye on the telephone indicator light in the office. After more time passed though, it was probably forgotten. Years went by and the telephone system in the area changed. Eventually, the direct line to the cemetery office was removed but thanks to very specific instructions in Sheets' will, and the money to pay for it, the telephone in the mausoleum remained connected and active.

A number of years later, Sheets' widow also passed away. She was discovered one day lying on her bed with the telephone clutched in her hand. In fact, she held the receiver so tightly that it had to be pried from her fingers. It was soon learned that she had experienced a severe stroke and family members assumed that she had been trying to call an ambulance when she finally died. A service was held and after a quiet memorial service, she was taken to the family mausoleum, where she would be interred next to her husband.

When cemetery workers entered the mausoleum, they received the shock of their lives. Nothing there was disturbed, they saw, except for one, very chilling item. Martin Sheets' telephone, locked away for all of these years, was hanging from the wall -- its receiver inexplicably off the hook!

Ghostly tales connected to persons who have been buried alive appear frequently in the annals of the supernatural and many of them are connected to the greater lore of a given location. For instance, one of the most terrifying tales of a Greenwood Cemetery in Central Illinois involves the spirited fates of a number of prisoners of war that were accidentally buried alive on the edge of the graveyard. This area is now considered one of the most haunted sites in the cemetery.

Grave Robbery

Beyond the fear of death itself, man has great concern over what becomes of his body after his spirit has departed from it. The fear of indignities being perpetrated on the body was a deciding factor for many years in cremations and the construction of private crypts and mausoleums.

Grave robbery is perhaps one of the most gruesome crimes to ever exist. In the late 1700's and early 1800's, the chances of being dug up and removed from one's coffin were much greater than your chances for being buried alive. The early history of grave robbery was created more out of necessity than desire. In those days, medical schools were faced with dire problems. A surgeon was only as good as his knowledge of anatomy and yet it was illegal in those days to dissect a corpse. Because of this, the schools were unable to legally procure an adequate supply of dead bodies for the teaching of medical students. Thanks to this, the schools had to depend on the services of loathsome men called "body snatchers", or more eloquently "resurrectionists", who would seek out fresh corpses in the local cemeteries. They would then sell the bodies to doctors and scientists for medical experimentation and teaching.

While body snatching started as a British phenomenon, it did happen in America too. The city of St. Louis has long been home to a number of medical schools and in the early part of the 1800's, all of them depended on "resurrectionist" activities to obtain cadavers of their anatomy and surgical classes. A surgeon at that time might have been jeered in the street as "old sawbones" and dissection of the dead for medical teaching was not seen as kindly, nor was it as understood, as it is in these more modern times. Eccentric surgeon Dr. William McDowell, who opened the McDowell Medical College in 1848, was so despised that he took to wearing a metal breastplate under his clothing in case one of his enemies shot at him on the street. He mounted cannons on top of the school and armed the students with muskets in case the local populace ever attacked them. He and his students often had to face down rioters and eject them from the school by force.

According to legend, there are few bodies that still remain today in several of the graveyards near the University of Maryland School of Medicine in Baltimore and cases of body snatching were even worse in New York. By the time that New York passed its anatomy law in 1854, grave robbers were emptying between 600 and 700 graves per year to supply the medical schools with cadavers. It was said that the worst city in America for body snatching in the 1800's was Cincinnati, because it had more medical schools than any other city in the west. It was estimated that over 5,000 bodies were stolen in the city alone.

As the years passed in the Nineteenth Century, more medical schools began to appear and as they did, the demand increased for cadavers to give the students hands-on lessons in anatomy. Today, medical schools require anywhere from 300 to 800 cadavers a year but state laws provide colleges with bodies and many people freely donate their bodies to science. This was not always the case though and so resurrectionists had to find bodies wherever they could. The medical schools often hired these men or equally as common -- the students did the body snatching themselves. On occasion, people were even murdered for their bodies.

Body snatching was not limited to areas around medical schools either. They were often taken from rural cemeteries and then shipped to the colleges that needed them. Most professional resurrectionists sold cadavers for about $5 each but they could go for as high as $30. Often, to save themselves the trouble of digging up the graves that had already been filled, body snatchers and medical students would make arrangements with devious undertakers and gravediggers, carrying away the corpses before the coffins ever made it to the cemetery. As the unsuspecting family was burying an empty, weighted casket, their loved one was being carried off to a medical school somewhere.

Body snatching became so prevalent that coffin makers began catering to those who feared for their loved one's remains. The manufacturers began making special containers to discourage grave robbers, from heavy metal coffins to caskets with locks on their lids and even what were called "torpedo coffins", which were equipped with explosive booby traps. For those who had little money, they turned to other methods to protect the dead. Embalming was not practiced until the late 1800's and so freshly buried bodies were preferred by resurrectionists over those that had started to decompose. With this in mind, families would hire (or would do it themselves) grave watchers to sit by the grave until the body was believed to have decomposed to the point that no medical school could use it.

Those whose bodies were not claimed, who died in a poor house or on a country farm or who were buried in a potter's field were most likely to have ended up on an anatomy table. These graves were most frequently raided, as were African-American cemeteries, especially in the South. Even private family burial plots in rural areas were not safe. Body snatchers often preferred these sites because they were isolated and there was less chance of discovery. City church burial grounds were less often affected. This was not because they were considered sacred but because there were in more populated areas.

Body snatching began to decline in the late 1890's, as most states had passed laws by this time that would provide medical schools with cadavers. Even so, body snatchers were still reportedly at work as late as the 1920's selling corpses to medical colleges in Nashville, Tennessee, Iowa City and to other places that could not afford to purchase bodies by legal means.

Many of the grave robberies committed in America though were not for the bodies in the graves, but for the valuables the deceased had been buried with. It was not uncommon in the 1800's and early 1900's for caskets to be found broken open in the local cemetery and the rings and jewelry of the corpse to have disappeared.

The standard operating procedures for such men would be to attend burials and wakes, looking for loot that would be placed in the casket with the body. The scouting trips also led to payments made to gravediggers and cemetery workers, who would pretend to close the graves after the services. A few shovels of dirt would be thrown down into the grave while the mourners were still present, just for good measure. Later, in the dead of night, the thieves would return to the graveyard and remove the valuables from the coffins. In addition to jewelry and personal belongings, other valuable prizes including gold-rimmed spectacles and the gold crowns from the teeth of the departed. These small amounts of gold were often melted down and sold on the black market.

Perhaps the most famous haunting connected to a grave robbery in American history involves the ghost stories associated with the tomb of Abraham Lincoln in Springfield, Illinois. In this case, we don't have just the grave robbery to explain why Lincoln's spirit might be restless either. As you will soon see, the posthumous wanderings of his corpse, and an ongoing mystery, may be more than enough to explain this haunting. You see, Lincoln's monument and tomb in Springfield's Oak Ridge Cemetery has long been a place of mystery, intrigue, speculation and bizarre history -- and from the very beginning, it was believed to be haunted by the ghost of the President himself.

Abraham Lincoln's monument & Tomb in Springfield, Illinois

Following his assassination in April 1865, the President's body was returned to Springfield and to a grave in a remote, wooded cemetery called Oak Ridge. The cemetery had been started around 1860 and it mostly consisted of woods and unbroken forest. In fact, not until after Lincoln was buried there was much done in the way of improvement, adding roads, iron gates and a caretaker's residence.

Lincoln was taken to the receiving vault of the cemetery and placed there with his sons, Willie, who had died during the presidency and Eddie, Lincoln's son who had died many years before. A short time later, a temporary vault was built for Lincoln and in seven months, on December 21, he was placed inside.

The new construction on a permanent tomb would last for more than five years and it was during this time that strange things began to be reported in the vicinity of Lincoln's resting place. A few days after the body was placed in the receiving vault, Springfield residents and curiosity seekers began to tell of sighting a spectral image of Lincoln himself wandering about near the crypt. The legends say that he was taking walks to investigate the broken ground where his tomb would someday stand. And the stories didn't end there either -- after the bodies were moved to the monument tomb, strange sobbing noises and sounds like footsteps were often heard at the site.

On September 19, 1871, the caskets of Lincoln and his sons were removed from the hillside crypt and taken to the catacomb. The dead president was laid to rest again, for another three years, while the workmen toiled away outside. On October 9, 1874, Lincoln was moved again. This time, his body was placed inside of a marble sarcophagus, which had been placed in the center of the semi-circular catacomb. A few days later, the monument was finally dedicated. Money had been raised for the groups of statues that were situated outside and the citizens of Springfield seemed content with the final resting place of their beloved Abraham Lincoln.

But then a new threat arose from a direction that no one could have ever predicted. In 1876, a band of thieves broken into the tomb and almost made off with the president's remains. They had planned to hold the body for ransom and only failed because one of the men in their ranks was a spy for the Secret Service.

It did not take long before the story of the Lincoln grave robbery became a hotly denied rumor, or at best, a fading legend. The custodians of the site simply decided that it was something they did not wish to talk about. Of course, as the story began to be denied, the people who had some recollection of the tale created their own truth in myths and conspiracies. Hundreds of people came to see the Lincoln burial site and many of them were not afraid to ask about the stories that were being spread about the tomb. From 1876 to 1878, custodian John C. Power gave rather evasive answers to anyone who prodded him for details about the grave robbery. He was terrified of one question in particular and it seemed to be the one most often asked- was he sure that Lincoln's body had been returned safely to the sarcophagus after the grave robbers took it out? Power was terrified of that question for one reason-- because at that time, Lincoln's grave was completely empty!

On the morning of November 1876, when John T. Stuart of the Lincoln National Monument Association learned what had occurred in the tomb with the would-be robbers, he rushed out to the site. He was not able to rest after the incident, fearing that the grave robbers, who had not been caught at that time, would return and finish their ghoulish handiwork. So, he made a decision. He notified the custodian and told him that they must take the body from the crypt and hide it elsewhere in the building. Together, they decided the best place to store it would be in the cavern of passages which lay between the Memorial Hall and the catacomb.

Later that night, Power and four members of the Memorial Association stole out to the monument and carried the 500-pound coffin around the base of the obelisk, through Memorial Hall and into the dark labyrinth. They placed the coffin near some boards that had been left behind in the construction. The following day, Power set to work digging a grave below the dirt floor. It was slow work, because it had to be done between visitors to the site, and he also had a problem with water seeping into the hole. Finally, he gave up and simply covered the coffin with the leftover boards and wood.

For the next two years, Lincoln lay beneath a pile of wood in the labyrinth, while visitors from all over the world wept and mourned over the sarcophagus at the other end of the monument. More and more of these visitors asked questions about the theft- questions full of suspicion, as if they knew something they really had no way of knowing.

In the summer and fall of 1877, the legend took another turn. Workmen arrived at the monument to erect the naval and infantry groups of statuary on the corners of the upper deck. Their work would take them into the labyrinth, where Power feared they would discover the coffin. The scandal would be incredible, so Power made a quick decision. He called the workmen together and swearing them to secrecy, showed them the coffin. They promised to keep the secret, but within days everyone in Springfield seemed to know that Lincoln's body was not where it was supposed to be. Soon, the story was spreading all over the country.

Power was now in a panic. The body had to be more securely hidden and to do this, he needed more help. He contacted two of his friends, Major Gustavas Dana and General Jasper Reece and explained the situation. These men brought three others to meet with Power, Edward Johnson, Joseph Lindley and James McNeill, all of Springfield.

On the night of November 18, the six men began digging a grave for Lincoln at the far end of the labyrinth. Cramped and cold, and stifled by stale air, they gave up around midnight with the coffin just barely covered and traces of their activity very evident. Power promised to finish the work the next day. These six men, sobered by the responsibility that faced them, decided to form a brotherhood to guard the secret of the tomb.

After the funeral of Mary Lincoln, John T. Stuart told the Guard that Robert Lincoln wanted to have his mother's body hidden away with his father's. So, late on the night of July 21, the men slipped into the monument and moved Mary's double-leaded casket, burying it in the labyrinth next to Lincoln's.

Visitors to the tomb increased as the years went by, all of them paying their respects to the two empty crypts. Finally, in 1886, the Lincoln National Monument Association decided that it was time to provide a new tomb for Lincoln in the catacomb. A new and stronger crypt of brick and mortar was designed and made ready. The press was kept outside as the Guard, and others who shared the secret of the tomb, brought the Lincoln caskets out of the labyrinth. Eighteen persons who had known Lincoln in life filed past the casket, looking into a square hole that had been cut into the lead coffin. Strangely, Lincoln had changed very little. His face was darker after 22 years but they were still the same sad features these people had always known.

The Guard of Honor lifted the casket and placed it next to Mary's smaller one. The two of them were taken into the catacomb and lowered into the new brick and mortar vault. Here, they would sleep for all time.....

"All time" lasted for about 13 more years. In 1899, Illinois legislators decided the monument was to be torn down and a new one built from the foundations. It seemed that the present structure was settling unevenly, cracking around the "eternal" vault of the president.

There was once again the question of what to do with the bodies of the Lincoln family. The Guard of Honor (who was still around) came up with a clever plan. During the 15 months needed for construction, the Lincoln's would be secretly buried in a multiple grave a few feet away from the foundations of the tomb. As the old structure was torn down, tons of stone and dirt would be heaped onto the grave site both to disguise and protect it. When the new monument was finished, the grave would be uncovered again.

When the new building was completed, the bodies were exhumed once again. In the top section of the grave were the coffins belonging to the Lincoln sons and to a grandson, also named Abraham. The former president and Mary were buried on the bottom level and so safely hidden that one side of the temporary vault had to be battered away to reach them.

Lincoln's coffin was the last to be moved and it was close to sunset when a steam engine finally hoisted it up out of the ground. The protective outer box was removed and six construction workers lifted the coffin onto their shoulders and took it into the catacomb. The other members of the family had been placed in their crypts and Lincoln's was placed into a white, marble sarcophagus.

The group dispersed after switching on the new electric burglar alarm. This device connected the monument to the caretaker's house, which was a few hundred feet away. As up-to-date as this device was, it still did not satisfy the fears of Robert Lincoln, who was sure that his father's body would be snatched again if they were not careful. He stayed in constant contact with the Guard of Honor, who were still working to insure the safety of the Lincoln's remains, and made a trip to Springfield every month or so after the new monument was completed. Something just wasn't right- even though the alarm worked perfectly, he could not give up the idea that the robbery might be repeated.

He journeyed to Springfield and brought with him his own set of security plans. He met with officials and gave them explicit directions on what he wanted done. The construction company was to break a hole in the tile floor of the monument and place his father's casket at a depth of 10 feet. The coffin would then be encased in a cage of steel bars and the hole would be filled with concrete, making the president's final resting place into a solid block of stone.

On September 26, 1901, a group assembled in secret to make the final arrangements for Lincoln's last burial. The casket was lowered down into the cage of steel and two tons of cement was poured over it, forever encasing the president's body in stone.

You would think that would be the end of it, but as with all lingering mysteries, a few questions still remain. The strangest are perhaps these: does the body of Abraham Lincoln really lie beneath the concrete in the catacomb? Or was the last visit from Robert Lincoln part of some elaborate ruse to throw off any further attempts to steal the president's body? And did, as some rumors have suggested, Robert arrange with the Guard of Honor to have his father's body hidden in a different location entirely?

Most historians would agree that Lincoln's body is safely encased in the concrete of the crypt, but let's look at this with a conspiratorial eye for a moment. Whose word do we have for the fact that Lincoln's body is where it is said to be? We only have the statement of Lincoln's son, Robert, his friends and of course, the Guard of Honor -- but weren't these the same individuals who left visitors to the monument to grieve before an empty sarcophagus while the president was actually hidden in the labyrinth, beneath a few inches of dirt?

And what of the stories that claim that Lincoln's ghost still walks the tomb?

Many have reported that he, or some other spirit here, does not rest in peace. Many tourists, staff members and historians have had some unsettling impressions here that aren't easily laughed away. Usually these encounters have been reported as the sound of ceaseless pacing, tapping footsteps on the tile floors, whispers and quiet voices, and the sounds of someone crying or weeping in the corridors.

Do the events of the past merely echo here in this lonely tomb? Or does the phantom of Abraham Lincoln still linger behind, wondering where his body might now be buried?

Unmarked Graves

Many burial grounds across the country are filled with unmarked graves. This is often caused by poor record keeping or graves that went unmarked because the occupants committed suicide or were criminals. Many researchers believe that graves that are left purposely, or accidentally unmarked, can cause cemeteries to become haunted as well. The annals of the supernatural are filled with stories of ghosts who walk because their graves have been left unmarked.

Rosehill Cemetery in Chicago was started in 1859 and remains one of the most beautiful burial grounds in the city. It serves as the final resting place for more than 1500 notable residents of the region.

As mentioned, ghostly lore is filled with tales of the deceased returning from the grave to protest the manner in which they were laid to rest and Rosehill boasts at least one legend of this type. In October 1995, a groundskeeper at the cemetery reported that he had seen a woman wandering about in the graveyard at night. She had been standing next to a tree, not far from the wall that separates the cemetery from Peterson Avenue. The staff member stopped his truck and got out. The cemetery was closed for the night and he was going to tell the woman that she had to leave and offer to escort her to the gate. When he approached her, he realized that the woman, who was dressing in some sort of flowing white garment, was actually floating above the ground! Before his eyes, she turned into a mist and slowly vanished. Not surprisingly, the groundskeeper wasted no time in rushing to the cemetery office to report the weird incident.

Strangely, a woman from Des Plaines, Illinois called the cemetery office the following day and requested that a marker be placed on the grave of her aunt, Carrie Kalbas, who had died in 1933. The grave site had previously been unmarked but the night before, the woman claimed that her aunt had appeared to her in a dream. She asked her niece to be sure that her burial place was marked because she wanted to be remembered. The aunt's grave was located in an old family plot and staff members went out to the site to verify the location and to see what type of monument was needed. They were amazed to find that the grave was located in the exact spot where the apparition had been reported the night before! The grave stone was ordered and the ghost was never seen again.

Desecration

Of all of the reasons why cemeteries become haunted, the desecration of graves remains probably the highest cause on the list. There are many graveyards that have been disturbed (in one way or another) and currently boast ghosts and hauntings. There are also many different ways that a cemetery can become disturbed. In some cases, nature plays a hand in the desecration as natural disasters take place that may unearth bodies or destroy grave sites.

For instance, located in Alton, was once the first prison in the state of Illinois. During the Civil War, it was turned into a penitentiary for Confederate prisoners. Conditions here were horrible and death and disease ran rampant. In 1863, thousands died from smallpox and during the height of the epidemic, a small island was commandeered on the Mississippi for use as a hospital camp. Hundreds of the men who died were buried on the island and were forgotten at war's end. As time passed, the island was washed away a small piece at a time by the changing currents of the river. The bodies and the graves were lost and today, only a small piece of land from the island remains against the Missouri shore. It is believed that the ghosts of the men who were interred on the island still haunt this area, along with the ruins of the former prison itself.

In most cases though, it is the hand of man that does the most damage to the resting places of the dead. The expansion of cities and homes can often be the culprit as new building sites are laid out without much thought as to what may have been present on the location before. Construction crews often uncover some gruesome surprises in the course of a day's work.

In other cases, the work of vandals has been cited or even perhaps the rumored "cultists" who practice their dark rituals in abandoned cemeteries. Such deeds are said to attract a negative energy to the location. Both of these have been said to play a part in the haunting of Bachelor's Grove Cemetery, one of the most haunted spots in the Chicago area.

Bachelor's Grove is located near the southwest Chicago suburb of Midlothian, tucked away at the edge of the Rubio Woods Forest Preserve. Many believe it to be the most haunted place in the entire region and this small, ramshackle burial ground has been the scene of more than 100 documented accounts of ghosts and paranormal phenomena.

The history of Bachelor's Grove has been somewhat shadowy over the years but most historians agree that it was started in the early part of the 1800's. In August 1933, the famous *Ripley's Believe it or Not* column featured a short piece on Bachelor's Grove Cemetery, stating that it was so unusual because even though it had been set aside as a burial ground for "bachelors only", there were also women buried here. Unfortunately though, the column was inaccurate and this has been just one of the many myths and misconceptions created about the cemetery over the years. The name of the cemetery came not from the number of single men buried here but from the name of a family who settled in the area. The lore about the "bachelor burial ground" dates back to 1833 or 1834 when a man named Stephen H. Rexford settled in the region with a number of other unmarried men. Allegedly, they began calling the place "Bachelor's Grove" but this has been widely disputed by historians, who believe the name "Batchelor's Grove" was already

in use at the time.

They believe that the name of the cemetery came from a settlement that was started in the late 1820's that consisted of mostly German immigrants from New York, Vermont and Connecticut. One family that moved into the area was called "Batchelder" and their name was given to the timberland where they settled, just as other timber areas like Walker's Grove, Cooper's Grove and Blackstone's Grove were named after families and individuals.

Regardless, the small settlement continued for some years as Batchelor's Grove, until 1850, when it was changed to "Bremen" by postmaster Samuel Everden in recognition of the new township name where the post office was located. In 1855, it was changed again to "Bachelder's Grove" by postmaster Robert Patrick but the post office closed down just three years later. Officially, the settlement ceased to exist and was swallowed by the forest around it.

The cemetery itself has a much stranger history -- or at least a more mysterious one. The land was apparently first set aside to be used as a burial ground in 1844, when the first recorded burial took place here, that of Eliza (Mrs. Leonard H.) Scott. The land had been donated by the property owner, Samuel Everden, and it was named "Everden" in his honor. Strangely though, this first burial is disputed by an article that appeared in the Blue Island Sun-Standard in August 1935. According to this story, the first burial was that of a man named William B. Nobles, who died in 1838. The last burials to take place are believed to be that of Laura M. McGhee in 1965 and Robert E. Shields, who was cremated and buried in the family plot here in 1989.

Regardless of exactly when the cemetery started, the first legal record of it appeared when Edward Everden sold the property to Frederick Schmidt in 1864. A notation in the records stated that all of the land would be sold excepting "one acre used as a grave yard". This makes it clear that the cemetery was already in existence and had been created by Everden, not, as the Schmidt family later tried to claim, by Frederick Schmidt. However, the Schmidt's did intend to expand the original property later on, but there is no evidence that this was ever done.

The last independent caretaker of the cemetery was a man named Clarence Fulton, whose family were early settlers in the township. According to Fulton, Bachelor's Grove was like a park for many years and people often came here to fish and swim in the adjacent pond. Families often visited on weekends to care for the graves of the deceased and to picnic under the trees.

Problems began in and around the cemetery in the early 1960's, at the same time that the Midlothian Turnpike was closed to vehicle traffic in front of the cemetery. Even before that, the cemetery had become a popular spot along a "lover's lane" and when the road closed, it became even more isolated. Soon it began to show signs of vandalism and decay and a short time later, became considered haunted. Although the amount of paranormal activity that actually occurs in the cemetery has been argued by some, few can deny that strange things do happen here. When the various types of phenomenon really began is unclear but it has been happening for more than three decades now. Was the burial ground already haunted? Or did the haunting actually begin with the destructive decades of the 1960's and 1970's?

The vandals first discovered Bachelor's Grove in the 1960's and probably because of its secluded location, they began to wreak havoc on the place. Gravestones were knocked over and destroyed, sprayed with paint, broken apart and even stolen. Police reports later stated that markers from Bachelor's Grove turned up in homes, yards and even as far away as Evergreen Cemetery. Worst of all, in 1964, 1975 and 1978, graves were opened and caskets removed. Bones were sometimes found to be strewn about the cemetery. Desecrated graves are still frequently found in the cemetery.

Was the haunting first caused by these disturbances? Most believe so, for even the early superstitions of the tombstone give credence to the idea that man has always felt that desecration of graves causes cemeteries to become haunted. Grave markers began as heavy stones that were placed on top of the graves of the deceased in the belief that the weight of it would keep the dead person, or their angry spirit, beneath the ground. Those who devised this system believed that if the stone was moved, the dead would be free to walk the earth.

There is no question that vandals have not been kind to Bachelor's Grove, but then neither has time. The Midlothian Turnpike bypassed the cemetery and even the road leading back to the graveyard was eventually closed. People forgot about the place and allowed it to fade into memory, just like the poor souls buried here.

Today, the cemetery is overgrown with weeds and is surrounded by a high, chain-link fence, although access is easily gained through the holes that trespassers have cut into it. The cemetery sign is long since gone. It once hung above the main gates, which are now broken open and lean dangerously into the confines of Bachelor's Grove.

The first thing noticed by those who visit here is the destruction. Tombstones seem to be randomly scattered about, no longer marking the resting places of those whose names are inscribed upon them. Many of the stones are missing, lost forever and perhaps carried away by thieves. These macabre crimes gave birth to legends about how the stones of the cemetery move about under their own power. The most disturbing things to visitors though are the trenches and pits that have been dug above some of the graves, as vandals have attempted to make off with souvenirs from those whose rest they disturb.

Near the front gate is a broken monument to a woman whose name was heard being called repeatedly on an audio tape. Some amateur ghost hunters left a recording device running while on an excursion to Bachelor's Grove and later, upon playback of the tape, they discovered that the recorder had been left on the ruined tombstone of a woman that had the same name as that being called to on the tape.

Coincidence? Perhaps, but it hardly seems likely.

Just beyond the rear barrier of the cemetery is a small, stagnant pond that can be seen by motorists who pass on 143rd Street. This pond, while outside of the graveyard, is still not untouched by the horror connected to the place. One night in the late 1970's, two Cook County forest rangers were on night patrol near here and claimed to see the apparition of a horse emerge from the waters of the pond. The animal appeared to be pulling a plow behind it that was steered by the ghost of an old man. The vision crossed the road in front of the ranger's vehicle, was framed for a moment in the glare of their headlights, and then vanished into the forest. The men simply stared in shock for a moment and then looked at one another to be sure that had both seen the same thing. They later reported the incident and since that time, have not been the last to see the old man and the horse.

Little did the rangers know, but this apparition was actually a part of an old legend connected to the pond. It seems that in the 1870's, a farmer was plowing a nearby field when something startled his horse. The farmer was caught by surprise and became tangled in the reins. He was dragged behind the horse and it plunged into the small pond. Unable to free himself, he was pulled down into the murky water by the weight of the horse and the plow and he drowned. Since that time, the vivid recording of this terrible incident has been supernaturally revisiting the surrounding area.

In addition to this unfortunate phantom, the pond was also rumored to be a dumping spot for murder victims during the Prohibition era in Chicago. Those who went on a "one-way ride" were alleged to have ended the trip at the pond near Bachelor's Grove. Thanks to this, their spirits are also said to haunt the dark waters.

For those searching for Bachelor's Grove, it can be found by leaving the roadway and walking up an overgrown gravel track that is surrounded on both sides by the forest. The old road is blocked with chains and concrete dividers and a dented "No Trespassing" sign that hangs ominously near the mouth to the trail. The burial ground lies about a half-mile or so beyond it in the woods.

It is along this deserted road where other strange tales of the cemetery take place. One of these odd occurrences is the sighting of the "phantom farm house". It has been seen appearing and disappearing along the trail for several decades now. The reports date back as far as the early 1960's and continue today. The most credible thing about many of the accounts is that they come from people who originally had no idea that the house shouldn't be there at all.

The house has been reported in all weather conditions and in the daylight hours, as well as at night. There is no historical record of a house existing here but the descriptions of it rarely vary. Each person claims it to be an old frame farm house with two-stories, painted white, with wooden posts, a porch swing and a welcoming light that burns softly in the window. Popular legend states that should you enter this house though, you would never come back out again. As witnesses approach the building, it is reported to get smaller and smaller until it finally just fades away, like someone switching off an old television set. No one has ever claimed to set foot on the front porch of the house.

But the story gets stranger yet! In addition to the house appearing and disappearing, it also shows up at a wide variety of locations along the trail. On one occasion it may be sighted in one area and then at an entirely different spot the next time. Author Dale Kaczmarek, who also heads the *Ghost Research Society* paranormal investigation group, has interviewed dozens of witnesses about the paranormal events at Bachelor's Grove. He has talked to many who say they have experienced the vanishing farm house. He has found that while all of their descriptions of the house are identical, the locations of the sightings are not. In fact, he asked the witnesses to place an "X" on the map of the area where they saw the house. Kaczmarek now has a map of the Bachelor's Grove area with "X's" all over it!

Also from this stretch of trail come reports of "ghost lights". One such light that has been reported many times is a red, beacon-like orb that has been seen flying rapidly up and down the trail to the cemetery. The light is so bright, and moves so fast, that it is impossible to tell what it really looks like. Most witnesses state that they have seen a "red streak" that is left in its wake.

Besides the aforementioned phenomena, there have been many sightings of ghosts and apparitions within Bachelor's Grove Cemetery itself. The two most frequently reported figures have been the "phantom monks" and the so-called "Madonna of Bachelor's Grove".

The claims of the monk-like ghosts are strange in themselves. These spirits are said to be clothed in the flowing robes and cowls of a monastic order and they have been reported in Bachelor's Grove and in other places in the Chicago area too. There are no records to indicate that a monastery ever existed near any of the locations where the "monks" have been sighted though, making them one of the greatest of the area's enigmas.

The most frequently reported spirit though is known by a variety of names from the "Madonna of Bachelor's Grove" to the "White Lady" to the affectionate name of "Mrs. Rogers". Legend has it that she is the ghost of a woman who was buried in the cemetery next to the grave of her young child. She is reported to wander the cemetery on nights of the full moon with an infant wrapped in her arms. She appears to walk aimlessly, with no apparent direction and completely unaware of the people who claim to encounter her. There is no real evidence to say who this woman might be but, over the years, she has taken her place as one of the many spirits of this haunted burial ground.

And there are other ghosts as well. Legends tell more apocryphal tales of a ghostly child who has been seen running across the bridge from one side of the pond to the other, a glowing yellow man and even a black carriage that travels along the old road through the woods.

Many of these tales come from a combination of stories, both new and old, but the majority of first-hand reports and encounters are the result of literally hundreds of paranormal investigations that have been conducted here over the last forty years. Many of the ghost hunters who come to this place are amateur investigators, looking for thrills as much as they are looking for evidence of the supernatural, while others, like Dale Kaczmarek and the *Ghost Research Society*, are much more on the serious side.

An enlargement of the photo taken by Mari Huff

Perhaps the most stunning photograph from Bachelor's Grove was taken in August 1991, during a full-fledged investigation of the cemetery. *Ghost Research Society* members came to the burial ground in the daytime and covered the area with the latest in scientific equipment, cameras, tape recorders and video cameras. All of the members were given maps of the cemetery and instructed to walk through and note any changes in electro-magnetic readings or atmosphere fluctuations. After the maps were compared, it was obvious that several investigators found odd changes in a number of distinct areas. A number of photos were taken in those areas, using both standard and infrared film. Nothing was seen at the time the photographs were taken, but once they were developed, the investigators learned that something had apparently been there!

In a photo, taken by Mari Huff, there appeared the semi-transparent form of a woman, who was seated on the remains of a tombstone. Was this one of the ghosts of Bachelor's Grove? Skeptics immediately said "no", claiming that it was nothing more than a double exposure or an outright hoax.

Curious, I asked for and received a copy of the photograph and had it examined by several independent photographers. Most of them would have liked to come up with a reason why the photograph could not be real, but unfortunately they couldn't. They ruled out the idea of a double exposure and also the theory that the person in the photo was a live woman who was placed in the photo and made to appear like she was a ghost. One skeptic also claimed that the woman in the photo was casting a shadow, but according to the photographers who analyzed the image, the "shadow" is actually nothing more than the natural shading of the landscape. Besides that, one of them asked, if she is casting a shadow in that direction, then why isn't anything else in the frame?

Genuine or not (and I think it is), this photograph is just one of the hundreds of photos taken here that allegedly show supernatural activity. While many of them can be ruled out as nothing more than atmospheric conditions, reflections and poor photography, there are others that cannot.

In the end, we have to ask, what is it about Bachelor's Grove Cemetery? Is it as haunted as we have been led to believe? I have to leave that up to the reader to decide, but strange things happen here and there is little reason to doubt that this one of the most haunted places in the Midwest.

Perhaps even more common than natural disasters and purposeful vandalism are ghostly tales connected to cemeteries that have been "removed" and then built over. With many old graveyards, all of the remains are seldom found, which often leads to problems later on. Growing up in Central Illinois, I found that this was especially true about two small cemeteries in Decatur, Illinois. The removal of these two burials ground would come back to "haunt" the city over and over again, even to this day.

Decatur is a town that is rather notorious for building over the sites of former cemeteries and such poor planning goes back even to the earliest days of the city. The city happens to rest on land where a number of American Indian burial sites are located. Centuries ago, the land around Decatur belonged to tribes within the large Illinwek Confederation. During this time, a number of these tribes settled in the area, although none of them lived within the boundaries of the future city limits. When the first settlers arrived, they would find this land abandoned by the Native Americans. They had used it for their burial grounds and the construction records of a number of local landmarks contains references to workers carting away boxes of Indian bones, skulls and relics.

Besides the Indian burial sites, sketchy records exist today to say that there were once a number of private and family cemeteries scattered throughout old Decatur. Most of these sites have been forgotten over the years. Early burial records in the city were largely nonexistent and many of the forgotten graves were marked with primitive wooden planks and they deteriorated in a few short years. It is not really surprising that many of these tiny graveyards faded from memory within a generation or two, but what of the secrets left behind by Decatur's first "official" cemetery?

Actually, there were two cemeteries located at this site and were located so close together that they have since been listed under the name of the larger of the two, the Common Burial Grounds. The other graveyard, King's Cemetery, was located nearby and accounts state that it was hard to tell where one ended and the other began. The two cemeteries were located on the far west side of the early Decatur settlement and today the corner of Oakland Avenue and West Main Street marks that area. The two cemeteries comprised several acres of ground and probably extended as far east as Haworth Street.

The exact size of the Common Burial Grounds is unknown but it was a part of the Amos Robinson farm. The Robinson family had settled in Decatur just a few years prior to 1836, when Amos Robinson died. He was buried in an orchard on his property, which later became part of the burial grounds.

King's Cemetery was platted in 1865 and was owned by John E. King. The cemetery ran alongside Haworth Street and extended down Wood to Oakland. The cemetery also lay on the edge of the old Robinson farm and as mentioned before, published accounts of that time stated that they were so close together that they were usually mistaken for one.

No one knows for sure when the first burials took place here but it was probably in the early 1830's. The cemeteries were used for many years but were finally closed down because of overcrowding in 1885. The land was sold off to the city to use as building plots for many of the homes and buildings that still stand in that area today. Once the sale went through, workmen were called in to remove the bodies to Greenwood Cemetery, a larger cemetery that was located on the city's south side.

However, these luckless workmen faced a problem. No one had any idea just how many people had been buried in the two cemeteries over the years, thanks to unmarked graves, poor records and lost grave markers and stones. The city pushed the move ahead and the workmen were advised to do the best they could with what information they had to work with. Construction was started a few months later and the old cemeteries were all but forgotten. But they wouldn't stay that way for long....

In 1895, while work crews were building an extension onto West Main Street, they discovered dozens of lost skeletons, the remains of caskets and buried tombstones. This was the first grisly find, but it would not be the last. For years after, new construction brought to light skulls, bones and pieces of wooden coffins. There were no clues as to just how many bodies had been left behind and these gruesome discoveries have continued for years, even up until today.

In 1935, a building on West Wood Street had its basement lowered and a broken wooden box that contained a complete skeleton was found beneath the dirt. Late that same year, a man working in his backyard found four skulls and three long bones in the spot where he planned to put a vegetable patch. This convinced him to find another location. The discovery of bones throughout the neighborhood became such a sensation that young boys organized "digging parties" and more remains surfaced each week. A 1938 newspaper report covered the furor over the lost cemeteries and even stated that Amos Robinson himself was still buried under a driveway on West Main Street.

In recent years, even Decatur's landmark restaurant the Blue Mill was not safe from rumors of strange discoveries. I was at the Blue Mill back in 1996 and was taken down into the basement by several staff members, who told me that a number of skeletons had been found beneath the floor a few years before. The story was never substantiated but these same employees believed the bones were tied into other weird happenings in the place. A number of ghostly encounters had taken place in the kitchen area and many of them were afraid to go down into the basement alone.

The Blue Mill closed down a few years ago and the buildings, which had been on the site since the 1920's, were torn down and the ground was excavated to make way for a new set of buildings and a much larger parking lot. Not surprisingly though, as work progressed, the crew began uncovering bones, skulls and pieces of tombstones that had been left behind from the old cemeteries more than a century before. The foremen on the crew pushed the men to plow the bones back under and to keep working but someone eventually leaked the finds to the local newspaper. The newspaper then contacted the Illinois Archeological Society, who immediately shut down the site until it could be inspected. Within days, small orange flags (designating spots where remains had been found) could be seen dotting the area where the new parking lot had not already been laid. The flags were later removed -- but the bodies never were. To this day, the parking lot can be found to come to a strangely abrupt end at the edge of the street, while a large part of the area lies open and covered with weeds. This entire area was once covered with orange flags and one has to wonder just how many other bodies were never found at all?

However, the former Blue Mill building was not the only place within the bounds of the former graveyards where reports of the restless dead occasionally come. Many of the people who work and live here believe that spirits, whose rest was disturbed years ago still roam this area today.

One family that was plagued by a disturbing ghost contacted a friend who claimed to have psychic abilities to identify the problem behind the knocking and pounding sounds in the house. According to the information the psychic gained through her "automatic writing", the ghost was that of a person who had been died long ago. His grave was now located beneath the front porch of the house and he wanted someone to help him. A short time later, they climbed beneath the porch with a shovel and began digging. It wasn't long before they discovered a number of scattered bones. They turned them over to the authorities and with the help of their pastor, arranged for a proper burial for them. The ghost troubled them no longer.

Another man that I spoke with lived on West Wood Street as a boy. He told me about an experience that he had many years ago. He was playing outside one afternoon and caught a glimpse of a man standing in the far corner of the lot. His features were blurry and his clothing was hard to make out. He said that the phantom figure only stood there for a few moments before he noticed something very strange about him -- that he was only visible to the knees and below that he faded away into nothing. The mysterious man soon vanished altogether.

An additional house, on West Main Street, is haunted by the ghost of a pale young girl who endlessly walks back and forth through the house. She seems oblivious to the people who live there now, as if she is from another time, but has also been seen skipping, running and playing with a small red ball. The occupants have also heard the sounds of knocks and whispers in the house on occasion. One has to wonder if she might be another of the specters from Decatur's two most famous "lost" cemeteries?

One of the most strange, but often overlooked, cases of cemetery disturbance took place in the town of Crosby, Texas in the early 1980's. That was at about the same time that the film *Poltergeist* was playing in movie theaters across the country. In the movie, spirits and strange activity besiege a family because their home was inadvertently built over the top of a cemetery. In Crosby, these same events were taking place, except this was no movie -- these events were happening for real!

The macabre story really began back in 1981 when Ben and Jean Williams moved into their brand new home on Poppets Way. It was located in the Newport subdivision of Crosby, an upscale housing addition. Within a few years, the Williams' and seven out of eight of the families who lived close to them would move away from the area. All of them did so at great expense, including the loss of their mortgages.

Shortly after the Ben and Jean moved into the house, they began to notice something odd about the place. Mostly it was the oppressive feeling that seemed to loom over the structure, but soon it was other things too. It all started naturally enough, but when combined, each of the events formed a more terrifying picture. Hundreds of ants began invading the house, followed by snakes that acted uncharacteristically hostile. Plants died for no reason and pets began acting very strangely.

Perhaps most odd were the sinkholes that began to appear in the yard. Located out near an oak tree that bore some peculiar markings, the depressions slowly widened and collapsed. Even when dirt was added to them, they refused to fill. No one noticed at the time how eerily the holes resembled open graves.

Then other, more mysterious and frightening, events began to occur. The toilets in the house suddenly began flushing on the own. Lights turned on and off without explanation and the garage door somehow began opening and closing itself. Ben and Jean separately began to hear footsteps pacing back and forth through the house. Both of them assumed that it was the other, but when they went to check, the found no one there. Tapping and knocking sounds were sometimes heard by not only the Williams', but by neighbors and visitors to the house too. Finally, a number of people began to report seeing shadowy shapes and what could have been apparitions in the yard.

Was the house haunted? If so, how could it be? The house had only been completed a short time before the family moved into it. What Ben and Jean and the other families in the neighborhood didn't know was just what had been located on the property before the subdivision was built.

In 1983, Sam Haney, a neighbor who lived near to the Williams house, contracted for a swimming pool to be built in his back yard. During the digging, two bodies were unearthed by workers. They later turned out to be the remains of a black man and woman. Unfortunately, this was only the beginning. According to local estimates there were dozens of bodies buried underneath the entire neighborhood.

Originally, the entire subdivision had been located on land that belonged to the McKinney family. Although long gone by this time, the McKinney's had been wealthy landowners and farmers and had maintained a large plantation and a number of slaves. One corner of the property had been given over to the slaves and was later used by their descendants, as a graveyard. A number of those descendants, along with a large local African-American community, now lived in the nearby town of Baird Station. The older people there had used the burial ground for many years and had called it Black Hope Cemetery. Some of the elderly folks had buried relatives there and easily recalled the location -- it was directly beneath the houses on Poppets Way!

After this frightening disclosure, Ben Williams went to see a man named Will Freeman, an older black man, who claimed to have carried out some of the burials. He said that the burials were often haphazard but that they always tried to bury on the higher ground and avoid the rocks and the boggy low spots. The Haney's and the Williams' later discovered their homes were located on this "higher ground". Freeman also told them that no one could really afford tombstones in those days and on one occasion when he had buried two of his sisters, he had chosen an oak tree as a marker. He had marked an arrow on the tree, along with some other carvings that he couldn't recall. Ben and Jean realized this tree was located in their yard.

By this time, Sam Haney was involved in a lawsuit against the Purcell Corporation, the developers of the land. The lawsuit was expensive and not going well, so the Williams' lawyer advised them to sell the house and get out. However, if they did try to sell it, they would have to disclose the fact that it had been built on top of the Black Hope Cemetery. They decided to wait and see what happened with the Haney suit, which would not come to trial until 1987, but they did try unsuccessfully to sell the house. Their attorney also tried pressuring the title and realty companies, ensnaring the property in mountains of red tape and legal hassles. What it boiled down to was that the house was impossible to sell -- and it was impossible to prove the graveyard existed. The only way to prove it was to dig and to dig for the bodies was illegal.

Meanwhile, the strange events in the house continued. The unexplainable sounds and incidents still occurred and the strange shapes were still seen both inside and outside of the house. The entire family was plagued by nightmares and several of the family pets mysteriously died.

Finally, Jean could stand it no more and she took a shovel from the garage and went out into the yard. She found the tree that had been marked so many years ago by Will Freeman and she started digging. Jean was only able to dig down a short distance before a terrible piercing pain stabbed through her back. She was forced to stop. Later that afternoon, her daughter, Tina, suddenly died. She had been in remission from cancer for some time but her health was fine. Tina's death was completely unexpected and remained unexplained.

Their nerves shattered, the Williams family fled the house and moved to Hamilton, Montana, where they owned a vacation home. They were convinced that if they stayed in the house on Poppets Way, the entire family would be destroyed. In the end, they lost their entire $18,000 down payment, seven years worth of mortgage payments and ruined their credit rating. In spite of this, they were glad to be out.

In May 1987, the Haney family lost their lawsuit against the Purcell Corporation. The jury that heard the case first awarded them $142,000 in damages but the judge nullified the verdict and left them with nothing. Purcell executives had testified that they knew nothing of a graveyard in the area and the judge ruled that Purcell had not been intentionally negligent -- despite the fact that rumors had placed the graveyard on the site for years before the development began.

As far as I know, the case was never settled and nothing was ever done to rectify the desecration of the Black Hope Cemetery.

The question still remains though as to how or why the disturbance of the graves causes the cemetery to be considered haunted. Is it because of natural or supernatural reasons? Ghost lore tells us that the spirits remain behind when their remains are disturbed and are unable to find rest. This may explain why desecrated cemeteries are so often believed to be haunted. But what if there was a natural explanation for the activity? As mentioned earlier, suppose the displacement of graves or physical remains releases an energy that might account for the bizarre happenings reported in cemeteries. Could this energy have seemed to our ancestors to mimic a "haunting"? Science tells us that all matter is energy and energy cannot be destroyed. Could this "energy" explain the phenomena that is reported?

The Mystery of Portals

My initial interest in cemetery hauntings (as mentioned earlier) began because of the ghostlore and weird legends that I found were often associated with burial grounds. And while this fascination continues, my paranormal research into cemeteries has led me in some strange and rather unusual directions. One of the things that I have continued to maintain throughout this book is that cemeteries are rarely haunted in the traditional way. In spite of this though, weird activity, hauntings, bizarre photographs and reports continue to come from graveyards all over the country. How and why can this be?

The theory behind some cemetery phenomena has been linked to what a few researchers call "portals" or "doorways". Dismissed by some and embraced by others, the idea of a portal is still mostly theory and conjecture but in my opinion, the idea explains a lot of things about cemetery hauntings and even some short-lived paranormal flaps or outbreaks.

The idea of a "portal" to another dimension is not a new one. It has been suggested that there exist places all over the world that serve as "doorways" from our world to another. These doorways may provide access for entities to come into our world. They may be the spirits of people who have lived before, or they may be something else altogether. Some researchers even believe that they could be otherworldly beings from some dimension that we cannot even comprehend. In famous cases like the "Mothman" or the "Mad Gasser" of Mattoon, Illinois, it may even be possible that such a portal opened for a short time in a specific area, allowing these figures to wreak havoc for a brief period, only to later vanish without a trace. Many of the readers of this book may have also read the book that I wrote about the infamous Bell Witch of Tennessee (*Season of the Witch*). If so, then the reader may be familiar with the theory that I have in that case about the haunting at the John Bell farm being a non-human entity that came through one of these doorways.

I know this all sounds far-fetched, but it may not be as strange as it seems. The entities that have been sighted, reported and even photographed around what many believe to be portals could be the spirits of the dead or perhaps something stranger. If locations like this do exist and they are some sort of doorway, it's possible that these spots may have been labeled as being "haunted" over the years by people who saw something near them that they couldn't explain, isn't it? I think it's possible that this has happened many times. In fact, I would even suggest that these places did not "become" haunted as traditional locations do (through death or tragic events), but had been "haunted" for many, many years already. This fits in well with the theories about haunted cemeteries that are not haunted in any traditional manner.

Many locations where groups of strange things happen seem to be "glitch" areas. An example of this would be Archer Avenue on the South Side of Chicago, Illinois. There are a number of haunted sites along this one roadway and many would consider it to be the most ghost-infested region of Chicagoland. There have been a variety of ideas that have been suggested as to why so many odd things happen here, from the fact that it was once an old Native American trail to the fact that Archer Avenue is almost completely surrounded by water. Some have also suggested that areas like Archer Avenue, or the portals in question, may be connected to what are called "ley lines".

The idea that a number of unusual spots are often located in a particular area, or along a straight line, was suggested by Alfred Watkins in 1925. The idea came to him when he was examining a map of Herefordshire, England and noticed an alignment of ancient sites. He gave such alignments the name of "ley", a Saxon word that meant "a clearing in the woodland". The lines (if they exist) are believed to be alignments or patterns of powerful earth energy that connect sacred sites such as churches, temples, stone circles, megaliths, burial sites and other locations of spiritual importance. The true age and purpose of such lines remain a mystery. Watkins suggested that all holy sites and places of antiquity were connected by ley lines and using an old Ordnance Survey, he claimed that the leys were the "old straight tracks" that crossed the landscape of prehistoric Britain and represented sites that were built from the very dawn of human settlement there.

After Watkins' theory was published, fascination with ley lines remained high until the 1940's, when it began to decline. Interest was revived two decades later and the idea of such lines remains a subject of speculation and debate to this day. Not surprisingly, most mainstream archaeologists and scientists dispute the existence of ley lines and say that Watkins contrived the whole thing using sacred sites from different periods in history. This would be true if the idea of such lines only dated back to the 1920's. As it stands, there should be sites that date from different periods in history if the lines had been there all along. Many contend that the ley lines mark paths of earth energy, which can often be detected by dowsing and which may have been sensed by early humans. For this reason, they chose to locate their sacred sites along the pathways and especially at points where the lines cross one another.

Points where the ley line paths intersect are believed to be prone to anomalies such as earth lights, hauntings and even UFO sightings. It is believed that the energy here is at its greatest and some might even describe such sites as portals.

Some of the most common sites alleged to be portals have been cemeteries. For years, ghost hunters and researchers have collected not only strange stories of haunted cemeteries, but dozens of anomalous photographs from them as well. In many cases, there seems to be no reason why the cemetery might be haunted unless it might somehow provide access for spirits, or entities, to pass from one world to the next. For this reason, some researchers, like my friend Barb Huyser, have started referring to these locations as "crossover points". In almost every case, there seems to be none of the historical reasons for the graveyard to be haunted -- no unmarked graves, natural disasters or desecration -- and yet phenomena is frequently reported.

Of course, some of the cemeteries are haunted in the traditional manner, but it's the ones that aren't that cause such a puzzle. Going back to what was mentioned earlier, it's possible that these sites were "haunted" long before the cemetery was ever located there. Might it be possible that some sort of "psychic draw" to the area was what caused our ancestors to locate a cemetery there in the first place? Perhaps they felt there was something "sacred" or "spiritual" about the place and without realizing why, placed a burial ground on the location and made it a protected spot. This would fit in well with the theories that many have about ley lines and their intersection points. They believe that the ancient inhabitants (in this case, our ancestors) felt the pull of the area and built their sacred sites along these lines or crossing points.

According to American Indian lore, the early inhabitants of this country chose their burial grounds in a conscious manner, looking for a place to bury the dead that was more closely connected to the next world. Many of these locations, including many disturbed sites, are now considered "haunted" or at least inhabited by spirits. They consciously chose these locations, again following the psychic draw of the spot.

So why not our own cemeteries? Could our own burial grounds have been chosen in the same way, although perhaps unknowingly? These sites could now mark doorways between this world and the next. In American culture, what more sacred sites exist than churches and cemeteries? Our ancestors may have placed their burial grounds on these spots as a way of protecting the location -- or perhaps because of something else that they sensed here. Is it possible that the settlers deduced that something was not quite right about the site and perhaps even believed that these strange feelings were of an evil or demonic nature? There has been a long tradition in this country about haunted or mysterious places being dubbed with "devil names" as a way of warning people away from something the discoverers did not understand. It's possible that superstitious settlers also felt that many of these portal locations were "evil" in some way, or of the Devil. Because of this, they attempted to "exorcise" the location by placing a holy or religious site upon it. This might explain the myriad of haunted churches that exist in this country and might also explain many of our seemingly spirit-infested graveyards as well.

Of course, the fear is that perhaps are ancestors may not have been as superstitious, or as mistaken, as we might first think. The strange entities that have been photographed around such sites could be the traveling spirits of the dead -- or they could be something far worse.

Cemeteries are not the only places to find these portals. I believe they may exist in other places too, including in places where we would least expect them. These "glitch" areas might be found anywhere, even under a home or building. In fact, these doorways, and the unknown entities that pass through them, might be the explanation for some of the strange sightings that have plagued paranormal research for years. For some time, investigators have attempted to dispel the myths that "ghosts are evil" and that they "hurt people", but what if we are wrong? Or perhaps even partially wrong?

Normally, I don't believe that ghosts hurt people. By that I mean that people involved in a haunting are not injured by the discarnate spirits of the dead. There are certainly instances of people being hurt though, but usually because they are struck by an object in a poltergeist outbreak or trip over a shifted piece of furniture.

In fact, you are more likely to be hurt running away from a haunted place than by the haunting that is taking place there.

But what about people who get hurt in other ways? These are the cases that worry everyone and the cases that give rise to the stories of "evil spirits" and dangerous ghosts. In some of these cases, we hear accounts of violent acts, terrifying visions and even strange beings that may have never been human at all. Can we always take such stories seriously? Perhaps not, but they are out there and what if these cases involve entities who are not ghosts at all? Could they be strange spirits who have passed into this world by way of the "portals" that we have been discussing?

This is interesting to think about. If this might be true, such a theory would certainly provide answers for puzzling cases when traditional methods of ghost investigations have not worked. It might also provide a solution as to how stories of "evil spirits", "demons" and even "negative ghosts" have gotten started.

Research into the idea of non-human entities is a subject of great controversy. For centuries, there have been tales of nature spirits and elementals who spring from the earth. They have never been human but choose to interact and to communicate with us. In more modern times, researchers have theorized that such spirits may actually be beings that pass between dimensions. They use the portals and doorways to pass back and forth and such spirits have a reputation for being both kind and benign, as well as dangerous and violent. As already mentioned, the passage of such beings between this world and another could provide an explanation for cases that are as far apart from one another as the infamous Mad Gasser, vanishing creatures and even haunted graveyards.

Who can say for sure at this point as to who or what these mysterious spirits may be and why places that should not be haunted, actually are? My interest in the possibility of portals began back in the middle 1990's and continues today. Below are two case studies of investigations that I have done in cemeteries that I believe were portal locations. Strangely, the entire cemetery could not be considered a portal in either case. This is something else that I have noted about such locations. Both of these cemeteries had certain areas in them where activity was the strongest. In fact, I would even go as far as to say that all of the activity in the graveyard was centered around this spot.

This seemed important to me because it not only seemed to indicate that the planners of the cemetery chose the location because of the psychical importance of it but that they also unconsciously highlighted the areas where the activity was the strongest. Following with my theory, I noted that these more active parts of the cemetery had been decorated with distinctive gravestones and architecture that set them apart from the rest of the graveyard. I'll go into this in more detail in the sections that follow.

Portal Case Study: Old Union Cemetery

My first investigation into a cemetery that I believe contains a portal area was in early 1996. The graveyard is known as Old Union Cemetery and it's located in a remote section of Central Illinois. The cemetery saw its first burials in 1831 and it closed down less than 100 years later in 1931 after a fire destroyed the Union Christian Church that was located at the edge of the grounds. As time passed, the road past the cemetery, which had once been a busy stage line between Bloomington and Springfield, Illinois, was abandoned and the graveyard was largely forgotten. Although it is well kept by workers from the local township, the cemetery is no longer visible from any road. The forest now surrounds it, hiding it away from history. Old records say that over 500 of the early residents of this area were buried in the grounds but less than 100 of their grave markers remain.

Old Union Cemetery first came to my attention thanks to reports from a sheriff's deputy and two independent witnesses who had worked for the local township. The police officer and the caretakers told me stories of glowing balls of light that were often seen among the tombstones of the cemetery grounds. In addition, the caretakers also told me of one part of the cemetery that they avoided working in if possible. Both of them told me, without knowing that anyone else had mentioned it, that one particular section made them feel very strange and uncomfortable. They had no reason to explain what bothered them about it, it simply made their flesh crawl.

This section of the cemetery was an area in the far corner of the grounds, almost touching the woods that loomed over the burial ground. The section was apparently some sort of private plot that contained a now unreadable tombstone and it was surrounded by an iron fence that was cast with the images of willow trees as a decorative motif. Each corner of the plot had a metal post to which the sides of the fence connected. The design of the posts was rather intricate as well, twisted and turned to stand about four feet tall.

I wanted to describe this fence in more detail because it was unlike anything else in the cemetery. Keep in mind, this is a simple, country cemetery with standard granite stones and very little in the way of decoration or design. This fenced-in plot was not only very much out of place (in regards to the architecture of the cemetery) but it was located in a very odd position within the grounds. The plot was located

The fenced area at the back of Old Union Cemetery. This photo was taken a couple of years after our initial investigation and after vandals had struck in the graveyard.

right at the edge of the woods, at least 20 yards away from not only the main portion of the cemetery, but from the closest other graves as well.

This fits in with the theory that I mentioned earlier about how the designers of the cemetery seem to have highlighted certain areas in ways that are unlike anything else that can be found in the graveyard. I don't think that it's any coincidence that the fenced area is the center (even the source) of the strange activity at Old Union Cemetery.

My first visit to the graveyard took place on a warm afternoon in the spring of 1996. There was nothing odd or spooky about the day and frankly, not much spooky about the cemetery itself either. I was accompanied to the graveyard by another investigator, who lived in the area and was able to track down the secluded location, and we drove back to the woods by way of an old farm road beside a field. We crossed a grassy area and then found ourselves rounding a curve and entering the cemetery itself. As mentioned, it was completely surrounded by the forest but aside from this, it looked a lot like just about every other small cemetery that you can find along country roads all over the Midwest. There were no signs of vandalism here nor anything else that might explain the reports of strange lights that so many people had spoken of in the area.

Our plan on that afternoon was to map out the cemetery and to look things over so that we could return one night for a full-fledged investigation. Neither of us wanted to show up here some night after dark and stumble into an open grave, so we thought it best to get a lay of the land. We spent about an hour walking around the area and poking into the woods to see what was on the other side of them. We found nothing but more woods and farm fields that lay some distance off. There are no houses in the immediate area, so when we did conduct our investigation, we knew that we could count on not picking up lights or sounds in the distance that might be coming from hidden structures.

One of the last areas that we looked over was the fenced-in section at the back of the cemetery. Perhaps it was my imagination at work, but this was the only area of the burial ground where I felt the least bit odd. I make no claims to any sort of psychic ability but it was hard not to wonder if I was feeling the same thing those caretakers had felt while mowing the grass around this small plot. Out of curiosity, my friend and I decided that we would set up a few pieces of equipment around the area and see if we detected anything with our tools that might explain the unusual reports.

The sun was just beginning to dip slightly below the tops of the trees as we unpacked the gear. The temperature that afternoon was in the lower 70's and it was quite comfortable in shirt sleeves. How then could I explain away what we discovered with the equipment? The first inkling that something was out of the ordinary around the burial plot came when I unpacked a TriField Natural EM Meter and placed it on the stone inside of the fence. The meter began to fluctuate back and forth, peaking suddenly and without explanation.

This particular TriField Meter is one of the best electromagnetic field meters on the market. Electromagnetic Field Meters (EMF Meters) are the most commonly used devices for ghost hunters today. Largely, they are also the most reliable. Electronic devices have been adapted to use in the paranormal research field as a way of giving confirmation of our instincts. They are also used to detect energy that we cannot see with the naked eye. Researchers believe that ghosts, or paranormal energy, are electromagnetic in origin. The energy that a ghost gives off (or uses) causes a disruption in the magnetic field of the location and thus, becomes detectable using measuring devices. For electronic devices to be useful in an investigation though, the researcher must search for corresponding activity to go along with the anomalies the EMF meter picks up. No single piece of evidence can stand alone, but coming up with several different things that are corresponding, like witness accounts, photographs, temperature changes and more, an investigation reveals some things that cannot easily be explained.

There don't seem to be any "ideal" readings when it comes to using these meters but it is worthwhile to search for sudden surges and drops that cannot be explained away. At one point, I was involved in the investigation of an allegedly haunted house that had been abandoned. It had no electricity, no running water, no gas lines and basically nothing artificial that could interfere with the detection equipment and produce false readings. In one corner of an upstairs room, my EMF meter suddenly began picking up a very strong energy field that I could not explain. The field was so strong that the needle on the meter was literally "buried", detecting readings that were completely off the scale. At first glance, it would seem that the meter was picking up some sort of artificial field, like a power line in the wall perhaps. The problem was, there was no power in the house!

At the same time that I was working with the meter, other investigators were recording a light fixture that was hanging in the hallway just outside the room. They were recording it because the light had suddenly starting moving by itself (at the same time I began measuring the energy field!). In addition, other investigators, outside of the house, took a number of photos that managed to catch some sort of activity around the outside of this upper level.

On another occasion, I was involved in an investigation of a cemetery that I already believed was haunted. Previously, other researchers and myself had been able to document strange happenings and had obtained a number of photographs here that could not be explained, even by commercial photographers. During this particular investigation, we set up detection equipment, motion detectors and an infrared video camera around a particularly active part of the graveyard. We began documenting the next several hours, keeping a close watch on the video monitor and noting any changes in the EMF detectors.

During the course of the evening, we managed to record what we felt were legitimate anomalies with the video camera (we also later learned that the still camera picked up activity too, but we didn't know this until the film was developed). These included small lights that moved on their own and in the opposite direction of any wind that may have been present and some odd flashes of light that we were unable to explain. But the strangest activity seemed to center on the EMF detectors. With chilling accuracy, we were able to show that the surrounding electromagnetic field actually dipped down each time one of the odd lights appeared on camera. They were not causing surges of energy, but seemed to be using the energy that was present to appear.

Investigations like this have convinced me that EMF detectors do work when hunting ghosts, or at least when tracking paranormal energy, and so the odd readings in Old Union Cemetery seemed to verify to me the reports from those who claimed this section of the cemetery was "haunted" in some way. Interestingly, it also seemed to verify the long-held belief that ley lines and their crossover points give off a natural energy that is detectable by not only humans, but by test equipment as well. There were no artificial reasons for there to have been any sort of readings on these devices in this remote cemetery. And yet both of us present were witnessing the changes on the scale.

Moments after the TriField meter began to behave erratically, my friend began working with a portable, infrared temperature scanner and he soon discovered that the temperature inside of the fenced-in area was almost 40 degrees colder than the air in the rest of the cemetery! But how could this be? And how does something like this work to pick up temperature readings when there was nothing to see with the human eye?

Infrared scanners, or non-contact thermometers, can track down a paranormal presence by taking instant temperature readings from a location and by detecting any changes that might be sudden or extreme. To state it simply, it checks for "cold spots" (unexplained temperature variances) that are believed to signal that a ghost is present. It is thought that a ghost uses the energy in a particular spot to manifest itself and by doing so, creates a cold mass. The energy may be invisible to the eye but still detectable using one of these devices.

Researchers have detected these cold spots, which can be very extreme, in both indoor and outdoor locations, from haunted houses to cemeteries. They have also collected a number of photographs that have been taken while the devices were picking up intensely cold spots. These "spots" were invisible and yet registered for the thermal scanner. The developed photos show the researcher pointing the gun-like device (seemingly at nothing) but, out beyond their reach, is an anomalous mist or light. My own experiences with photos like this has convinced me that there are useful applications for these devices in paranormal investigation.

Not everyone is convinced though. In spite of interesting evidence, many researchers have argued that these thermometers can only work when they come into contact with something solid. However, there is evidence to the contrary because by pointing the probe straight into the sky, you can get a reading of the moisture and temperature in the air. So, obviously, this is not a case of it coming into contact with anything solid. In addition, I have documented evidence to say that firefighters sometimes use these thermal scanners to record the temperature of a fire. As fire is not a solid object, and yet the probes still works, so what can it be recording?

I do not argue the fact that the device does need to come into contact with something to register a reading. However, in the research that I did after the first investigation at Old Union Cemetery, I spoke to a technician who worked for the makers of one of the best IR probes on the market. During our discussions, she explained to me how the device worked and that it had to make contact with something to register a reading. After showing her the photos that I had of strange mists that were giving off cold readings at the time the photos were taken, she agreed that such a "mass" could give off the temperature changes necessary to register on the device.

She explained that the thermometer reads the infrared energy of an object and converts that into a temperature. A basic hand-held thermal scanner is set at a level of about 98% of the energy given off. The good news is that rock, bricks, trees and cemetery headstones are also at about this same level and that's why these devices work so well for paranormal investigations. Based on the evidence that we have so far, it seems that "spirit energy" is on a different level than that and that's why it can be picked up using one of these devices.

The temperatures that my friend was picking up inside of the fenced area ranged from around 30 to 36 degrees. This was at a level of about five to six feet off the ground and he was careful to make sure that the infrared beam of the scanner was not pointing off into the woods. In order to assure himself of this, he stepped sideways and pointed the thermometer so that the beam did not cross above the fenced area as it passed by. When he did this, he recorded a temperature of 68 degrees, which agreed with the ambient temperature of the cemetery.

We also took a number of photographs to document the area that day but nothing out of the ordinary turned up in them. However, this would not be the case as we continued our investigations at this location.

We returned to the cemetery a short time later for the first of several investigations. As with the first trip, all of the activity that we documented with our equipment centered around this same part of the cemetery.

The fenced area also seemed to be the source for small, glowing balls of light that turned up in the developed photographs from the place. During what turned out to be our second investigation, which lasted about two hours, we managed to come back with 14 unusual photos, all of which were later sent to an independent lab for analysis. They had no explanation for the balls of light and stated that they were not developing flaws or anything wrong with the film itself. The balls of light were seen hovering, or captured in motion, in several areas of the cemetery. Most were photographed near the fenced section. Other photos showed investigators pointing their infrared temperature scanners directly at the gold-colored globes. Strong temperature drops were being experienced by the equipment, although nothing was seen by the naked eye at the time. Once again though, this would change as well.

I returned to the cemetery about three months later in the company of two other investigators. We arrived in the late afternoon to once again test the area where the fenced section is located for additional daytime activity. I have always maintained that if a location is really haunted, then it's going to be active both in the daylight and after dark. I think it's a common misconception that hauntings only take place at night -- and I think Old Union Cemetery certainly dispels that myth!

Shortly after we unpacked our equipment, one of the other investigators announced that he had seen movement around the center of the graveyard. Thinking that it might have been a bird, he asked us to keep watch with him for a few minutes. As we stood watching, I suddenly saw a yellowish-colored blur streak past us and vanish near the woods. The other two saw the image as well and this single light was followed by others. Amazingly, we were watching the cemetery's "spook lights" with not only our naked eyes -- but in the daylight as well. Even when we had been in the cemetery at night, we had not seen the lights (which in the photos seemed to give off a glow) but we saw them in the daylight instead. What made this day different than the others when we had been present?

I have no idea but I can tell you that it never happened to me again. At no time after this, in subsequent investigations, did I ever see the strange lights, or anything else that I would consider to be paranormal. However, I did again bring back some weird photos of the place. Recently though, a friend of mine who visited the cemetery also reported seeing the lights in the daytime. When he told me about them, he had no idea that the lights had been reported during the daylight hours before. Thinking quickly, he managed to snap a couple of quick photos as the lights buzzed past him. The photos were blurry but if you looked at them closely, the eerie globes were visible.

The "real" Graveyard X -- Or is it??

Portal Case Study: Anderson Cemetery (a.k.a. Graveyard X)

Over the past several years, I have probably received more requests for information about, and directions to, the elusive burial ground known as "Graveyard X" than I have any other site that I have investigated. And while I am still not going to reveal its location within these pages, I will pass on to the curious that while some readers may think they know the location of this mysterious cemetery, it's likely that they do not. It has been pointed out to me on numerous occasions that there is more than one Anderson Cemetery in Illinois (where this one is located) but all that I can tell you is that I made an agreement not to reveal the whereabouts of this cemetery when I first starting doing research here.

In addition, to prevent the cemetery from being overrun by would-be "ghost hunters" and vandals, I have done much to cover my tracks in regards to this place, even going as far as to weave several locations into one and offering photographs that are misleading at best. It has been pointed out as well that both in the photos and in the documentary that was filmed in "Graveyard X", the cemetery is very recognizable. And I will agree that it is -- but one of the basic rules of filming any sort of television program is that separate sections of the show can be filmed in many areas and then edited to appear as one. Artistic license can be taken with the historical aspects of the place as well.

Of course, I can't say one way or another just what has occurred here in regards to keeping the location of the cemetery secret but I will urge the reader not to take anything that they think they know for granted.

With all of that said though, let me assure you that Anderson Cemetery (as we'll call Graveyard X here) is a very haunted place. In fact, it was because of my investigations at this place that I first began to research more deeply the idea of "portals" and doorways between this world and another. I could find no other explanation for the strange events that had been reported here, the eerie happenings, the bizarre photographs and first-hand accounts. There was no reason for this cemetery to be haunted -- and yet it was.

Anderson Cemetery is not a place that you are going to find on any maps. It is a typical rural cemetery that is well hidden by curving back roads, thick woods and wind-swept fields of grain. It's not a place that most people would go to, or would care to find, unless they had relatives buried there and had a reason to visit. Unlike many other cemeteries that are regarded as haunted, it is not vandalized and is in fact in good condition, well-maintained by the local township crew and still in use today.

Over the years, I have visited literally hundreds of places that are alleged to be haunted, but by all indications, Anderson Cemetery may be one of the most actively haunted spots that I have been to. Strangely though, its history suggests nothing that would have made it become that way. It is located on land that once belonged to a local farmer named Anderson. Prior to 1867, the graveyard was nothing more than a wooded section of his property. It did not become a burial ground until the internment of a small child took place there. A family that was passing through the area on their way west came to the Anderson house with a child that had fallen ill and died. They asked if the child might be buried somewhere on the farm. Anderson selected a clearing in the woods where a high knoll was located and on this site the cemetery was started. The small hill can still be seen in the cemetery today, although any grave marker made for the young girl has long since deteriorated over time.

I first heard about this cemetery several years ago from a man who had grown up in the area where it is located. For some time, there had been stories about people reporting strange lights and unusual sounds in the cemetery at night. It is very isolated and surrounded on three sides by heavy woods, so it was unlikely these lights and noises were coming from a nearby farmhouse or road. It was also supposed to be haunted, a claim that was met with much skepticism by the man who told me about it.

It was not until his made his own trip the cemetery that he began to believe there might be something behind the tales that he had been told. One night, he drove out to the graveyard and stayed for several hours. A short time after he arrived, he got his first glimpse of one of the eerie lights. It floated up from behind one of the graves, flashed for a moment, and then vanished seemingly into nowhere. Soon, he saw several more of them but could find no explanation as to what they might be. Stunned, he attempted several times to photograph them, but he was sure that his camera and reflexes were too slow to catch them. When his film was developed though, he got the surprise of his life.

The finished photos showed what can only be called a number of "misty shapes and apparitions". I confess that when I saw these photographs and heard the man's stories about the graveyard, I was intrigued. In fact, I was intrigued enough to schedule an investigation to the site with members of the American Ghost Society. The location was so hard to find though that we had to meet with the original witness in a nearby town and literally follow him to the cemetery.

We arrived at the cemetery just about the time the sun was going down, which is not an optimal time to arrive, as you will discover later in this guide. In spite of this, we were able to map out the cemetery and to coordinate enough so that we were not on top of one another and were able to use equipment and to photograph the area without interfering with the other researchers.

The first investigation paid off with little in the way of documented evidence except for several strange photographs. Several of them were taken by my wife, Amy, and myself. One of the ones that I snapped that night clearly appeared to be a white, human-like face that looked directly into the camera. It was pretty unnerving to say the least. Some time later, it was sent to the Kodak Laboratories for an explanation. However, they had no idea what the weird image might be. They merely stated that it was not a problem with the film, the developing or the camera. They refused to comment on what the images might be though, especially the one that looked so much like a human face.

My research into this cemetery continued and I began looking for any history about the place that might provide a clue as to why the cemetery was haunted. I also began speaking to people in the area, including residents and police officers who patrolled the area, about their own experiences with the graveyard. I continued to hear the accounts of the strange lights and of the sound of voices that could be heard in the cemetery at night. According to my sources, the voices of children at play were sometimes heard, literally coming from nowhere. This eerie sensation was experienced by six independent witnesses that I spoke with and has since been verified by others as well. I should add that I have searched diligently for a logical explanation as to where this sound could be coming from but there are no houses near the cemetery -- and why would children be playing and laughing near the cemetery in the middle of the night, when several of the witnesses have reported the sounds?

I returned to Anderson Cemetery the following summer to conduct another investigation during the daylight hours. I unpacked my equipment and began trying to monitor the cemetery, searching for anything out of the ordinary. I found it after about an hour. There was one particular part of the cemetery where the temperature was noticeably colder than anywhere else, in fact about 40 degrees colder! Remember that this was a summer afternoon and the temperature that day (according to a gauge that I brought with me) was 89 degrees. The temperature in this area of the cemetery was only 53. How could I explain this away naturally?

Using the maps and charts that we had put together during our various investigations, I marked the area from which the cold temperatures were from. I discovered that not only were the unusual temperature readings confined to one

section of the cemetery, but so were the readings that we had picked up with our equipment, as well as the strange photographs that had been taken. All of the activity at the cemetery came from one small area that was roughly the shape of a triangle. The angles of the line were marked with a stone bench at one corner, a large, arched stone at another and strangely, the third corner was marked with the largest stone in the cemetery. Like the fenced area at Old Union Cemetery, all of these stones were unlike anything else that could be found in the graveyard. Stranger yet, the tallest stone that marked the third corner of the triangle was located on top of the mound where the original grave in the cemetery was located. It was this small hill, located in the woods, where Anderson had buried the little girl around who the cemetery was started. If we take the theory of the portal seriously, then this can be no coincidence.

More than a year after I first began delving into the strangeness of Anderson Cemetery, I returned there in the company of ghost researcher Bob Schott, who was filming an installment of the now defunct series "Adventures Beyond". We were accompanied to the graveyard by Tim Harte and Mike Hollinshead, creators of a sophisticated computer tracking system. The device was designed to take readings in an alleged haunted location and then analyze the gathered data and determine the nature of the haunting. The system reads changes in electromagnetic fields, temperature changes, visible light, seismic vibrations and other areas. The experiments with this system are closely controlled and monitored with motion detectors and video cameras. To try and cover all of the possibilities with this experiment, we decided to do it using the computer system to monitor an old-fashioned séance.

A table was set up and a small group of average (non-psychic) people gathered around it with a Ouija board. These people were completely unaware of the past history of the place and were asked to simply try and communicate with anything that might be present. Whether you believe in the validity of Ouija boards or not, it was a fascinating, and somewhat chilling, experiment. In a relatively short time, the sitters claimed to be in contact with something supernatural. Later, they would say that at times, the pointer on the board was moving so fast that their fingers were not even touching it! It should be noted that later viewings of the film that was shot that night would confirm that this occurred. Stranger still, the spirited communicator claimed to be that of a small child who had been buried there before it was a cemetery. What was so strange about this is that, as you might remember, the first burial that took place here was that of a little girl who had died while passing through the area. Not a single one of the people involved in the séance knew this at the time! I was the only person who possessed this information and I was not involved in the séance except as a monitor. I was passing on no information to the sitters who were present. Coincidence? Perhaps, but it seems unlikely.

It seems especially unlikely when considered in connection with the results achieved by Tim and Mike's computer system. According to the read-outs and graphs, there were things occurring in the cemetery during the séance that could not be explained! These anomalous spikes and dips were totally out of the ordinary and showed severe fluctuations in electromagnetic radiation that could not be explained by natural means. Even stranger still was the fact that these fluctuations were occurring in response to

A photo taken during the filming of "Adventures Beyond". Bob Schott is shown at right and the members of the séance are Nancy Napier, Teresa Hall & Charles Hall in the foreground.

the questions asked by the sitters. It seemed as though some sort of intelligent energy was present in the graveyard.

"I couldn't explain why this was happening," Tim Harte later told me in an interview. "The readings were completely unexplainable. Whatever was going on, it seemed to occur at the same time the people at the table would ask a question. The computer would show a massive change then, pause for a moment, and then spike again. It was almost like something was answering."

As the séance was taking place, other pieces of equipment were being used to monitor the area, in addition to the computer system. TriField Natural EM Meters had been placed around the séance table and the electromagnetic field around the table actually dipped and spiked in response to the questions being asked with the Ouija board, just as the computer system monitors did. We also photographed the area heavily, all during the séance, and managed to capture a number of photos that showed small balls of light that were hovering in the vicinity of the table.

And not all of the strange photos were taken during the séance itself. Prior to the start of the investigation, Amy actually snapped two Polaroid photos that were very difficult to explain. One of them showed a white mist that surrounded the computer system that Tim and Mike were setting up and the other was taken of one of the researchers standing next to the tallest obelisk in the cemetery, which is the third corner of the "paranormal triangle" here. Just on the other side of the gravestone was a large, glowing light that seemed to be the size of a basketball! Obviously, none of us saw it but it managed to be picked up by the emulsion of the film.

The séance was also monitored using a television camera that had been fitted with a Generation III Night Vision lens, which was reportedly five times more sensitive than the equipment used by the U.S. Military during the Gulf War. The lens was so advanced that it had not been available on the civilian market until a short time before the investigation. It had been loaned to Schott by the manufacturer, a company that deals specifically with sensitive government and military contracts. The company that made the equipment later took a look at a copy of the film that we shot that night in the cemetery and were puzzled by what they saw. They, along with other film experts, ran the clip over and over and put it through all sorts of tests to determine if it had been hoaxed or if it was merely an accidental image that had been caused by camera flashes or some sort of reflection. In their final report on the footage, they stated that they had no explanation for the strange anomaly and that it could only be paranormal in origin.

The image that was filmed was documented using not only the television camera, but also by several handheld infrared temperature detectors. The séance was monitored using these detectors, in the hands of Bob Schott and myself. We circled the table and took readings directly from the center of the séance. Impossibly, on this warm summer night, we picked up temperatures that dipped down as low as 10 degrees above zero! How was this possible? I have no idea but it was all documented on film and the readings were recorded using not only different temperature scanners but scanners made by totally different companies.

The startling image that appeared on the film came at a high point in the séance. After more than 30 minutes of strange readings, inexplicable replies from the Ouija board and strong temperature drops, one of the participants in the séance, Charles, announced that he felt something cold creeping across his back. During a playback of this video shot that night, I discovered that Charles actually said this several times before I heard him and went to check it out.

I hurried around behind where Charles was sitting and aimed the infrared beam of the temperature scanner at his back. If you have ever worked with one of these devices and have aimed it at a person's body, you usually get a reading that is only a few degrees below the person's body temperature, thanks to the clothing they are wearing. That was not the case this time however. Even though it should be absolutely impossible, I pulled the trigger on the scanner and it registered a reading of only 14 degrees! On the tape of the investigation, you can clearly hear me announce, "Bob, I have 14 degrees on Charlie's back."

And if this was not strange enough, it was about to get stranger. After the investigation was over and the film from the television camera was being analyzed, it was discovered that the Night Vision scope had picked up something very strange at the exact same time that the cold chill moved across Charles' back. At the same moment that I announced to Bob what was happening with the temperature device, the camera recorded a white, human-looking face that appeared just above his left shoulder! As I mentioned, this film was analyzed closely by the company that created the scope and they had absolutely no explanation for it.

In my opinion, something supernatural occurred that night in Anderson Cemetery. Was it ghosts? I don't know, but whatever it was, I have never forgotten it. To this day, the graveyard remains a peculiar and curiously haunted place. The strangeness of the haunting is rivaled only by the fact that it really seems to have no reason to be haunted, and yet it is. Perhaps the lingering questions here can be best answered by more research and investigation into the mystery of Portals and crossover points? This is an area where there remains much work to be done and I hope that my own small contributions will open the door for others to continue this research into the future.

3. Researching Cemetery History
Do the Answers to the Haunting Rest in the Past?

As mentioned already, conducting paranormal research in cemeteries really shouldn't be that much different than conducting an investigation in someone's home or in a building. Every investigation has to be organized and there has to be a point to it, otherwise we can't legitimately call it "research" or even an "investigation". To be able to conduct an actual investigation, we have to have rules and criteria to go by. The ghost hunter should have his own checklist of items to be studied at the site because while wandering around in a cemetery taking pictures is fun, it does not constitute an actual investigation.

You should choose the site for the investigation by not simply picking a cemetery at random. Despite what some people apparently believe, not every cemetery is haunted. However, you can narrow down the sites to locations with dark history or at least with accounts of paranormal events from the past. Choosing cemetery sites to investigate is much like choosing other types of sites, although in this case, you will not have the home owners around to help you out with their experiences. Your best bet is to keep your ears and your options open. You may be surprised at how many people have ghost stories to tell about local cemeteries, what might be around in the old folklore or what might be heard by everyday people who have encountered the unusual. Keep in mind that my own interest was piqued at Old Union Cemetery by some township groundskeepers and a sheriff's deputy. Who knows where your first inkling of a story might come from?

In the past, the one thing that has set the investigation of cemeteries apart from investigations of homes and buildings is that researchers have had such a hard time tracking down the history of the sites. This has been one of the reasons why this type of research has never really been considered "legitimate". Hopefully though, the information in this chapter will help to change that.

The sections ahead have been designed to help ghost researchers compile as complete and as accurate a picture of the haunted graveyards they are investigating as possible. After the researcher has learned of the possibility of the haunting, it is now up to him or her to try and discover why the place might be haunted. In many cases, as has been pointed out already, no real reasons may exist but the historical background of any location is essential to the investigation. Obviously, we cannot jump to the conclusion that the cemetery is haunted because it is a portal spot or crossover location without examining all of the facts at our disposal. It's possible that the haunting activity might have a cause behind it after all. Perhaps the ghost that has been seen stalking the grounds is not a nameless spirit from another dimension at all but rather a convicted murderer who was buried there in an unmarked grave after his execution?

In this case, as with haunted houses, the history of the site may be the key. I have often been asked whether or not I believe modern technology has convinced non-believers that ghosts exist? Do the gadgets, cameras and sensitive meters actually convince skeptics that ghosts are really out there? Honestly, I don't think that technology has done all that much for the non-believers, other than to convince them that a lot of people don't know how to use cameras correctly! Technology has really done more for those who already believe than for anyone else. Unfortunately, so many things can go wrong with these meters and cameras that many mistake their readings and their mysterious "orbs" for ghosts -- when they are actually not. Don't get me wrong, I think technology certainly has its uses but I think that many ghost hunters are ignoring the skills that they really need in favor of "gee whiz" gadgets.

Technology is unlikely to ever "prove" that ghosts exist. We can gather all sorts of evidence with it and when compiled together with corresponding activity, it become pretty convincing. But is it "proof"? At this point in time, the only way that we can really prove the existence of ghosts is through history. In other words, find a location that is alleged to be currently haunted. Then contact people who have been involved with the site both currently and in the past. In a perfect situation, they will tell you that the exact same things are happening at the place now and also happened there in the past -- even though these people have never met, do not know one another and have not compared stories. How can we dismiss such claims?

Before we can worry about whether or not a place is really haunted though -- we have to find the place first.

For me, the search for historical evidence of ghosts has never been that tough. There are two things in my life about which I have always maintained a strong interest -- ghosts and history. The study of history has always been a close second for me, just behind ghosts, and one of the best ways to research the background of a haunted place is through its history. As mentioned though, you have to find the location first. There are many worthwhile places to search for ghosts and I have written about some of the best ones in the past, including houses, old theaters, schools and colleges and of course, cemeteries.

Needless to say, there are many other spots but just from the ones that were mentioned here, it's obvious that they have the opportunity to be very historical spots. Nearly every town and city in America has at least one place that is not only a historical site but one that is alleged to be haunted as well. How can you find these places? Start out by checking your local newspapers everyday, especially during the

Halloween season, when "ghost stories" make good filler for unimaginative news writers. There is always a chance that a good location, or a newly unearthed one, could appear there.

You can also check books about haunted places in your area. A good ghost hunter will usually spend a lot of time collecting books on ghosts and if you are like me, you take every opportunity to pick up often obscure regional books, sometimes about places where you have never been and don't plan to go. In many cases, these books will offer you a lead.

As I mentioned at the beginning of this chapter though, when dealing with local haunts, the best way to find out about possible sites is to let people know you are looking for them. Spread the word around that you are interest in hearing local ghost stories and checking out haunted places. Try to get interviewed in the local newspaper on the subject. As mentioned already, reporters are always looking for something spooky around Halloween and this is a great time to make yourself known. You can also join a local ghost research group and if one doesn't exist, start one. This is a good way to find haunted graveyards and spooky locations, as people will often perceive credibility in an organization (even a small one) when they may not in an individual.

Once you spread the word around that you are interested in ghosts, you will undoubtedly start to get calls from people who will want to tell you about haunted places. Hopefully, you will run across some chilling stories from some local cemetery to check out -- and hopefully, you will not dismiss them as simply folklore. Even the most often repeated legends and folk tales got started for a reason and it's very possible that your local story of the "vanishing bride" began because someone encountered something they could not explain in the graveyard.

Your job now, as a competent researcher, will be to try and figure whether there is any truth to the story or not. And if there isn't, then what events may have occurred that would have caused the story to get started. This is where ghost hunting becomes even more like detective work. All you need to get started is a little direction and a few tools -- sturdy notebook, a sharpened pencil, a magnifying glass for examining documents, a lot of curiosity and plenty of energy. Searching through the past can be a tiring job but well worth the time and effort.

Start off easy and check out what the local historians or even people who live nearby know about the history of the place. Be prepared for some inaccurate information though. There is a chance that if this is a place that has long been regarded as "haunted", the information they give you could be shadowed in a suggestive way. You'll also want to talk to neighbors who have been in the area for a long time. These local residents may also know if there is any local folklore about the place. This type of information is rarely scientific and usually only partially accurate, but don't discount it totally. Folklore can often point the researcher in the right direction, although sometimes by a meandering path.

Your next step should be checking to see if anyone else has ever traced the history of the cemetery in question. You might be able to find a history of the graveyard at the local library or perhaps even better, at the local genealogical society. One of their best sources for information about people comes from the cemetery and they will often have files or books that contain burial records and even inscriptions from local cemeteries. You also might find information at the local newspaper. Many newspapers have a research division too but they will also charge exorbitant prices for assisting you.

But all cemeteries, just like people, have a past. You may find clues to what you are looking for right under your nose -- within the confines of the cemetery itself. The story that the graveyard might tell, if researched correctly, may be a compelling one.

As you can see, there is much to learn from the examination of a graveyard's past and I hope the information in the sections ahead will assist you in making your own discoveries. But keep in mind that none of the how-to information is this book is presented as being the final word on the subject. I want this guide to merely serve as material that the individual researcher can take, change and adapt to work for them in their particular circumstances. Good luck with it!

Exploring the Cemetery

If you have heard about a cemetery that may be haunted, you are going to want to do two things: first, to visit the cemetery for yourself and second, to research the history of the place so you can get a better feel for its background.

Once you have decided on your possibly haunted cemetery, and believe that it seems worthwhile to organize an investigation, you should start the investigation by visiting the location in advance during the daylight hours. There are many things that need to be studied in detail and since most investigations take place at night, the option of studying the place will not be available to you then.

Before you go out to the site though, here are some tips that will hopefully make the experience much more productive. First, use some thought when planning the time of year for both the scouting expedition and the investigation. The best time to go is in the early spring or the fall. You should wait until after the snow, cold weather and freezing rain are no longer a problem. Bad weather can wreak havoc on both your photographs and your equipment. In addition, the weeds have not grown up in spring and snakes are not usually a problem either early or late in the season.

Cemeteries are also excellent place to find not only ghosts but all of the following -- sunburns, poison ivy, chiggers, ticks and mosquito bites. When visiting these sites, be sure to bring sunscreen, for when even a deceptively shady graveyard can have you roasting, sturdy walking shoes and bug repellant.

Also, be sure to be careful to watch for hills, uneven ground (graves tend to settle) and even open graves. In the years that I have been researching cemeteries, I have not only known two different people who have broken limbs while exploring in cemeteries -- in the daytime, mind you -- but even one person who was injured after falling into an open grave at night.

If there is a caretaker's office at the cemetery, be sure to stop in and ask for maps and any available literature about the cemetery. We'll discuss permissions for your investigations later on in the chapter. If you plan to do any headstone rubbings, ask the caretaker's permission for that as well. Technically, the stones belong to the family members of the person buried beneath them, but it never hurts to establish a good rapport.

Later on, we'll discuss more in detail about what you should do during the daytime to prepare for the investigation but in your first scouting expedition, you'll want to get an overall feel for the place. Be sure to take plenty of photographs, stroll through the graves and try and search out the older sections. Take your time in doing this and get a feel for the different kinds of markers that are on the grounds, the landscape and anything else that might play a role in the history of the place.

As a method of determining a complete history of the graveyard, you will want to discover what type of cemetery it is. There is a more detailed discussion of this in Chapter One, but the following is a breakdown of various types of burial grounds:

1. Church Cemetery

America's first cemeteries were the churchyards of New England the East Coast and it's here that you will find the oldest burials. The tradition of church burials was started in Europe and carried on in America. When the churchyards became too crowded and the conditions unsanitary, town cemeteries were started. After that, land was usually set aside on the borders of towns where the cemeteries would be located. The early churchyards will not usually be laid out in neat rows like later cemeteries. The alignment of the graves tended to be haphazard and close. In many cities, and often in rural settings, churchyards are still in use today but those located away from the East Coast tend to me more organized and less crowded than the original sites.

2. Family Plots

Family plots, or private burial grounds, would often hold the remains of not only the immediate family who owned the land, but also friends, neighbors and extended relatives as well. Family burial grounds were most common in the old South, where plantation living made it impractical to take a body for miles to churchyard or town cemetery, but they can be found in other locations as well. The burial plots were normally located on a person's property, usually in a garden or an orchard, and often on high ground. In towns and cities, many private burial grounds were absorbed by larger ones or bodies were moved to new locations as the town grew around them. Many others were lost altogether and were built over, often leading to gruesome finds in later years. In some states, it is still legal to bury the bodies of loved ones on private property (especially in the South) and so it's not uncommon to find homes with small fenced-in graveyards in front.

3. Garden Cemetery

The Garden Cemetery movement (as detailed in Chapter One) began in Paris and later extended to America. The popularity of the movement came at a time when American attitudes toward death were changing from the grim reality of it, as typified by the skulls, wings and dark characters of early tombstones, to finding beauty in death. This beauty was portrayed in the statuary and monuments and soon in the landscape architecture of the cemetery itself. Garden Cemeteries are easily identified by the park-like setting of them, with pathways, ponds, trees, foliage and benches for visitors. Before public parks were common, people came to the cemeteries on weekend afternoons to relax, walk, have picnic lunches and even make love under the shade trees. Even the names of the cemeteries began to emphasize the beauty and back-to-nature settings with names like Greenwood, Laurel Hill, Spring Grove, Forest Lawn, Oak Ridge and others. Garden Cemeteries tend to be huge, sprawling places and maps are always suggested if one is available.

4. Rural Cemetery

Growing up in the country in Illinois, rural cemeteries were the first types of graveyards that I was exposed to. These types of cemeteries are a true piece of Americana and are easily found on the highways and back roads of the country. On many occasions, you'll find them well hidden along gravel roads and at the end of dirt tracks, abandoned and forgotten by the local populace. Other times, they will be on the edge of a small town, or a mile or two from town, and often on small hills to protect them from spring floods. It is rare to find large monuments or mausoleums in them because most of these cemeteries are small, which makes them simple to investigate but difficult to research the history for. In these cases, it's best to check with the local genealogical society for information or to talk with some of the old-timers in the area.

5. Urban Cemetery

Most modern urban cemeteries are "public" cemeteries that are operated by the cities in which they can be found. Because most of them are not very historic or picturesque, they have largely been ignored over the years by researchers. The rows and rows of mostly ordinary markers tend not to get too much attention and for this reason, little documentation is available about them, even at the cemetery office itself.

6. Memorial Parks

The first Memorial Park was established in Southern California in 1917 (Forest Lawn) and the movement has since spread all over the country. There is nothing inspiring about this type of cemetery -- which is really the point. The flat, grassy lawns with their flush, stone tablets were designed to eliminate all suggestions of death. There are no monuments and no grave mounds and the markers are all situated against the ground so that lawn mowers will pass right over them. The goal was to give the cemetery a more park-like landscape but what it succeeded in doing was erasing all of the personality from the graveyard.

7. Military Cemetery

The first large military cemetery in the country was established in Pennsylvania in 1863, shortly after the Battle of Gettysburg doomed the fate of the Confederacy. It was here that President Abraham Lincoln gave his famous "Gettysburg Address" and consecrated the place as hallowed ground. There are currently 119 National Cemeteries in the United States, including Arlington Cemetery, and all of them are filled with rows of rows of identical stone markers, marking the graves of men killed in battle and who were discharged from military service. The history of these cemeteries, especially those associated with the battlefields, can easily be obtained and offer a rich tale for the researcher. Many of them are as haunted as the battlefields that are located nearby.

8. Potter's Fields

Potter's Fields are graveyards where the country or the city buries the poor, the unknown, the unclaimed, criminals, suicides and illegitimate babies. Most often they are buried in mass graves or in individual graves with no marker. A potter's field is the greatest example of anonymity, a place where the names of the dead, if known, are usually placed only on the coffin itself. A pit is loaded with coffins until it is full and then the entire mass grave is given a single, numbered marker. No mourners are present when the earth is smoothed over this grave and no clergyman is there to offer a prayer for the dead. They can be stark, forbidding places. One of the most famous potter's fields is Hart Island, off the shore of New York City, and its story will be told in the final section of the book.

As you are exploring the cemetery, you will want to try and get oriented with the general design of the site. One of the most common customs regarding cemetery layout is that most are on an east-west axis. The inscription on the monument might face east or west though. Many times, they face west so that visitors are not standing on the grave to read the inscription but they can be anywhere, so check the back and all of the sides too. Many ornate monuments, or those with lengthy stories to tell about the people buried beneath them, may have inscriptions on practically every surface. Some graves also have footstones, which makes it obvious which direction the body was placed, but most are laid with the head to the east and the feet to the west. This tradition follows the idea that the eastern sky will open on the Day of Judgment and the dead will rise from their graves to face the east. I once ran across a monument in which the deceased, who was a devout Christian, had been placed inside of it, standing up and facing the east. He wanted to be among the first of the dead to rise when Christ returned!

In an earlier chapter, I offered some details about the symbols that can be found on gravestones in American cemeteries, but what about the decorations that are left behind by visitors to the graveyard? Flowers are obviously the most common items left behind but there are many other, much stranger, items that are placed on graves as well. It is not uncommon to find holiday decorations on recent graves and many place toys and small gifts on the graves of children. Some African-Americans leave broken dishes and pottery on graves to symbolize a shattered life and often the pieces of crockery will have come from the dishes last used by the deceased. Light bulbs and lanterns are sometimes left to stand for the lighting of the way to the afterlife and shells and coins are often left behind as well, although normally to signify good luck for the living.

Some items that are left behind have special meaning to the graves where the objects are deposited. For instance, flowers and unusual messages are often left on the grave of accused murderer Lizzie Borden in Fall River, Massachusetts. Cigars and bottles of booze are often cleaned away by cemetery caretakers from the grave of Al Capone at Chicago's Queen of Heaven Cemetery. The grave of cave explorer Floyd Collins, who died after being trapped in a branch of Kentucky's Mammoth Cave, is often decorated with candles and waterproof matches -- the cave explorers best friends. Outside Chicago, the grave of Mary Alice Quinn, who was believed to have miraculous healing powers, is constantly surrounded by candles, religious icons, coins and prayer cards as the living pray to have her intercede on their behalf. Some visitors also claim to experience the supernatural scent of roses while in the presence of this grave.

Grave Stones & Markers

Grave stones and cemetery markers will provide us with the greatest amount of information that we will be able to find about the history of the graveyard, while we are actually at the site. For this reason, it's best that we understand as much as we possible can about them. Listed below are the items that you are most likely going to find on cemetery stones:

- The name of the deceased
- birth date and date of death
- birth place and place of death

- relationships / marriage information
- artwork and / or epitaph

Other information may appear as well, including service in the military, fraternal or service orders, life accomplishments and perhaps even a short biography of the deceased but the items above are the most common. Many graves will have footstones as well, which may have no engravings or perhaps only the initials of the deceased.

It should also be noted that just because there is a stone in the cemetery, it does not mean that the person is actually buried there. The marker could be simply a memorial that was placed there by loved ones. The body could have been lost in an accident or disaster and never recovered. Cemetery records, if they exist, should reveal that information. You can watch for clues on the tombstones that say something like "Sacred to the Memory of.." and while this is not a sure indicator, stones are usually inscribed with certain words and phrases for a reason.

Cemetery gravestones act as a road map to the past but unfortunately, vandals, pollution and the weather can destroy these vital links. Weathering is a natural decaying process that affects porous objects that are left outside. When water gets into the cracks of a tombstone and freezes, it tends to expand, causing stress on the marker, especially older and more fragile ones. This makes the stone much more susceptible to accidents and damage from lawn mowers and rakes that are wielded by cemetery caretakers. Wind, rain and sun can do damage also and since the force of our weather patterns seem to move from west to east, many markers, especially marble ones, become eroded and are no longer legible. In Chicago, and other cities around the Great Lakes, some of the most fragile statues and monuments have been placed inside of heavy glass boxes to protect them from the cold winds and weather from the lakes. Lichen and moss and other plants that grow on the stone's surface can cause damage also, further weakening the marker.

Types of Gravestones
In spite of all of the damage that may have been done to older tombstones in a cemetery, from broken stones to weathering, or even if a good portion of it has sunken into the ground, you can still get an idea as to when the stone was placed based on the composition of the stone and the lettering that is on it. The type of stone that it is will also tell you if it is a replacement marker or an original. For instance, a granite stone with a death date before 1880 is not an original marker.

Prior to 1650
During this time period, graves were marked with either wood or field stones. The wood markers would have, of course, deteriorated by this time but the field stones might remain. However, nearly all of them were uncarved, rough-cut rocks

and boulders that generally only bore the initials of the deceased and perhaps a year of death.

1660's - 1850s'

Tombstones from this era were generally made from sedimentary rock, like red and brown sandstone or limestone, as well as slate. Sandstone and limestone weather very easily and for this reason do not hold up well. Slate is more resistant to the weather but it does tend to flake and peel. Inscriptions at this time were generally carved in Roman lettering. Wooden markers and crosses were also used during this time period but few remain today.

Early 1800's - 1850's

A bluish-gray slate stone came into use about this time and inscriptions began to appear that used an italic script lettering. Unfortunately, italic lettering does not weather well and as a result, many of these types of stones are almost impossible to read. Roman lettering soon returned in popularity (especially to the stone cutters) because the italics were too hard to carve.

1830's - 1890's

Although the first uses of it date back to the 1700's, marble became very popular during this time period and beyond. It was easy to use and Italian stone cutters specialized in ornate stones and beautiful statuary, including life-sized figures, angels and even likenesses of the deceased. Unfortunately though, marble is especially prone to staining and weathering and the wear tends to leave the inscriptions unreadable and causes once polished monuments to appear dull and lifeless. In the early 1850's, the use of photographs secured to tombstones began. The majority of the images were life portraits but in some cases, postmortem photographs were also used.

1880's - 1910's

Soft, gray granite and metal markers began to be used during this time period and raised lettering on the granite became popular. The soft granite weathers somewhat and lichen and moss take root to it quite easily. Around this same time, the method of sandblasting the stones took the place of carving by hammer and chisel. This signaled the end of a great cemetery art form and the decline of the "celebration of death".

1920's - Present Day

In keeping with the idea that death should be more orderly and sanitized than even before, our favorite type of grave markers have followed suit. Today, most stones are depressingly similar to one another and aside from special, customized stones, most only come in a few specific shapes and almost without fail, are made from polished granite. This type of marker is easily to clean, weathers well and generally withstands lichen and moss. These types of markers blend right in to the modern urban cemeteries, never standing out from one another and fading into row after row of nearly identical monuments.

Photographs on Tombstones

The tradition of including portraits of the deceased on their grave markers has literally come full circle over the past 200 years. The precursor to actual photographs was to have a portrait of the deceased carved into the stone. They were usually small, cameo-type portraits with wings on either side of them to show that the deceased had gone to heaven. As soon as photography was invented in the 1840's though, families began thinking of ways to secure photographic portraits onto the stones. Postmortem photographs were rarely ever used in those days, unless the deceased was a child who had not lived long enough to have an actual photo taken. In 1851, Solon Jenkins Jr. or West Cambridge, Massachusetts patented an idea for a memorial tombstone that featured a locket-type setting with the photograph inside. Visiting family members could slide aside a protective cover that cleverly shielded the daguerreotype from the elements.

Unfortunately, few photographic stones from this time period still exist, although patents and advertisements from the era suggest that they were very popular. Sadly, most have been destroyed by vandals and relic seekers over the years. Most older stones that still have portraits on them are porcelain or ceramic photographs that only date back to the 1920's.

Because so many of the stones like this have been damaged over the years, leaving a gaping and unsightly cavity behind, many cemeteries have rules against placing memorial photographs on grave markers. Monument makers have since come up with a new way to include portraits, and even panoramic scenes, on stones that do not require photographs. As I mentioned, this has come full circle from the beginning of the tradition in that the images are once again being carved onto the stones themselves. A trip through a modern cemetery might reveal portraits of the deceased on the markers, automobiles, mountain vistas and in one rural cemetery that I visited, a tractor and farm machinery.

Military Markers

Before and during the Civil War, most soldier's markers were nothing more than wooden boards with rounded tops that bore the name and description of the man buried beneath it. The markers were far from durable and were only expected to last for about five years. It was not until 1865, when more than 100,000 soldiers were buried in our national cemeteries, that the government gave any thought to abandoning the old wooden markers. A debate began that lasted for seven years over whether the graves should be marked with marble or by iron that was coated with zinc. (Ironically, any markers that had been placed before the debate began were now gone with a life expectancy of only 5 years!) The marble stones won out in 1873 but the stones have changed many times over the years. Here is a timeline of the different types of military stones that have been used:

1873

This type of stone is referred to as a Civil War-type marker and was used in all military cemeteries. For the known dead, the stones were usually made from polished marble (or some other durable stone), were four inches thick, ten inches wide and twelve inches high above the ground. The tops of them were slightly rounded. The number of the grave, rank, name of soldier and name of state were carved on the front in a raised shield. These markers were furnished for soldiers in the Federal Army only. For the unknown dead, markers were made from polished marble or stone, were six inches square and thirty inches long. The number of the grave was carved into the top. Stones were also furnished for the unmarked graves of soldiers from the Revolutionary War, the War of 1814, the Mexican War and the Indian Campaigns in the west. Congress also authorized furnishing stones for unmarked graves of veterans in private cemeteries as well.

1899

In 1899, markers were also authorized for those killed in the Spanish-American War and for veterans of the conflict. These stones were designed to be the same as the Civil War markers but the words "Spanish-American War" were added.

1903 - 1904

In 1903, the stone sizes for markers were changed, making them 39 inches high, 12 inches wide and four inches thick. In October, the use of simple stone blocks for marking the graves of the unknown dead was discontinued and graves began to be marked with the same design as for the known dead. The following year, Congress authorized headstones for unmarked graves of civilians who were buried in post cemeteries.

1906

Headstones began to be furnished for the graves of Confederate soldiers who had died, primarily in Union prison camps and hospitals, and were buried in military cemeteries. Congress approved the same size and material for the Confederate stones but the shield was not included and the tops of the stones were pointed instead of rounded. Legend has it that the pointed top was to prevent any Yankees from sitting on the Confederate stones.

1918

A new headstone was approved in this year and became known as the "General" type. It was designed to be used on all veteran's graves, save for those from the Civil War and the Spanish-American War. The new stones were made from American white marble and was slightly rounded on top. They were 42 inches long, 13 inches wide and four inches thick. The inscription on them included the name of the soldier, rank, regiment, division, date of death and the state he was from. Religious emblems were also adopted for use on these types of stones but were limited to a Cross and a Star of David.

1929 - 1930

Two changes were made for Confederate veterans in these years. In 1929, Congress authorized the Confederate marker for use in private cemeteries and also approved the inscription of a Confederate Cross of Honor that could be carved in a small circle on the front of the stones. The emblem would appear over the standard inscription of the soldier's name, rank, company and regiment.

1936

Flat, marble military markers were approved for cemeteries that only allowed that type of gravestone. The new markers were 24 inches in length, 12 inches in width and were four inches deep. The marker was placed flush against the ground and the inscription ran parallel to the greatest dimension of the stone. The inscription included the soldier's name, rank, organization, date of death and a religious emblem. Granite markers of this type were approved in 1939 and in 1940, flat bronze markers also began to be used.

1941 - 1945

During the years of World War II, granite markers came into use for soldiers of any war and dates of birth began to be added to the inscriptions. Also, in 1945, the words "World War I" or "World War II" also began to be added. Between 1951 and 1954, the word "Korea" began to be added to the stones of men who died during this conflict or whose death was attributable to service in Korea.

1964

The word "Vietnam" began to be added to stones of those men who died in Vietnam or whose death was attributable to service there. This was used during the duration of military activities in that country and eventually was retroactive back to 1954. The word "Korea" was also approved on headstones of military personnel and veterans who were on active duty during the period from June 1950 to July 1954.

1983
The words "Lebanon" and "Grenada" were authorized for those killed during these military actions.

1990
The words "Panama" and "Persian Gulf" began to be used for those killed in action.

False Crypts, Table Tombs, Ovens & Grave Houses
While tombstones and grave markers are the most common types of monuments that stand above the ground in cemeteries, they are not alone. Statuary are also common in most larger graveyards and in cemeteries that enjoyed their heyday in the late 1800's or early 1900's, you are likely to find an overabundance of marble angels, mourning statues and more.

Mausoleums can also be found in many larger cemeteries and some smaller ones. These expensive tombs enjoyed their heyday during the Victorian "Celebration of Death" era and for the most part, were the exclusive resting places of the wealthy dead. On occasion, the deceased was cremated and the urn placed in the mausoleum but most commonly, the caskets themselves were placed inside. Most mausoleums are kept locked and usually the cemetery caretaker, or family members, hold the key. You will also find that many mausoleums will have glass doors that will allow the visitor to seen inside. It's not uncommon to find flowers, chairs, photographs and even personal items resting inside.

Mausoleums, crypts and tombs are only infrequently used today, except in coastal areas, like New Orleans, where underground burial is unheard of because of the water table. The dead here are entombed in family vaults, benevolent society mausoleums and crypts that are commonly known as "ovens". These vaults also serve as the outer wall of the older cemeteries. In order to entomb someone in a wall vault, the marble plaque must be removed and then the layer of brick and plaster behind the plaque must be broken open. After that, any casket that is already inside must be removed and disposed of. In the past, these caskets were burned for fear of contagion but today, they are merely thrown away. Any human remains found in the old casket are then placed back in the vault and moved to the rear or side to make room for the new coffin. The piles of remains in these vaults may be the mingled bones of a number of generations. The wall vaults are referred to as "oven vaults", thanks to the fact that the barrel-shaped crypts look like brick baker's ovens. Ironically though, the vaults do act literally as ovens too. In cooler climates, one year and one day would not be enough time for a corpse to decompose. However, in southern regions, the temperature inside of one of these brick wall vaults can reach several hundred degrees between the months of May and

September. Such temperatures are a great aid in accelerating decomposition. Many of these wall vaults are not actually owned, although some are. In most cases, families with less money rent the vaults for burial. As with a home or an apartment, if the rents are not paid on the vaults, the occupants are then evicted.

There are also a few other items that you might run across while exploring the cemetery, depending on the graveyard you are in. One of the most commonly asked questions that I get from people about cemeteries concerns the false crypts (also known as "chest tombs" or "box tombs") that look like small, one person, above-ground tombs. The crypt is usually on a base of brick or stone, on top of which is an inscribed slab. The box, no matter how it might look, is actually empty and the body is interred beneath it, underground. The flat slab beneath the box was once referred to as a "wolf stone" and its purpose was to keep wolves and other animals from digging up the grave. The false crypt serves no real purpose, other than for design.

Another oddity is the tabletop tomb, which looks just like a stone table. This is also a false crypt and the body lies beneath it, The table is a flat, inscribed slab that rests on four or six pillars and date back to Colonial times. The only real purpose behind them was to protect the grave from vandals, animals and the weather.

Surveying the Cemetery

One of the best ways of finding out about the cemetery is through records, newspapers, local census records and county histories but you can also get an equally good sense of time and place by surveying the cemetery itself. When you do this in conjunction with your research on paper, the cemetery will literally come alive for you. By surveying the site and reading though the tombstones (especially in smaller cemeteries) you should be able to determine many details about much of the following:

Where the Dead Came From

On some headstones, you will find information on where people buried in the cemetery migrated from, such as places of birth or inscriptions that tell of moving from one place to another. You can also use such information, including family names, to determine where their country of origin may have been.

Family Groups

In many cemeteries, you will find family plots conveniently marked by fences or stones that separate them from other parts of the cemetery. You may also want to note the names of those buried within the plots whose names do not match. Later research will likely reveal they are part of the family by marriage. I once discovered some interesting facts when I found a large family plot on the edge of a cemetery. Research revealed that it actually pre-dated the rest of the graveyard and had been a private burial site that was eventually absorbed by the larger cemetery. As it turned out, the family's mansion was actually right behind the private plot through a patch of woods and a path had once led to it from the house. I was glad that I checked into it too --- because family lore had it that the place was haunted!

Occupations & Trades

Cemetery inscriptions and stones can also give you a sense of the type of work that was done by those buried there. City directories and census records might be more thorough but artwork and epitaphs can also give you a sense of business and trades. Years ago, I ran across the tombstone of a man who worked for the railroad and had been killed. His obviously grieving family gave a detailed description of the accident and where and when it had occurred. I failed to write down the story and have regretted it ever since.

Epidemics & Disasters

A survey of gravesites can also give you an idea of how the people buried in the cemetery were affected by epidemics that swept through the region. If you find a number of graves that are dated 1918, it's possible that many of the deceased died during the Spanish Influenza epidemic of that year. A number of graves that share the same date means that a check of the records could reveal a cholera, smallpox or any other common frontier epidemic could have also occurred.

Floods, hurricanes, tornadoes, fires, mine accidents and other tragedies often claim the lives of a large number of people. On many occasions, the victim's tombstones will tell the story of the disaster, or at least that it occurred. If not, another check of records from a date that appears on many stones will likely provide the information that you need.

Life Expectancy

While you are in the cemetery, use your notebook to take a random sampling of about 40 gravestones that belong to adults that were at least 21 years of age when they died. Write down just the birth and death years and then sort them out by sex. Total the ages of the men and women and then divide that number by the number of individuals of each sex. This number that you come up with will give you an average age at death for men and women of the community. To be totally accurate, you would have to go through the entire cemetery and do this but this random sampling will at least give you an average for the community.

Economy

The general design and look of the cemetery can you tell you much about the local economy, from present to past. If the place is rundown or ill-kempt, then chances are that things are not good at the moment. The older stones can speak for the past as well. If there are a number of elaborately carved markers and mausoleums, then it was (at least at some point) a wealthy community. But if you find rocks and slabs instead of markers, homemade gravestones or temporary markers from funeral homes that are still in place after many years, then the place has been economically depressed.

The History of the Cemetery & It's Occupants

Surveying and exploring the cemetery grounds is likely to give you pages and pages of information and believe it or not, most of it will be worthwhile, no matter how confusing it might seem at first. A few years back, I spent nearly a week in a large cemetery, going over every section of it, a grave at a time. I photographed everything of interest and used a large notebook to write down the names and inscriptions of those I believed would be of interest to the history of the town and cemetery. Keep in mind, that I did this with a fairly practiced eye -- meaning that I knew what kinds of monuments and burial plots to look for. However, most of the names that I jotted down meant nothing to me at the time.

After I finished exploring the graveyard, and had completed my survey, I began to research the names that I had compiled. Even though very few of them meant anything to me when I was trudging through the cemetery, the names on the list ended up belonging to politicians, city founders, early pioneers, generals, Civil War heroes, a famous Methodist circuit rider and even an ambassador to a South American country! I learned more about the history of the area from my trip to the cemetery that I had previously learned from books and documents about the town.

More importantly (at least for our purposes here), I was also able to track down some authentic history behind some of the ghost stories that I had heard about various parts of the cemetery. I was then able to actually link the tales to some real people who were buried there. For this reason, I continue to believe that, even with cemeteries, the history is the key to determining the ghostly activity at a place.

As with a haunted house, city directories can also provide information about the graveyard with not only listing those in charge of the cemetery in the past but also the local funeral homes, undertakers and monument companies. All of these companies have the potential to have records for the cemetery. If they are no longer in business, the local historical society may have access to their past records.

County, Local and Family histories may also provide information and as mentioned before, the local genealogical society can provide a wealth of information about the cemetery, from burial lists to epitaphs and even maps.

Here are some other areas worth checking to glean some additional information about the graveyard and about the people buried there:

Cemetery Plat Maps

While it may be hard to find plat maps (again, check the genealogical society) for old and defunct cemeteries, those graveyards still open for interments should have a map or register so that grave diggers don't accidentally dig a grave where another is still in use. You can check for copies of such maps at the cemetery office or at a town or county office. Cemetery maps normally give the names of the person or person occupying the graves and other details, such as the date of burial. This may be important if you survey of the cemetery pointed toward evidence of some unmarked graves in some areas.

In other cases, and with most maps that I have run across, the plots on the map are numbered and to find out who is buried where, you have to compare the map to the cemetery deeds (see next section).

This type of information is vital when visitors and workers at the cemetery are experiencing phenomenon in one particular area and are unable to link it to any one person or event in particular. By tracking down the owners of the surrounding plots, this is the first link in the chain to establishing who might be haunting the spot. From there, more detailed information will be needed about the owners, which is more research in itself, but this will at least get you started in the right direction.

Cemetery Deeds

In the same way that purchasers receive a deed showing the ownership of a piece of property they have bought, those who purchase a cemetery plot also received a deed. A copy of it is usually recorded with the town or county where the cemetery is located and the other copy is stored with the cemetery sexton. In the record, you will find the names of the buyer and seller, the amount paid for the plot, the lot number and where it is located in the cemetery. This is the next likely step in research following the obtaining of a cemetery plat map.

Cemetery Transcriptions

As I have mentioned already, one of the best place to find more information about the cemetery is at the local genealogical society. Genealogists love cemeteries and graveyards are, in addition to records rooms and in front of their computers, the place where they spend the bulk of their time tracking down family histories. Over the years, many genealogists have taken the time to copy down cemetery inscriptions -- and I mean from *entire* cemeteries -- and have often had them privately printed into books that are stored in the local library or genealogical society so that others will have access to them. However, since this has been done on a hit and miss basis, not all transcriptions are the same, as some may be in manuscript form while others may be only index cards.

WPA Historical Records Survey

Between 1935 and 1943, the Works Progress Administration (WPA) Historical Records Survey undertook a cemetery survey project that was done on a county by county basis across the country. Unfortunately though, not every county took part in it so the end results varied. The finished products ended up being in all different types of formats from typed files to manuscripts to card files. Some contain tombstone inscriptions, cemetery obituaries, death notices and maps of the cemeteries, while others may have only included veterans or those killed in wars. To make matters more confusing, the WPA cemetery surveys are not centrally located, Because it was done on a local basis, they can only be found in county repositories and state library archives.

Cemetery Records

The person in charge of the cemetery and its records was once known as the "sexton", but today is called the superintendent. Years ago, such a person might also handle the bell-ringing duties to announce a person's death or would dig the graves in the cemetery himself. Today, he is usually in charge of a crew of people who maintain the grounds, handle burials and record the deceased that are buried on the property. The sexton's records typically give the name of the deceased, the date of the burial and often, the exact location of the grave in the cemetery. In addition, the records sometime list the original purchaser of the burial plot and who is responsible for the upkeep of it, such as a relative living in the area. When researching stories from a ghostly viewpoint, this just may be vital information if that person's relative is suspected of being the resident haunt. You can often find these records in the cemetery office itself or filed at the town or city hall.

I should add though that cemetery records, deeds and transcriptions may not always have all of the information that you need. As I mentioned at the start of this chapter, the information here will not provide all of the answers and over time, I have found that no matter how hard you search -- sometimes the answers are just not there. In one case, I was looking for information about an entire cemetery that had been closed down and moved. The company that constructed on the original site of the cemetery had not only found human remains while they were building, but the structure that was completed on the site was known for being haunted.

The only records that I could find stated that the cemetery, which had been a potter's field for the local poor house, had been closed down in 1913 and moved to a larger cemetery. The remains from the old site had been buried in a common grave on the grounds. Strangely, I was completely unable to find any records of the relocation (only that it had been done) and despite an extensive check of the cemetery records and plat maps, I was unable to discover where the mass grave was located on the grounds. The cemetery superintendent, who had been at his position since the early 1970's, was just as stumped as I was and even took it upon himself to continue the research and see if the remains were actually sent to another cemetery in the area. To this day, they remain "missing"!

Bringing the Dead to Life

After you have been to the cemetery and have pored through the records trying to link the burial plots or sections to those buried there, you now have to try and find out more about the people whose identities you have discovered. There are many ways to find out more about their lives, including at the library, through city directories and of course, at the local genealogical society but our focus here will be on their deaths. As most readers are undoubtedly aware, the majority of those who return to haunt the earth do so because of their death and usually when and how it occurred. I have pointed out several times already that most cemetery ghosts are linked to events that happened after death, rather than before, but our research should be complete enough to delve into the final days of those buried within the cemetery ,or section of the graveyard, in question.

For the purposes of our example here, we will assume that you are trying to track down more information about a single person that is buried in a section of the graveyard. As part of the example, let's assume that there is a private burial plot where visitors to the cemetery and cemetery workers have reported seeing a ghostly figure. After tracking down as much information as you can about the cemetery, and prior to conducting an on-site paranormal investigation of the spot, you will want to learn all that you can about the life and death of the individual who is interred in the plot.

If the subject died since the early years of the Twentieth Century, when statewide vital registration became common, you will probably find a death certificate on file for them in a local office. If the person died before that though, there are still other records that you can find to establish dates and information about his death. Following are different types of sources for death-related information that may assist you. Not all of them will be relevant to your individual search but each will help you to get a little closer to what you are looking for. Here are some excellent places to start the search:

City Directories

As the reader may have noticed already in this book (and in some of my other research guides), city directories are an excellent place to begin an investigation into the history of a person or a site. With places, the directory, which is an alphabetical listing of inhabitants and businesses in a town, offers a "reverse directory", listing street addresses and who once lived there. Obviously, this can be essential to a haunted house investigation but when searching for information on people, it is even easier to use. Information will vary in the books from city to city but you may find the person's death listed or, as in some cases, a list of all the deaths that occurred in the city over a given year. A clue to watch for is a man's name being listed and then disappearing from the following year's directory with his wife listed as "widow" or "widow of..." Remember though, just because a name is removed does not mean the person died. He could have simply moved or was missed for that year, so be sure to check the next several following years as well.

Obituaries

Your next likely step, after determining a death date and a place or residence for the subject, is to check for information listed in the newspaper obituary. Obituaries are like small biographies and are often written for the newspaper by funeral homes or by the relatives of the deceased. They will often tell something about the deceased and his remaining family, as well as details about funeral services and where he was buried. The cause of death may or may not be listed in the obituary but you can watch for clues within the notice as to what may have happened. Words like "died suddenly" might indicate an accidental death, a murder or suicide or possibly just a heart attack or a stroke. The words "lingering" or "long illness" could suggest cancer, heart disease or tuberculosis.

The best news might be when someone who ordinarily would not end up on the front page of the newspaper ends up there because they died in an unusual way. If your subject did die in a strange way, be sure to look for an article to go along with the obituary. A few years ago, I was researching a haunted house and found that the original owner had committed suicide. When I found the article that went along with the death notice, I found that he had killed himself in remorse over a crime that he had committed -- or so the police believed. There actually had been some questions left unanswered concerning his method of suicide, leaving some to believe that he may have actually been murdered instead. What better reason was there for his ghost to linger behind?

Death Certificates

Death certificates are the official documents that record people's deaths and were first created to determine the frequency and distribution of fatal diseases. Many states did not have such a plan in place until the early part of the last century but modern death certificates are completed by several people. If a person dies in a hospital or other institution, then a nurse or staff member fills in the time and date of death. The doctor fills in the cause and then the funeral director, or one of their staff members, fills in the rest. The information then is retyped onto a new, blank form and then is returned to the doctor for their signature. After that, the funeral home then goes to the registrar for a burial permit. Usually, the funeral home will keep a copy of the certificate on file.

Death certificates, which are filled with vital information, can be confusing and hard to decipher but the more modern they are, the more they are likely to contain. Sometimes, information can be in error and often the cause of death can be obscured or covered up to protect a person's reputation or privacy. This is especially common with older certificates. For example, instead of "suicide", you might find the cause of death was listed as "accidental" or instead of "abortion", you might find "uterine bleeding". On older certificates, causes of death will often use archaic words for diseases so be sure to have some sort of glossary on hand while attempting to decipher them.

Funeral Home Records

While this is a possible source for research, it's not a likely one. Many funeral homes will not have a problem accommodating you for research on people who have been dead for many decades, they are unlikely to grant you access to anything recent. Funeral home records are private and so they are within their rights to restrict or deny access to records. And because they are private, the content in the records will vary from one location to another and from one time period to another as well.

Institutional Records

If your subject died in a hospital, asylum, tuberculosis sanatorium, poor house or prison, then his death would have been recorded in that institution's records. These registers, which usually predate state ward registrations, may be kept in a separate death book or among the other entries in the main register book. Information is going to vary in them from one place to the next and certainly from one time period to another. In many cases, the institution (especially with asylums and tuberculosis hospitals) will have closed down years ago and so finding the records may be tricky. To find out if the records still exist, contacted the town, city or county, or even the state historical society. They may have some idea to help you find them.

Autopsy Records

Many death certificates can tell you if an autopsy was performed on your subject and it that record will then be filed with the hospital or with the coroner's reports (see next section). Hospital records are considered private and you can usually only get access to them if you are related to the deceased. Each hospital has its own policy as to hoe long it keeps records. An autopsy is performed when a cause of death is uncertain, questionable or suspicious. If the medical examiner suspects something unusual, then no consent is needed from the family for an autopsy. The details of these records are fascinating and just may provide many clues to the researcher in search of the strange.

Coroner's Records

If you should learn from your research that your subject died in an unusual way or under strange circumstances, you will want to check and see if a coroner looked into the case. Both medical examiners and coroners investigate suspicious deaths and the position of coroner predates that of medical examiners. The coroner, an elected position, was responsible for examining dead bodies for any sign of foul play. No special education was required and it was not necessary to be a doctor. By the late 1800's, many states and cities began replacing the position of coroner with that of medical examiner, who is required to be a physician. Some locations still use the elected coroner position or a combination of both.

If the coroner decided that the death appeared to be from criminal negligence or murder, then he held what was called an inquest and the records of these affairs hold huge amounts of information for both crime buffs and ghost researchers. Juries were appointed and witnesses were called to testify. The postmortem findings (autopsy records) were included as well. Most coroner's reports are open to the public and should be followed up with newspaper research. There might be an obituary that was written or if the death was unusual, an entire report. If the death turned out to be murder or linked to a crime, there also be subsequent articles and possibly even court records if the case went to trial.

As you can see from the preceding pages, research and investigation into possibly haunted cemeteries can be just as "legitimate" as the research that is being done in other haunted sites -- as long as it is done the right way. As mentioned, wandering aimlessly through a graveyard at night, just snapping photographs, is not the way to do worthwhile research. However, we have been able to show that by using even a fraction of the information that we have listed here, your cemetery research can go in all sorts of new and fascinating directions.

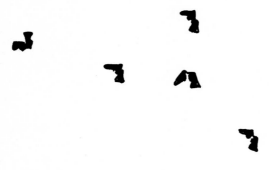

4. Paranormal Research
A How-To Guide for Your Cemetery Investigation

Once all of your preliminary research has been finished, there is still much to be done before the actual investigation takes place. Some of that will mean returning to the cemetery for some additional surveying and exploration, although this time it will be specifically in regards to the vigil that your investigation team will be carrying out on the grounds.

You will need to return to the cemetery again and once more, bring your notebook and pen with you. There are a number of things that have to be noted about the graveyard and the surrounding area before you can return at night. Make sure that this step is carried out during the daylight hours so that everything can be seen in detail. You will be coming back after dark for the investigation, so all of this data will need to be compiled now. Here are some steps for you to follow:

1. Draw a map of the location, as close to scale as possible. Be sure to mark any landmarks or noticeable spots on the map so that other team members will be able to easily locate them. This may mean trees, mausoleums, easily identifiable grave markers and monuments and anything else that the team can use to orient themselves between the cemetery and your map.

2. Take note of the location's surroundings. Be sure to notice what might be seen from the location during the investigation. If woods surround the cemetery, check and see if there are houses on the other side of the trees. Even a small amount of light (or sound) from a home or farm could appear to be anomalous in any photos that might be taken or on any recordings that your group might make.

3. Take many photographs of the site in the daytime. That way, any night time photos can be checked for location and compared to areas that might be active.

After leaving the site, there is more preparation work that needs to be done. One of the most important things can be accomplished by speaking with local authorities. It is imperative that if you are planning to conduct an investigation in a public location, that you find out what the state and local laws say about trespassing in a cemetery after dark. In most cases, unless the site is otherwise posted, you will be asked to leave the cemetery if bothered by law enforcement officials. If the cemetery is posted, then you could be arrested or fined. Never go into a cemetery that is posted against night time trespassing unless you have permission to be there!

4. Try to get permission in writing from the owners of the location to conduct investigations at the site. Few cemeteries are privately owned and most belong to the local community (or the township in rural areas). You can speak to the on-site superintendent about this. You might also contact the local police department and let them know that you will be at the site as a courtesy. This may be very important if you are unable to get written permission. If you can get permission, take the letter with you to the site.

5. After selecting the site and getting your clearances (if applicable), carefully put together a team of people to accompany you to the location. As with any other investigation, you will want to put together people who can take photographs, run the equipment, use the video camera...etc. Be sure not to tell them what to expect before the vigil. If they witness anything at the site that matches previous reports, this will strengthen your suspicions about the place being haunted.

6. Once your team has been put together, I recommend preparing a variety of equipment that you want to take with you. Your team should be no larger than 7-9 people and no less than 5. Here is a list of some equipment that I believe is worth taking along (in addition to extra batteries and essential items from your "ghost hunter's kit"):

- Flashlights (one for every team member)
- clipboard, paper, pencil & copies of the location maps
- EMF detectors and IR temperature probes
- Cameras (one for every team member)
- At least one video camera, capable of IR filming in total darkness
- PIR (Passive Infrared) motion detectors
- hygrometer (measure humidity in the area)
- Thermometer (check weather conditions for the vigil)

Beyond this basic list, you should add whatever pieces of equipment that you feel would be useful in your particular location or investigation. Just be sure that you have a practice run with any new or unfamiliar equipment prior to the investigation. This is also suggested with new cameras and probes as well. Most likely, you will be working in uncomfortable and dark conditions and it is important that the investigators be familiar with the equipment before arriving at the location.

7. Before you leave for the investigation, consider using the map that you have already made to decide where you would like to first set up the equipment. This might be based on previous reports from the location or insights by the team member who previously visited the site. No matter what, it will give you a place to start from and a "game plan" for the investigation.

Photographing the Cemetery

One of the most important parts of your investigation will be the photographs that are taken and later examined for evidence of the paranormal. For this reason, it is vital that your entire team is well aware of your "protocols" for using cameras in your investigations. Spirit photography involves many kinds of advanced techniques that can be used to try and capture ghosts and "spirit energy" on film and several basic ones as well. The following is some information for best using your camera in cemeteries and also some methods and ways to be sure that what you are getting on film is actually something paranormal.

To start with, it shouldn't matter what sort of technology you are using to try and obtain spirit photos if the photos themselves cannot stand up to the scrutiny of a practiced eye. In other words, just because someone claims that they have a photo of a ghost, does not necessarily mean that they do. Often, anyone with any experience with photography at all can spot the claims of those who want to "believe" they have a ghost photo. There are many problems that can occur, even with the most simple cameras, from double exposures, tricks of light, camera straps, lens refractions and even obvious hoaxes.

But how does taking photographs of ghosts actually work? How do ghosts end up on film when that cannot be seen with the human eye?

Unfortunately, no one really knows just how ghosts end up on film. Some believe that it has something to do with the camera's ability to freeze a moment of time and space in a way that the human eye cannot do. This may also combine with the intense energy pattern of the ghost, which somehow imprints itself through emulsion onto the film itself. This is the reason why many researchers recommend that the ghost hunter does not load his film into his camera until he actually reaches the place that he plans to investigate.

In addition to those theories, it has also been suggested that ghosts, or paranormal energy, may be at a different spectrum of light than we are used to. This light spectrum may be one that is not visible to the human eye and yet the camera manages to sometimes pick it up. This may be the reason that infrared film is often suggested as the best film to use when hunting ghosts.

Once again, these are only theories. It may be a combination of any of these methods and for all we know, every one of is correct -- or perhaps none of them are. As with anything else to do with the paranormal, few researchers are ever in complete agreement as to how something works. Most ghost hunters simply find a method for producing ghost photographs and then adapt it to work in their own research. Most often though, ghosts are captured quite by accident, leaving no clues as to why a particular photo was successful.

Each photo that is taken and is displayed should be under intense scrutiny by the researcher before he presents it to the public. There are hundreds of terrible photos out there that claim to be authentic. Most of them are not and this sort of shoddy ghost research is damaging to every ghost investigator who is trying to provide legitimate evidence that ghosts exist.

In order to be sure that your own photos are genuine, it's important for you to have a good working knowledge of cameras, films and natural lens effects. I encourage anyone to go out and purchase standard books on photography. You should know your camera, your shutter speeds and what can happen with lens refractions, light reflections and arcs. By doing this, you have protected yourself from the arguments of the debunkers and perhaps have spared yourself some embarrassment by finding your own flaws in some of your photos. Once you understand the natural effects that can occur, you will be confident about the photos you are taking.

I also recommend that you try experimenting with what fake photos look like. Try bouncing your camera flash off of a reflective surface and see if you can make "orbs" appear. Try taking photos in the rain and in poor weather conditions. Also, drop various things like flour, dust and water in front of your lens and try photographing your camera strap to simulate many of the photos that are out there. I think that you will be amazed to find that you have debunked a number of photos that you may have previously thought were genuine.

The Trouble with Orbs

There are a number of different types of photographic anomalies that turn up on film in cemeteries. Many researchers believe that these types of activity portray actual ghosts, but I cautiously refer to it as "paranormal energy" on film, simply because there are so many unknown variables when it comes to paranormal photography. Some of the strange images on photos that turn up include eerie rays of light, floating objects, mists and shapes and even apparitions that appear to be human, but perhaps the most common images are the so-called "orbs".

They don't always turn up in cemeteries either and actually seem to have an annoying habit of showing up almost anywhere. They have become the most commonly reported types of "paranormal photos" claimed by ghost hunters today. Despite what you might see and hear though, there is absolutely no hard evidence whatsoever to suggest that orbs are in any way related to ghosts. Yes, they do often turn up in photos that are taken at haunted locations, but as you'll soon see, many of these photos have been called into question. However, I do think that legitimate photos of paranormal lights (or orbs, if you prefer) exist. These photos do show a type of paranormal phenomena, but just what type that is remains to be seen.

As mentioned, orb photos are the most commonly seen "ghost photos" today and you will probably see more photos on the Internet of these purportedly "mysterious" balls of light than of anything else. While I do believe that genuine photographs of paranormal orbs exist, they are not as common as many people think. An "orb photograph" is usually one that is taken in an allegedly haunted place and somewhere within the photo is a hovering, round ball. Some of these orbs, or "globes", appear to be giving off light, while others appear to be transparent.

Despite the claims, the majority of orb photos are not paranormal at all, but merely refractions of light on the camera lens. This occurs when the camera flash bounces back from something reflective in the range of the camera. When this happens, it creates a perfectly round ball of light that appears to be within the parameters of the photo but is actually just an image on the lens itself. Many people often mistake these orbs for genuine evidence of ghosts. These false orbs can also be created by bright lights in an area where the photo is being taken, by angles of light and by many types of artificial lighting.

So, how do you tell a real "orb" photo from a false one?

There are a number of determining factors, not the least of which is corresponding activity. By this I mean, photographing an orb just after recording a sharp temperature drop, or some other event that can be documented. In every aspect of paranormal research, corresponding activity, and documentation of the activity, is vital to the success of the investigation and to authenticating the activity, evidence and especially the photographs.

The investigator should also look at the photograph itself. In doing so, watch for orbs that are especially bright or are especially dense (in other words, you can't see through them). This is important in determining which are genuine orbs because false orbs are readily identified by the fact that they are always very pale white or blue in color and are very transparent. Also watch for orbs that appear to be in motion. This can be a very good sign that the image is genuine. I have seen a number of photos that are believed to be genuine in which the orb actually moved several feet during the time when the shutter of the camera was open. In situations like this, it's hard to believe that the anomalous object could be anything other than paranormal in origin.

As mentioned though, one of the things that I have noticed about orb photos is that the majority of them seem to be taken in cemeteries. I have often been openly critical of ghost hunting in cemeteries. By that I mean, actually just going out to cemeteries and shooting photographs and hoping to capture something on film. While this is great for the hobbyist, I don't feel that it's serious research. Needless to say, I have been harshly criticized for this view. In spite of this, I have not changed my mind about the fact that random "ghost hunting" is not an investigation. And if this isn't reason enough to discourage this kind of activity, I now have another reason for taking this view.

One of the problems that I have had with this type of ghost hunting is the photos that often come back from it. Ghost hunters, with no idea of any corresponding evidence, often come back from cemeteries with copious numbers of orbs in their photos. Again, I do feel that some orbs constitute paranormal energy, but most don't, so I decided to try something out on my own.

With three other researchers, I went out to a cemetery that we picked at random on a warm summer night and took several rolls of film. We had no readings, stories or reports to justify the decision, but just took photos anyway. After having them developed, we discovered a number of the photos were filled with semi-transparent orbs.

On a hunch, we then went to a nearby football field that was roughly the same size as the cemetery we had already visited. We walked around for a few minutes and again shot a few rolls of film. I was unfortunately not surprised to find that these photos were also filled with orbs. Was the football field haunted? Of course not!

What we did was walk around both areas and stir up dust and pollen from the grass. When we took the photos, these particles in the air caught the reflection of the camera flash and appeared to be "orbs". We also discovered that such photos could be taken after walking or driving on a dusty road. The dust particles would reflect the light, just as moisture can do, and make it seem as though the air was filled was "orbs"!

I can't help but feel that this might explain some of the photos that have been taken in cemeteries that have been thought to be paranormal in origin. Does it explain them all? No, it doesn't, but such tests and experiments beg all of us to be careful in our research. As I have always maintained, there exist no experts on ghosts or paranormal photography. My thoughts are that if we can discover the ways to rule out the false photos, we have a much better chance to discover which ones might be genuine.

Why Not Digital Cameras?

In this book and in other writings that I have published, I have always stated that it is my philosophy to try and rule out any natural explanation for activity before considering that it might be a haunting. This is not because I am a debunker but because I am looking for authentic evidence of the paranormal. I don't make any false claims about being an "expert" but try to base my knowledge on genuine evidence and not on what I want, or wish, ghosts to be. I try to caution other ghost hunters about presenting questionable photos and materials that cannot stand as evidence. I believe that anything we call "evidence" should be approached with caution. That is not to say that these things cannot be genuine, but unless there is other evidence to back it up, it cannot (and should not) be presented as proof of the paranormal.

With those statements in mind, let's discuss why digital photography should never be used in paranormal research and why it cannot produce irrefutable proof of the paranormal.

Before we get to why digital cameras should not be used in ghost hunting, let me just say that I have nothing against the cameras themselves. I understand the benefits of them. They provide instant images, there is no wasted film or development costs. In most cases, you can actually see the photo in a matter of seconds after it was taken. I admit that saving time and money are positive points but unfortunately, the negative points to digital cameras outweigh the good ones, at least when it comes to their use in the paranormal field.

I realize that digital cameras continue to be used in ghost research and thankfully, not all ghost hunters are using them incorrectly. These cameras are excellent for documenting a location and also as a secondary, back-up camera. This is how a digital camera should be used and that's what many ghost hunters are using them for. Many readers misunderstand my objections to them and see this as nothing more than a diatribe against digital cameras -- but it's not. I see absolutely no problem with using digital cameras, as long as they are used in the correct way.

The problem comes when the digital camera is the only camera used in an investigation. This incorrect use of the camera had led to some disastrous results for the credibility of paranormal investigations. Many ghost hunters are out snapping hundreds of digital photos at random, using nothing else for their "investigation" but the camera. They are presenting digital images as absolute proof of the paranormal and by doing so, are making a mockery out of the real investigations that are going on. Fortunately, these people are in the minority when it comes to paranormal investigators, but they are still out there, wreaking havoc with every digital photo they claim is authentic.

Just remember, no matter what some people claim, digital cameras can never be used to provide evidence of the paranormal. Here's why:

1. Some time back, I began to notice that digital cameras almost always seemed to capture images of "orbs". This made me curious, especially in light of the fact that 35mm cameras that were being used in the same investigations would capture nothing at all.

I began to research some of the mechanics behind digital technology and I contacted tech support people at three companies that made digital cameras. They had no idea that I was talking about ghost photos but only knew that I had been taking photos in dark locations and that my digital pictures were coming back with what looked like "balls of light" in them. These were actually my own photos too. I had been experimenting with a digital camera and had been suspicious of the results that I was getting. All of the activity that I found seemed to be "orbs" and they appeared to be very prevalent, appearing in places that had no reports of being haunted (my backyard, for instance).

I had noticed that upon close examination, many of the alleged "orbs" in my pictures appeared to be spots where the image had not filled in all of the way. I was not surprised to hear from the three companies that I spoke with that this would explain what I was seeing in the pictures. According to the tech support people, all three of the (unrelated) companies had been experiencing this with their cameras when they were used under low-light conditions. It seemed that when they were used in darkness, or near darkness, the resulting images were plagued with spots that appeared white or light colored and where the digital pixels had not all filled in. In this manner, the cameras were creating "orbs", and they had no paranormal source at all.

2. Another major reason why digital cameras are useless for paranormal research is because of film emulsion. Emulsion on traditional film is based on infrared light values and the temperature associated with that light value. A digital camera cannot determine these values, it simply creates an image based upon the tones it receives from the reflection of light off of the subject matter. Due to the fact that we still don't really know how ghosts end up on film anyway, I think that we would be taking a major risk by assuming that it has nothing to do with the energy being imprinted on the film itself. If this is true (even in some cases), then digital cameras will not work for ghost research.

And here's the main reason why digital cameras cannot be used for legitimate paranormal research! You can ignore everything else that has been written here, but this is the essential information!

3. To be able to analyze a photo and to be able to determine the photo's authenticity, two things are needed -- a print of the photo and its negative. A digital photo can provide neither of these essential elements. In the past, many researchers have had photos and negatives studied by professional photo outlets. In many cases, these photos have been authenticated and have been accepted as genuine during non-destructive testing. There were no flaws in the film, they stated, and no explanation for the resulting images. To be able to do this analysis, each of the labs required both a print of the picture and its negative. Both of these are needed to prove that a photo is genuine because it must be possible to reproduce the photo and to show that no tampering or alterations have taken place. Obviously, this cannot be accomplished with a digital camera, especially in light of the fact that electronic images are easily changed and altered. It is impossible to prove they are authentic.

To put it simply, we have to accept the idea that we are always going to get more authentic and truer images when light is printed onto emulsion film than when it hits a CCD chip, because with a digital camera, the image has to be processed by a microchip. Every single one of us has experienced computer problems at one time or another and with a digital camera, we are taking a chance that an extraordinary image that we have captured is nothing more than an ordinary computer glitch.

Let me just say that I have taken a lot of criticism for this opinion about the use of digital. Some readers have contacted me to ask why I simply can't take the word of the ghost researcher that their digital image was not altered and that it is truly authentic? Why must I ask for a negative and a print to say that the photo is actually evidence? I have been told that this isn't fair and that I am expecting too much. Once again, I disagree with this. Unfortunately, I am unable to just take someone's word for it that the digital image is real. Here's why:

For me to view images that have been taken with a digital camera and that have been sent to me by a reputable ghost researcher, I can be reasonably sure, after ruling out that the images cannot be artificially or naturally explained, that the images are genuine, reliable and authentic. I feel this way about their authenticity because I am working with another person in the paranormal field and who may have a good reputation in the ghost research community. I can take their word for it that the images have not been altered and in fact, there may have been several other researchers present at the time the photo was taken who can also vouch for the integrity of the photo and the investigation. I can feel confident about the image in a case like this, but...

What is the person is not a reputable ghost hunter?

Or what if the person is someone that I don't know at all?

And most importantly, how can I expect to be able to show this image to someone outside of the ghost research field and expect them to take it seriously? This person will likely not know the photographer and will be unable to just "take their word for it" that the photo is authentic. To ask such a person to examine the photo under these conditions is pointless. The only examiner of a photo like this can be someone who is already a ghost researcher and that's the problem. Are we only working in ghost research to be able to show our results to other ghost hunters? Are we only doing this to make ourselves, and other researchers, feel good about what we are doing? Or are we doing it to present evidence to the general public that ghosts are real and that there is something viable about the research that we are conducting?

I have always been of the opinion that this is what ghost research is all about and that only reliable evidence that we have carefully examined should be presented if we are to make claims about it being both paranormal and authentic. Digital cameras cannot provide evidence that does not require us to just "take the investigators word for it". It's just like never conducting an investigation alone --

you always have to have something to back up your claims and in the case of paranormal photography, you need that negative and print. Whether or not you or I believe a digital image is authentic or not doesn't matter. As long as there is a chance (thanks to the lack of hard evidence) that it is not, the debunker will always have a way to undermine what we are doing.

Digital cameras certainly have their place and a number of benefits. I just don't think that they can benefit the study of the paranormal beyond being a secondary camera. For this reason, I suggest that all ghost hunters approach digital photos with caution. The images they produce may, or may not be, genuine but it's better to be safe now than to be sorry later on.

Photography How-To Guide

Often ghost hunters ask me to suggest cameras and film for ghost hunting but there really doesn't seem to be a definitive type of either one to use. I have seen remarkable photos that have been taken with everything from expensive 35mm cameras to instant cameras to even cheap, disposable cameras. Obviously, cost is almost always a determining factor in choosing a camera, but remember that while an $800 camera may be of a better quality than a $200 one, it is the person behind the lens who makes all the difference. The quality of the equipment does not reflect the quality of its owner, so never be ashamed of the type of camera that you use in your investigations. And don't be belittled by someone with a camera bag full of high-tech toys either. When he starts bragging about how much equipment he has, ask to see his photographs rather than his camera. It's the results that matter, not what he uses to get them.

There are many different kinds of cameras manufactured today but the most popular 35mm cameras are two basic types. One of them is the "point and shoot" camera, which is very simple and is completely automatic in its operation. The other camera type is the Single Lens Reflex camera (SLR). This type is larger and more complex to operate but is a favorite for most professional and amateur photographers. I usually recommend to people that they use a model of camera that is most comfortable for them, regardless of the type. When it comes to film, I usually suggest Kodak 400 ASA film (and sometimes higher speeds) for overnight, outdoor investigations, depending on the strength of your camera flash. There are three basic methods of photography to consider when photographing cemetery investigations:

Color Film

This is the simplest and most basic method of cemetery photography during nighttime investigations. Use a 400 ASA speed Kodak film, along with your camera flash, to obtain results. This is a small grain film, so enlargements will not be difficult and it is fast enough to use under low light conditions. You may want to experiment with your camera at night and make sure this is a high enough speed film for your particular model of camera.

Black & White Film (No Flash)

If you prefer to try and experiment without the flash, thus eliminating the chance for false orbs and lens refractions, you will want to use the a 400 ASA film made by Tri-X or Kodak. This film is ideal because it is more sensitive to ultraviolet light and so you have a better chance of possibly picking up something unseen by the human eye.

Infrared Film

One of the most reliable, but most difficult to use types of film and photography is infrared. There is a lot of experimentation and money involved with using it but this type of film is sensitized to light that we can see with the naked eye, as well as light that is of a different wavelength of radiation and is invisible to us. The film allows you to see, literally, what is beneath the surface, or what the human eye cannot see. Infrared does not detect heat, but rather sees and photographs radiation. It can actually "see" a level of radiation that is one spectrum below thermal radiation and this is radiation caused by electromagnetic fields. Because we believe that paranormal energy also lurks in this same "dead zone", infrared film becomes a very helpful tool in ghost hunting.

However, infrared film does require special filters to use, must always be kept refrigerated, requires special processing and must always be loaded and unloaded into the camera under conditions of absolute darkness. Also, most automatic cameras cannot be used with infrared film. There in an infrared sensor inside most models to make sure that the film advances properly. This sensor will badly cloud your film.

Photography Hints & Tips

When conducting investigations, remember that photographing ghosts is not an easy process. Many investigators only use a camera when they encounter anomalous readings on their equipment and still others cover the location with their camera to document as much as they can. You just never know what might turn up on your developed film. Do plan to use a lot of film when you are ghost hunting. It is a common fact that it sometimes takes dozens (or even hundreds) of snapshots to come up with even one paranormal photo that you can feel is genuine. With this being the case, try not to get discouraged if every investigation fails to turn up a "ghost photo". Just because you don't get any results with your camera, doesn't mean the location is not haunted. The camera is just like any other tool in your ghost hunting kit. The results that you achieve with it do not stand alone and it's always possible that you won't find anything with your camera, even though your other equipment says that something is there.

And when the camera does work, you still have to be careful. Turning to the camera for proof of ghosts does not insure against mistakes and many ghost hunters are fooled into believing that some erroneous photos are real. We have all seen dozens of photos that supposedly show ghosts and paranormal energy but that actually do not. Be careful to do your research and know how to tell "accidental" photos from the real thing. Here are some things to be careful of when experimenting with ghost photographs:

1. Be careful that you have nothing protruding in front of the camera lens. Believe it or not, this can be anything from a finger to clothing, items around you in the cemetery like trees, bushes and the edges of tombstones and even hair. People with long hair should make sure that it is pulled back tightly or tucked under a hat. Loose hair that ends up in front of the camera lens (which may be unseen by the photographer) and which gets illuminated by the flash can look pretty eerie.

2. Be sure that your lens is clean and covered when not in use. Even a small drop of rain, dirt or moisture that ends up on the lens can show up on the developed print. This would not be seen through the viewfinder, so you would never know that it was there.

3. Make sure the weather is cooperating with your photographs. By this, I mean to make sure that it is not raining or snowing. Round balls of glowing light that are photographed during a rain storm are not exactly overwhelming proof of the supernatural.

4. Make sure that conditions are not damp, promoting moisture or fogging, on your camera lens. This is why I always mention bringing along temperature and humidity gauges to an outdoor investigation site. You can check and see if "fog-like" images that later turn up on film could have a natural explanation.

5. Be sure to point the camera away from reflective surfaces when using a flash. Avoid mirrors and windows in a house and bright or polished surfaces when working outdoors. The light from the flash bouncing off this surface can refract back onto your camera lens and create "orbs" that are not of paranormal origins. This can often happen with reflective tombstones, especially polished granite, which easily catches the light.

6. Make sure you know where your camera strap is at all times. Notice how many so-called "ghost photos" that you see look like camera straps? That's because most of them are! Notice how those "anomalous" images always come from the right

side of the camera, where the strap is normally located? I suggest taking the strap off your camera or at least leaving it around your neck, where it belongs.

7. No matter where you are taking photographs, be sure to use a photographic log sheet to keep track of where the photos were taken, who took them and whether or not they were taken randomly or because some strange activity was occurring at the time. This can be very important when it comes to analyzing the photos and looking for corresponding activity at the site.

The Investigation

Before the investigation actually begins, you may want to go over some ground rules with your team. Here are some suggestion about things to keep in mind while getting the investigation organized:

1. Never take on an investigation like this alone. A good team is required for legitimate research. Not only is safety important in an outdoor or an isolated location, but it is essential to have more than one person to authenticate evidence and incidents that might occur.

2. Never trespass in a location without permission. As mentioned earlier, you should try and get permission from the caretaker of the cemetery, or county officials, before the investigation. If this cannot be done, get in touch with the local police department or sheriff's department about the investigation. This is a good idea to do no matter what, even if for nothing other than courtesy and professionalism.

3. Do not drink or smoke prior to or (especially) during the investigation. The majority of evidence from the night comes in the form of photographs that have been obtained with corresponding evidence. If a team member is smoking, even if the smoke does not appear in any photos, it can destroy the credibility of any evidence that might be obtained.

4. As with any other investigation, arrive at the scene with skepticism and make an effort to find a natural explanation for any phenomena that occurs.

5. During the investigation, be sure to write down and make a note of anything that occurs, no matter how small it seems. I suggest creating a logbook for the investigation. A logbook can be prepared in advance and should contain the following information:

- Date and Time of the Investigation

- Name and location of the site
- Investigators / team members present
- weather conditions (temperature / humidity / barometer readings and even the wind speed... check the local weather service before leaving home)
- Detailed list of the equipment being used

Each of the team members should receive a copy of the log sheet, along with the map of the location. An additional sheet should also be added with times listed along the left side. On the right, blank spaces should be inserted so that any phenomena that occurs can be noted next to the corresponding time. You need to consider a photographic log as well (especially when working with infrared film) so that you can keep track of when and where your photographs were taken.

6. Finally, leave the location exactly as it was when you found it. Be sure that you do not leave any trash behind and also be sure that nothing is done to physically disturb the site, such as knocking over a tombstone. Even accidents can have a grave effect on the opportunity that you might have for future investigations at this site and others.

Once you arrive back at the cemetery that night, you are going to want to get a "feel" for the place and to set up a base of operations. I suggest finding a central location that is easily recognized by all of the team members. Here, you can leave your equipment cases and any non-essential items that do not need to be carried about the cemetery or location. If possible, try to arrive at the site before dark so that all of the team members can get a look at the place. Hopefully, the map that you made will have noted any hazards that might be encountered (like an open grave) but if not, this will give everyone a chance to see things for themselves.

Once this is done, you should start setting up any stationary equipment that you plan to use, like Tri-Field meters and motion detectors. Position the instruments in locations where they will not be moved and have each team member make note of where everything is so that they will not stumble over it later. Make sure the equipment is in a place where it is most likely to encounter phenomena. If nothing occurs after a set period of time (say, one hour), then try moving it to another spot. If hand-held equipment encounters something in a different place, trying moving the stationary equipment to that area as well.

Once the equipment is in place, it is time to get started.

1. It is best to try and split the investigators into separate teams. You may have noticed that when I noted the ideal number of investigators that I suggested an odd number of people. I feel that one person should always be in charge of monitoring the stationary equipment. It does not have to be the same person for the entire

investigation, but this should always be someone's job. He or she should take notes of anything that occurs and if more than one camera is available, keep a video camera monitoring this equipment.

2. The rest of the researchers should be split up into teams of two and should begin checking out the rest of the location with various other types of equipment. Remember that you are not here to randomly snap photographs! You should be searching for all manner of activity and photographing any anomalies that may occur in order to provide corresponding evidence. It might be best that one member of the team handles the equipment and the other team member holds the flashlight and the investigation log. This person can keep track of anything unusual that occurs and mark the location of the occurrence on the map.

3. Ideally, the vigil will last from 2-4 hours (depending on the amount of activity recorded) and this means that the location will have to be covered almost continuously during this time. Try to refrain from too many breaks and from leaving the equipment unwatched. There is no pattern as to when something paranormal might occur and the investigator has to be constantly aware.

4. If strange activity is found during the course of the night, the investigators should compare notes and try to pinpoint the most active areas of the location. Using the map that you have drawn, it becomes possible to see what areas of the location boast the most anomalies. For the last hour of so of the vigil, it is suggested that all of the equipment and the cameras be focused on this area.

It has been my experience with cemeteries in the past, that much of the activity seems to center around a particular area. There may be no reason for this, unless we consider the theories of "portals" or "doorways", as we discussed in an earlier chapter. It is possible that you might discover a lot of strange phenomena is taking place in a localized section of the graveyard.

Even though the investigation ends for the night, it is far from over. All of the data that you collected has to be gone over, the tapes watched and the photos developed. In an investigation such as this, you have a unique situation in that you rarely have any eyewitness testimony to collect. For this reason, the material that you have collected becomes even more important and essential to any theories that you might develop about the haunting.

Also important are follow-up visits to the location. There can be much to learn from returning to the cemetery again, especially if anything strange occurred during your first outing -- and sometimes what seemed "strange" may turn out to be something different altogether. This is something that *American Ghost Society* researcher David Ford can attest to and what occurred in one cemetery that he was investigating is a perfect of example of trying to rule out every possible explanation for what seems to be ghostly activity.

David began conducting research in a St. Louis, Missouri area graveyard after he was contacted by the cemetery management about a crypt that refused to stay locked at night. No matter how many times they locked it up, the door was always found standing wide open the next morning. The caretaker wanted to put a chain on the gate to keep it closed, and to keep out the teenagers that he believed were opening it, but knew this would be unsightly on the door of what was an architecturally beautiful tomb. His alternate plan was to then stake out the tomb at night, hiding in another nearby crypt that offered a direct view. He called David on the afternoon following his stakeout in shock, swearing that before his own eyes, he had seen the two cast-iron gates on the tomb swing open "as if something unseen from the inside of the tomb had placed its hands on the bars and pushed."

David went down and examined the crypt the next day. He checked out the gates themselves, the rest of the tomb and spent about two hours interviewing the caretaker about what he had seen. The following day, the caretaker again reported that the gates had opened in the night, as they did the next night as well. By this time, the caretaker was refusing to stake out the cemetery at night by himself. David quickly agreed to accompany him and he and the caretaker established a watch on the tomb in question.

They sat through most of an uneventful night and then just before dawn, David spilled coffee all over himself as the two gates slowly and deliberately swung open!

In the days that followed, David checking into everything, from the family that was interred in the crypt to the maintenance log of the caretakers, the type of stone used to make the crypt and even the type of iron the gates had been forged from. He also took temperature readings and kept a nightly log of the events as they were reported. It would be his careful investigating and his repeated return visits to the cemetery that would finally solve the mystery. This is what had happened:

Just a few weeks before the occurrences began, some extensive tree trimming had taken place in the area of the cemetery where the tomb was located, exposing it to great amounts of sunlight for the first few hours of the day. The tomb was located in a ring of crypts at the highest point in the cemetery and a water main had broken in the area the winter before. The east side of the crypt (which caught the morning sun) was slanted almost 10 degrees from the west side. The slant had been caused when the water main break washed away much of the sandy soil here, causing the crypt to settle. The angle put additional pressure on both halves of the tomb's iron gate, which weighed more than 100 pounds each. The deadbolt lock used to secure the gate was made from decorative brass, and unlike most metals, brass contracts when it is heated -- even by several hours of the morning sunlight. The hole in the foundation where the gate was also secured by a rod -- also made from brass -- was filled with dirt and debris.

In short, the ghost was "exorcized" from the crypt by installing a new steel deadbolt on the gates and cleaning out the rod hole out of the dirt that had gathered in it over the years. It became "a ghost story that wasn't"!

If paranormal occurrences in your own cemetery of research do happen, definitely plan to do follow-up investigations. And when you do, you might consider working with different investigators (as well as the same team members) and try to focus your investigations on the areas of the location that were the most active. You might see an increase in activity, or possibly even a decline. If this occurs, continue the same methods that you used in your initial vigil and see if the phenomena has moved to a different area.

Just remember that an investigation of this sort can quickly deteriorate into a circus if it is not handled properly. It is extremely important that the goals of the group remain focused and that the vigil is organized and well thought out. This is the only way that an outdoor, or cemetery, investigation can be considered successful and the only way that it can be considered to be legitimate ghost research.

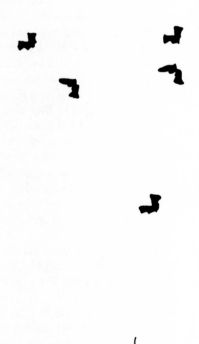

5. Field Guide to Haunted Graveyards

The final section of the book is a "field guide" to haunted cemeteries all over America. At this time, I feel that this is the most complete list of sites available but even so, I make no claims that it is complete. I am sure that there are tales of cemetery ghosts that have managed to elude me. There are many haunted places that remain unknown and encounters that have never been talked about. So, I cannot claim to have uncovered every haunted burial ground in the country but I do feel this listing will introduce you to some that you have never heard of before.

I owe this "travel guide" to a great many sources that assisted my research, from books to personal accounts, but a great many of the stories were sent to me by people who answered a general call for graveyard stories and encounters. You will find over 200 different, allegedly haunted cemeteries listed and reviewed in the pages to come and I actually had to narrow that list down from the several hundred that I received. Many of the stories and locations that were sent to me were either too hard to find further information on, too sketchy or in some cases, mere urban legends that were completely untrue. Keep in mind though that even after searching through my files for the best places, I cannot guarantee the truth behind every single story. In each case, the stories were passed on to me as being true but I leave the reader to make the final judgment for himself. The reader will find many similarities among a number of the stories from weeping women to glowing tombstones, ghostly brides, flickering "spook lights" and more. There also seems to be an epidemic in our country of people who kill their entire families in cemeteries and choose these secluded spots to commit suicide -- or so many would have you believe!

Regardless of the questionable nature of some of the legends associated with these sites, do not dismiss them off-hand as mere "campfire stories" and local folklore. Remember that these stories often get started for a reason and so the haunting may be more real than we might first assume.

I hope that you enjoy these sites and if you do go out to find them, remember never to trespass on private property and to take away nothing but photographs and memories and leave nothing behind but footprints, as they say. Any place that you find listed here will likely require permission to visit or investigate. In addition, many of them are patrolled by the authorities and trespassers will be prosecuted. Go

Alabama

Bladon Springs

The Bladon Springs Cemetery is the burial place of a man named Norman T. Staples, a steamboat captain and ship designer who committed suicide in 1913. He is buried here with the bodies of his wife and several of his children and legend has it that Staples haunts this place, protectively watching over the graves of his family. But this was not where his ghost was first seen.

Staples was a wealthy and successful riverboat captain and in 1908, built a huge vessel, the *James T. Staples* in honor his father. A few years before his crowning achievement, he married Dora Dahlberg but unfortunately, his family life did not go as well for him as his career did. Staples was an inattentive husband and rarely home. In spite of this, Staples and his wife soon had two children, a boy named James Alfred and a little girl they called Mable Claire. Before Dora could recover from James' difficult birth, the boy had gotten sick and had died. They grieved but this did not stop them over the next few years from having four more daughters, Beatrice Alice, Bertha, Melanie and Mary Faye, and a stillborn son, who was buried next to his brother.

In 1907, Staples was desperately trying to complete the James T. Staples but then tragedy struck his family. During that cold winter, all of the children came down with a fever. Bertha and Mable would not survive it .

Every penny had gone into the construction of the ship and little did Staples know, but the heyday of the steamboat was just about to end. To make matters worse, a company called the Birmingham and Gulf Navigation Co. was putting small operators out of business. Staples managed to keep the company operating until December 1912. Shortly after Christmas tough, his creditors called in his loans and effectively shut Staples down for good. On January 2, 1913, Captain Staples committed suicide, unable to cope with the loss of his lifelong dream.

The creditors who had taken away the *James T. Staples* were having problems of their own trying to operate the ship. Deck hands and crew were reporting that the ghost of Captain Staples was haunting the ship. A shadowy figure was clearly recognizable as the late captain and the firemen stated that he moved around the boiler room with a purpose, as though he belonged there, and then suddenly he vanished. Frightened, the firemen all quit their jobs and after hearing the story, many of the other workers left too. With great difficulty, the new owners got another crew together. This time, it was made up of men who had never worked with Staples and knew nothing about the sighting of his ghost on the boat.

One day, the boat departed from Mobile and headed north. The trip proceeded uneventfully until they reached Powe's Landing, a port about one hundred miles from Mobile. The crew was unloading freight and the passengers were taking their noon meal. All was calm and then suddenly, one of the boilers in the ship's bow exploded with a tremendous roar! The steaming hot water shattered the decking and gushed over the crew and passengers, killing many of them instantly. The front of the ship burst apart and the river became a frothing, writhing scene of horror. Dozens were killed, including the captain and first mate, scalded beyond recognition.

In what seemed like moments, the *James T. Staples* burst into flames and began drifting out into the river as the ropes securing it to the dock slowly burned. With fire dancing up from the hull, the ship sluggishly moved down the Tombigee until it came to a point almost in line with the Bladon Springs Cemetery, where Norman Staples was buried. Then, with a great shudder, the vessel sank to the bottom of the river. Twenty-six people had died in the disaster and another twenty-one had been seriously injured.

A full-scale investigation of the accident followed and the *James T. Staples* was hauled up from the riverbed and inspected. The conclusion was reached that the boilers had malfunctioned, but no one was able to explain why. They had been inspected in December and had been in perfect working order. Strange stories soon came to be told. Many remembered the sightings of Norman Staples' ghost in the boiler room of the ship.

With the ship gone, the ghost of Captain Staples apparently left the river and took up residence in the Bladon Springs Cemetery. Over the years, visitors to the graveyard have reported the apparition of a man matching his description near his gravesite. They say that he sits there, holding his head in his hands as if he has some great regret. They wonder what keeps the ghost here, watching over the graves? Could it that he wishes he had spent more time with his children in life, or something much worse?

There are those who say that Captain Norman Staples will never rest. Eternal peace will always elude him because of his actions in 1913 that caused the deaths of passengers on the James T. Staples -- actions carried out from beyond the grave.

Hauck, Dennis William - Haunted Places: The National Directory (2002)
Taylor, Troy - Beyond the Grave (2001)

Bladon Springs is located in Choctaw County in southwestern Alabama and the cemetery is located outside of town about eight miles off Highway 6.

Claiborne

The ghosts of 12 Federal horsemen have been seeing riding near the old McConnico Cemetery near Claiborne. The first sightings occurred in the autumn of 1865 on Mount Pleasant Road near the cemetery have continued sporadically ever since. The first to ever encounter the ghost riders were Captain Charles Locklin and his wife, who were out for a drive in their carriage early one morning when two columns of Union soldiers on gray horses passed on either side of them. They noticed that each of the riders wore white gloves and had their hands crossed on the pommel of the saddle in front of them. Strangest of all, each of the silent men wore a white bandage wrapped tightly around their head.

Locklin, and those who have since encountered the ghosts near the cemetery, believe that they are the spectral victims of a Confederate guerilla named Lafayette Seigler, who gained a reputation for ambushing Union patrols during the Civil War. Seigler was also known for the fact that he cut the ears off the men that he and his guerillas killed, which explained the bandages that the ghosts had been seen to wear.

Windham, Kathryn Tucker - Jeffrey Introduces 13 More Southern Ghosts (1987)

Claiborne is in Monroe County in the southwestern section of the state. The town lies just along the Alabama River.

Kinston

The ghost of an old square dancer is said to sometimes appear under the shelter that was constructed over his tomb in Harrison Cemetery. The old man was named Grancer Harrison and he was a local cotton farmer from Virginia who built a large plantation bordering the Pea River back in the 1840's. He often held huge parties at his grand mansion house and neighbors from three counties would come for barbeques, horses races and especially square dancing, which Harrison particularly loved. In fact, he asked that when he died, he be buried in his dancing shoes and clothes and that instead of a coffin, his body be placed on his favorite old feather bed. He also had a brick tomb built for himself, large enough to accommodate the bed, and then covered it with a protective wood shelter that would keep out the weather.

After his death, locals have reported the sounds of lively fiddle music coming from the tomb and the sounds of shoes dancing on the stone floor inside. The stories have continued for over a century and no natural explanation has been found for them.

Windham, Kathryn Tucker - Jeffrey's Latest 13: More Alabama Ghosts (1987)

Kinston is located in southeastern Alabama, in Coffee County. Harrison Cemetery is located just outside of town on the opposite side of Cripple Creek.

Mobile

Although the potter's field that once stood here no longer exists, a living testament to a hanged man's innocence is still haunted by his ghost. Charles Boyington was hanged for the murder of his best friend, Nathaniel Frost, on February 20, 1835. The two friends had been together on many nights at the old Church Street Graveyard and so when Frost was found stabbed to death there, it was believed that the two men had gotten into an argument and that Boyington had killed him in a fit of anger. The man proclaimed his innocence but no one believed him.

After a quick trial, at which Boyington continued to claim that he had not killed his friend, he was sentenced to hang. According to the legend, he stood on the gallows and announced that an oak tree would spring from his grave to show that he had truly been an innocent man. He was buried in the potter's field near the wall of the Church Street Graveyard, only about 60 yards from where his friend's body had been found. Within a few months, a tiny oak tree sprouted over his grave and it still stands today.

Strangely, the tree has survived many disasters that have claimed other trees in the area and the stories say that the cries of Charles Boyington has still be heard moaning and sobbing as the wind rustles through its branches. Today, the potter's field is gone, having been replaced by a playground, but it stands at the edge of a parking area, still marking the grave of what may have really been an innocent man.

Windham, Kathryn Tucker - Jeffrey's Latest 13: More Alabama Ghosts (1987)

Mobile is located at the extreme southwestern tip of Alabama and the oak tree stands at the edge of a gravel parking lot on Bayou Street. It is the only Live Oak tree in the area with wooden posts around it.

Winfield

After the death of Robert Musgrove in 1904, he was buried in the Musgrove Chapel churchyard in Winfield, Alabama. Not long after, a strange image appeared on his tombstone as a testament to the love that was felt for him by a woman.

Robert Musgrove was born in 1866 and was raised in Fayette County, Alabama. He grew up loving trains and as a young man, he began working for the railroad. He was a hard worker and well-liked and started working his way up through the ranks from conductor to brakemen to fireman. After a number of years, he was promoted to the rank of engineer on the St. Louis and San Francisco Railroad. The train on which he was an engineer ran between Memphis and Amory, Mississippi and Robert's good looks had women waiting for him in both destinations. He became involved with a number of women of questionable character until one night when he was attending a party in Amory. There, he met a stunning young woman named Maude and it wasn't long before the two of them fell in love. Within six months, they were engaged to be married.

Both families were delighted with the engagement and arrangements were made for the two of them to be married at Musgrove Chapel, a church that had been built by Robert's family in Winfield. Unfortunately, their wedding plans were cut short one night in April 1904. Somehow, something had gone wrong and crossed signals had two trains approaching each other head-on along the same route. One of them was speeding toward Amory and the other was headed on the same track toward Memphis. They collided and Robert was killed instantly in a massive explosion.

Maude was devastated by his death. She never married and each year, on the anniversary of Robert's death, she came to the cemetery and placed flowers on his grave. This continued up until the time of her own death, nearly 50 years later -- and then people began to notice that something unusual had happened at the grave.

One day in 1962, as people were leaving Musgrove Chapel, someone walking past the graveyard noticed what looked like the silhouette of a woman on Robert Musgrove's obelisk. Other people gathered around the tombstone and agreed that it did appear to be a woman's shadowy form on the marker. Soon, word quickly spread about the strange tombstone and people from all over the area came to see it. The Musgrove family tried to remove the image with soap and water. They scrubbed and scoured the stone with brushes, but it did no good. When these efforts failed, they hired a stonemason to try sandblasting it. Although this method did erase the shadow, the spectral image of a woman returned after a year and is still visible on the marker today. Visitors who go to the cemetery can find the outline of a grieving girl still kneeling in prayer over her lost love.

Bingham, Joan & Dolores Riccio - More Haunted Houses (1991)
Brown, Alan - "Seeing is Believing" / Ghosts of the Prairie (1999)

Windham, Kathryn Tucker - Jeffrey's Latest 13: More Alabama Ghosts (1987)

The town of Winfield is about an hour north of Birmingham and the Musgrove Chapel Cemetery is near Winfield, along the Luxapaillila Creek in north Fayette County.

Alaska

Talkeetna

One of the most famous resident haunts of this Alaskan town is of Mike Trepke, an old gold miner who died alone in his cabin by his claim on Birch Creek one rainy September years ago. The problems began when the locals brought his body back into town to be buried, His grave was dug on the edge of town one day but the funeral had to be postponed because of the constant rain. When they returned to the graveyard the following day, the grave had filled with a couple of feet of water overnight. The Talkeetna residents had to stand on the coffin to hold it down and eventually were able to pile enough dirt and rocks on it to sink it beneath the murky water.

According to the legend, his ghost began to return soon after, looking for a warm, dry spot. The miner's ghost is further bothered by his daughter's refusal to honor a pact he had made with his wife. The couple was to be buried side by side, but when his wife died in Oregon, the daughter buried her mother there instead. Later, the daughter reportedly sold the land where Trepke was buried. In the early 1980's when a new owner took over the land, he decided to find the miner's grave and relocate it at the town cemetery.

A Talkeetna resident recalled how the casket stank and dripped water when they pulled it out of the ground. The coffin was placed in the landowner's driveway that night, until it could be moved the next day but, according to the story, it was mysteriously transported to the landowner's kitchen overnight. He awoke the next morning to find there, still dripping water. The house has been haunted ever since.

Talkeetna is located north of Anchorage and a short distance from the Denali National Park.

Other Haunted Alaska Cemeteries

Birch Hill Cemetery (Fairbanks) is reported to be haunted by the ghost of a young girl who is seen wearing a white dress that appears to have come from the early 1900's. Many Gold Rush miners and pioneers are buried in this graveyard and she is thought to be perhaps the daughter of an early miner who perished from a disease.

Kenai Cemetery (Kenai) The ghost of an old man, who some say is a miner named Arthur Johnson, has been seen here maintaining the graves in the section where he is buried. He is reportedly mistaken for a living person until the visitor notices that he is transparent. There is also a legend that claims there are a number of unmarked graves in the back part of the cemetery that belong to servants who were brought here to dig for gold by a wealthy man. When the claims ran dry, the stories say that the servants were murdered so that they would not have to be fed and cared for any longer. Their ghosts are believed to walk here as well.

Arizona

Ehrenberg

The Ehrenberg Cemetery has been reported haunted since at least 1908, when author Martha Summerhayes first wrote about the ghosts who haunted the already desecrated graves here. She lived just a short distance away at the time and often spoke and wrote of the apparitions that lingered here, waving and calling to her and others who lived nearby.

Since that time, others have had unsettling experiences within the confines of the little place as well, telling of glowing lights that have been seen, rank smells that seemed to engulf them (and which had no explanation) and more of the same specters first reported nearly a century ago. One of them, a little girl, has been spotted carrying a rag doll and looking very pale and sickly. It has been suggested that she may be the daughter of an early settler who died from one of the many epidemics that plagued the west in the late 1800's.

Robson, Ellen - Haunted Arizona (2003)

Ehrenberg is located in western Arizona, not far from the California border. The cemetery is on the edge of town along Poston-Parker Road.

Tombstone

The town of Tombstone is located in southwestern Arizona and during the 1880's gained infamy as one of the most famous silver boomtowns of the Old West. During this period, the eyes of all Americans were focused on the events that took place here, from the first silver strike to the bloody gunfights in the town's dusty streets. The death toll in Tombstone reached such epic proportions in 1882 that President Chester A. Arthur even threatened to declare martial law in the city. It was a rough and dangerous place and certainly lived up to its reputation as one of the wildest towns in the west.

As seems to be the case with many violent locations, the number of ghosts who still linger in Tombstone may outnumber the permanent living population. Many of them, it is believed, don't even yet realize they are dead and continue looking for the next fight, the next drink, or even the next roll of the dice. Such a present, and such a past, makes Tombstone one of America's most haunted small towns.

Tombstone got its start on April Fool's Day 1877. On that afternoon, a prospector named Ed Schiefflin rode into Fort Huachuca in the San Pedro Valley and announced that he intended to look for silver in the Apache country. The soldiers scoffed at his plans and did all they could to dissuade him from such a dangerous endeavor. All that he would find, they told him, would be his tombstone. Schiefflin spent the entire next summer staying away from the Apache Indians and seeking ore. By October, he was out of supplies, his clothing was in tatters and he had nothing left. Just as he was about to give up, he discovered the first vein of pure silver. It was only seven inches wide, but more than fifty feet long. He called the strike Schiefflin's Lucky Cuss and he produced $15,000 per ton of rich silver. Partnering with his brother Al and an assayer named Dick Gird, they founded the Tombstone Mining District.

Soon, other miners and prospectors began flocking to the area and Tombstone began to boom. The prospectors attracted the suppliers, the saloonkeepers, the gamblers and the whores. It wasn't long before Tombstone became known as the place to find just about any vice known to man. Saloons such as the Oriental and the Crystal Palace operated 24 hours a day. John Clum, editor of the *Tombstone Epitaph*, once wrote that "Tombstone is a city set upon a hill, promising to vie with ancient Rome, in a fame different in character but no less important."

The most famous years of Tombstone were the days of Wyatt Earp and his brothers, who faced off against the Clanton's, the McLaury's and other cattle rustlers and outlaws. Americans are very familiar with the story of the legendary gunfight that took place at the O.K. Corral and with the three things that made the town famous -- gambling, violence and the death. It would be here that western legends would be created and it was also here that many of them would come to an end. Tombstone's Boot Hill Cemetery was an unforgiving place.

Long after the Earp's moved on and the Clanton's had faded into history, stories have continued to be told about haunted places in Tombstone, from the Bird Cage Theater to Boot Hill. It is at this famous little cemetery where visitors claim to have encountered the ghosts and hauntings of yesterday. Many of the men who were killed and buried here do not rest in peace. Eerie lights have been reported here, flickering in and out of the grave markers and tumbleweeds, and the apparitions of shadowy figures have been seen as well.

Spirits linger in this town that's "too tough to die".

Taylor, Troy - No Rest for the Wicked (2001)

Tombstone is located in the far southeastern corner of the state.

Arkansas

Little Rock

Mount Holly Cemetery is likely the most historically significant cemetery in Arkansas. It is the final resting place of senators, Confederate Generals, governors and of course, ghosts. The graveyard was established in 1873, which is less than a decade after Arkansas became a state, to give the growing city more burial space. Today, it is known for being the burial place of executed 17-year-old Confederate spy, David O. Dodd, as well as five Confederate generals and countless Confederate soldiers. Dodd is the most famous of the Civil War causalities resting here. He was arrested at the Ten Mile House near Little Rock and sentenced to hang by Union occupation forces after a brief trial. Dodd was called "the boy hero of the Confederacy" and a grave marker calls him "boy marty."

Also buried there are 10 former Arkansas governors, 6 United States senators, 14 Arkansas Supreme Court justices and 21 mayors of the city. You can also find the graves of Sanford C. Faulkner, the original "Arkansas Traveler," William E. Woodruff, the founder of the *Arkansas Gazette*, the wife of Cherokee chief John Ross and Pulitzer Prize winner John Gould Fletcher to name a few.

If you are looking for ghosts, you are in luck there also, because the cemetery draws nearly as many paranormal enthusiasts as it does history buffs. There have been many reports of ghostly incidents here, from strange lights to eerie sounds that cannot be explained. Some visitors even claim that a few of the statues here move about on their own -- and bizarrely, some of the photographs that have been taken seem to attest to that also. There are also reports of a ghostly flute that has been heard and sightings of a man in dark clothing have also taken place. He is sometimes seen near several tall monuments but whenever anyone takes a second look, he has always vanished.

Galiano, Amanda - Walk With the Dead : Mount Holly Cemetery (2003)

Little Rock is located in the center of the state and Mount Holly is open to the public and located on 12th street in the downtown area. It was listed on the National Register of Historic Places in 1970.

Other Haunted Arkansas Cemeteries

Avon Cemetery (DeQueen) is said to have haunted well that is located in the center of the graveyard. Years ago, before this was a cemetery, there was a story that told of a woman who came to the well to draw water and as she did, she placed her small child on the stone edge of the well. The baby tumbled over the side and plunged into the dark water below. She drowned before the frantic mother could summon help. Since that time, the legends say that the sound of a baby crying can be heard coming from the well on certain nights. There are also stories of a woman's ghost who has been seen running through the cemetery in the darkness. It is believed to be that of the baby's mother, still trying to bring help for the drowning child.

California

Hollywood

The lure of "Tinseltown" has been a part of America since the first silent film makers came west to the small town of Los Angeles at the turn of the century. What began as a scheme for movie maker Mack Sennett to make some extra money with a low-cost housing area called "Hollywoodland" became a movie colony for artists, writers and actors who came west to make it big. Today, Hollywood remains not so much a place as a state of mind. However, it still retains a strange allure for those with an interest in history and hauntings and for those interested in the screen legends of long ago.

The history of the region is a dark journey through tales of crime, corruption, death, murder, and of course, Hollywood-style scandal. Nearly every tale of ghosts and hauntings in Hollywood involves some sort of terrible crime or an unsolved murder. The dark tales of Hollywood's most haunted cemetery are no exception.

This classic graveyard was known as Hollywood Memorial Park for years but has become more recently known as "Hollywood Forever". It boasts the graves of many silent film stars and legends of the silver screen like Douglas Fairbanks, Rudolph Valentino, Tyrone Power, Cecil B. DeMille, Clifton Webb and others. This park is so geared to the celebrity of Hollywood that it even passes out maps to the star's graves at the front office. And some say that if you stay in the cemetery after dark, you might even be able to get your map personally autographed! You see, Hollywood Memorial Park is one of the most haunted sites in the area...

One ghost who wanders this cemetery is that of actor Clifton Webb, who was best known for playing "Mr. Belvidere" in the film *Sitting Pretty* and as newspaper columnist Waldo Lydecker in *Laura*. Webb is said to divide his time between haunting the graveyard and his former home in Beverly Hills. Webb was a long-time believer in life after death and hosted many séances in his home. Many later owners of the house, and visitors to the cemetery, claim to have encountered his spirit. If Clifton Webb does haunt this place, he does not do so alone. The hauntings at Hollywood Memorial Park are reportedly so strong that they have even affected Paramount Studios, which is located next door.

One haunted spot in the cemetery is the grave of actress Virginia Rappe, a barely-remembered starlet who would be completely forgotten today if not for her unwilling part in one of the greatest Hollywood scandals of all time. But what tragic events have caused her spirit to linger behind? To answer that question, we have to look back to the doomed history of the man who was accused of her murder, Fatty Arbuckle.

Roscoe "Fatty" Arbuckle was an overweight plumber in 1913 when Mack Sennett discovered him. He had come to unclog the film producer's drain but Sennett had other plans for him. He took one look at his hefty frame and offered him a job. Arbuckle's large appearance, but bouncing agility, made him the perfect target for Sennett's brand of film comedy, which included mayhem, pratfalls, and pies in the face. He was soon making dozens of two-reelers as a film buffoon and audiences loved him. He made one film after another, all of them wildly successful, and also made a rather substantial fortune, going from a $3-a-day job in 1913 to over $5000 by 1917, when he signed with Paramount.

Virginia Rappe came to Hollywood around 1919. She was a lovely brunette model who caught the eye of Mack Sennett and he offered her a job with his company. She soon went to work on the studio lot, taking minor parts and soon earned a part in the film *Fantasy* and later met Fatty Arbuckle and appeared with him in *Joey Loses a Sweetheart*.

Soon, Virginia was noticed by William Fox, shortly after winning an award for "Best Dressed Girl in Pictures" and he took her under contract. There was talk of her starring in a new Fox feature called *Twilight Baby* and Virginia certainly seemed to be on her way. Fatty had taken a shine to Virginia soon after meeting her and insisted that his friend, Bambina Maude Delmont, bring her along to a party celebrating his new $3 million contract with Paramount. Fatty decided to hold the bash in San Francisco, which would give him a chance to try out his new custom-made Pierce-Arrow on the drive up the coast. On Labor Day weekend, two car loads of party-goers headed up the coast highway, including Fatty, several friends and an assortment of starlets. They arrived in San Francisco late on Saturday night, checking into the luxurious Hotel St. Francis. Fatty took three adjoining suites on the 12th floor.

Shortly after arriving, Fatty made a call to his bootleg connection and the party was on, lasting all weekend. On Labor Day afternoon, which was Monday, September 5, 1921, the party was still going strong. The crowd had grown to about 50 people, thanks to Fatty's "open house" policy. Around three in the afternoon, Fatty, who was wearing only pajamas and a bathrobe, grabbed Virginia and steered the intoxicated actress to the bedroom of suite 1221. Bambina Maude Delmont later testified that the festivities came to a halt when screams were heard in the bedroom. She also said that weird moans were heard from behind the door. A short time later, Fatty emerged with ripped pajamas and he told the girls to "go in and get her dressed...she makes too much noise". When Virginia continued to scream, he yelled for her to shut up, or "I'll throw you out the window".

Bambina and another showgirl, Alice Blake, found Virginia nearly nude and lying on the unmade bed. She was moaning and told them that she was dying. Bambina later reported that they tried to dress her, but found that all of her clothing, including her stockings and undergarments were so ripped and torn "that one could hardly recognize what garment s they were."

A short time later, Virginia slipped into a coma at the Pine Street Hospital and on September 10, she died. The cause of her death almost went undiscovered. The San Francisco Deputy Coroner, Michael Brown, became suspicious after what he called a "fishy" phone call from the hospital, asking about a postmortem. He went over personally to see what was going on and walked right into a hasty cover-up. He was just in time to see an orderly emerge from an elevator and head for the hospital's incinerator with a glass jar containing Virginia's female organs. He seized the organs for his own examination and discovered that Virginia's bladder had been ruptured, causing her to die from peritonitis. Brown reported the matter to his boss and both agreed that a police investigation was called for.

The hospital staff was grilled as to what they knew and they reluctantly reported the strange incidents that brought Virginia to the hospital. Soon, the newspapers also carried the story and Fatty Arbuckle was charged with the rape and murder of Virginia Rappe. The public was soon in an uproar and Arbuckle's films were pulled from general release.

Held without bail, Fatty waited in the San Francisco jail while his lawyers sought to have the charges reduced from murder to manslaughter. Film tycoon Adolph Zukor, who had millions at stake with Arbuckle, contacted San Francisco District Attorney Matt Brady in an effort to make the case go away. Brady was enraged and later claimed that Zukor offered him a bribe. Other friends of Fatty called the D.A.'s office and suggested that Arbuckle was being punished because some starlet drank too much and died. They assumed they were helping Fatty's case, but the result was just the opposite. Brady grew angrier with each call on Fatty's behalf and by the time the case went to trial, he was livid.

The trial began in November 1921 with Arbuckle taking the stand to deny any wrong-doing, although his attitude toward Virginia was one of indifference. He never bothered to express any remorse or sorrow for her death. His lawyers were even more to the point, making every effort to paint Virginia as "loose", suggesting that she slept around in New York, South America, Paris and of course, in Hollywood. After much conflicting testimony, the jury favored acquitting Fatty by 10-2 after 43 hours of deliberating. The judge declared a mistrial.

A second trial was held and this time, the jury was hung at 10-2 for conviction. Fatty was now out on bail and was forced to sell his Los Angeles home and fleet of luxury cars to pay his lawyer fees.

Despite the hard work of Brady, who wanted to convict Arbuckle very badly, Fatty was finally acquitted in his third trial, which ended on April 22, 1922. Thanks to confusing testimony by 40 drunken witnesses and no physical evidence Fatty was finally a free men. Fatty may have been free, but he was hardly forgiven. Paramount soon canceled his $3 million contract and his unreleased films were scrapped, costing the studio over $1 million. Fatty's career was finished and he found himself banned from Hollywood.

Arbuckle would never act in the movies again and the public would never allow him to forget his fall from grace either. People shouted "I'm Coming, Virginia" when they recognized him on the street and laughter often greeted him in restaurants and shops. In his forced retirement, Fatty also took to drinking quite heavily and finally, he died in New York on June

28, 1933.

Innocent or guilty? We'll never really know for sure, but in the state of mind called Hollywood, it didn't really matter. Arbuckle had managed to change the image of Hollywood from one linked to dreams to that of one forever linked to scandal.

And now we return to Hollywood Memorial Park and the ghost of Virginia Rappe. I would imagine that there is little doubt in the mind of the reader as to why Virginia's spirit may be a restless one. In addition to losing her life during the horrifying incidents of that fateful Labor Day, Virginia lost her reputation as well. The press was nearly as cruel to her as they were to Fatty Arbuckle.

So, it's not surprising that her ghost still lingers behind. Visitors who come to Hollywood Memorial Park have reported hearing a ghostly voice that weeps and cries out near Virginia's simple grave. It is believed by many to be her ghost, still attached to this world, and still in anguish over her promising career, which was cut short -- just like her life.

Ghosts in Hollywood are not confined to the cemeteries. Many of the old-time movie studios have their own ghostly tales but without a doubt, the most haunted of them is Paramount. Over the years, the ghostly sightings and strange reports here have become as much a part of the legend of the place as the movies themselves. Being the last major studio actually located in Hollywood, Paramount makes the perfect setting for ghostly activity. It is located right next door to Hollywood Memorial Park. The stories say that some of their spirits have been seen walking directly through the walls from one lot to the next.

Hollywood Memorial Park is located closest to stages 29 through 32. The reports of spirits seen entering the studio lot describe them as wearing clothing from the 1930's and 40's. Out of all of sound stages in that area, Stages 31 and 32 seem to have the most activity. Footsteps are often heard tapping through stages that have been secured for the night and it is not uncommon for equipment to turn on and off and operate by itself.

Paramount Studios has many entrances and some of them are walk-in gates, like the one at Lemon Grove, located a few feet from the cemetery. It is here where many of the ghosts from the graveyard are also said to enter the studio lot. Some of them, according to guards posted here, actually appear as heads that poke through the cemetery wall and then disappear. Others actually walk through the gate itself, like the ghost of silent film star Rudolph Valentino.

Valentino was considered the greatest Latin heartthrob of the 1920's. He made a number of successful films but died early in his career at the age of only 31. When news leaked of his death in 1926, crowds of adoring fans mobbed the funeral home where his services were held, people everywhere were heartbroken and several passionate admirers even committed suicide.

Not surprisingly, a number of legends have sprung up around Valentino and his ghost. One such legend grew up around his crypt in Hollywood Memorial Park, where he was buried. It seems that since the demise of the star in 1926, a "Lady in Black" has put in an appearance at his tomb and each week, leaves a fresh bouquet of flowers. There is no way to know if this might be the same woman after all of these years, but regardless, the flowers have never stopped coming. I visited Hollywood Memorial Park a few years ago and visited the crypt. Not surprisingly, fresh flowers were still appearing each week.

There are also the "spirited" tales as well. In fact, Valentino may be the most well-traveled ghost in Hollywood. He is reported to haunt his former home in Beverly Hills,

"Falcon's Lair", Valentino Place, an old apartment building that used to be a speakeasy in the 1920's and a place frequented by the actor, his former beach house in Oxnard, and of course, Paramount Studios. Valentino was a driving force at Paramount in his day and rumor has it that he was buried in his white costume from the film, The Sheik, for which he is best remembered. Whether he was or not, it is in this costume that his ghost is sometimes reported.

In addition to Valentino, other Hollywood Memorial ghosts sometimes appear at the gates. This does not please the security guards at all, especially those who work the night shift at the Lemon Grove gate. The gate is located at the northeast corner of the studio lot facing Lemon Grove Avenue and a wall is all that separates it from the cemetery. It is here where most of the uninvited visitors are usually seen but these sightings are mostly harmless, leaving the officers confused over where the "trespasser" disappeared to. These sightings can also leave a few rattled nerves however.

One night, a veteran security guard was working the late night shift. Most of the guards know everyone who comes in an out of the gates because they see them every day. On this evening, the guard noticed an unfamiliar face lurking about. He followed the man to a corner of the wall to the cemetery and thinking he had him cornered, he waited for the suspicious visitor to come out. After a minute or two, he looked around the corner -- just in time to see the man vanish into the cemetery wall! From that time on, he refused to work the Lemon Grove gate at night.

Bingham, Joan & Dolores Riccio - More Haunted Houses (1991)
Taylor, Troy - Beyond the Grave (2001)

Hollywood Memorial Park / Hollywood Forever Cemetery is located behind Paramount Studios at 6000 Santa Monica Boulevard in Hollywood. Maps of the cemetery are located at the office.

Sacramento

Established in 1849 as one of the first "Garden" cemeteries on the West Coast, the Old City Cemetery is the oldest in the region. There are a number of well-known people from the region buried here, including John A. Sutter, a gold rush pioneer and founder of Sacramento, as well as more than 300 victims from a cholera epidemic in 1852. There are more than 36,000 people buried in this graveyard and many of them are still believed to walk today. This can be a place of great beauty -- and of strangeness as well. The cemetery is also the final resting place of William Stephen Hamilton, son of Alexander Hamilton, the nation's first treasurer. He is one of the cemetery's most restless residents. He died in 1850, was exhumed twice, and buried three times.

One of the most unusual events reported here involved the exhumation of the bodies of John Wesley Reeves and his daughter Ella. They had been buried more than 100 years before in iron coffins and when caretakers opened their graves, they found the bodies of Reeves and his daughter to be amazingly preserved. Thanks to a perhaps a combination of the caskets, the soil and the ground temperature, their still smooth skin held its natural color and their clothing looked just like new.

One of the alleged ghosts in the cemetery is that of William Brown, a railroad engineer who died on September 26, 1880, after saving hundreds of lives. Brown was aboard his locomotive one night when he learned that a fatal switching error had the passenger train heading onto a ferry wharf that led into San Francisco Bay. He was able to get the passenger cars unhooked from the locomotive, just before the entire train would have plunged into the water. As it happened, the engine toppled over the edge of the wharf, taking Brown along with it. When the bay was dredged for the locomotive, they found Brown still holding onto the controls. He had died in a last minute effort to brake the heavy machine. His restless ghost has haunted the graveyard ever since and he has often been sighted walking near his burial site, his hands deep in his pockets and seemingly deep in thought.

Another ghost is that of May Woolsey, a young girl who died at the age of 12 in 1879. Her parents, both believers in the Spiritualist movement, were convinced that they made contact with the girl after her death. She assured them that she was not really lost but merely waiting for them on the other side. Her ghost has often been reported near her monument in the cemetery. Oddly, a trunk of her toys and personal belongings were discovered behind a secret wall in her home in 1979. Her ghost is believed to haunt this house also and the trunk is now on display at the Sacramento History Museum.

Hauck, Dennis William - Haunted Places: The National Directory (2002)
Personal Interviews & Correspondence

Sacramento is the capital city of California and is located in the central part of the state. The cemetery is located at 10th and Broadway in the downtown area.

San Diego

El Campo Santo Cemetery is located in the Old Town district San Diego. As far as ghosts go though, there are few places in the area that can rival this small and secluded graveyard. While it is restored today, this tiny cemetery has seen more than its share of desecration over the years. The tiny enclave is located between two commercial buildings and behind a low, adobe wall. The bare grounds are filled with white wooden crosses and a number of stone monuments in honor of the city's early Hispanic and Anglo settlers.

Until July 1998, there was also a scattering of white crosses that were painted on the sidewalk and on the roadway outside of the cemetery itself. These painted marks had been meant to symbolize the presence of other graves. They were burial places that had been violated by the pavement that had been so recklessly placed there years before. Many feel that this disregard may be the reason the cemetery is so haunted today.

Founded in 1849, this Catholic burial ground once held 477 bodies. According to author John Lamb in his book San Diego Specters, the graveyard began to fall into decline when the fortunes of San Diego's Old Town district began to decline and the population departed for what was the more prosperous New Town. Soon, weeds began to grow and overtake the grounds and the sun and the weather destroyed the simple wooden grave markers. Before long, it was impossible to tell just who was buried where and at what point the graveyard ended and the open land began. The first real desecration to the cemetery came in 1889, just two years after the last burial took place here, when a street car company constructed one of their lines through a portion of the cemetery.

Over the next few decades, a problem was realized and those who saw a threat to the cemetery banded together and built a low wall to protect a portion of the burial ground. It did little good though. In 1942, a dirt lane called San Diego Avenue was covered with pavement.

This roadway passed along the front of El Campo Santo and a number of graves vanished beneath the new pavement. When questioned, local officials claimed that workers were unaware of the boundaries of the cemetery and hadn't deliberately desecrated it. This was unlikely and descendants of the original settlers repeatedly complained and petitioned the city government to acknowledge what had happened. Finally in 1993, technicians using ground-piercing radar discovered at least 18 graves below the street. They were then marked with white crosses, until July 1998, when a new coating of asphalt was applied to the street. The markings were obliterated and not replaced and strangely, ever since that time, there has been an increase in mysterious car alarms activations along this stretch of roadway.

There has also been an increase in the sightings of apparitions as well.

El Campo Santo has been considered haunted for many years. It is a small and gloomy place and definitely has an atmosphere where one might imagine a bevy of spirits would dwell. Not surprisingly, for over 50 years, residents of the area and visitors have claimed to see phantoms appearing among the scattered white markers and passing along the sidewalk outside the cemetery gates. There are many reports of strange activity in nearby buildings and as mentioned, car alarms shriek without any explanation -- other than that they are parked above forgotten graves.

Lamb, John - San Diego Specters (1999)
Taylor, Troy - Beyond the Grave (2001)

The remains of the cemetery are located near the center of the commercial district in Old Town San Diego at the 2400 block of San Diego Avenue. It once extended as far as Old Town Avenue.

Other Haunted California Cemeteries

The exclusive Westwood Memorial Cemetery (Beverly Hills) is reportedly haunted by the ghost of one of America's most famous movies stars, Marilyn Monroe. She died tragically in August 1962 from a drug overdose but some believe that she was murdered, which may be why her ghost remains behind. Marilyn's apparition is sometimes seen near her crypt , as is a hazy, glowing cloud, which may also be a manifestation of her ghost.

The Pioneer Cemetery (Colma) is believed to be haunted by a watchful ghost. The stories say that the phantom of a woman in a burgundy dress watches over the Schieffer family plot in this old settler's burial ground. There are only a handful of marked graves in this section, belonging to three members of the Schieffer family, William, Charles and Mary, who died at the ages of two, 42, and 27 respectively. However, the ghost who haunts this plot is that of an older woman with gray hair, which is parted in the middle and pulled back into a bun. There is no clue as to who this woman might be. She is reportedly seen from the roadside, beckoning to passersby as if wanting someone to come and sit with her.

Greenwood Cemetery (Greenwood) is located in El Dorado County and has been heavily vandalized over the years. According to reports, it is now haunted by the ghost of a tall man with huge hands, who is seen walking through the overgrown burial ground. He appears to be searching for something but according to witnesses, he has also been known to chase and attack those who come here with the intent to harm the cemetery. The old Mortuary building in town is also believed to be haunted, as is the local "hanging tree" that stands in front of it. The ghosts of a woman and a young boy have been seen standing beneath the tree and entering the front door of the former mortuary. On some nights, witnesses also claim to have seen a body dangling from the branches of the tree. When they look again, the image disappears.

The Old Yorba Linda Cemetery (Yorba Linda) is believed to be haunted by a female ghost who has been dubbed the "Pink Lady" over the years. She appears here, according to the legend, on June 15, during every even-numbered year. Her specter is said to walk through the cemetery, only to pause for a moment near an unmarked grave, where she weeps in silence. The ghostly woman is thought to be Alvina de Los Reyes, the daughter of Bernardo Yorba. She died in a carriage accident in the late 1800's, while returning home from a formal party.

Colorado

Central City
Located on a lonely hilltop on the north side of the city is an old Masonic Cemetery that for many years has played host to a ghost -- or at least that's what everyone believed. The eerie lady in black first began appearing here back in 1887, after the death of John Edward Cameron. The young man had died after suffering from "heart paralysis" on November 1 and as a Freemason, was buried with honors in the cemetery. Strangely, an unknown woman in a black dress and a heavy mourning veil attended the funeral. No one from the area recognized her but she wept openly and left a large bouquet of flowers on the grave. Rumors spread that the mysterious woman had been a jealous lover who may have poisoned the young man -- but soon the story changed and by 1899, they were convinced the woman was a ghost. In fact, some even believed that she might have been Cameron's lover, who had committed suicide after he married another. The stories continued to be told as the woman returned to the gravesite every year on April 5 and November 1 to place fresh flowers -- and then would simply vanish.

By October 1899, plans were hatched to try and catch the woman when she returned to the grave. On November 1, a dozen of the townspeople waited for her and just after sundown, she appeared. As she leaned down to place the flowers on the grave, two of the men attempted to grab her but she managed to slip past them and disappear over the top of the hill.

As the years have passed, the lady in black has continued to return to the Masonic Cemetery to place flowers on the grave of John Cameron. Although many have tried to catch up with her over the years, she remains as elusive now as she was more than a century ago.

Martin, Maryjoy - Twilight Dwellers: Ghosts, Ghouls and Goblins of Colorado (1985)

Central City is located in Gilpin County, about 20 miles west of Golden.

Denver

Denver's Cheesman Park seems to be a place of peace and tranquility. The rolling lawns and stately trees offer an oasis of shade and quiet among the busy streets of the city. All seems to be well here -- but is it?

Cheesman Park is a place that some say hides a legacy of horror. There is no disputing the fact that it has long been considered haunted and for reasons that few readers will not understand. You see, this beautifully landscaped park was built over the desecration of the old City Cemetery. This was a dark period in Denver history and as with other such sites, ghosts and hauntings were born from it. However, this was not merely a desecration, nor was it just a case of a few buildings being constructed over some old burial sites. This episode was a scandal that rocked the city government, outraged the public and filled with the newspapers with lurid tales. Cheesman Park is a place that has long been considered as being infested with ghosts.

In 1858, a man named William Larimer set aside 320 acres of ground that were to be used as a cemetery in the new and growing city of Denver, Colorado. He named the cemetery Mount Prospect and sites on the crest of the hill were to be set aside for the rich and influential residents of the city. Paupers and criminals were to be buried on the far edges of the graveyard and ordinary people would find burial spots somewhere in the middle.

The first burials to take place here were the victims of crime and violence. A Hungarian immigrant named John Stoefel had come to Denver to settle a dispute with his brother-in-law and ended up murdering him. After a short trial, Stoefel was dragged away by a mob and hanged from a cottonwood tree. He and his brother-in-law were then taken to Mount Prospect and their bodies were unceremoniously dumped into the same grave. Murder victims and those killed in accidents continued to be buried in the lower sections of the cemetery and the name Mount Prospect began to fall out of use. Most people simply referred to the place as the "Old Boneyard" or "Boot Hill". The cemetery failed to gain the respect and reverence that William Larimer intended for it to have.

As time passed though, Denver began to flourish, with large fortunes being made in silver mining and real estate. Embarrassed by the unseemly reputation of the local cemetery (and names like Boot Hill), the city fathers decided to re-name the graveyard the City Cemetery in 1873. Even the new name though couldn't hide the fact that it was becoming an eyesore. Lack of interest and care had caused the cemetery grounds to revert back to nature. Tombstones had fallen over, prairie dogs had burrowed into the hills and cattle were allowed to graze among the graves. Some time before, affluent families had started burying their loved ones at the newer Riverside and Fairlawn Cemeteries and were leaving the City Cemetery to paupers, criminals, transients and unclaimed smallpox and typhus victims from the local pesthouse.

Meanwhile, ownership of the cemetery passed from Larimer to a cabinetmaker named John J. Walley, who soon went into the undertaking business. He did little to improve the situation in the cemetery and with new homes and mansions being built nearby, the city government was being pressured to do something about it. They soon found a way to pull a fast one over on owner John Walley. Out of the blue, someone in the U.S. Government discovered that the cemetery was on land that was part of an Indian treaty that dated back to before 1860. This made the United States the legitimate owner of the property and in 1890, they sold it to the city of Denver for $200.

The city soon went to work. During Walley's ownership, the cemetery had been divided into three sections. The city's portion had deteriorated but the Catholic and Jewish sections continued to be well-maintained. Soon after the city took over the land, the Jewish churches removed their dead from the graveyard and leased the land to the City's Water Department. The Catholic Church purchased their own land and kept the cemetery in excellent condition until 1950.

The following summer, City Hall announced that all interested parties should remove their dead from the City Cemetery for burial elsewhere within 90 days. Some were reburied by concerned family members but more than 5,000 of the dead were forgotten and went unclaimed. In the early spring of 1893, preparations were made to remove these bodies. At that time, Denver's mayor, Platt Rogers, who worried about the health hazards of opening the graves, was out of town. Ordinances were passed to release funds for the removal and an unscrupulous undertaker named E.F. McGovern was awarded the contract. He specified that each body would be dug up and then placed in a new box at the site, but the box was to only be 3 1/2 feet long and one foot wide. Upon delivery of these boxes to Riverside Cemetery, McGovern would be paid $1.90 each.

In March, McGovern's men went to work. Curiosity-seekers and reporters came out to watch and at first, things were orderly and smooth but it didn't take long for the work to become careless. According to the legends, an old woman came down to speak to the men and told them that they should whisper a prayer over every body that was unearthed or the dead would return. Needless to say, the workmen laughed at her, but they had a hard time concealing their obvious unease. Their haste also allowed souvenir hunters and onlookers to help themselves to items from the caskets. The bodies that had not decayed sufficiently enough to fit into the small wooden boxes were broken apart and shoveled out of the old caskets.

And none of these people (including the workmen) were immune to fear. One workmen, a man named Jim Astor, claimed that he felt a ghost land atop his shoulders. He was so frightened that he threw down a stack of brass nameplates that he had looted from old coffins and ran for his life. He did not return to the site the following day. People who lived in the homes nearby began to report spectral manifestations in their houses and confused spirits who knocked on their doors and windows throughout the night. In the darkness, low moaning sounds could be heard over the field of open graves -- a sound that can still sometimes be heard today.

By the time that Mayor Rogers returned to town, the local newspapers were running front page stories about the atrocities being committed at the cemetery and the general state of corruption at City Hall. The stories brought to light that there were discrepancies between the number of re-burials being charged to the city and the actual number of boxes being delivered to Riverside Cemetery. The matter had become a full-blown scandal and with the help of the health commissioner, he brought the project to a halt. An investigation was launched, leaving the gaping holes in the ground unfilled. Eventually, the rest of the bodies would be forgotten -- and they are still there, under the surface of the park's grounds and gardens.

In 1907, work was completed to turn the City Cemetery into Cheesman Park. It was named in honor of Walter S. Cheesman, a prominent citizen of Denver. Two years later, the marble pavilion shown in the postcard (top of article) was constructed in his memory. In 1950, the Catholic Church sold its adjacent cemetery and an orderly removal took place. Since then, that portion of the land has become Denver's Botanical Gardens. What was once the

Jewish section of the cemetery is now Congress Park.

But despite the passing years of peace, the ghosts who were disturbed more than a century ago have returned, or perhaps have never left at all. Many people who come to the park (and don't know its history) speak of feelings of oppression and sadness, even in these peaceable surroundings. Others still claim to occasionally sight the misty figures, strange shadows and apparitions of the dead. These ghostly images wander in confusion, perhaps wondering what has become of their final resting places. One has to wonder if they will ever find peace?

Martin, Maryjoy - Twilight Dwellers: Ghosts, Ghouls and Goblins of Colorado (1985)
Taylor, Troy - Rest in Peace? Hauntings of Denver's Cheesman Park (2002)

Cheesman Park is located in downtown Denver in the Civic Center area. It is bounded by 8th and 13th Avenues, near University Boulevard.

Fairplay

There is strange tale told of Buckskin Cemetery, which is located in Laurette, a few miles away from Fairplay, Colorado. It is a tale of a tragic death, a restless ghost and the body of a dead man that for many years refused to stay in the ground. The spectral force that propelled the bones is believed to linger in the small graveyard today.

Gold was discovered in a narrow valley located a few miles west of Fairplay in August 1860 by Joseph Higginbottom, David Greist, M. Phillips, W.H.K. Smith, D. Berger and A. Fairchild. A district and town were named "Buckskin Joe" for Higginbottom, a mountain man and trapper who had long been known by this nickname. The camp kept this name for many years, although it was sometimes just known as "Buckskin" and for awhile as "Laurette", a combination of the names of the only ladies here in 1861, Laura and Janette Dodge. As word of the gold discovery spread, more women came to the area but the men in the area still outnumbered the ladies by seventy to one. Even then, most of the women attracted to this mining camp were "soiled doves" and as rough as the men who flocked to the gold strike.

One story of the cemetery involves a man named J. Dawson Hidgepath, who came to Buckskin to find gold and a wife in 1863. He became a nuisance to most of the working girls as he attempted to get them to marry him. He even approached married women, arriving at their homes uninvited and unconcerned about their husbands. Trouble seemed to follow him everywhere. His professed love for a singer and dancer named Julia Cotton got him tossed in the creek. His adoration for Lulu Wise, a working girl, got him a beating from her employer. His advances toward a woman staying at the Argyle House only gained him a knock on the head from her husband's revolver. In addition, his gold claim never seemed to pay off as others nearby did, making Hidgepath all the more miserable. In the end, his search for love and wealth ended in disaster.

On July 23, 1865, Hidgepath's broken and lifeless body was found at the bottom of the west side of Mount Boss, where he had apparently fallen several hundred feet while trying to prospect on the mountainside. The eccentric character was laid to rest in Buckskin Cemetery but he didn't stay at rest for very long. Soon after he was buried, Dawson's bones were discovered on the bed of a dance hall girl in town. How they could have gotten there, no one knew, but assuming that it was some sort of tasteless prank, they were returned to his grave in the cemetery.

In the following months, Hidgepath's bones began appearing about town on a regular basis. It was as though the lovesick miner refused to stay in his grave. The skeleton was reportedly found in women's kitchens, parlors and even in their beds. Some of the women claimed to hear a voice asking them to be Hidgepath's wife, while others stated that the bones were accompanied by a sprig of flowers. Each time, the men of Buckskin reburied the mysterious bones. Once they dug a deeper grave, but it didn't matter. Next, they placed a large, flat rock over the hole, but somehow they managed to escape again.

Eventually, as the mines played out, the town of Buckskin faded into obscurity. However, this did not stop the roving skeleton. Now, the bones sought out women in the town of Alma, a boomtown less than two miles from Buckskin that had sprang up in 1872. Soon, the ladies here also began to receive amorous visits from the now-legendary bones. By this time, they had become the talk of the state and each time they managed to escape from the grave, the story was told in every saloon in the region!

By 1880 though, the local folks decided that the incidents had gone on long enough. Late one night, a handful of men removed Hidgepath's skeleton from his grave and took it to Leadville, where the bones were tossed into an outhouse. What happened next is anyone's guess, but according to the legend (or is it a tall tale?) Hidgepath's bones are resting today in the Buckskin Cemetery. How they managed to get back there is unknown but perhaps a young lady of Leadville got a little more than she bargained for when she went to use the outhouse one day?

Hauck, Dennis William - Haunted Places: The National Directory (2002)
Martin, Maryjoy - Twilight Dwellers: Ghosts, Ghouls and Goblins of Colorado (1985)

Fairplay is in Park County and Alma is located two miles west of it, although it is little more than a ghost town today. Buckskin Cemetery is actually in the town of Laurette, eight miles northwest of Fairplay in the Pike National Forest.

Silver Cliff

One mile south of the little town of Silver Cliff sits an old graveyard that has become known as a site for one of America's greatest unexplained mysteries. During the daylight hours, the Silver Cliff Cemetery is a tranquil place and gives no indication that many unsolved questions have plagued the burial ground since 1880. It is not until darkness falls that the cemetery becomes quite eerie and it is not until then that the "ghost lights" begin to appear.

These mysterious lights have been observed in the old miner's cemetery for more than a century, intriguing several generations of tourists and the residents of Silver Cliff, which is located in the Wet Mountain Valley. Silver Cliff is little more than a ghost town today, boasting only a few hundred inhabitants, but in its heyday, it was a bustling town of more than 5,000 people. Once the mines stopped producing though, the population dwindled but the ghost lights remained.

The lights, which appear as white balls of illumination, have been talked about for years. In the earlier days, the stories were spread by word of mouth, but in 1956, an article appeared about them in the *Wet Mountain Tribune*. It wasn't long before people from all over Colorado began coming to the small cemetery. The reports rarely varied and described tiny, dim lights that would flash on and off, popping up and then vanishing. Sometimes they would be little more than a twinkle and other times they would move about horizontally. If a visitor tried to approach them, they would always stay out of reach and no source could ever be determined as to their origin.

Skeptics dismissed the lights as nothing more than reflections, but in the older parts of the cemetery (where the lights usually appear), there are no reflective stones. Still, in order to counter this explanation, residents of Silver Cliff, and even those in nearby Westcliff, deliberately agreed to shut off their lights for an evening. Even the streetlights were shut off, plunging the area into blackness -- but the lights still appeared.

A Denver scientist named Charles H. Howe had tried to discover a source for the lights in 1895. He journeyed to Silver Cliff in the company of a photographer, Joseph Collier, and an electrical engineer named John Crawford. They studied the lights for an entire week in May and saw the lights on two of the seven nights. On both nights, the sky was overcast and there were no light reflections from town.

Other have tried to explain the lights as being nothing other than the reflections of the stars overhead. In 1988, a reporter and an electrical engineer investigated the phenomenon and stated that the lights were just that, obvious overhead reflections. Unfortunately, this did not take into account the sworn statements of witnesses who had seen the lights on overcast evenings or, like Silver Cliff resident Bill Kleine, had observed them on nights when there had been a thick fog.

Another explanation maintained that the lights were merely "swamp gas" or "will-o'-the-wisps", effects caused by marshy places and decaying matter. Ray de Wall, the publisher of the *Wet Mountain Tribune*, adamantly disagreed. He stated that the cemetery was on a dry ridge and that yucca and cacti grew on the graves. This would rule out wet conditions causing the lights to appear.

So, if we agree that the lights remain an enigma, why are they appearing? Many of the old-timers of the area believe that the ghost lights have a supernatural, rather than a natural, explanation. According to the legends, the cemetery became the burial ground for many of the men who died while working in the mines of the region. The flickering lights of the graveyards are said to be the small lights that used to be worn on the miner's hats. They appear because they are manifestations of the restless souls of the miners -- still looking for the bonanza they never found during their lifetime.

The Silver Cliff lights gained national attention in August 1967 when an article was published about them in the *New York Times*. This got the attention of *National Geographic* Magazine and assistant editor, Edward J. Linehan. He featured a piece about the lights in the August 1969 issue of the magazine. Linehan drove to the cemetery in the company of Bill Kleine, the mentioned area resident and the proprietor of the local campground. Kleine had seen the lights on many occasions and he directed the writer to park the car. They climbed out and stood in silence for several minutes. As they walked through the cemetery, they saw something start to appear. Linehan looked and saw the lights start to flicker. "Dim, round spots of blue-white light glowed, ethereally among the graves", he later wrote. He and Kleine walked about in the cemetery, pursuing one ghost light after another, for the next fifteen minutes. No matter how hard they tried, they were unable to catch them.

Strangely, the lights remain just as elusive today as they were in 1969. Even the most logical and persistent seekers of an explanation for the lights have been forced to admit that they have no answers. No one had been able to get close enough to examine them and despite many attempts, the lights refuse to be photographed.

Over the years, many attempts have been made to discredit the supernatural powers of the lights but until a logical explanation can be reached, the more romantic of us will still wonder about the signal lights of the lost miners.

Hauck, Dennis William - Haunted Places: The National Directory (2002)
Linehan, Edward - National Geographic magazine article
Martin, Maryjoy - Twilight Dwellers: Ghosts, Ghouls and Goblins of Colorado (1985)
Taylor, Troy - Beyond the Grave (2001)

Silver Cliff is located in Custer County in south central Colorado. The cemetery is near Rosita in the foothills of the Wet Mountains.

Connecticut

Easton & Monroe

According to legend, the same "white lady" appears in cemeteries and along roadways in these two towns. In Monroe, the eerie apparition is said to be reported in Our Lady of the Rosary Chapel Cemetery and along nearby Pepper Street. Most of the sightings are the same in that she is seen wearing a white gown, walking among the tombstones or approaching passing cars along the street. She began to be reported first about 50 years ago and has been seen continuously ever since. In 1993, a local fireman "struck" the ghost with his pickup truck as he was driving by. Shaken, he left the vehicle to see if anyone had been injured but there was no woman to be found. Some believe that she is the ghost of a Mrs. Knot, whose husband was murdered near Easton in the 1940's. It has been suggested that her spirit is still searching for that of her husband's.

The White Lady has also been reported at nearby Union Cemetery in Easton. In addition to her ghost, the graveyard has gained a fearsome reputation over the years and many ghosts are reportedly seen here, from that of a little girl to apparitions in dark robes. Tales of a monastery and ritual murders nearby have proven to be groundless but it is believed that authentic- -- and very strange -- things do take place here.

One of the strangest types of reports come from visitors to the cemetery who claim to have encountered solid and seemingly life-like spirits here, who talk, look and behave just as if they were alive. It is not until the person vanishes that they realize they have been talking to a ghost. Acquaintances of people who are buried here say that the ghosts they have encountered look and interact with them just as they did when they were alive.

Hauck, Dennis William - Haunted Places: The National Directory (2002)
Personal Interviews & Correspondence
Warren, Ed & Lorraine - Graveyard (1992)

Easton is located in southwest Connecticut and the cemetery can be found on Highway 59, near the Easton Baptist Church. Monroe is just north of Bridgeport..

Pomfret Area

There is a haunted cemetery located in a small village in New England, but it's not a village that you will find on any map. You see, even today, in places that are as populated as Connecticut, it is still possible for towns to become "lost". One such town, called Bara-Hack, is in a place that is so remote and mysterious that only the strange stories told about the place keep it from being lost altogether.

The lost village of Bara-Hack is located deep in the northeastern woods of Connecticut, close to Abington Four Corners and in the Pomfret township. It can only be found by following a seldom-used trail that runs alongside Mashomoquet Brook. If you ask most people in the region, they will have never heard of Bara-Hack but ask them about the "Village of Voices" and you are much more likely to get a positive response.

Two Welsh families settled the isolated village around 1780 and the name of the place, Bara-Hack, is actually Welsh for "breaking bread". Legend has it that one of the first settlers was Obadiah Higginbotham, a deserter from the British army. He was accompanied by his friend, Jonathan Randall, and his family and both men came to the Connecticut wilderness from Rhode Island.

The Randall family brought slaves with them to the new settlement and according to the stories, the slaves were the first to notice that the village was becoming haunted. As the first of the populace began to die, the slaves claimed that their ghosts returned to the local cemetery. They reportedly saw them reclining in the branches of the graveyard trees at dusk. These were the first ghost stories of Bara-Hack, but they would not be the last ones.

Obadiah Higginbotham started a small factory called Higginbotham Linen Wheels and the mill made spinning wheels and looms until the time of the Civil War. The factory failed after the war and the residents began to slowly drift away from the area. By 1890, the last date recorded on a stone in the graveyard, the village was completely abandoned.

However, travelers and passersby still came through the area and almost immediately after the town died, people began to report strange things were going on in the remains of Bara-Hack. It was not ghosts that they saw though; it was the ghosts that they heard. According to stories and reports, those who came to the ruins of Bara-Hack, and the local graveyard, could still hear a town that was alive with noise. Although nothing would be visible, they could hear the talk of men and women, the laughter of children, wagon wheels passing on the gravel road, farm animals and more. The stories continued and now, more than a century after the town was abandoned, the sounds are still being heard.

Over the years, many people have visited Bara-Hack, although it remains a fairly unknown place in New England lore. Few people have ever written about it and even fewer have ever investigated the claims made by generations of curiosity-seekers. Perhaps the most extensive investigations were carried out by college students in 1971 and 1972. The group was led by then student Paul F. Eno, who wrote about their adventures in *Fate* magazine in 1985 and in his book *Faces in the Window* (1998). The group was escorted to the site by Harry Chase, a local man who had a long interest in the history of the area and in the mysteries of the vanished village. Chase had documented his own explorations of the town with photographs that dated back to 1948. The blurs and misty shapes that appeared in some of the photos have been deemed "unsettling" to say the least.

According to Eno, the groups of students documented many bits of puzzling phenomena. Although the village site was isolated, well over a mile from the nearest house, the students often heard the barking of dogs, cattle lowing and even human voices coming from the dense woods. They also reported the frequent sound of children's laughter coming from the Bara-Hack graveyard.

It was hear that the group had their most unnerving encounters. Eno wrote that for more than seven minutes his group "watched a bearded face suspended in the air over the cemetery's western wall, while in an elm tree over the northern wall we clearly saw a baby-like figure reclining on a branch." One member of the group claimed that his hat was pulled off and was tossed up into a tree here. In addition, another member, who was a middle-aged man that had come along as an advisor on cameras and equipment and quite definitely a skeptic, was physically restrained by an unseen force. He could move, he said, but not in the direction of the cemetery. He could not explain what had happened to him, other than to say that he felt as though he had been "possessed".

Finally, just as Eno's group was departing, they claimed to hear the sounds of a rumbling wagon and a teamster shouting commands to his animals. The sounds began at the cemetery and then moved away, fading off into the dense and mysterious forest.

Eno, Paul F. - Faces in the Window (1998)
Myers, Arthur - The Ghostly Register (1986)
Taylor, Troy - Beyond the Grave (2001)

Bara-Hack can be found from the intersection of Highway 44 and Highway 97 in Pomfret township in northeastern Connecticut. Take Highway 97 north and to the left of Mashomoquet Brook and then follow a dirt road about a quarter mile to the settlement.

District of Columbia

Our nation's capital is undoubtedly one of the most haunted cities in America. The ghosts of Washington are among some of the most famous in the annals of the supernatural and are made up of names that have shaped the country's history. Even the cemeteries and burial grounds of Washington have spellbinding stories to tell.

Located east of the U.S. Capitol building and along the banks of the Anacostia River is Congressional Cemetery, the final resting place of not only some of our nation's leaders but a number of historical figures of the past. The cemetery was started in the early 1800's when Congress purchased hundreds of lots at the Washington Parish Burial Ground of the Christ Episcopal Church. Back then, it was nearly impossible for bodies to be shipped back home, so any congressmen who died In Washington would be buried here. Special markers were even designed so that the graves would be uniform in appearance.

Later on, as it became possible for cadavers to be transported, many of those buried in Congressional Cemetery were claimed by their families and the remains were relocated home. The distinctive markers then became "cenotaphs", grave monuments erected in honor of someone whose body lies elsewhere. This has become the case with such men as Presidents William Henry Harrison, John Quincy Adams and Zachary Taylor, among others.

However, many notables are still buried here and some, like John Phillip Sousa, allegedly do not rest in peace. Sousa was born in Washington in 1854 and music was always his life. By the age of thirteen, he had been apprenticed to the Marine Band, the official band of the President of the United States. Thirteen years later, he was appointed the leader of the prestigious band and it was during this time period that many of his most famous marches were composed. Among them were *Semper Fidelis* and of course, *The Stars and Stripes*

Forever. Sousa later resigned and formed his own band.

The great musician was always a perfectionist and established a new level of professionalism for marching and concert bands. He was also a musical inventor, devising a tuba-like instrument that he called the "Sousaphone". He designed it from a large bass tuba with a circular coiling and an upright bell. He gave a "big bold brassy" sound to the marches that a traditional tuba could not match.

Sousa's tomb is located in the southwest corner of Congressional Cemetery and it overlooks a bridge that bears his name over the Anacostia River. Legends say that over the years, people have heard the sounds of a deep bass horn being played on foggy nights. The music comes from the cemetery and from the vicinity of Sousa's tomb. The stories say that it is the sound of John Phillip Sousa still trying to perfect the tones of the "Sousaphone".

Another reportedly restless spirit of this cemetery is that of the famed photographer Mathew Brady. He was at the height of his career when the Civil War began, with fashionable galleries and studios in New York and Washington. His reputation was so great that he was known world-wide and would, throughout his career, preserve the images of eighteen U.S. Presidents. When rumors reached Brady in 1861 that a battle was going to take place just south of Washington, he hastily equipped a wagon with equipment and supplies and, like many other curious residents of the city, set out for Manassas.

During the war, Brady invested his own money in documenting the devastation following the battles. He financed twenty-two photographic teams in every theater of the war, a move that brought him not success, but financial disaster. By 1865, Brady had spent his entire fortune and was in debt for supplies that had long since been used. The views of the war were not good sellers amongst the general public. To make matters worse, the War Department, although it made use of the photographs, balked at paying for them and Congress failed to see that Brady was reimbursed for any of them.

By the end of the war, Brady was exhausted, depressed and disillusioned. His wife, Julia, was in poor health, his business was in ruins and his life in shambles. Now, younger photographers competed for business and misfortune seemed to plague Brady at every turn. Julia finally passed away in 1887 and while Brady mourned, he continued to work in his Washington gallery, hoping that his views of the war might someday gain wider acceptance.

In the summer of 1885, Brady began to talk of a New York exhibit that would feature his Civil War photographs. He believed it would be his long-awaited triumph and would restore his faltering reputation. Over the following winter, he moved to New York and began extensive preparations for the show. Tragically, Brady died of a kidney ailment in January 1896, never realizing the fame that would someday come. He died alone, in poverty, in the small room of a New York boarding house.

As if his lonely death were not enough, Brady would suffer another indignity. When his body was returned to Washington, he was not buried in the National Cemetery at Arlington where so many of the statesmen and soldiers whose portraits he had preserved had been laid to rest. Instead, he was buried in Congressional Cemetery, next to the very men who had fought to keep him from being reimbursed for his expenses during the war.

In the years after his death, legend had it that a frail, bearded man, dressed in a wrinkled overcoat and slouch hat, was seen wandering the cemetery. He walked about and peered at the inscriptions on the cenotaphs, reading the names of those whose photographs he took years before. These men were immortalized by a tragic figure who, in death, would become known as one of the greatest figures of the Civil War. They say that Mathew Brady's ghost walked for many years, never content in the fact that his legacy was never realized during his lifetime. And some say that he still walks today.

Located in northwest Washington is Rock Creek Cemetery, which holds the grave of Marian Hopper Adams. There is no inscription and no date on her grave marker but it is topped by an unusual statue that was commissioned by her husband, Henry Adams. The statue was created by Augustus Saint-Gaudens, a premiere American sculptor of the late 1800's. Before his death in 1907, he created some of the most honored works in America, including the figure of Diana that once topped Madison Square Gardens and monuments to American heroes and statesmen like Lincoln and Sherman. One of his greatest pieces of work was this memorial for Marian Adams. Marian, called "Clover" by her friends, had fallen into a dark depression after the death of her father in 1885. In December of that year, she committed suicide by drinking potassium.

Henry Adams plunged into despair and in search of comfort, traveled to Japan in June 1886 with his friend, artist John La Farge. When he returned from his trip, he decided to replace the simple headstone that he had ordered for his beloved "Clover" in Rock Creek Cemetery with a more elaborate memorial. He turned to St. Gaudens and asked him to create something that would never be "intelligible to the average mind".

The endeavor took over four years, frustrating Adams, but creating what some called "one of the most powerful and expressive pieces in the history of American art, before or since". It was placed in the cemetery in 1891 and Adams was delighted with both the design and the setting. However, cemetery officials found the mysterious figure of a woman in a full-length veil to be disturbing and at first would not let the marker be placed. Thanks to Adams' influence though, they reluctantly agreed. The statue was never officially named, known as the "Adams Memorial" and later by the more popular name of "Grief". The stories for this nickname vary. Some say that the statue was dubbed this by St. Gaudens himself and others say Mark Twain, who viewed the memorial in 1906, coined the name.

Strangely, Marian's grave monument was something of an enigma. Henry Adams refused to ever speak publicly about his wife's death and would never officially name the monument. He also refused to acknowledge its popular nickname. Thanks to Adams' silence and the fame of his esteemed political family (he was the grandson of President John Quincy Adams), many became curious about the monument. Adams furthered this curiosity by refusing to have an inscription placed on the monument and by placing it behind a barrier of trees and shrubs. The challenge of finding it only fueled the public interest, first by word of mouth and later in guidebooks and magazine articles. The grave became a popular site for the curious, especially as the statue was so unnerving to look at.

Stories persisted for years that the Adams' house, especially the area around the fireplace, where Marian's body had been discovered, was haunted -- but soon those stories grew to encompass the area around her grave as well. According to the stories that were spread by cemetery visitors, the ghost of Marian Adams appeared near the statue at dusk and they continue to be told today.

Alexander, John - Ghosts! Washington Revisited (1998)
Taylor, Troy - Beyond the Grave (2001)

Florida

Key West

One of the strangest cemetery stories of all time has its roots in the Key West Cemetery but it did not begin there. In 1931, a Key West radiologist named Carl von Cosel became obsessed with one of the tuberculosis patients at the sanitarium where he worked. Her name was Maria Elena de Hoyos. She was a beautiful, 22-year-old woman and von Cosel fell in love with her at first sight.

Von Cosel hoped to marry her, but before she could respond to his attentions, she weakened and died just days before Halloween. He begged the family not to bury her under the ground. Fearing contamination of her body from groundwater, he built a mausoleum for her in the nearby cemetery and had her properly embalmed. He visited the cemetery everyday and had "conversations" with her. He even left a phone in the mausoleum so he could speak to her while away. Finally, he decided to remove her corpse from the crypt and take her to his home.

The funeral home had done a poor job with the embalming but by this time, von Cosel was claiming that Elena's ghost was directing him in what to do to recreate her body. He first brought in a regular supply of preservatives and perfumes, but Maria Elena's corpse eventually began to deteriorate. Using piano wire to string her bones together, von Cosel replaced her rotted eyes with glass eyes and her decomposed skin with a mixture of wax and silk. As her hair fell out, he used it to make a wig to put on her head. Stuffing her corpse with rags to keep her from collapsing and dressing her in a bridal gown, he kept her by his side in bed at his small home on Flagler Avenue. He even went so far as to insert a tube into her decrepit corpse to serve as a vagina for making love. He also played a small organ for her as she "slept."

This continued for seven years and before long rumors began to circulate that something very strange was going on at von Cosel's house. Eventually the stories reached Elena's sister, Nana, and went she went to investigate, she was horrified by what she found. As she peered into the window of his house, she saw von Cosel playing a melody on the organ and in bed next to him was a fully reconstructed Elena wearing a wedding dress. She had been dead for nine years by this time. Stunned and sickened, she called the police.

Von Cosel was arrested, but the statute of limitations had run out on his crime of grave robbing, so he was set free. Elena's body was put on display at a local funeral home and people from all over Florida came to see her. Soon, the story was national news. Heartbroken, von Cosel moved to central Florida, where he sold postcards of his beloved. Hours after he had fled from Key West, an explosion blew up the tomb that he had built for Elena. She had never been put back in it though. Maria Elena's body had been divided into a number of sections and each one of them was buried secretly in undisclosed locations. Some believe that they rest in the local cemetery, but no one knows for sure. The three men who carried out the burials have since taken the secret to their graves.

It was said that even after Elena was taken away from von Cosel though, he was unable to forget her. When he eventually died in 1952, he was found in a room with a large doll in his arms that was wearing Elena's death mask.

Harrison, Ben - Undying Love (1997)

Sloan, David - Ghosts of Key West (1998)

Other Haunted Florida Cemeteries

Spring Hill Cemetery (Brooksville) is an old African-American cemetery that dates back to the middle 1800's. There have been many stories told about the site over the years, including stories of a lynched man who has been seen hanging from a tree in the graveyard and stories of groups of spirits that have been seen standing together in the dark of night. There is also a story that states that the cry of an infant can be heard here on certain nights.

There is the ghost of a man named Benjamin Miles who reportedly haunts the Rouse Road Cemetery (Orlando). This local settler died in the late 1840's and was buried here in an unmarked grave. Since that time, he has been seen by cemetery visitors as a shadowy figure in old-fashioned clothing -- and many believe that he is a dangerous and violent spirit. According to local legend, his presence is accompanied by a chill in the air and the cry of an owl, which serves as a warning that his ghost is near. The sightings all take place at night and usually in the cooler weather months of fall and winter.

The famed Huguenot Cemetery (St. Augustine) is believed to be one of the most haunted cemeteries in the southeast and it is certainly one of the oldest. The grounds of the graveyard are believed to be haunted by a headless apparition, whose story dates back to the early 1800's. A caretaker came into the cemetery one morning and discovered that one of the tombs had been vandalized and the body of the occupant pulled out. The corpse's head had been removed and had been apparently taken away by the vandals, for it was never found. The body was re-interred but sometimes, during the evening hours, the ghostly figure of the headless man is still seen roaming throughout the grounds. Sightings began not long after the crypt was first broken into and they continue to this day.

Oaklawn Cemetery (Tallahassee) has been the site of a number of unusual reports that come from the Phillips Mausoleum. The tomb was erected in the early 1900's by Calvin Phillips, one of the city's most eccentric characters. The mausoleum is unusual in its own right and was one of the first to be built in the graveyard. It stands more than 20 feet high and has a small minaret atop it. According to the legend, Phillips literally crawled into his own coffin when he died. It had been placed in the crypt in advance of his death and he allegedly left a key with one of his friends so that they could lock the door behind him after he died. Since that time, there have been a number of reports of strange sounds and mysterious lights in the vicinity of the tomb.

Georgia

Milledgeville

Located in this very haunted town is Memory Hill Cemetery, a small, twenty-acre piece of land that was set aside as a graveyard back in 1803. This historic site holds the remains of a number of people associated with Georgia history, including famed southern author Flannery O'Connor. And, if the stories are true, it holds a few ghosts as well.

One unusual resident of the cemetery is William Fish, who once lived in the town of Hardwick, just outside of Milledgeville. In 1872, Fish's wife and daughter contracted typhoid and both of them died slow and agonizing deaths. In despair, Fish constructed a brick mausoleum in which they were interred. For the next several months, he continued to mourn, unable to overcome his depression. Not long after the mausoleum was finally completed, he placed his old rocking chair inside of it, closed the iron door, sat down in the chair and shot himself with a revolver. He was soon placed next to his wife and child and the three of them will be together for eternity. Although Mr. Fish has still been unable to rest. Legends of the cemetery say that if a visitor knocks on the iron door of this small crypt, sometimes an answering knock will be heard in reply.

Perhaps the most famous grave in this cemetery belongs to a "witch". The occupant, Dixie Haygood, was born in Milledgeville in 1861 and according to the stories, possessed amazing supernatural powers as a psychic medium. It was said that she could cause a piano to move about a room and chairs to rise up into the air. While in a trace, she could find lost objects for members of the audiences who came to seen her and she had an ability that could prevent five men from lifting her small body off the floor. On one occasion, Dixie was said to have lifted a table holding several men and she was able to command the chairs around it to leave the room. Her audience watched in amazement as one by one, the chairs slid off the stage. Some of the spectators even checked to make sure there was nothing physical propelling them. Dixie would often simply place her hands on the back of a chair and without holding onto it, make it rise from the floor. A dozen men were unable to break her hold on the object without twisting or jerking it away from her.

During her career, Dixie allegedly performed for the tsar of Russia, Queen Victoria of England, governors of Georgia and even United States presidents. She became a well-known southern medium but one day, it all came to an end. Stories say that Dixie eventually went crazy and records show that she was a patient at the Central State Hospital for the Mentally Insane when she died. She was then laid to rest next to her husband in Memory Hill Cemetery.

Since that time, her grave has become a popular spot for ghost hunters and curiosity-seekers because the legends say that her spirit still lingers nearby. Before her death, Dixie was said to have placed a curse on many of the local families, including the Yates family, whose burial plot is located next to hers. For the past century or so, a sinkhole has appeared in the Yates' plot every year just before Christmas. The hole is so bad that the gravestone of Mr. Yates and one of his daughters sinks out of sight. Many blame this odd phenomenon on the winter rains and in the past, city crews have filled the hole with cement, gravel and stones. No matter what they do, the hole always comes back.

Taylor, Troy - Beyond the Grave (2001)

Milledgeville was once the capital of Georgia and is located in Baldwin County in the central part of the state.

St. Simons Island

There is no question that the state of Georgia is a very haunted place. Ghost stories here abound, both in the small towns and in the large cities. One haven for ghostlore is a line of islands that stretch along the southeastern shore of the state. These "Golden Isles" are filled with both history and hauntings but none of them can claim as many ghostly tales as St. Simons Island can.

There are a number of famous stories on the island that have been passed along for generations. But of all of these tales, there is no other account as famous as that of the light that appears in the Christ Church Cemetery. Today, there are few island residents who can remember the full name of the woman in the story. In spite of this, nearly all of them can tell you the legend of the woman whose fear of the dark prompted her husband to place a lighted candle on her grave every night.

According to the story, Emma, on whose grave the candle glows, was always afraid of the dark. Growing up, it had been her greatest childhood fear. Each night as she was growing up, a lamp was always left next to Emma's bed with a glowing candlestick inside. Even as Emma grew older, her fear remained. She began to develop an anxiety about running out of candles in the house and she started hoarding the discarded stubs in case her family's supply ever ran out.

Except for her incredible fear of the dark, Emma was a normal, happy and very attractive young woman. She had many friends and was invited to all of the social occasions on the island. One evening at a party, Emma met a young man named Phillip. He had recently moved to Brunswick, Georgia from the Carolinas to work in a cotton brokerage firm. He and Emma fell in love and not long after, they were married at Christ Church. Phillip soon learned to live with Emma's intense fear of the dark and never complained about the candle that was left burning beside their bed each night. They lived a very happy life and after a few months, moved from Brunswick to Frederica on St. Simons Island. Phillip went to work managing his father-in-law's plantation and his shipping company.

Time passed and one day Emma was busy making candles when she accidentally spilled hot wax on her arm. She was badly burned and for some reason, the wound did not heal properly. An infection set in and despite care from the local doctor, she came down with blood poisoning. In less than a week, Emma died.

Phillip was heartbroken. Every night, for as long as Phillip lived, he made a solitary journey to the graveyard and he placed a candle on Emma's grave. He never wanted her to be without the light that she had always needed. When the weather was rainy or windy, he placed it inside of a glass lamp, but he never failed to leave a light for her. His friends and neighbors sadly remarked on his faithfulness and they always explained the significance of the candle to strangers who asked about it.

When Phillip finally joined his beloved wife in death, he was laid beside her in Christ Church Cemetery. For several nights after he died, people passing by the graveyard still saw the familiar light on Emma's grave. They were startled at first but then realized that some of the neighbors were simply carrying on the tradition of placing a candle there. However, a few discreet inquiries soon disclosed that no one on the island was responsible for this new light as no one was taking candles to the grave. The source for the eerie light was, and remains today, a mystery.

Since Phillip's death, literally hundreds of people on St. Simons Island have seen a glowing light that looks just like a candle flame appearing near an old grave in Christ Church Cemetery. A brick wall that has been built now hides the graves from those who pass on the road. However, those who walk back into the graveyard at night and stand beneath the Spanish moss that hangs from the ancient oaks still tell of occasionally seeing a strange, flickering light among the tombstones. Emma still has her light -- and she always will.

Taylor, Troy - Beyond the Grave (2001)

St. Simons Island is located about an hour south of Savannah, along Georgia's east coast. It can only be reached by the Brunswick toll bridge but is well worth the trip.

Other Haunted Georgia Cemeteries
A strange phenomenon occurred for many years at the New Enterprise Freewill Baptist Church Cemetery (Bainbridge) as people who lived nearby often reported seeing what was described as a "ball of fire" hovering over the graveyard. The strange image came to be regarded as a portent of death in the area, as after the fire ball was reported, someone would always die within a few days. The land surrounding the cemetery also came to be haunted by a black dog. This huge animal was extremely vicious and left no tracks behind. It would often be heard howling in the night and one evening, a local family saw and heard the dog but when they tried to follow it over a muddy field, they found that it left no trail.

Bonaventure Cemetery (Savannah) started out as a private estate that was built in the 1750's by Colonel Mulryne. The mansion, Bonaventure, was landscaped with beautiful hanging terraces and surrounded by hundreds of live oaks. The colonel's daughter married into the Tattnall family and they remained in the house for the generations to follow. The two families remained loyal to England during the Revolutionary War and returned to Britain, save for Mary's son, Josiah, who fought for the Colonies. After the war, he became prominent in Georgia and was later elected as governor. Years later, during a party given by Josiah, Bonaventure burned to the ground. It was never rebuilt and was later turned into a cemetery. To this day though, cemetery visitors will sometimes report the sounds of laughter and dinner ware from a party that is taking place somewhere on the grounds. In truth, the party does not exist -- except as a final, ghost remembrance of days at Bonaventure long past.

Illinois

Alsip
A menacing figure began to be reported around St. Casimir's Cemetery in Alsip, a south suburb of Chicago, in the middle and late 1970's. The first sighting occurred in 1978 when a man was driving past the cemetery on Pulaski Road one night and spotted a figure standing just inside of the cemetery fence, draped in a long, black cape. The figure had its back to the driver, but the young man couldn't help but slow down to get a closer look. As he did, the man turned around to face him, revealing a ghastly white face above the neck of the cloak. The sinister looking man bared his teeth at the driver and the fellow in the car sped off.
Around June 14 and 15, the figure was seen again, this time by neighborhood teenagers, who added that he was now seen in the same cape, but also with a top hat on his head. The local police believed that it was nothing more than a prank to frighten the local children, but they became concerned after two police reports stated that the man had approached, chased and threatened youths on two separate occasions. According to the reports, the man was described as being "six feet tall, extremely thin with broken teeth and wearing dirty, muddy

clothing." Both reports also said that he had a "disgusting odor" about him, to go along with the hat, cape and makeup. The sightings were apparently kept quiet in the 1970's to "prevent hysteria" but similar sightings continue today.

Taylor, Troy - Haunted Chicago (2003)

The cemetery is located along 111th Street in Alsip, a south suburb of Chicago.

Alton

The Alton City Cemetery, located at the top of Monument Avenue, is believed to be the third oldest ongoing cemetery in the state of Illinois. It is a beautifully landscaped and well-maintained burial ground in the heart of the old part of the city. The rolling hills are shaded by large trees and the entire place is confined by high limestone walls and iron fences. It is a peaceful place but there are also intriguing sections of the cemetery as well. One of them, which is now forgotten, was the "Stranger's Ground", where it is believed that non-residents were buried in the early days. During the Civil War and in the years before it, many soldiers from Illinois, Kansas, Missouri and Iowa were buried in the cemetery but all were re-interred in the National Cemetery on the east side of the burial ground in 1938. Many of the graves here include Union prisoners and guards who died at the Alton penitentiary during the smallpox epidemic that swept through the prison during the war. Interestingly, this section of the cemetery has been the source of a ghost story. According to accounts, there have been a number of sightings here of a man dressed in a Union officer's uniform from the Civil War. Could he be one of the men who died here during the smallpox epidemic at the penitentiary?

According to rumor, there is also a ghostly woman in black who haunts the Grandview public mausoleum that is located in the Alton Cemetery. This rather daunting old building has been around for many years and is not open to the general public. The stories persist however that a woman in a long black dress has been seen walking down the hallways during services and internments that have been held here.

The other ghostly tale is a little stranger - and much sadder. According to eyewitnesses, there is the ghost of a little girl that has been seen along the south side of the Alton Cemetery, where there is a monument to the Hayner and Haskell families. The witnesses who have seen this phantom girl (and strangely, this story came from three different sets of witnesses who did not know one another), all claim that she plays in the cemetery near this stately family plot. In each case, the witnesses to the little girl's appearance have not been the adults who passed on their story to me but rather their children who have seen her. All of these children have stated that they have "played with the little girl" or have spoken with her in the cemetery. In each case though, the parents never saw a thing, despite the fact that the sightings took place during the daylight hours and their children always insisted that the girl looked completely solid and not like a ghost at all. She is believed to be the ghost of a little girl named Lucy Haskell, who died at the age of nine from diphtheria. She is buried nearby in the cemetery and it has been suggested that perhaps she still returns, visible only to children, as she tries to recapture some of the joy and happiness that she lost when her life ended at such a young age.

The cemetery also has a story of a vanishing hitchhiker. She has been called the "woman in white" and even the "phantom bride" by those familiar with the tale. Over the years, it has faded from memory but it was passed on to me by an older gentleman who has lived in the area all his life. According to his version of the tale, the story got started back during the time of World War II. He was a taxi driver in those days and the story started making the rounds after an incident reportedly occurred with another driver. After it happened, the drivers started to avoid picking up passengers around the Alton Cemetery - or at least they stopped picked up young women in white who hailed from the cemetery's west gate.

One driver had picked up just such a young girl one night and drove her to the address that she gave him. Once they arrived, she asked him to go up and ring the bell, then inquire for the man who lived there. The man came out, but when the driver told him of the girl waiting in the cab, he immediately asked for her description. When the driver described the girl to him, the man shook his head sadly. This was obviously not the first time that a driver had appeared on his doorstep. The young girl, he explained to the taxi driver, was his wife - but she had died many years ago and had been buried at the Alton Cemetery. After hearing this, the driver raced back to the cab and jerked open the door but the woman was gone. The driver fainted away on the spot. After that, young women in white stood little chance of hailing a cab near the entrance to the graveyard.

Taylor, Troy - Haunted Alton (2003)

Alton is located in the southwestern part of Central Illinois, near where the Mississippi, Illinois and Missouri Rivers meet. It is regarded as "one of the most haunted small towns in America". The city cemetery is located at the top of Monument Avenue, overlooking the river.

Arcola

Chesterville is a small town that no longer appears on maps of the state. The village still exists though and is located a short distance away from Decatur and just west of Arcola, which is in the heart of Illinois Amish country. Most of the remaining residents of the town are of the Amish and Mennonite faiths, religious orders that shun the use of electricity and modern conveniences. Located just outside of the village, and across an ancient, one-lane bridge, is the small Chesterville Cemetery. It is in this secluded graveyard that a traveler can find a "witch's grave". The story goes that it once belonged to a young woman who was regarded as a witch in the community.

According to local lore, the "witch's grave" belongs to a woman who once lived in Chesterville, although her name is no longer recalled. She was very liberal-minded and liked to challenge the Amish faith, speaking out against the treatment of women in the area. Thanks to this, she was branded a witch. She continued to disobey the elders of the church and was banished. As few ever questioned the decisions made by the church elders, rumors quickly spread through the community that she practiced witchcraft, was a servant of the devil and worse. Soon after, she disappeared. A short time after she vanished, the woman was discovered dead in a farmer's field. Regardless of what may have happened, the authorities ruled that her death was from natural causes. The body was placed in the local funeral home and people from all over the countryside came to view the "witch's body". They were terrified that she would come back to life.

Eventually, she was buried in the Chesterville Cemetery and a tree was planted on her grave so that her spirit would be trapped in the tree. Today, that tree still stands and many still believe that if the tree ever dies, or is cut down, the "witch's" spirit will escape and take her revenge on the town. A fence was later placed around the grave site to make sure that people stayed away from it. Since that time, her ghost has been reported to still appear nearby, never venturing out beyond the confines of the fence that traps her near the gravestone.

Taylor, Troy - Haunted Illinois (2001)

Chesterville is located in a rural area outside of Arcola. The cemetery is outside of what little remains of the town today. It can be reached by way of a small, one-lane bridge and the "witch's grave" is surrounded by an iron fence on the edge of the graveyard.

Barrington

Strange tales that seem to mix elements of folklore and authentic accounts of the paranormal come from a place called White Cemetery in northern Illinois. This small graveyard, and the surrounding Cuba Road area near Barrington, has gained a rather strange reputation in recent years.

White Cemetery is a small burial ground that is located just east of Old Barrington Road. It dates back as far as the 1820's, but no records exist to say when it started to gain the attention of those with an interest in the unexplained.

For many years, it has been reportedly haunted by eerie, white globes of light that have been seen to hover and float among the tombstones. Witnesses to these anomalies have ranged from teenagers to average passersby, many of whom have gone to the local police and have described not only the glowing lights, but hazy figures too. The lights are said to sometimes float along through the cemetery, drift over the fence and then glide out over the surface of the road. The hazy human-like figures have been spotted along the edge of the fence and lingering near stands of trees. They tend to appear and then vanish at will. Both types of the phenomenon have been investigated and studied by ghost hunters and researchers for some time, but no explanation has been discovered as to their source.

Taylor, Troy - Haunted Chicago (2003)

Barrington is a northwest suburb of Chicago and the cemetery is located on Cuba Road, which is just east of Old Barrington Road.

Champaign-Urbana

Located just east of the twin cities of Champaign and Urbana, Illinois is a cemetery that has been told of in local legends, and at the University of Illinois, for many years. The graveyard is called Clements Cemetery and is said to be home to a ghost that has been dubbed "the Blue Man". For many years, students from the college and the surrounding area have made late night treks to the cemetery, hoping to catch a glimpse of the ghost. It is said that he only appears by the light of the full moon and that if you should see him, he will be glowing with a translucent, blue color.

The story of this ghost has been around for nearly 150 years. In 1841, a man was found to be hanging, either from suicide or a lynching, near the cemetery. Since that time, this stranger's ghost has said to be haunting the area. How much truth is there behind this story? No one knows. I have never actually met anyone who claims to have seen the Blue Man, but then again, you have to wonder just how the story got started in the first place if he never existed at all...?

Clements Cemetery is located east of Urbana, Illinois. Travel east on University Avenue and then north on High Cross Road until you reach the cemetery.

Chicago

Graceland Cemetery came about because of the closure of the Old City Cemetery in Chicago, which is now Lincoln Park. The cemetery was started in 1860 by real estate developer Thomas B. Bryan and it was located far away from the city proper along North Clark Street. There are a number of Chicago notables buried in Graceland, including John Kinzie, Marshall Field, Phillip Armour, George Pullman, Potter Palmer, Allan Pinkerton, Vincent Starrett, writer and creator of the "Baker Street Irregulars", architect Louis Sullivan and many others.

Graceland is also home to several ghost / supernatural stories. One of these legends however, remains puzzling to both cemetery buffs and ghost hunters alike. It involves the strange story of the ghost who has been seen in the vicinity of the underground vault belonging to a man named Ludwig Wolff. The tomb has been excavated from the side of a mildly sloping hill at the south end of the cemetery and according to local legend, it is supposedly guarded by the apparition of a green-eyed dog that howls at the moon.

There are two very different stories connected to "haunted" grave monuments in Graceland. While one of them has widely become accepted as a folk legend, the other one finds a surprisingly receptive, and believing, audience.

The first tale concerns the statue that was placed over the resting place of a man named Dexter Graves. He was a hotel owner and businessman who brought an early group of settlers to the Chicago area in 1831. He passed away and was buried but his body was moved to Graceland in 1909. At that time, a statue that was created by the famed sculptor Lorado Taft was placed on his grave. Taft christened the statue "Eternal Silence" but the brooding and menacing figure has become more commonly known as the "Statue of Death".

The figure was once black in color but over the years, the black has mostly worn away, exposing the green, weathered metal beneath. Only one portion of it remains darkened and that is the face, which is hidden in the deepest folds of the figure's robe. It gives the impression that the ominous face is hidden in shadow and the look of the image has given birth to several legends. It is said that anyone who looks into the face of the statue will get a glimpse of his or her own death to come. In addition, it is said that the statue is impossible to photograph and that no camera will function in its presence. Needless to say though, scores of photos exist of the figure so most people scoff at the threats of doom and death that have long been associated with "Eternal Silence".

Without a doubt, the most famous sculpture (and most enduring ghost) of Graceland is that of Inez Clarke. In 1880, this little girl died at the tender age of only six. Tradition has it that she was killed during a lightning storm while on a family picnic. Her parents, stunned by the tragic loss, commissioned a life-size statue of the girl to be placed on her grave. It was completed a year later, and like many Chicago area grave sculptures, was placed in a glass box to protect it from the elements. The image remains in nearly perfect condition today. Even in death, Inez still manages to charm cemetery visitors, who discover the little girl perched on a small stool. The likeness was cast so that Inez is seen wearing her favorite dress and carrying a tiny parasol. The perfectly formed face was created with just the hint of a smile.

It is not uncommon to come to the cemetery and find gifts of flowers and toys at the foot of her grave. The site has become one of the most popular places in the cemetery, for graveyard buffs and curiosity seekers alike.

You see, according to local legend, this site is haunted. Not only are their stories of strange sounds heard nearby, but some claim the statue of Inez actually moves under its own power. The most disconcerting stories may be those of the disembodied weeping that is heard nearby but the most famous are those of the statue itself. It is said that Inez will sometimes vanish from inside of the glass box. This is said to often take place during violent thunderstorms. Many years ago, a night watchman for the Pinkerton agency stated that he was making his rounds one night during a storm and discovered that the box that holds Inez was empty. He left the cemetery that night, never to return. Other guards have also reported it missing, only to find it back in place when they pass by again, or the following morning.

Taylor, Troy - Haunted Chicago (2003)

The cemetery is located at the corner of Irving Park Road and Clark Street on Chicago's North Side.

Chicago

Rosehill Cemetery began in 1859, taking its name from a nearby tavern keeper named Roe. The area around his saloon was known for some years as "Roes Hill". In time, the name was slightly altered and became "Rosehill". After the closure of the "dreary" Chicago City Cemetery, where Lincoln Park is now located, Rosehill became the oldest and the largest graveyard in Chicago and serves as the final resting place of more than 1,500 notable Chicagoans, including a number of Civil War generals, mayors, former millionaires, local celebrities and early founders of the city. There are also some infamous burials here as well, like that of Reinhart Schwimmer, the unlucky eye doctor and gangster hanger-on who was killed during the St. Valentine's Day Massacre. Another, more mysterious grave site, is that of young Bobby Franks, the victim of "thrill killers" Nathan Leopold and Richard Loeb. After his death, Bobby Franks was buried at Rosehill with the understanding that his lot number would never been given out to the curious. To this day, it remains a secret, although visitors will sometimes find the site by accident among the tens of thousands of graves in the cemetery.

There are also a number of deceased Chicagoans who are not peacefully at rest here and they serve to provide the cemetery with its legends of ghosts and strange happenings.

Perhaps the most famous ghostly site on the grounds is the tomb belonging to Charles Hopkinson, a real estate tycoon from the middle 1800's. In his will, he left plans for his mausoleum to serve as a shrine to the memory of himself and his family. When he died in 1885, a miniature cathedral was designed to serve as the tomb. Construction was started and then halted when the property owners behind the Hopkinson site took the family to court. They claimed that the cathedral tomb would block the view of their own burial sites. The case proceeded all of the way to the Illinois Supreme Court, which ruled that the other families had no say over what sort of monument the Hopkinson family built and that they should have expected that something could eventually block the view of their site. Shortly after, construction on the tomb continued and was completed. Despite the fact that the courts ruled in the favor of Hopkinson, it is said that on the anniversary of the real estate investor's death, a horrible moaning sound can be heard coming from the tomb, followed by what appears to be sound of rattling chains.

Ghost lore is filled with stories of the dead returning from the grave to protest wrongs that were done to them in their lifetime, or to continue business and rivalries started while they were among the living. Such events have long been a part of the lore of Rosehill's community mausoleum.

The Rosehill Cemetery Mausoleum was proposed in 1912 and the cemetery appealed to the elite businessmen of the city for the funds to begin construction. These men were impressed with the idea of a large and stately mausoleum and enjoyed the thought of entire rooms in the building that could be dedicated to their families alone and which also could be decorated to their style and taste. The building was designed Sidney Lovell and is a massive, multi-level structure with marble passageways and rows upon rows of the dead. It is filled with a number of Chicago notables from the world of business and even architect Sidney Lovell himself.

Two of the men also laid to rest in the building are Aaron Montgomery Ward and his bitter business rival, Richard Warren Sears. One has to wonder if either of these men could rest in peace with the other man in the same structure, but it is the ghost of Sears who has been seen walking through the mausoleum at night. The business pioneer has been spotted, wearing a top hat and tails, leaving the Sears family room and walking the hallways from his tomb to that of Ward's. Perhaps the rivalry that plagued his life continues on after death?

Rosehill has also been plagued with odd monuments and unusual stories connected to them. One legend that attracts visitors to a Rosehill monument is connected to the tombstone of Mary Shedden, who was allegedly poisoned by her husband in 1931. Those who find the stone may have to use their imaginations a little but they will likely see two startling visions within the stone of the monument itself. One is the young and happy face of Mary Shedden --- and the other is her grinning and cadaverous skull! Skeptics dismiss the tale, saying that the illusion of "faces" is nothing more than the stone's material playing tricks on the eye, but others are not so sure.

One of the most famous mortuary statues in the cemetery, or at least one of the most visited, is the monument to Lulu Fellows, a young woman who died at age 16 in 1833. Visitors who come here often leave behind coins, toys and tokens to the girl whose monument bears the words "Many Hopes Lie Buried Here". A number of visitors claim that they have encountered the smell of fresh flowers around this life-like monument -- even in the winter, when no fresh flowers are present.

Another "statuary spirit" that comes from Rosehill Cemetery and while this burial ground boasts a number of ghosts, perhaps the most romantic and tragic tale involves the grave of Frances Pearce. This striking monument was moved from the old Chicago City Cemetery to Rosehill many years ago and depicts the life-sized images of Frances and her infant daughter. Both of them are reclining, with the little girl in the arms of her mother, atop the stone. The figures are encased inside of one of the already described glass boxes. Frances was married to a man named Horatio Stone around 1852. The two of them were said to be very much in love and lived a happy life together. Then, in 1854, Frances tragically died at the age of twenty from tuberculosis. To make matters worse, her infant daughter followed her to the grave four months later. Horatio was nearly destroyed by these terrible events and he commissioned sculptor Chauncey Ives to create a memorial sculpture to be placed on their graves in the City Cemetery. Later, both the remains and the memorial were moved to Rosehill. According to local legend, on the anniversary of their deaths, a glowing, white haze fills the interior of the glass box. The stories go on to say that the mother and daughter are still reaching out from beyond the grave for the husband and father they left behind.

Another sad and tragic figure here is that of Philomena Boyington, the granddaughter of architect William W. Boyington, who designed the gothic gates that lead into the cemetery. According to the stories, people who sometimes pass by the cemetery at night will see the face of Philomena peering out at them from the window to the left and just below the bell tower of the Ravenswood gates. It has been said that the young girl often played near the site when the gates were being constructed back in 1864. She died of pneumonia not long after the structure was completed and she has haunted the place ever since.

Taylor, Troy - Haunted Chicago (2003)

Rosehill Cemetery is located at 5800 North Ravenwood on Chicago's North Side.

Decatur

Located in the southern part of Decatur is the city's oldest and most beautiful graveyard, Greenwood Cemetery. The beginnings of Greenwood Cemetery are a mystery. There is no record to say when the first burials took place in the area of land that would someday be Greenwood. It was not the city's first official burial ground, but the Native Americans who lived here first did use it as a burial site, as did the early settlers. The only trace they left behind were the large numbers of unmarked graves, scattered about the present-day grounds.

As mentioned in the introduction to this book, the "lost years" of Greenwood seem to have spawned most of the eerie tales of the place. The story of Greenwood's most famous resident ghost, the Greenwood Bride, begins around 1930 and concerns a young couple who was engaged to be married. The young man was a reckless fellow and a bootlegger, who was greatly disapproved of by his future bride's family. One summer night, the couple decided not to wait any longer to get married and made plans to elope. They would meet just after midnight, as soon as the young man could deliver one last shipment of whiskey and have enough money for their wedding trip. Unfortunately, he was delivering the bottles of whiskey when he was murdered. The killers, rival businessmen, dumped his body into the Sangamon River, where two fishermen found it the next morning.

The young woman had gone to the arranged meeting place the night before and she had waited until daybreak for her lover. She was worried when she returned home and devastated when she later learned that he had been killed. She became crazed with grief and began tearing at her hair and clothing. Finally, her parents summoned the family doctor, who gave her a sedative and managed to calm her down.

She disappeared later that night, taking with her only the dress that she planned to wear in her wedding. She was found wearing the bridal gown the next day, floating face down in the river, near where her lover's body had been pulled ashore. She had taken her own life near the place where her fiancée's had been lost, perhaps hoping to find him in eternity.

A funeral was held and her body was laid to rest on a hill in Greenwood Cemetery. It has been said however, that she does not rest here in peace. As time has passed, dozens of credible witnesses have reported encountering the "Greenwood Bride" on that hill in the cemetery. They claim the ghost of a woman in a glowing bridal gown has been seen weaving among the tombstones. She walks here with her head down and with a scrap of cloth gripped tightly in her hand. Occasionally, she raises it to her face, as if wiping away tears.

Located on the edge of the forest that makes up Greenwood's northwest corner is an old burial plot that sits upon a small hill. This is the plot of a family named "Barrackman" and if you approach this piece of land from the east, walking along the cemetery's narrow roads, you will find a set of stone steps that lead to the top of a grassy hill. There are four, rounded stones here, marking the burial sites of the family. Little is known about the Barrackman's, other than the four members of this family are buried in Greenwood. No records exist about who they were, when they may have lived here or even about what they may have accomplished in life. We simply know their names, father, mother, son and his wife, as they are inscribed on the identical tombstones. As mentioned, two of the stones bear the names of the Barrackman women, and although no one really knows for sure, it may be one of these two women who still haunts this burial plot.

According to many accounts, collected over the years from dozens of people who never knew one another, a visitor who remains in the cemetery as the sun is going down may be treated to an eerie, and breathtaking sight. According to the story, the visitor is directed to the Barrackman staircase as dusk falls on the graveyard. It is said that a semi-transparent woman in a long dress appears on the stone steps. She sits there on the staircase with her head bowed and appears to be weeping, although she has never been heard to make a sound. Those who do get the chance to see her, never see her for long. She always inexplicably vanishes as the sun dips below the horizon. She has never been seen in the daylight hours and never after dark -- only just at sunset.

Located on a high, desolate hill in the far southwest corner of Greenwood Cemetery is a collection of identical stone markers, inscribed with the names of the local men who served, and some who died, during the brutal days of the Civil War. But not all of the men buried here served under the Stars and Stripes of the Union Army. There are a number of dark secrets buried here.

During the years of the Civil War, a great many trains passed through the city of Decatur. It was on a direct line of the Illinois Central Railroad, which ran deep into the south. The line continued north and connected to a railroad that went to Chicago. Here, it reached Camp Douglas, a prison for Confederates who were captured in battle. Many trains came north carrying Union troops bound for Decatur and beyond. Soldiers aboard these trains were often wounded, sick and dying. Occasionally, deceased soldiers were taken from the trains and buried in Greenwood Cemetery, which was very close to the train tracks. In 1863, a prison train holding southern prisoners pulled into Decatur. It was filled with more than 100 prisoners and many of them had contracted yellow fever in the diseased swamps of the south.

The Union officers in charge of the train had attempted to separate the Confederates who had died in transit, but to no avail. Many of the other men were close to death from the infectious disease and it was hard to tell which men were alive and which were not. The bodies were removed from the train and taken to Greenwood Cemetery. They were unloaded here and their bodies were stacked at the base of a hill in the southwest corner of the graveyard. This location was possibly the least desirable spot in the cemetery. The hill was so steep that many of the grave diggers had trouble keeping their balance. It was the last place that anyone would want to be buried.

The men hastily dug shallow graves and tossed the bodies of the Confederates inside. It has been said that without a doctor present, no one could have known just how many of the soldiers had actually died from yellow fever -- were all of those buried here actually dead? Many say they were not, some of them accidentally buried alive, and this is why the area is the most haunted section of Greenwood.

Reports from eight decades have revealed unexplainable tales of ghosts and strange energy lingering around this hill. Visitors who have come here, many of them knowing nothing about the bizarre history of this place, have told of hearing voices, strange sounds, footsteps in the grass, whispers, cries of torment and some even claim to have been touched or pushed by unseen hands. There are also the reports of the soldiers themselves returning from the other side of the grave. Accounts have been revealed over the years that tell of visitors to the cemetery actually seeing men in uniform walking among the tombstones -- men that are strangely transparent.

Taylor, Troy - Where the Dead Walk: History & Hauntings of Greenwood Cemetery (2002)

Greenwood Cemetery is located at the dead end of Church Street in Decatur, which is located in the center of the state.

Dupo

A phantom woman reportedly haunts the road near the now abandoned Gaskill Cemetery near Dupo. The cemetery is in a secluded spot off of old Route 3 between Cahokia and Dupo and beyond a road called Cement Hollow. There used to be an old house that stood nearby but it was torn down years ago and replaced by a newer one. The cemetery can be found along a bluff that overlooks Route 3 but it is private property and trespassers are discouraged. This is mainly because of the condition of the place, with its overgrown grounds, sunken graves and toppled tombstones. Vandals and time have taken their toll on the graveyard and it is plagued by a ghostly tale as well.

According to the story, the spirit of a young woman can sometimes be found wandering along the roadway at the bottom of the bluff attempting to flag down ride from passing cars. Those who have picked her up in the past have been directed to an address outside of Dupo but the girl always vanishes from the car long before they reach it. The legend of the ghostly girls states that she was killed in an accident many years ago and was buried in Gaskill Cemetery. Her spirit is now trying to get someone to take her back home because she misses her family so badly.

Taylor, Troy - Haunted Alton (2003)

Dupo is located in southwestern Illinois and the cemetery is located between Dupo and Cahokia, just off Route 3.

Evanston

A mysterious figure, with possible connections to the past, haunts a stretch of roadway that leads into the gates of Calvary Cemetery, located along the North Shore in Evanston. This old Catholic Cemetery rests on the edge of Lake Michigan and is located between two large universities, Loyola in Chicago and Northwestern in Evanston. For this reason, students from both of these colleges have been unlucky enough to travel Sheridan Road at night and to encounter the phantom as he crosses the roadway to the graveyard gates.

According to the story, motorists following the "S" curve that passes between the cemetery on one side and Juneway park and beach on the other are often startled by a disheveled, wet and tired-looking figure as he pulls himself from the rocky water and staggers across the road to the graveyard. He often stumbles from the water and barely pulls himself across the road. In some reports, he even drags a strand of seaweed behind him, further adding to his drowned appearance.

While a legend among those who live along the North Shore, his identity remains unknown. The tales have it that the man was a drowning victim who met his death in Lake Michigan many years ago (the sightings began in the 1950's). His body was apparently washed ashore near this site and his ghost has remained here ever since. Some believe that perhaps he is buried in Calvary Cemetery and his spirit is now trying to make its way to his grave -- or that the man was never buried at all and for this reason, struggles to make it to consecrated ground. Regardless, who he really is remains a mystery, although this has never stopped anyone from speculating.

Some believe that the phantom may be connected to a plane crash that occurred in nearby Lake Michigan in May 1951. An instructor from the Glenview Naval Air Station experienced engine problems and had to bail out of his aircraft. He landed in the lake just a short distance from Northwestern University. He was spotted alive and waving his arms as a signal for help, but unfortunately, he drowned before anyone could get to him. Two days later, his body was found washed up on the rocks near the cemetery. Could it be this lost soul who now haunts the roadway leading into the cemetery. Many local residents believe so and in fact, have even dubbed the ghost "the Aviator".

Others believe that while this figure did haunt the roadway for a number of years, sightings abruptly came to an end in the 1960's and that he has not been seen since. Apparently though, while sightings have been few and far between in recent years, they do continue and the Aviator has been seen as recently as 1997

Taylor, Troy - Haunted Chicago (2003)

Calvary Cemetery is located on Sheridan Road in Evanston, a northern suburb of Chicago.

Evergreen Park

A phantom hitcher haunts the roadways near the Evergreen Cemetery in Evergreen Park, a Chicagoland community. For more than two decades, an attractive teenager has been roaming out beyond the confines of the cemetery in search of a ride. A number of drivers claim to have spotted her and in the 1980's a flurry of encounters occurred when motorists in the south and western suburbs reported picking up this young girl. She always asked them for a ride to a location in Evergreen Park and then mysteriously vanished from the vehicle at the cemetery.

According to the legends, she is the spirit of a child buried within the cemetery, but there is no real folklore to explain why she leaves her grave in search of travelers, nor what brings her to the suburbs and so far from home. In addition to seeking rides in cars, she is resourceful enough to find other transportation when it suits her. In recent years, encounters with this phantom have also taken place at a bus stop that is located directly across the street from the cemetery. Many have claimed to see a dark-haired young girl here who mysteriously vanishes. On occasion, she has also climbed aboard a few Chicago Transit Authority buses as well.

One evening, a young girl climbed aboard a bus and breezed right past the driver without paying the fare. She walked to the back portion of the vehicle and sat down, seemingly without a care in the world. Irritated the driver called out to her, but she didn't answer. Finally, he stood up and walked back toward where she was seating. She would either pay, he thought, or have to get off the bus. Not surprisingly though, before he could reach her, she vanished before his eyes.

According to reports, other shaken drivers have had the same eerie experience at this bus stop. The other drivers have also seen this young girl and every single one of them have seen her disappear as if she had never been there in the first place.

Taylor, Troy - Haunted Chicago (2003)

Evergreen Cemetery is located on South Kedzie in Evergreen Park, a Chicago suburb.

Forest Park

A mysterious hitchhiker ghost haunts the vicinity of Jewish Waldheim Cemetery (now re-named Waldheim Cemetery), located at 1800 South Harlem Avenue in Chicago.

The story of the ghost states that she was a young Jewish girl who attended dances at the Melody Mill Ballroom, formerly on Des Plaines Avenue. The place was one of the area's favorite spots for ballroom dancing, from the 1920's to the middle 1980's. The girl who became the spirit was said to be a very attractive brunette with bobbed hair and a dress right out of the Roaring 20's, hence the spirit's nickname of the "Flapper Ghost". This fetching phantom has been known to hitch rides on Des Plaines Avenue and most often has been seen near the cemetery gates. Some travelers passing the cemetery even claimed to see her entering a mausoleum that is located off Harlem Avenue.

The ghost seems to have had a real-life counterpart, although her name has been lost to time. She was a lovely girl and a regular at the Melody Mill Ballroom until she died of peritonitis, the result of a burst appendix. The girl was buried at Jewish Waldheim and she likely would have been forgotten, to rest in peace, if strange things had not started to happen a few months later. The events began as staff members at the Melody Mill began to see a young woman who looked just like the deceased girl appearing at dances at the ballroom. A number of men actually claimed to meet the girl here (after her death) and also to have offered her a ride home. During the journey, the young woman always vanished.

Although recent sightings have been few, the ghost was most active in 1933, during the Century of Progress Exhibition, and again in 1973. In the early 1930's, she was often reported at the ballroom, where she would dance with young men and ask for a rides to her home at the end of the evening. Every report was basically the same. A young man agreed to drive the girl home and then she would give him directions to go east on Cermak Road, then north on Harlem Avenue. When they reached the cemetery, the girl always asked for the driver to stop the car. The girl would explain to them that she lived in the caretaker's house (since demolished) and then get out of the car. One man stated that he watched the girl go towards the house but then duck around the side of it. Curious, he climbed out of the car to see where she was going and saw her run out into the cemetery and vanish among the tombstones.

Another young man, who was also told that the girl lived in the caretaker's house, decided to come back during the day and to ask about the girl at the house. He had become infatuated with her and hoped to take her dancing again on another evening. His questions to the occupants of the house were met with blank stares and bafflement. No such girl lived, or had ever lived, at the house.

More sightings took place in the early 1970's and one report even occurred during the daylight hours. A family was visiting the cemetery one day and was startled to see a young woman dressed like a "flapper" walking toward a crypt, where she suddenly disappeared. The family hurried over to the spot, only to find no girl and nowhere to which she could have vanished so quickly.

Another strange sighting took place in 1979 when a police officer saw a beautiful girl walking near the ballroom on a rainy night. He asked her where she was going and she replied "home". He offered her a ride and she directed him to go east on Cermak Road. He later reported that he asked her a number of questions but she always just changed the subject and steered the conversation to how much she liked to dance and how much she enjoyed going to the Melody Mill. The girl then directed him to an apartment building near the cemetery entrance. After the girl got out of the car, she vanished near a covered doorway and the policeman, shocked, got out and went after her. He was sure that she could not have gotten into the building so quickly and was even more surprised to see no wet footprints on the dry sidewalk below the building's awning.

Since that time, sightings of the "Flapper" have been few, and this may be because the old Melody Mill is no more. The days of jazz and big bands were gone by the 1980's and attendance on weekend evenings continued to slip until the place was closed down in 1985. It was later demolished and a new building was put up in its place two years later.

Taylor, Troy - Haunted Chicago (2003)

Waldheim Cemetery is located on South Harlem in Forest Park, a suburb of Chicago.

Hillside

In Hillside, just outside of Chicago, is Mount Carmel Cemetery. In addition to being the final resting place of Al Capone, Dion O'Banion and other great Chicago mobsters, the cemetery is also the burial place of a woman named Julia Buccola Petta. While her name may not spring to mind as a part of Chicago history, for those intrigued by the supernatural, she is better known as the "Italian Bride". Julia's grave is marked today by the life-sized statue of the unfortunate woman in her wedding dress, a stone reproduction of the wedding photo that is mounted on the front of her monument. The statue marks the location where Julia's apparition is said to appear. Not surprisingly, the ghost is clad in a glowing, white bridal gown.

Julia Buccola grew up on the west side of Chicago and when she and her husband married, they moved to a more upscale Italian neighborhood. Eventually, she became pregnant with her first child but complications set in and she died giving birth to a stillborn child in 1921. Because of the Italian tradition that dying in childbirth made the woman a type of martyr, Julia was buried in white, the martyr's color. Her wedding dress also served as her burial gown and with her dead infant tucked into her arms, the two of them were laid to rest in a single coffin

Julia's mother, Filomena, angrily blamed her daughter's husband for the girl's death and she claimed the body and buried her with the Buccola's at Mount Carmel Cemetery. Shortly after Julia was buried though, Filomena began to experience strange and terrifying dreams every night. In these nightmares, she envisioned Julia telling her that she was still alive and needed her help. For the next six years, the dreams plagued Filomena and she began trying, without success, to have her daughter's grave opened and her body exhumed. She was unable to explain why she needed to do this, she only knew that she should. Finally, through sheer persistence, her request was granted and a sympathetic judge passed down an order for Julia's exhumation.

Two Photographs from the grave marker of Julia Buccola Petta show her on the day of her wedding, wearing the bridal gown that she was buried in and the condition of her body when it was exhumed six years after her death.

In 1927, six years after Julia's death, the casket was removed from the grave. When it was opened, Julia's body was found not to have decayed at all. In fact, it was said that her flesh was still as soft as it had been when she was alive. A photograph was taken at the time of the exhumation and shows Julia's "incorruptible" body in the casket. Her mother, and other admirers, placed the photo on the front of her grave monument, which was constructed after her reburial. The photograph shows a body that appears to be fresh, with no discoloration of the skin, even after six years. The rotted and decayed appearance of the coffin in the photo however, bears witness to the fact that it had been underground for some time. Julia appears to be merely sleeping. Her family took the fact that she was found to be so well preserved as a sign from God and so after collecting money from other family members and neighbors, they created the impressive monument that stands over her grave today.

What mysterious secret rests at the grave of Julia Petta? How could her body have stayed in perfect condition after lying in the grave for six years? No one knows, but not surprisingly, reports have circulated for years claiming that a woman in a bridal gown haunts this portion of the cemetery.

Some of the stories come from students at Proviso West High School, which is located just east of the cemetery on Wolf Road. They have reported a girl walking in the cemetery at night and they are not alone. A number of people in a car traveling down Harrison Street were startled to see a woman passing through the tombstones one night. Thinking that it was simply a Halloween prank, they stopped the car for a closer look. They did not become unnerved until they realized that, even though it was pouring down rain, the girl was perfectly dry. They didn't choose to investigate any closer and immediately drove away.

Taylor, Troy - Haunted Chicago (2003)

The cemetery is located at 1100 South Wolf Road in Hillside, a southwest suburb of Chicago.

Justice

Bethania Cemetery in Justice, in southwest suburb of Chicago boasts at least two mysterious figures that haunt the grounds and the streets nearby. Bethania is a largely German cemetery and it is located along very haunted Archer Avenue.

One of the most common phantoms to appear here is seen on the 79th Street side of the cemetery. Just past the maintenance entrance to the grounds, motorists have often reported seeing the harmless figure of an elderly man as he rakes and burns leaves along the side of the road. These sightings normally occur during the fall, so it's not the time of year that it happens that seems so odd to the people who spot this scene -- it's the time of day! Those who are driving by are often puzzled as to why this old man would be out working in the cemetery between 2:00 and 4:00 in the morning. However, as the witnesses slow down to have a look in the rearview mirror, or even glance back in his direction, they discover that not only is the old man gone, but so are the piles of burning leaves. So far, no one has been able to provide an explanation as to why this odd figure is being seen here, nor even who he might be.

Bethania's other phantom figure is more on the unnerving side. He haunts the far southwestern edge of the cemetery, located along Cork Avenue. Several reliable witnesses have reported that they have seen a blood-covered man running from a nearby model home and waving a flashlight as he goes. He flees the edge of the graveyard towards oncoming traffic, whirling the flashlight as he goes, as if trying to flag down one of the passing cars.

One witness stated that the bloody man had run right out in front of his car, forcing the witness to swerve wildly to avoid hitting what he believed was a flesh and blood person. The sighting was so real that he could see the injuries to the man, the blood on his clothing and at one point, the light from the phantom flashlight temporarily blinded the driver. The witness regained control of his car and as he swerved back into his lane, he quickly looked back in his rearview mirror. Amazingly, he was stunned to see the bleeding man stumble into the path of another car, still waving the flashlight. The second driver did not react as quickly though and the first witness watched in shock as the car passed directly through the figure without even slowing down. The bloody man then staggered to the side of the road, crossed a shallow ditch and then vanished as he reached the cemetery fence.

The identity of this strange figure also remains a mystery and no research has even been able to discover if a murder or accident occurred near here that might explain the horrific apparition.

Taylor, Troy - Haunted Chicago (2003)

The cemetery is located at 7701 South Archer Road in Justice, a south suburb of Chicago.

Justice

A "woman in white" haunts one of the area's most foreboding graveyards, a place called Archer Woods Cemetery. For years, the female phantom has been reported at this wooded burial ground, especially back in the days when it was a desolate spot along Kean Road. She does not wander the roadway flagging down passing motorists however, although she is usually spotted by those who drive by the cemetery at night.

Those unwitting travelers, passing along Kean Road, are often greeted by the sound of a woman loudly sobbing in despair. When they stop their vehicles for a closer look, they see a woman in a white gown wandering near the edge of the graveyard. She is always said to be weeping and crying and covering her face with her hands. She is normally only seen for a matter of seconds before she disappears.

In addition to the "Weeping Woman", Archer Woods is also said to be home to another, more terrifying, specter, an old-fashioned hearse. This black coach is said to be driverless but pulled by a team of mad horses. The hearse itself is made from black oak and glass and carries the glowing coffin of a small child as cargo. Residents of the area have been reporting this bizarre "ghost hearse" for years and it is often seen along nearby Archer Avenue.

Taylor, Troy - Haunted Chicago (2003)

The cemetery is located along Kean Road in Justice, a south suburb of Chicago.

Justice

Resurrection Cemetery in the Chicago suburb of Justice has become known as the center of one of the greatest ghost stories of all time. The story of the ghost who has come to be known as "Resurrection Mary" began in the 1930's. It was around this time that drivers along Archer Avenue started reporting strange encounters with a young woman in a white dress. She always appeared to be real, until she would inexplicably vanish. The reports of this girl began in the middle 1930's and started when motorists passing by Resurrection Cemetery began claiming that a young woman was attempting to jump onto the running boards of their automobiles.

Not long after, the woman became more mysterious, and much more alluring. The strange encounters began to move further away from the graveyard and closer to the O Henry Ballroom, which is now known as the Willowbrook. She was now reported on the nearby roadway and sometimes, inside of the ballroom itself. On many occasions, young men would meet a girl at the ballroom, dance with her and then offer her a ride home at the end of the evening. She would always accept and offer vague directions that would lead north on Archer Avenue. When the car would reach the gates of Resurrection Cemetery, the young woman would always vanish.

More common were the claims of motorists who would see the girl walking along the road. They would offer her a ride and then witness her vanishing from their car. These drivers could describe the girl in detail and nearly every single description precisely matched the previous accounts. The girl was said to have light blond hair, blue eyes and was wearing a white party dress. Some more attentive drivers would sometimes add that she wore a thin shawl, or dancing shoes, and that she had a small clutch purse.

But who is this young woman, or at least who was she when she was alive?

Most researchers agree that the most accurate version of the story concerns a young girl who was killed while hitchhiking down Archer Avenue in the early 1930's. Apparently, she had spent the evening dancing with a boyfriend at the O Henry Ballroom. At some point, they got into an argument and Mary (as she has come to be called) stormed out of the place. Even though it was a cold winter's night, she thought, she would rather face a cold walk home than another minute with her boorish lover. She left the ballroom and started walking up Archer Avenue. She had not gotten very far when she was struck and killed by a passing automobile. The driver fled the scene and Mary was left there to die. Her grieving parents buried her in Resurrection Cemetery, wearing a white dress and her dancing shoes. Since that time, her spirit has been seen along Archer Avenue, perhaps trying to return to her grave after one last night among the living.

Mary was soon making regular appearances along Archer Avenue and stories of motorists who have picked her up have become commonplace over the years. Dozens of young men have told of picking up a girl, or meeting her at the ballroom, only to have her disappear from their car. The majority of the reports seem to come from the cold winter months, like the account passed on by a cab driver. He picked up a girl who was walking along Archer Avenue one night in 1941. It was very cold outside, but she was not wearing a coat. She jumped into the cab and told him that she needed to get home very quickly. She directed him along Archer Avenue and a few minutes later, he looked back and she was gone. He realized that he was passing in front of the cemetery when she disappeared.

During the middle 1970's, the number of Mary sightings began to increase. People from many different walks of life, from cab drivers to ministers claimed they had picked her up and had given her rides. It was during this period that Resurrection Cemetery was undergoing some major renovations and perhaps this was what caused her restlessness.

The stories continued but perhaps the strangest account of Mary was the one that occurred on the night of August 10, 1976. This event has remained so bizarre after all this time because on this occasion, Mary did not just appear as a passing spirit. It was on this night that she left evidence behind.

A driver was passing by the cemetery around 10:30 that night when he happened to see a girl standing on the other side of the gates. He said that when he saw her, she was wearing a white dress and grasping the iron bars of the gate. The driver was considerate enough to stop down the street at the Justice police station and alert them to the fact that someone had been accidentally locked in the cemetery at closing time. Two officers responded to the call but when they arrived at the cemetery gates, was no one was there. The graveyard was dark and deserted and there was no sign of any girl. But an inspection of the gates, where the girl had been seen standing, did reveal something unusual. They found that two of the bars in the gate had been pulled apart and bent at sharp angles. To make things worse, at the points on the green-colored bronze where they had been pried apart were blackened scorch marks. Within these marks was what looked to be skin texture and handprints that had been seared into the metal with incredible heat.

The marks of the small hands made big news and curiosity-seekers came from all over the area to see them. In an effort to discourage the crowds, cemetery officials attempted to remove the marks with a blowtorch, making them look even worse. Finally, they cut the bars off and installed a wire fence until the two bars could be straightened or replaced.

The cemetery emphatically denied the supernatural version of what happened to the bars. They claimed that a truck backed into the gates while doing sewer work at the cemetery and that grounds workers tried to fix the bars by heating them with a blowtorch and bending them. The imprint in the metal, they said, was from a workman trying to push them together again. While this explanation was quite convenient, it did not explain why the marks of small fingers were clearly visible in the metal.

The bars were removed to discourage onlookers, but taking them out had the opposite effect and soon, people began asking what the cemetery had to hide. The events allegedly embarrassed local officials, so they demanded that the bars be put back into place. Once they were returned to the gate, they were straightened and painted over with green paint so that the blackened area would match the other bars. Unfortunately though, the scorched areas continued to defy all attempts to cover them and the twisted spots where the handprints had been impressed remained obvious until just recently, when the bars were removed for good.

On the last weekend in August 1980, Mary was seen by dozens of people, including the Deacon of the Greek Church on Archer Avenue. Many of witnesses contacted the Justice police department about their sightings. Squad cars were dispatched and although the police could not explain the mass sightings of a young woman who was not present when they arrived, they did find the witnesses themselves. Many of them flagged down the officers to tell them what they had just seen.

In October 1989, two women were driving past Resurrection Cemetery when a girl in a white dress ran out in front of their car. The driver slammed on the brakes, sure that she was going to hit the woman, but there was no impact. Neither of the women could explain where the apparition had disappeared to.

During the 1990's, reports of Mary slacked off, but they have never really stopped altogether. Even though sighting and encounters have slacked off in recent years, they still continue to occur today. While many of the stories are harder to believe these days, as the tales of Mary have infiltrated our culture to such a degree that almost anyone with an interest in ghosts has heard of her, some of the stories still appear to be chillingly real.

Taylor, Troy - Haunted Chicago (2003)

Resurrection Cemetery is located along Archer Avenue in Justice, a south suburb of Chicago.

Lebanon

There are also said to be two haunted cemeteries in Lebanon, Illinois. At one of them, a cross-eyed ghost is said to stare at passing motorists while the other is home to a slightly more chilling spirit.

The story goes that a young man is driving past the cemetery at night and spots a young girl in the road ahead of him. He slams on his brakes and tries to stop before hitting her, but he can't. He hears the terrible thud as she hits the front of the car and rolls beneath it. He manages to stop the car and he jumps out to look for her, but he can't find her. Mystified, he searches the surrounding roadway and the ditch, but the girl is nowhere to be found. The tale continues with the man going to the local police station to report the accident. He explains to the officer on duty what happened and that he needs help to go back and look for the little girl. The officer shakes his head and smiles sadly, then explains to the young man that the girl was killed there by a car five, ten years before. Her ghost is sometimes still seen there on foggy or rainy nights. Still in shock, the man leaves the police station and walks outside. On his way to his car, he happens to look down and notices something strange - imprinted in the bumper on the front of his car is the mark of a very small hand.

Taylor, Troy - Haunted Alton (2003)

Lebanon is located in southwestern Illinois, about 30 minutes southeast of St. Louis.

Lemont

Archer Avenue is undoubtedly one of the most haunted stretches of road in Chicago. There are a number of locations along this road, including cemeteries, homes and businesses, which boast more than their share of ghosts. The paranormal activity on the roadway seems to be anchored at both ends by cemeteries, both of which have their own ghost stories. One of them is the famous Resurrection Cemetery and the other, lesser-known, burial ground is St. James-Sag. This old Indian trail is thought to possibly be the location of a "ley line" that attracts strange activity. The Indian trail was turned into an actual road in the 1830's. Irish workers on the Illinois-Michigan Canal completed the construction. Most of them lived near

Lemont, at the southern end of Archer Avenue.

Here is located the St. James-Sag Church and burial ground, which dates back to around 1817, a few years before Archer Avenue was built to follow the route of the canal. Most of the men who worked on the road and canal moved out of Chicago and became parishioners of the church.

The site of the church and burial grounds has a long history in Chicago. The site marks the second oldest Catholic Church in northern Illinois and dates back to 1833. Before that, Marquette and Jolliet were the first white men to see this area, later known as the Sag Ridge and when they arrived in 1673, the local Indians were using it as a burial ground. For this reason, the site was already sacred ground when Marquette offered a mass here in the year of his arrival. The site became a mission and a French signal post in the late 1600's. The present parish was established not by the French, but by the Irish when, as mentioned earlier, so many of them moved into the region as workers on the canal.

The first church was constructed in 1833 and was a simple log cabin that stood on the highest point of the ridge. In 1850, it was replaced by the limestone building that is still in use today. The pale yellow building stands on top of the hill, just a short distance from the newer rectory and stands watch over the hundreds of graves scattered about on the hills below. It is an idyllic scene and could easily be part of the Irish countryside, rather than a landscape from the southwest side of Chicago.

Supernatural events have been reported at St. James-Sag since around 1847. It was at this time when the first sightings of the "phantom monks" took place here. These stories continued for decades and there were many reliable witnesses to the strange activity. One of them, a former rector of the church, admitted on his deathbed that he had seen ghosts roaming the cemetery grounds for many years.

One cold night in November 1977, a Cook County police officer was passing the cemetery and happened to turn his spotlight up past the cemetery gates. He claimed to see nine hooded figures floating up the cemetery road toward the rectory. Knowing that no one was supposed to be in the cemetery, he stopped and yelled out the window at them to come back toward the road. If they did not, they would be arrested for trespassing. The figures simply ignored him and continued up the road toward the church and rectory.

Quickly, he grabbed his shotgun and ran around the gate and into the graveyard. He pursued what he first thought were pranksters into the graveyard but while he stumbled and fell over the uneven ground and tombstones, the monk-like figures eerily glided past without effort. He said that he nearly caught up with them when "they vanished without a trace". Unable to believe what had just happened, he searched around the area for any trace of the figures but found no one. Finally, he returned to his squad car to write up his report. The paperwork that he filed merely stated that he had chased some trespassers through the cemetery but he always maintained that what he had seen was beyond this world.

Another legend of St. James-Sag is likely what gave the burial ground its ghostly reputation in the first place. This story concerns a phantom hearse that is possibly the same vehicle seen on Kean Road and at nearby Archer Woods Cemetery. The description of the vehicle is the same, from the black horses to the glowing coffin of a child, and was first reported back in 1897. According to a report in the Chicago Tribune, two musicians spent the night in a recreation hall that is located at the bottom of the hill below the St. James-Sag rectory. They were awakened in the early morning hours by the sound of a carriage on the stones outside. They looked out and saw the macabre hearse. They became the first to report the eerie vehicle, but they would not be the last.

Taylor, Troy - Haunted Chicago (2003)

St. James-Sag Church & Cemetery are located along Archer Avenue in Lemont, a southwest suburb of Chicago.

Midlothian

This south Chicago suburb is home to one of the most haunted cemeteries in America, Bachelor's Grove Cemetery. The story of this eerie graveyard can be found in Chapter 2 of the book.

Millstadt

There have been stories for years about the glowing tombstone at Mount Evergreen Cemetery in Millstadt. The stories say that a young woman was murdered near the tombstone many years ago and that her blood now makes the tombstone glow. She was allegedly stabbed to death by an insane cemetery groundskeeper but unfortunately, there are no facts to back up the tale.

Another variation of the story claims that another woman was killed while trying to ward off the spirit of the murdered woman. She was supposed to go up to the tombstone and drive a stake into the ground next to it, which would chase the woman's ghost away. However, when she hammered the stake into the ground, it snagged on the hem of her dress and tripped her. She believed that it was a spectral hand from beyond the grave and the story says that she died on from fright on the spot. Now, her ghost also haunts the area, still trying to drive the stake into the ground to ward off the other spirit.

Taylor, Troy - Haunted Alton (2003)

Millstadt is located in southwestern Illinois, southeast of St. Louis

Oakley

Peck Cemetery is located in the woods near the small Central Illinois town of Oakley. More about this haunted graveyard can be found in the introduction to this book.

Steger

Calvary Cemetery in Steger is home to a rather mysterious figure. This figure haunts the roadway in front of the cemetery gates and may just be re-playing an incident from the past. The burial grounds are located on the north side of Steger Road and near the south edge of the Sauk Trails Woods Forest Preserve, near Chicago. It's a fairly secluded area and roads here are often shrouded in darkness from the overhanging trees. Which makes the strange occurrences along the roadway all the more unnerving…

According to witnesses, sightings of the cemetery's phantom figure occur after turning east on Steger Road from Western Avenue. This is a dark, rural roadway and there are no streetlights of any kind here until the driver actually enters a residential area further up the road. It's along this dark stretch of drive though, near the cemetery entrance, where the motorists suddenly encounter the figure of a young boy who is a riding his bicycle in the middle of the road! Everyone who experiences this phantom never imagine that he is anything other than a careless little boy -- until they realize he is apparently out riding his bike in the middle of the night!

These late night encounters nearly always end up in near collisions and accidents as the driver tries to avoid hitting the boy. They are stunned as he appears out of the darkness, riding casually down two lanes of traffic, and often have to slam on their brakes or swerve quickly. After recovering from their near miss, they attempt to find the boy and reprimand him for his dangerous behavior but there is never any boy to be found. He has simply vanished into the night.

Who this phantom boy might be is unclear but many believe that he may be the spirit of a child who was killed on this same roadway in the past. Perhaps he was struck and killed by a passing motorist one night and is now replaying his final moments again and again -- or perhaps the figure appears a warning. Perhaps the ghost is appearing to drivers to caution them to look for other children who might share his same fate someday if a motorist comes over one too many hills in the darkness, only to find another careless bicyclist on the other side?

Taylor, Troy - Haunted Chicago (2003)

The cemetery is located at Steger Road and Western Avenue in Steger.

Tower Hill

One of the strangest mystery spots in Central Illinois is undoubtedly Williamsburg Hill. It is located near the small communities of Tower Hill and Shelbyville and it is not hard to find, for it rises to its highest point at 810 feet, making it the highest elevation in that part of the state. To drive across the hill today, you would see no evidence of the history that is hidden in this remote spot. Williamsburg Hill just seems to rise out of nowhere on the prairie and is covered by a heavy stand of trees.

The village of Williamsburg, which was also called Cold Spring for a time, was laid out in 1839 by Dr. Thomas Williams and William Horsman. It was located on the south side of the large hill and for about 40 years, was a bustling community of about four square blocks. At one time, there were two churches, a doctor's office, a saloon, a post office, a blacksmith shop and a number of modest homes. The Main Street of the community was once part of the "Old Anglin' Road", a stage route that ran from Shelbyville to Vandalia. It was this stage line that brought prosperity to the village for many years. Some say the community died out when the Beardstown, Shawneetown and Southeastern Railroad bypassed the village in 1880. However, others believe that the town was abandoned for much darker reasons, attributed to the strangeness of Williamsburg Hill itself. Today, there is nothing left of the village, save for a few old gravel pits. The land where it once stood has long been plowed under and trees have covered the area where homes once stood.

One of the strangest locations remaining on the hill is a place called Ridge Cemetery. This rugged graveyard can be found on the highest summit of Williamsburg Hill. The desolate burial ground has many tilted stones, thanks to the sharp hills, and also bears evidence of both vandalism and unmarked graves. The cemetery can be found by watching for a massive microwave tower, located just east of the burial ground.

Ridge Cemetery has been part of the lore that makes up Williamsburg Hill for many years and has long been considered a frightening place. It is located back off the main road and down a wooded lane that is very dark for those curiosity-seekers who venture down it at night, braving the sheriff's deputies who regularly patrol the road and graveyard. Cases of vandalism, and some say darker things, have forced the authorities to close the place after dark. There have been reports of cultists using the cemetery and this has sparked both gossip and concern in small, surrounding towns.

Other stories of the burial ground are more ghostly in nature. Many of these tales speak of strange lights and apparitions in the vicinity of the graveyard and the woods beyond it. In the forest, there are a number of forgotten graves that have been hidden by time. There are also anecdotes concerning the old road that leads back to the cemetery, namely stories of a bobbing red light and a spectral old man who vanishes if anyone tries to approach him.

In addition to the many stories told by visitors to Williamsburg Hill, there are also the incidents that occur involving those who still live here. Many of them will state that strange things happen here on a daily basis, as if the landmark that rises from nowhere out of the prairie acts as some sort of signal beacon, or magnet, for strange activity. Past accounts tell of ghostly figures on the roadways, animal mutilations and unexplained lights in the sky. So what makes Williamsburg Hill so strange and haunted and why has it been the source for so many legends over the years?

It's possible that the huge microwave tower on the hill could offer some clues, even if some of the stories were already being told before the tower was ever built. Could some of the phenomena be attributed to the tower? Is it possible that the strange lights, glowing balls of energy and eerie apparitions are some sort of side effect from the magnetic field around this structure? It has also been suggested that the tower may be attracting the paranormal phenomena, instead of creating it. Perhaps lost spirits are feeding off the energy given off by the tower, resulting in the myriad of stories that plague the place?

Or maybe, as was suggested earlier, the strangeness was already here, attracted by the natural landscape of the hill? Who knows? Regardless, if any of the numerous stories about Williamsburg Hill have even a semblance of truth to them, then the place is infested with ghosts!

Taylor, Troy - Haunted Illinois (2001)

Williamsburg Hill and Ridge Cemetery are located near Tower Hill in South Central Illinois.

Worth

An often visited grave is located in the Chicago suburb of Worth and at Holy Sepulchre Cemetery. It is said to have mysterious benevolent properties. In fact, it is said be able to heal the sick and the dying. Many people feel that this is a sacred place and is made so because the grave holds the final remains of a young girl named Mary Alice Quinn. Over the years, hundreds have claimed to experience miraculous healings here, while others speak of strange occurrences that can only be paranormal in nature. Because of this, Mary's grave and tombstone have been the subject of visits by religious pilgrims and supernatural enthusiasts alike.

Mary was a quiet child who died suddenly in 1935, when she was only 14. Born in 1920, she was one of three children of Daniel and Alice Quinn. As a young girl, she was diagnosed with a heart condition and became devoutly religious, devoted to St. Theresa, who claimed to have a mystical experience when she saw a religious image appear on her wall. After that, she became known in her neighborhood for curing the sick. While on her deathbed, Mary told her parents that she wanted to come back and help people after her death. The faithful say that she has done just that. Soon after her death, she was said to have mysteriously appeared to a number of people in the Chicago area. Throughout the 1930's and 1940's, it was not uncommon to hear of new Mary Alice Quinn sightings.

On one occasion, a sick nun at Mary Alice's former school claimed that she was visited by an apparition of the girl and cured. Others who claimed to see her said that her apparition had a glowing veil over her face. This was attributed to being a "veil of grace", a supernatural manifestation that is found in cases of people who are saints. Witnesses also began to tell of the spectral scent of roses that surrounded the healings and the apparition sightings. This is noteworthy because of Mary Alice's devotion to St. Theresa, whose motto had been "I will let fall from heaven a shower of roses." For years after their daughter's death, Daniel and Alice Quinn hoped that the numerous reports of healings and strange phenomena attached to their daughter would attract the attention of the Catholic Church and that the girl might someday be considered for sainthood herself. They distributed literature and holy cards and helped to provide documentation for the few articles that were written about Mary Alice in Catholic journals.

And while there has been no official interest from the church, Mary Alice's following continues to grow among believers. Today, her healing powers are said to have taken on another manifestation and one that surrounds her grave marker. When she passed away, she was secretly buried in a cemetery plot that belonged to the Reilly family. It was thought that this might keep her burial place a secret and prevent the graveyard from being overrun by curiosity seekers intent on finding her resting place. Word soon spread though and a gravestone was eventually cut with her name on it. Since that time, thousands have come to the site, many of them bringing prayer tokens, rosaries, coins and photos to leave as offerings and to ask that Mary intercede for them in prayer. Many claim to have been healed of their afflictions after visiting the grave and others have been healed by extension. They claim to have found relief from one of the many spoonfuls of dirt that has been taken from Mary's burial site.

Strangely, the phantom scent of roses has been reported filling the air around the gravestone, even when there are no roses anywhere around. The smell is said to be especially strong in the winter months, when the scent of fresh roses would be impossible to mistake. Many visitors have alleged this smell over the years and some of them even say that it is overwhelming. The faithful claim that this unexplainable odor is proof that Mary's spirit is still nearby and interceding on their behalf. Her love and charity continues, even decades after her death.

Taylor, Troy - Haunted Chicago (2003)

The cemetery is located west of Cicero Avenue, between 111th and 115th Streets in Worth, a southwest suburb of Chicago.

Other Haunted Illinois Cemeteries

The Fairmount Hills Cemetery (Willow Springs) is located along Archer Avenue and is across the street from a restaurant and former speakeasy, which legend has it, was once operated by crime boss Al Capone. The club was said to have been populated by gangsters and bootleggers and an escape route was allegedly located in the basement that allowed the mobsters to run out through a tunnel in case the police showed up. The stories had it that the tunnel exited across the street in the Fairmount Hills Cemetery and most specifically, in the White Mausoleum that was located here. The mausoleum itself was the source of many rumors and stories over the years, as it was believed to be haunted. Visitors to the cemetery often claimed that the sound of music could be heard coming from inside of the locked tomb. But could the ghostly music have actually been sounds that were coming through the escape tunnel from across the street? The stories of the tunnel have never been proven but strangely (just before this writing) the restaurant was closed down and drug charges were filed against many of the staff members. At the same time, the White Mausoleum was inexplicably torn down by cemetery officials and the foundation filled with concrete. Were the stories true after all?

A very unusual grave marker can be found in St. Omer Cemetery (Ashmore). This monument, which has the shape of a ball on it, is said to be the gravesite of a witch who was killed many years ago. In order to keep her in her grave, the death date that was inscribed on the stone was February 31. Over the years, stories have circulated that claim the stone will give off an unearthly glow on certain nights. I have seen nothing to validate this part of the story -- but the unusual date is authentic!

Oak Hill Cemetery (Taylorville) is home to a stone that refuses to stay still. The monument was constructed around 1910 and bears the family names of Richardson and Adams. It is not an unusually unique monument, as there are many like it in cemeteries across America. It is simply a large marble ball that has been placed on top of a pedestal at the center of a family plot. It is so nondescript that it has been a forgotten ornament in this cemetery for many years. Then, local people began to notice that it moved. The stone ball, which weighs several hundred pounds, is set into a granite base and is not designed to rotate. Somehow though, it has managed to move and has turned to expose the rough bottom of the sphere. It was at this spot where workmen attempted to seal the stone to the base. Caretakers were puzzled. It would take several men with pry bars to move the granite ball and yet somehow, it has happened -- and it continues to move today. Visitors to the cemetery can see where the rough, round area at the bottom of the sphere has become visible, thanks to the movement of the stone. They can also return to the cemetery on another occasion and see the rough spot facing in another direction.

Indiana

Bloomington Area

Elements of folklore and the supernatural pervade the story of one of the most famous haunted cemeteries in the state of Indiana. Located off of Old State Highway 37 in the

Morgan-Monroe State Forest is a small, abandoned cemetery around which a number of eerie legends have appeared.

It is called Stepp Cemetery and it is a desolate and lonely place that can be found at the end of a narrow, dirt trail that winds back into a veritable wilderness. Such a place would have long been forgotten if it wasn't for the weird tales that are still told about it. Only two dozen of so grave markers remain here and all of them are old and crumbling, as no one has been buried in this tiny graveyard in decades. Along the southern edge of the grounds is a row of tombstones and nearby is a worn tree stump that looks to be vaguely in the shape of a chair.

Depending on which version of the Stepp Cemetery legend that you hear, one of these graves seems to be the focus of the paranormal activity in the cemetery. The stories vary, but one part of them all stays the same -- each of them tells of a ghostly woman who watches over the gravesite, and the cemetery, in the darkest hours of the night. Over the years, scores of people have claimed that she is seen in the darkness, seated on the old tree stump that is found nearby. There, she waits silently, watching over and protecting the grave of her loved one.

The history of this cemetery is nearly as mysterious as the ghost who is found here. No one really seems to know when the burial ground was started, or by whom. Forest rangers will tell visitors that some area families founded it, but local rumors state that a now defunct religious cult called the "Crabbites" may have had some connection to it. Apparently, this peculiar sect conducted services that included snake handling, speaking in tongues and sex orgies. Local lore has it that a deputy from the area once stated that he had been called to the cemetery late one night to break up a particularly bizarre Crabbite ritual. The story says that he had to use a bullwhip to settle things down.

The legend of the spectral woman is just as strange. It tells of a young woman who came to the region from the east. Her husband went to work in one of the local quarries and they settled down and had a daughter. One afternoon, her husband was killed in a dynamite explosion at the quarry and was buried in Stepp Cemetery. After that, her daughter became her entire life and she watched over her constantly as she got older, attended school and later met a young man of her own. But unfortunately, her happiness was not to be. One rainy night, when coming home from a date, the young couple was killed in auto accident. In a repetition of the earlier tragedy, the daughter too was buried in Steep Cemetery. Her mother would never recover from the girl's death.

Soon, she began to make nightly treks to the cemetery, where she would sit for hours, talking to her dead husband and daughter as if they were still alive. An old tree stump that was near to the graves made a comfortable, makeshift chair for her visits. It was here where locals who passed by the cemetery began to see a woman in black sitting and weeping as the sun fell from the sky. It was said that if anyone approached her, she would run away and hide in the woods and would not return until they had gone. Soon, local residents began to avoid the graveyard, as it was believed the woman was crazy.

Eventually, she too died and, according to the legend, was also buried in Stepp Cemetery. Her spirit is still said to be restless today though, lingering in the graveyard and watching over the remains of her family. Many people believe that her ghost can still be seen at Stepp on nights of the full moon, when the woman in black returns to the stump and is visible to those of us still among the living. Those who doubt the legend to be true should take into account the many strange sightings that have taken place over the years. The most chilling encounters take place when visitors leave the cemetery shaken after having seen a black figure rise from the old tree stump and turn toward them in the darkness. The descriptions they give of the woman in black are strikingly similar as well. She is said to have long, white hair, although she is not old, but rather the color was bleached from her hair by shock.

Those who do not see the mournful apparition still often have their own tales to tell. It has been said that strange sounds sometimes emanate from the cemetery grounds. Law enforcement officials and park rangers are said to have received reports of a woman sobbing in the cemetery at night. When they go to check and see if anyone is injured or ill, they find that no one is there.

While the stories have changed many times over the years, it does seem possible that the story of the woman in black may have been based on a real event that occurred many years ago. True or not though, Stepp Cemetery has become a landmark in the Morgan-Monroe State Forest and is a popular stop for ghost hunters, curiosity-seekers and those with an interest in eerie folklore.

Many of those who come here wonder if the story of the ghostly woman can be true? Perhaps the story is just a compelling piece of Hoosier folklore, or perhaps not. Those who are convinced that the tale is merely the creation of someone's imagination often confess to a feeling of doubt when they see the twisted tree stump that looks remarkably like a chair on the far side of the cemetery. If the old stump truly exists, they ponder, can they woman in black exist as well?

Marimen, Mark - Haunted Indiana (1997)
Taylor, Troy - Beyond the Grave (2001)

Steep Cemetery is located outside of Bloomington and the entrance is located next to a curved stone wall at the side of Old State Highway 37 in the Morgan-Monroe State Forest. A dirt path leads back to the cemetery.

Terre Haute

In addition to being the resting place of Martin Sheets and his mausoleum, as described in an earlier chapter of the book, Highland Lawn Cemetery is also a place where one of the great graveyard legends of the region can be found. If you happen to be in the area around this cemetery at night, and hear a dog bark, you may just be hearing the legendary voice of Stiffy Green, Indiana's favorite graveyard ghost.

In the early 1900's, Stiffy Green was a familiar character around Terre Haute. He was the constant companion of a man named John Heinl, an elderly gentleman who was well-liked in town. He too was familiar figure as he strolled about the city each day in the company of his little bulldog. Stiffy Green was so named thanks to his unusual, stiff-legged walk and the fact that he had startling, green-colored eyes. The little dog was friendly, yet fiercely protective of his master, never allowing strangers to get too close.

In 1920, John Heinl passed away. While his death was a cause for sadness in the community, no one was hit harder by it than Stiffy Green. The poor creature was heartbroken and he refused to leave his master's side, even during the funeral services and after Heinl was entombed at Highland Lawn. Eventually though, two of Heinl's friends decided to take in the dog and care for him. They took him to their house in Terre Haute and introduced him to his new home.

Within a few days, Stiffy Green had gone missing. He was found a few hours later lying in front of the door to the Heinl mausoleum, silently watching over his master's burial place. John's friend placed a leash on the dog and took him back home again but less than a week later, the dog was missing once more. He was always discovered again, several miles away, in the cemetery. Over the next month or so, this became a standard routine. If the dog could not be found around the house anywhere, his new owners always knew where he was. Eventually, they just gave up and let Stiffy Green take up residence in the graveyard. They brought him food and water and allowed him to stay there.

Not long after this, they began to realize that the dog was not eating. He paid little attention to the bowl of water either, preferring to sit nearly motionless at the entrance to the tomb, barring anyone from entering it. He stayed there in the rain and cold and never shirked what he seemed to feel was his duty. And it was there, on the cold stone step, that the body of Stiffy Green was eventually found.

As word of the loyal dog's death spread, Heinl's friend pondered what to do with the animal's body. They certainly didn't want to simply dispose of their friend's constant companion but they weren't certain he should be entombed as a human would be either. Finally, they reached a compromise. A fund was established and the dog's body was taken to a local taxidermist. The dog was then stuffed and mounted into the sitting position that he had maintained outside of the tomb for so many months. His eyes were left open and his bright green eyes were replaced with glass ones that managed to capture the gleam of the originals. When the task was completed, Stiffy Green was placed inside of the Heinl tomb, right next to the crypt that held the remains of his beloved companion.

And seemingly, this would be where our story ends -- but it's not.

Several months after Stiffy Green's death, a caretaker was leaving the cemetery on a warm evening. Just as he was opening the door to his car, he heard the bark of a dog from the direction of the Heinl mausoleum. Thinking that something about this seemed odd, he decided to go and have a look. As he neared the tomb, the sound got louder and then he suddenly realized why the bark seemed so strange, and so eerily familiar. He had heard this dog barking before. It was the bark of Stiffy Green!

But that was impossible, he realized, the poor animal had died many months ago. The bark must have been his imagination, he decided and walked back to his car. He would think no more about this until other people started to report the same barking from the area around the tomb.... and they would report something else too.

According to the legends, many people have heard the barking of a small dog in Highland Lawn Cemetery in the evening hours. It always seems to come from the direction of the Heinl mausoleum. A few of them have also reported that Stiffy Green does not wander the cemetery alone. They also claim to have seen the figure of an elderly man strolling along between the tombstones, sometimes smoking a pipe and sometimes just smiling as he looks away into the distance. While the old man's description sometimes varies, the witnesses never disagree about the fact that he is always accompanied by a small stiff-legged bulldog -- with piercing green eyes.

Marimen, Mark - Haunted Indiana (1997)
Taylor, Troy - Beyond the Grave (2001)

Terre Haute is located in western Indiana, just off Interstate 70. The cemetery is located east of town on Wabash Avenue.

Other Haunted Indiana Cemeteries

Gypsy Cemetery (Northwest Indiana) is located in a remote and secluded area and is not listed here with directions in order to prevent any further vandalism and trespassing at the site. The site is actively haunted though and has a peculiar legend attached to it. While the truth behind the legend is debatable, it is regarded as a genuinely haunted place. As with many such locations, it's possible that the legend was created to explain the very real happenings that occur here.

The story goes that the cemetery was started sometime in the 1820's by a band of local gypsies who made the small piece of land their temporary home. The gypsies had caused some trouble with the local townspeople, which led to the locals telling the leader of the gypsies that they had two days to leave. Since this was the time of an influenza outbreak, the leader had argued that they were unable to move because their people were ill but the townspeople demanded that they pack up and depart. When the deadline was up, a number of locals journeyed to the site to see if the gypsies had disbanded. To their surprise, they had found a makeshift cemetery. The gypsies had departed, but they had left behind their dead. Since that time, the local populace has taken over the small cemetery.

Over the last several decades, there have been many odd occurrences reported here. Perhaps one of the strangest is the story of a campfire that is sometimes seen from the street and that disappears and reappears. When investigated the next day, there are no remains of a fire ever there. In addition, balls of light that are blue in color are said to chase passing cars and then vanish without a trace. A number of unusual photographs been taken here as well.

Park Cemetery (Fairmount) draws thousands of people to it every year. They don't come looking for ghosts though but rather to visit the grave of American movie idol James Dean, who was buried here in his hometown after being tragically killed in his Porsche in 1955. Dean's grave is a simple one and many fans take home handfuls of dirt with them from the site. In addition, many claim that the ghost of Dean is often sensed and witnessed near his grave.

Iowa

Iowa City

Oakland Cemetery is the location of one of the most famous "cursed" grave monuments in American history. For those who have grown up in the area, a nighttime visit to the "Black Angel" is almost a rite of passage, a necessary part of growing up and facing your darkest fears. To many, who can often recite dark tales of the "Angel", the story is little more than a local legend. However, the Black Angel does have a very real history -- and according to some, there is reason to be afraid of her!

Teresa Feldevert commissioned the bronze statue in 1911 as a monument for both her husband Nicholas and her teenaged son, Eddie. Many consider it to be one of the greatest works of art in the area, having been created by Daniel Chester French, the same sculptor responsible for the gigantic statue of Abraham Lincoln at the memorial in Washington.

Yet, despite the artistry, the gleaming bronze memorial weathered and darkened to a foreboding black color. All attempts to restore the nine-foot tall figure with outstretched wings have failed miserably. The black remains and according to legend, grows a shade blacker every Halloween. No one knows how the stories of death and curses got started, but perhaps they came about because of the appearance of the statue itself. The eyes of the figure are truly eerie with swirled irises that seem to bulge from the blankness of the rest of the eye. They seem to stare at the visitor from beneath strangely drooping eyelids -- an effect that can be unnerving at best.

Many years ago, stories began to be told of this bronze creature. It seems that anyone who touches the statue risks the pain of death, except for virgins, who are reportedly immune to her power. It is also said that vandals who have attempted to deface the monument have come down with mysterious, and sometimes fatal, ailments. A number of people have told personal stories of the angel over the years, most of them recounting apparitions spotted in the cemetery, strange sights and sounds around the monument and stories of those who have tempted fate, seeking out proof of the paranormal, only to vanish without a trace. Some claim that looking directly into the mysterious eyes of the Angel at midnight will result in a fatal curse upon the gazer. Others maintain that the curse is transmitted only if a person actually touches the statue. Still, concrete accounts of anyone being cursed are nonexistent at best.

One of the most popular stories told concerns a group of young men who tested the supposed "evil powers" of the site by urinating on the angel. As the legend holds, they were involved in a four-car accident later that night. Truth or fiction?

One has to wonder if there is any truth to these legends at all? It's doubtful, but who can really say for sure? As nearly every legend has some basis in fact, I can't help but wonder (once again) how this story got started in the first place.

Taylor, Troy - Beyond the Grave (2001)

Iowa City is located in the southeast part of Iowa and the cemetery is located at 1000 Brown Street.

Ottumwa

The Mars Hill Church and cemetery are located near Ottumwa, Iowa. The church was built in 1850 and is said to be one of the oldest, still operating, churches in the state. The congregation meets here once each year as the church is in a very remote and secluded location. The area of the church and the cemetery has been the scene of much vandalism and desecration over the years and is it also said to have been used by occult groups for ritual ceremonies. American Ghost Society Representative Nancy Napier traveled to Mars Hill in July 1998 and reported that some evidence of occult practice did exist and she found many gravestones that were stained with rings of candle wax. As in many other locations where such activity has been reported, stories of ghosts and hauntings abound here as well.

Before arriving at the church and cemetery, visitors cross a narrow bridge, which has it's own story. It is said that many years ago, a young woman had her baby baptized in the church and then for some reason, walked to the bridge and threw in into the water, drowning the child. Legends say that on certain nights, you can hear the sound of a scream while crossing the bridge.

The cemetery is located southeast of Ottumwa. Follow Route 63 south and then left onto Copperland Road. Turn right on 100th Avenue and watch for the cemetery entrance on the left side.

Washta

There is a sinister tale to tell about one of the tombstones located in the Washta Graveyard. The story of this tombstone dates back to the early 1900's and centers around an elderly couple named Heinrich and Olga Schultz and their mysterious farm hand, Will Florence. The old couple owned and operated a small farm outside of town and they were well liked in the community. Schultz had hired Will Florence during the haying season, despite the fact that many of his friends and neighbors were suspicious of the stranger.

There was no clue as to where Florence had come from and the man revealed little information about himself. He did say that he had been recovering from some medical problems in Texas and while he claimed to have worked outdoors in the past, he was clumsy and obviously inexperienced at farm work. Schultz continued to show the man kindness though and he patiently instructed him with his chores. Unfortunately, Florence repaid that kindness with murder.

One day, word came to the farm that failure was eminent at the bank in town. Fearing for his savings, Schultz went into Washta and withdrew most of his money. On his way out of town, Schultz waved a friendly greeting to one of his neighbors and that was the last time he was seen alive.

Three days later, a friend decided to check on the old couple because no one recalled seeing them for several days. He stopped by the house and opened the front door to find Heinrich and Olga lying on the kitchen floor in a huge pool of blood. Both were dead and their heads had been split open by an ax. The house had been wrecked and all of the money withdrawn from the bank was gone. And so was Will Florence...

The authorities were quickly notified and Florence was tracked down a few days later in Nebraska. He was arrested and returned to Washta for questioning. Convinced of his guilt, the local prosecutor convened a grand jury and pushed for an indictment. Sadly, there was just not enough evidence to hold him for the crime and the officials were forced to let him go. He vanished from town and was never seen again.

A short time later, a strange story began making the rounds in Washta. It was said that a face was starting to appear on the tombstone of Heinrich and Olga Schultz. Many believed that it was the face of their murderer. To make matters even more intriguing, those who saw it swore that it was the face of Will Florence. The story was told and re-told and people flocked to the cemetery to see the gravestone. More and more of them, some grudgingly, admitted that the cloudy face that was forming in the stone appeared to be that of Florence. Was it the power of suggestion, or was the tombstone somehow changing to show the face of the man who killed the elderly couple?

A marble dealer was brought to the cemetery to examine the stone and try to explain what was happening to it. He reported that the features were developing because of "atmospheric influences of the rust and veins in the marble". He predicted that the face would grow plainer, and it did. He believed that the strange event was caused by perfectly natural means, but local folks weren't so sure.

Finally, after much urging, two police detectives agreed to visit the cemetery and examine the stone. They soon returned with other officers. Even the most skeptical of them agreed that the face in the marble did resemble Will Florence. That was enough to convince them to take a closer look at the case. When they did, they discovered new evidence that had been overlooked the first time. The new evidence solidly implicated Will Florence and a warrant was put out for his arrest. He was never found though -- Florence simply vanished from the pages of history. I would like to think that he got just what he deserved. I'd also like to think that whatever happened to him took place at just about the same time that his face was being stamped on the tombstone of Heinrich and Olga Schultz.

Scott, Beth & Michael Norman - Haunted Heartland (1985)
Taylor, Troy - Beyond the Grave (2001)

Washta is located in the northwest portion of Iowa and the hillside burial ground can be found in Cherokee County, near Washta.

Other Haunted Iowa Cemeteries

The Oak Hill Cemetery (Cedar Rapids) is said to be haunted by the ghost of a young Czech girl named Tillie, who was buried in the potter's field section of the graveyard many years ago. She is most often seen walking through the gravestones carrying a flickering candle but some stories do circulate that claim she has tried to pull people inside of some of the mausoleums here on occasion.

The Lutheran Cemetery (Milford) has a strange bend in the fence that surrounds it that many have attributed to an unnatural, perhaps paranormal, energy. In the early 1900's, a maintenance crew that was putting up the fence on the cemetery border found that a strange force prevented them from their work. Shovels bent, tools broke and the ground simply refused to be turned as they were trying to sink one of the fence posts. The frustrated men finally brought in heavier equipment and dug up the entire section, only to find that an unrecorded burial had taken place at the fence line. Today, the west fence of the cemetery turns at the fourth post to avoid the haunted piece of ground.

Kansas

Alma

Stories and legends surround the Alma Cemetery, which was, according to one of the stories, once the property of a local farmer who was urged to sell the place to the town for a burial ground. The farmer continually refused and finally, one day as he was drawing water from his well, he slipped and fell (or was pushed) in and he drowned. The stories say that the local sheriff covered up the incident and the land became the local graveyard soon after. The legends say that the farmer's vengeful ghost has been here ever since and that he enacts his revenge on those who come here through a "devil's chair".

The story of a so-called "devil's chair" is not a new one and it is certainly not limited to this one cemetery. It is one of the most enduring of the graveyard legends and involves the stone seats that can be found in scattered graveyards in mostly the Midwest and Great Plains regions. Many people accept the stories connected to these chairs as factual, offering second-hand reports and accounts as proof.

The story of the "Devil's Chair", or at least the modern version of it, began in the

Appalachian Mountains of the middle 1800's. Legend had it that on certain nights, a chair would rise from the ground in the local graveyard. Anyone who sat down in this chair could make a pact with the Devil and receive his or her heart's desire for the next seven years. At the end of that time, the Devil would return and take the hapless victim's soul. The legend has changed and modified over the years, taking on a more simple mythology. The stories now state that if you sit down in one of these chairs, you are sure to die within the next year. Whether or not such a statement is true is not for me to say, although most of the chairs that are mistaken for "Devil's Chairs" have nothing to do with the supernatural. Most of these chairs are simply what were called "mourning chairs" during the Victorian era. They were usually placed next to the grave of the recently deceased by a relative, creating a more comfortable place to sit when visiting the grave site.

The story of the chair in the Alma Cemetery has been tied into the ghost of the farmer who once owned this land, making it both a chilling and localized version of the story.

Alma is located in the central part of the state, between Manhattan and Topeka.

Lawrence Area

There are graveyards across America that defy all definitions of a "haunted cemetery". They are places that go beyond the legends of merely being haunted and enter into the realm of the diabolical. They are places said to be so terrifying that the Devil himself holds court with his worshippers there -- and in the case of Stull Cemetery in Kansas, is one of the "gateways to hell" itself!

But just how terrifying are these places? While there are few of us who would challenge the supernatural presence of a place like Bachelor's Grove, there are some who claim that Stull Cemetery does not deserve the blood-curdling reputation that it has gained over the years.

Stull Cemetery, and the abandoned church that once rested next to it, is located in the tiny, nearly forgotten Kansas town of Stull. There is not much left of the tiny village, save for a few houses, the newer church and about twenty residents. However, the population of the place allegedly contains a number of residents that are from beyond this earth. In addition to its human inhabitants, the town is also home to a number of legends and strange tales that are linked to the crumbling old church and the overgrown cemetery that can be found atop Stull's Emmanuel Hill. For years, stories of witchcraft, ghosts and supernatural happenings have surrounded the old graveyard. It is a place that some claim is one of the "seven gateways to hell."

The legends say that these stories have been linked to Stull for more than 100 years, but none of them made it into print until the 1970's. In November 1974, an article appeared in the University of Kansas student newspaper that spoke of a number of strange occurrences in the Stull churchyard. According to the article, Stull was "haunted by legends of diabolical, supernatural happenings" and the legends asserted that the cemetery was one of the two places on earth where the devil appears in person two times each year. It said that the cemetery had been the source of many legends in the area, stories that had been told and re-told for over a century. The piece also went on to say that most students learned of Stull's diabolical reputation from their grand-parents and older individuals, but that many of them claimed first-hand encounters with things that could not explain. One student claimed to have been grabbed by the arm by something unseen, while others spoke of unexplained memory loss when visiting the place. Like many other locations of this type, the tales of devil worship and witchcraft also figured strongly into the article. But were the stories actually true?

Not according to the residents of Stull, who claimed to have never even heard the stories before. They were bemused, annoyed and downright angered that such things were being said about their town. The pastor of the new church in Stull, located right across the road from the old one, indicated that he believed the stories to be the invention of students at the university.

But such stories have a strong hold on people, as evidenced by the reaction to the article that claimed that the devil would appear in Stull Cemetery on the night of the Spring Equinox and again on Halloween. On March 20, 1978, more than 150 people waited in the cemetery for the arrival of the devil. The word also spread that the spirits of those who died violent deaths, and were buried there, would return from the grave. Unfortunately, the only spirits that showed up that night came in bottles and cans -- but this did not stop the stories from spreading.

All through the 1980's and up until today, stories have been told about Stull Cemetery and as time has passed, most have grown more horrifying and hard to believe. The problem seems to be that the cemetery has a lack of real, documented accounts of strange activity. The weird tales seem to be little more that "urban legends" and second-hand stories from teenagers and college students.

The legends say that the Devil has been appearing here since the 1850's and insist that the original name of the town was "Skull" and that the later corruption of that into "Stull" was simply to cover the fact that the area was steeped in black magic. It was said that the witchcraft-practicing early settlers were so repentant about their past deeds that they changed the name of the town. In truth, the town was called "Deer Creek Community" until 1899, when the last name of the first postmaster, Sylvester Stull, was adopted as the name of the village. The post office closed down in 1903, but the name stuck.

In 1980, an article appeared in the *Kansas City Times* that added further fuel to the rumors about Stull Cemetery and the abandoned church. The article was quoted as saying that the Devil chose two places to appear on Earth every Halloween. One of them was the "tumbleweed hamlet" of Stull, Kansas and the other, which occurs simultaneously at midnight, is someplace on the "desolate plain of India." From these sites, according to the article, the Devil gathers all the people who died violent deaths over the past year for a prance around the Earth at the witching hour.

But why in Stull? The article adds that he appears in Stull because of an event that took place in the 1850's, when "a stable hand allegedly stabbed the mayor to death in the cemetery's old stone barn. Years later, the barn was converted into a church, which in turn was gutted by fire. A decaying wooden crucifix that still hands from one wall is thought to sometimes turn upside-down when passersby step into the building at midnight..." The story neglects to mention that, historically speaking, neither the Deer Creek Community nor Stull have ever had an official mayor.

One of the strangest stories about Stull supposedly appeared in *Time* magazine (it didn't) in either 1993 or 1995 (depending on the version you hear). This story claims that Pope John Paul II allegedly ordered his private plane to fly around eastern Kansas while on his way to a public appearance in Colorado. The reason for this, the story claims, was that the Pope did not want to fly over "unholy ground".

The legends grew and by 1989, the crowd at the graveyard on Halloween night had become so overwhelming that the Douglas County sheriff's department had to station deputies outside to send people on their way. They handed out tickets for criminal trespass to anyone caught on the property. It was believed that nearly 500 people came to the cemetery on Halloween night of 1988, doing damage to the church and gravestones, prompting a police response the following year.

As time passed, the local residents grew more irritated that vandals and trespassers were wreaking havoc in the cemetery where their loved ones and ancestors were buried. Finally, a chain link security fence was installed around the grounds and although the area is still regularly patrolled, the visits have died down somewhat, at least outside of October. In addition, there have been the signs posted against trespassing here and locals have made it clear that visitors are not welcome.

So, what about the stories? Were they true or the work of some student writer's imagination? Is the cemetery at Stull really haunted -- or is the "haunting" merely the result of an "urban legend" gone berserk? That's a hard question to answer. Although undoubtedly the vast majority of the tales about the cemetery have been manufactured from horror fiction, they still beg that now-familiar question of how such stories got started in the first place? Is there any truth to the stories at all?

We have no idea and local residents are not talking. Strangely, although property owners have spoken out against both vandals and the macabre stories, they have done little to try and end the legends for good. Why chase away those who come to the cemetery at midnight on Halloween to see the Devil appear? Why not simply "control the chaos" and allow the curiosity-seekers to see that no spirits will run rampant on that fateful night? On Halloween night of 1999, reporters from a local newspaper and a television news crew joined a group of onlookers at the cemetery. Sheriff's deputies were on hand, but did not ask anyone to leave until 11:30pm. At precisely this moment, an unknown representative for the cemetery owners appeared and ordered everyone to leave the property. The officers had no choice but to go along with their wishes and the reporters and spectators had to leave. As Stull Cemetery and the land around it is private property, there was no option but to comply. The owners stated, through the representative, that they did not want media attention brought to the graveyard because it attracts vandals. But couldn't they have furthered their cause by allowing the camera crew to show that the Devil did not appear at midnight, thus debunking the legend forever?

In April 2002, the stories of the place took another twist. According to the Lawrence newspaper, the *Journal-World*, the old stone church was mysterious torn down on Friday, March 29, 2002. The building had been standing vacant 1922 and it has been badly damaged by vandalism over the years. In 1996, the remnants of the roof blew off and a few years later, a large crack also opened in one of the stone walls after the church was struck by lightning. It remained standing though until it was destroyed in 2002. A man named Major Weiss, who owns the property, along with two other people (who he declined to name) said that he did not authorize the abandoned church to be destroyed. Those who live nearby stated that they were also unaware of the demolition, although one of them did say that a wall of the church had collapsed about two weeks before. As of this writing, the mystery of who destroyed the old church remains unsolved!

Heitz, Lisa Hefner - Haunted Kansas (1997)
Taylor, Troy - Beyond the Grave (2001)

The town of Stull is located about ten miles west of Lawrence, Kansas in the northeast part of the state. It can be found by traveling west on Route 40 and then traveling straight west to Stull. The town can be found on the northwestern edge of Clinton Lake and close to the Clinton State Park. Visitors to the cemetery are advised to go there at their own risk.

Topeka

One of the strangest legends of Kansas is that of the Albino Woman who haunts the Rochester Cemetery in Topeka. Over the course of at least three generations, she has been a figure of terror to residents of Topeka, north of the Kansas River.

This ghostly woman has long been a part of local lore and the Albino Woman is said to be a startling apparition with white skin, red-rimmed eyes and tangled pure-white hair that falls to her waist. She is usually seen wearing a long white dress and is often accompanied by a dog. She wanders the area surrounding Rochester Cemetery and has also been seen along back roads and in isolated spots in the vicinity. But who is she? No one really seems to know, although older residents of North Topeka recall a real albino lady who lived and worked in the area in the 1930's and 1940's. In addition, people who live near Rochester Cemetery also remember a "crazy lady" with white hair who lived in the neighborhood for some time. Many believe these two individuals may have "merged" to create the stories that are still told today about a supernatural being.

The stories of the Albino Woman have changed many times over the years. In the early accounts, she was always seen as a benign figure, a wandering soul who may have been a real person but was seen as an outcast because of the odd way that she looked. It was always said that she roamed the streets, never talking to anyone, and that in the mornings, she stood in her yard and silently watched the children pass by on her way to school. A woman named Mrs. Cook, a resident of Lower Silver Lake Road, once told a reporter that an albino woman lived next door to her at one time and that neighbors largely avoided her because of her unfriendly demeanor. The local children often taunted the woman, although they were deathly afraid of her. Mrs. Cook added that the woman had lived alone and had no relatives.

The very real albino woman died in 1963 and after that, the stories of the legendary creature took a different turn. These new tales had the Albino Woman as a ghostly apparition. Stories emerged from people who claimed to see her white figure drifting along roadways at night. The sightings usually occurred on a route from the Seaman district to the cemetery where the woman was buried.

On April 11, 1966, a man named Paul Bribbens reported that a white ghost appeared in the front yard of his home along this same road. "It kept talking in a woman's low monotone," he said. "I couldn't make out a word of it. Like she was stark raving mad or something." Paul's dogs, at the sight of the apparition, climbed underneath his front porch and could not be coaxed out. Bribbens called the sheriff's department, but by the time the officers arrived, the ghost had vanished.

Reports continued to come in from area residents, visitors and people who worked in the neighborhood. They stated that a "glowing white woman" was walking the streets at night. Several employees of the local Goodyear Tire Factory and the Boy's Industrial School saw the ghost regularly as it walked along the banks of Soldier Creek. A long-time Topeka resident, who lived just west of the school on Highway 24, reported that whenever the ghost came near, "everything would become very quiet". He said that animals in the vicinity always seemed to know it first and would cower in fear. He warned others about being out alone and on foot when the Albino Woman was nearby.

The ghost was also sighted quite often in Rochester Cemetery, but in the 1970's and 1980's, the stories changed again. Up until this point, the ghost of the Albino Woman had always been a little frightening, but never threatening or violent. All that was about to change though. She had now become a more terrifying apparition and malevolent in her actions. The legend now incorporated the idea that she was searching for her lost children. If she didn't find her own though, well, anyone's children would do!

The fearsome spirit was said to be attacking and scaring young couples parked in cars too. They would often be terrified by a rapid tapping on the window, only to look up and seen a white, red-eyed face on the other side of the glass. Often, motors stalled and headlights failed when the ghost was lurking nearby, which could prove hazardous to the drivers and passengers in the automobile.

In recent times, the legend of the Albino Woman has faded somewhat. Perhaps people have started to realize the changing versions of the story have the ring of the true "urban legend" or perhaps the ghostly woman herself has indeed moved on. Who knows? Regardless, the Albino Woman will always be at least a small part of the ghostly lore of Kansas.

Heitz, Lisa Hefner - Haunted Kansas (1997)
Scott, Beth & Michael Norman - Haunted Heartland (1985)
Taylor, Troy - Beyond the Grave (2001)

Sightings of the Albino Woman have occurred on Lower Silver Lake Road and Rochester Road, as well as at Rochester Cemetery. The area is surrounded by Soldier Creek, a Goodyear plant, a boy's school and Lower Silver Lake Road.

Kentucky

Bardstown

The Federal Hill Cemetery in Bardstown is the site of a moving gravestone that seems to be influenced by the spirit of the man who is buried beneath it. It is located here in Bardstown and it has acquired a rather unusual legend over the last 150 years.

This stone is placed over the grave of John Rowan, one of historic America's most prominent men. He was a state judge in Kentucky, served seven terms in the legislature and was elected to the United States Senate. He was also Kentucky's Secretary of State and the chief justice for the court of appeals. His cousin, Stephen Foster, is probably the best remembered songwriter of the 1800's and Rowan's former mansion, Federal Hill, is now a popular tourist attraction. It was at Federal Hill that foster wrote "My Old Kentucky Home" and the house was given this nickname many years ago.

Tragedy plagued Rowan throughout his life. When he was a boy, he was so sickly that his family never expected him to live very long. Hoping that the robust country might invigorate the puny child, Rowan's father, William Rowan, moved the family west to Kentucky. Here, enrolled in Dr. James Priestly's school, John began to thrive and not only improved physically but intellectually as well. He became a brilliant scholar and studied law in Lexington and was a well-known lawyer by 1795. A few years earlier, Rowan met Ann Lytle and the two married. The land on which Federal Hill was constructed was deeded to Rowan by his father-in-law in

1794. Throughout the early 1800's, the Rowans hosted a number of dignitaries, including Henry Clay, James K. Polk, James Monroe and others.

Tragedy came to Federal Hill in July 1833 when four members of the Rowan family and 26 slaves died during a cholera epidemic. Rowan's oldest son, John, had just been appointed as Secretary of State for President Andrew Jackson. He had stopped at Federal Hill to pay a visit to his family on the way to Washington. Unfortunately, he came down with cholera and died with the others.

When Rowan died in July of 1843, he expressly stated that he wished to have no monument or stone placed on his grave site. He felt that since his parents had been buried without grave markers, he would be disrespecting their memories if he were given an honor they had not received. He felt that his home at Federal Hill stood as more than enough monument to his memory. His family and friends ignored this request however, believing that such a great and prominent man deserved a suitable marker to grace his final resting place. He was buried in Bardstown Cemetery, then later moved to Federal Hill Cemetery (near his home) and a tall, obelisk-shaped stone was placed at the site.

A short time after work was completed and the monument was placed at the site, it suddenly toppled over for no apparent reason. Members of the family, already disturbed by the talk that had gone around about the controversial marker, quickly summoned a stonemason to repair the marker and put it back into place. The workmen were puzzled by how the stone could have fallen. Someone suggested that perhaps the ground had settled or that tree roots had knocked the stone over. They hesitantly agreed, but remained unconvinced. Soon after, rumors began to circulate about the stone's mysterious movements.

Within a month or two, the masons received word that their services were needed once more. John Rowan's gravestone had again fallen over. Several of the workmen refused to return to the cemetery. The stone was fixed, but soon after, it fell over again. It tumbled off its base and fell directly onto the ground where Rowan lay. More rumors began to spread that the unhappy spirit of John Rowan had returned and was knocking over the marker that he had not wanted placed there in the first place. It continued to fall over on a regular basis and finally, frightened stone masons refused to return to the cemetery at all. Repair of the stone was left in the hands of the cemetery workers.

Inexplicably, workmen and caretakers are still trying to keep the stone in place today. It continues to fall over for no apparent reason. Why? No one seems to know, but it's just possible that John Rowan meant exactly what he stated in his will -- that he forbid a monumental stone of any kind to be placed on his grave!

Taylor, Troy - Beyond the Grave (2001)

Bardstown is about thirty miles south of Louisville, Kentucky, which is just over the Southern Indiana border.

Pikeville

There is said to be a spirit who looms over Pikeville, Kentucky and she has become such a part of the lore of the city, and surrounding Pike County, that students at nearby Pikeville College can tell you a dozen different versions of how this ghost died, how she lived and how she makes her spectral presence known in the local graveyard. Unfortunately, few of these stories are actually true - the truth may be much more frightening - but there are those who maintain that the ghost of a young woman named Octavia Hatcher still haunts this place. And since her death in 1891, has never rested in peace.

Pike County, Kentucky is nestled in the hills that rise to meet the Appalachian Mountains. It is a secluded region in the extreme southeastern corner of Kentucky and it is rich in coal, hardwood timber and the medicinal herbs of the mountain region. It is also rich in the lore, history and legend of the area as well. It was in Pike County that the famous Hatfield-McCoy Feud took place, which has appeared in books, magazines and on film throughout the years.

But the Hatfield's and the McCoy's were only two of the prominent families in the Pike County region and were far from the only clan to leave a lasting impact on Pikesville and the surrounding area. Perhaps Pikeville's most important family was that of the Hatcher family, which was founded in the area by James Hatcher.

James Hatcher (or Uncle Jim) as he was known later in life, was a wealthy land owner and prominent business figure in the Pikeville region. He was one of nine children born in September 1859 to A.J. and Mary C. Layne Hatcher at the mouth of Beaver Creek in Floyd County. He moved to Pikeville early in life and attended school there.

Hatcher entered into business in Pikeville at the age of 18 and opened a warehouse for good brought in on the river. At one time, he handled nearly all of the merchandise that was hipped via steamer to the city. He became associated with several other businessmen in building a steamer called the "Mountain Girl", which was considered the finest boat on the river - but also one of the biggest financial failures as well. Hatcher never let this deter him however and he also went into the contracting business, which led to his erecting the courthouse in Pikeville in 1886.

Hatcher also became a pioneer in the southeastern Kentucky timber business, long before the coming of the railroads and before coal was discovered in the area. He used hundreds of rafts to float lumber down the Big Sandy River to the Ohio and then on to markets in Cincinnati, Louisville and Evansville. Much of his profit was invested in land and he soon became one of the largest individual landowners in the valley. He later opened the James Hatcher Coal Co. and accumulated great wealth in this industry as well. He also became a prominent figure in Democratic political circles, served a term as the Clerk of the Pike County Court and in 1932, was elected railroad commissioner for the district.

In 1931, he opened the Hotel Hatcher on Main Street in Pikeville and it became known as one of the showplaces of the Big Sandy river region. The spacious lobby of the place included a museum that displayed ox-yokes, ancient hand-made furniture, antique weapons and utensils used by the early settlers. The lobby also boasted a huge fireplace and the walls were covered with historical photos, illustrations, maps and information about Pike and Floyd Counties.

James Hatcher passed away in his home next to the Hotel Hatcher in October 1939. He had been ill for several weeks, having just celebrated his 80th birthday. The funeral was held at the hotel and scores of his friends and relatives were in attendance, as was Kentucky Governor A.B. Chandler, Lieutenant Governor Keen Johnson and a number of other state officials.

Hatcher was buried in the family plot at Pikeville Cemetery, in a casket that he had especially constructed for him. There is no indication as to what specifications the coffin had been designed with but one has to wonder if it might have had some sort of safety release that would allow the person inside to escape in the event of premature burial. As the reader will soon see, Hatcher had every reason to be plagued by this fear....

In 1889, at the age of 30, James Hatcher was married in Pikeville to a young woman named Octavia Smith, the daughter of Jacob Smith, an early settler. Their life together would be tragically brief and their union would produce one son, Jacob, who was born shortly before his mother died. The baby died soon after he was born, possibly leading to the depression and illness that preceded Octavia's own death.

And it is the death of Octavia Hatcher that has created a legend that is still very much a part of Pikeville. The Hatcher baby, Jacob, was born in January 1891 and only lived for a few days before he died. A short time later, Octavia took to her bed, likely suffering from depression, and was quite ill. The illness took a turn for the worse in April of that same year and she slipped into a coma. The doctors were unable to determine a cause for it and when she died on May 2, it was thought that she had perished from an unknown illness.

The funeral services were held and almost immediately carried out. It was an unseasonably hot spring and as Octavia was not embalmed , no was time was wasted in placing her in her grave at the Hatcher family plot. James had just suffered a terrible double tragedy -- but his grief was not yet over.

Several days after Octavia's death, several other people began suffering from the same coma-like symptoms that Octavia exhibited at the time of her death. The illness was apparently a sort of sleeping sickness that was brought on by the bite of a certain fly. When news of this began to spread, Hatcher and members of his family (some of them doctors) began to worry that this may have been the same illness that Octavia had contracted. Their fears turned to panic as they realized that she may have been buried alive.

An emergency exhumation was conducted and Octavia's casket was opened. They found the poor young woman in a horrific state. Apparently, the coffin had not been airtight and she had managed to survive for a few days, trapped beneath the ground. The lining on the lid of the coffin had been torn and shredded by Octavia's bloody nails and her face had been scratched and contorted into an expression of terror. She must have awakened from her sleep to find herself trapped in the casket. Then, unable to escape, she had undoubtedly succumbed to a terrifying death!

Octavia was reburied but James' heart was broken. He had a expensive monument erected on the site, a tall stone that bears a likeness of Octavia standing atop it. At one time, a carving of her baby had been placed in the statue's arm, but in more recent times, vandals have managed to break the arm off and the infant lies on the ground next to the marker.

As the years passed, the strange and unsettling story of Octavia Hatcher's final moments began to be told and re-told in Pikeville. Eventually, as is the case with many legends, the story was twisted and changed until much of the truth was lost. The most commonly told revision of the story had it that Octavia had died while she was still pregnant. The story went that, during the funeral, the mourners heard an odd sound coming from inside of the coffin. When they opened the lid, they found that the baby, Jacob, had been born to the dead woman. He only lived a short time and then died himself. Obviously, this story is untrue and a glance at the Hatcher family gravesite would reveal that Jacob's death preceded Octavia's by several months.

As the story of Octavia Hatcher continued to spread, the tale took on a more "urban legend" quality. Students from the college and teenagers from around the area often went to the cemetery on Halloween night to drink and scare one another. They claimed that the statue would come to life on certain nights and frighten trespassers out of the graveyard. It was during this period that someone broke off the arm that held the stone infant.

Pranksters also went to the trouble of climbing onto the monument to bother the statue themselves. This gave birth to yet another, and perhaps most popular, version of the story. According to this version, Octavia's spirit was angry at the people of Pikeville for allowing her to be buried alive. Because of this, she would literally turn her back on the city on the anniversary of her death. On these nights, the statue mounted on her grave marker would turn on its pedestal and would face the opposite direction from where it had been previously. This story was accepted as truth for many years until it was finally revealed that the nocturnal movements were the work of clever college students.

Even after story after story about Octavia was debunked, this never seemed to quell the rumors that spread about the cemetery being haunted. People who visited the site, and most especially, those who lived on the hill where the graveyard was located, often spoke of hearing strange cries in the darkness and about spotting a misty apparition in the vicinity of Octavia's grave. Finally, in the middle 1990's, the Hatcher family placed a stone in the cemetery that contained accurate information about Octavia's death and placed her statue on a new marble base. They also enclosed the area with a fence, hoping to keep out the trespassers and vandals.

And while the additions to the gravesite have managed to keep out the unwanted, they have done nothing to curb the continued stories of ghosts and supernatural manifestations around the plot. Many people who live on the hill near the cemetery tell of strange incidents that take place in the cemetery. Many of them expressed a fear to come into the graveyard, especially at night, and there is a solid belief that the ghost of Octavia Hatcher still walks here. One couple, who had lived nearby for more than 30 years, stated that they had noticed something very odd in recent months. According to their account, they heard the sound of woman weeping, coming from the direction of the burial plot on several nights. A check of the area revealed absolutely no one in the cemetery.

Another couple, who had moved to the neighborhood a short time before, said that they were told by others in the community to expect parties and trespassers in the cemetery at night but that they had yet to see anyone around. However, one evening they walked out into the graveyard themselves because they thought they heard a kitten crying in the darkness. As they approached the Hatcher plot, where the sounds were coming from, the crying stopped.

So, does the ghost of Octavia Hatcher walk in the Pikeville Cemetery? Or are the stories nothing more than local myths? According to a number of reliable witnesses, unexplained things still take place around the place where her life ended in terror. Could witnesses who claim to feel depressed and anxious around the grave be experiencing the young woman's final moments? Or is the apparitions reported around the grave the spirit of Octavia as she still searches for peace?

That is, of course, up to the reader to decide, but if you ever get the chance to visit the Pikeville Cemetery, you should visit this site for yourself. Haunted or not, this is a place where a tragic young woman deserves a moment or two of silent recognition for a life cut too short and a death that came far too early.

Taylor, Troy & Herma Shelton - The Legend of Octavia Hatcher: The Girl Who Turned Her Back on Pikeville (2002)

Pulaski County

One haunted graveyard rests on a hillside in Pulaski County. According to old-timers in the area, this burial ground holds the grave of a witch. Visitors here will find the grave to be isolated from the rest of the stones here and an iron fence with a gate surrounds it. The old, weather-beaten tombstone bears the name of Katherine Tyler. She died, it reads, in 1899 at the age of only nineteen.

A large oak tree has grown up alongside the fence, its roots twisting and gnarling toward Katherine's gravestone. The tree's branches also reach out for the grave of another, located a few yards away from the enclosure. This gravesite belongs to John Tyler, Katherine's father, and the man who abandoned her not long after the death of her mother.

Katherine gained her reputation as a "witch" when she was about twelve years old. She began making predictions about her neighbors, which came eerily true, and seemed to possess the power to read minds. She always seemed to know when a farm animal was going to get sick or die, when crops would fail, what neighbor was going to have an accident and other things that no ordinary child would know. Not surprisingly, soon after Katherine began to exhibit her strange gifts, people began to avoid the Tyler farm and talk among some of the locals turned threatening. Fearful, John Tyler abandoned his daughter and his farm and left the area. He would not return until after her death.

Katherine began to spend more and more time alone. She walked and wandered in the woods for hours and even days at a time. The stories said that the animals were not afraid of her and that she became a part of the forest herself. Gradually, as time passed, her hair grew long and her eyes wild and feral. The Tyler farm slowly crumbled and so did Katherine's mind. It was said that neglect and loneliness caused her to go insane.

As her sanity slipped away, strange things began to happen in the neighborhood. Cows refused to give milk, crops failed, farm animals died for no reason, large snakes, of an unknown species, were seen and huge birds began to appear in the area. After a few years of these unnatural occurrences, the superstitious locals decided that Katherine was a witch. They were determined to either drive her out of the area, or kill her. They would do anything to save their farms and homes.

A group of men gathered one night and they went out to the old Tyler farm. The house and the outbuildings had fallen into disrepair over the past several years and now lay huddled at the edge of an overgrown clearing. No lights burned in the windows of the house. They called out for Katherine, but she did not appear. Gathering their courage, they broke open the door and went inside. What they discovered makes this particular story even stranger....

They found Katherine inside of the house. She was dead and her body was lying on the bed. Strangely, the frightening wild woman was gone and had been replaced by an angelic-looking young woman who was dressed in beautiful, expensive clothing that no one had seen before. It was as if Katherine had, in her death, turned back the hands of time and the past seven years had been erased. No one ever learned what caused her death, or how the change to her appearance had taken place.

Because of their fear, the locals refused to have Katherine buried in the local graveyard. When John Tyler learned of his daughter's death, he returned to the area and buried her, with his own hands, a few yards outside of the graveyard. It was he who built the iron fence around the site but it was the locals who erected the pointed gravestone over her resting place. This type of stone is said to be the indication that a witch is buried there.

The stories go on to say that the oak tree over Katherine's grave began to grow a few months after her burial. They say that the long limb of the tree that reaches out toward the grave of John Tyler is a manifestation of the girl's love for the father who abandoned her. She still reaches out to him, they say, from beyond the grave.

Taylor, Troy - Beyond the Grave (2001)

Pulaski County is located in the south central part of the state.

Other Haunted Kentucky Cemeteries

Oak Grove Cemetery (Paducah) is said to be haunted by a young woman named Della Barnes. Legend has it that she was murdered by her fiancée in a jealous fit of rage and that he cut off her finger to retrieve the expensive engagement ring that he had given her. History tells another story though -- that she was accidentally poisoned by a doctor who was treating her. Her ghost has walked her ever since, wandering through the cemetery, carrying a small, glowing light. She vanishes whenever she is approached.

Ridge Cemetery (Glasgow) is said to be haunted by the ghosts of two feuding brothers who killed one another in an argument in the graveyard back in the 1880's. Their ghosts are still believed to haunt the place and locals say that they make their presence known with the sound of a small, tinkling bell.

Louisiana

Metairie

Located on the outskirts of New Orleans is a place called Metairie Cemetery and it has always been known as the most fashionable burial ground in the city. It became the epitome of the classic Victorian graveyard, which was far removed from the jumbled chaos of graveyards in New Orleans. Originally a racetrack, the grounds were converted to their present use in 1873 by Charles T. Howard, president of both the New Orleans Racing Association and the Louisiana State Lottery. The circle of the racecourse became the main drive of the cemetery and other roads were laid out, ponds were dug and flowers and trees were planted. Metairie remains an opulent park-like cemetery and holds the grave and tombs of the wealthiest people in the city. It now serves as the final resting place as not only famous local citizens but also a number of Confederate leaders as well, including General Pierre Beauregard, General Richard Taylor, General Fred N. Ogden and General John Bell Hood. At one time, Jefferson Davis was also buried here, but his body was removed.

The most interesting tomb in Metairie does not belong to any Confederate leader or wealthy politician. However, it does belong to "royalty"-- to Josie Arlington, the once reigning Queen of Storyville. For years, the tomb of Josie Deubler, also known as Josie Arlington, has attracted more people to Metairie than any other monument in the cemetery. In fact, curious crowds have sometimes forced police officers to remain all night on the spot to maintain order.

During the heyday of the Storyville district, Josie was the most colorful and infamous madam of New Orleans. In this center of vice is where Josie operated her house of ill repute and became very rich. The house was known as the finest bordello in the district, stocked with beautiful women, fine liquor, wonderful food and exotic drugs. The women were all dressed in expensive French lingerie and entertained the cream of New Orleans society. Many of the men who came to Josie's were politicians, judges, lawyers, bankers, doctors and even city officials. She had the friendship of some of the most influential men in the city, but was denied the one thing she really wanted -- social acceptance.

She was shunned by the families of the city and even publicly ignored by the men she knew so well. Her money and charm meant nothing to the society circles of New Orleans. But what Josie could not have in life, she would have in death. She got her revenge on the society snobs by electing to be buried in the most fashionable cemetery in New Orleans, Metairie Cemetery. She purchased a plot on a small hill and had erected a red marble tomb, topped by two blazing pillars. On the steps of the tomb was placed a bronze statue that ascended the staircase with a bouquet of roses in the crook of her arm. The tomb was an amazing piece of funerary art, designed by an eminent architect named Albert Weiblen, and cost Josie a small fortune. Although from the scandal it created, it was well worth it in her eyes.

Tongues wagged all over the city and people, mostly women, complained that Josie should not be allowed to be buried in Metairie. There was nothing they could do to stop her though and nothing was ever said to Josie's face. The construction of the tomb had achieved just what she had wanted it to do -- it had gotten the people's attention!

No sooner had the tomb been finished in 1911, than a strange story began making the rounds. Some curiosity-seekers had gone out to see the tomb and upon their arrival one evening, were greeted with a sight that sent them running. The tomb seemed to burst into flames before their very eyes. The smooth red marble shimmered with fire, and the tendrils of flame appeared to snake over the surface like shiny phantoms. The word quickly spread and people came in droves to witness the bizarre sight. The cemetery was overrun with people every evening, which shocked the cemetery caretakers and the families of those buried on the grounds. Scandal followed Josie even to her death.

Josie passed away in 1914 and was interred in the "flaming tomb", as it was often referred to. Soon, an alarming number of sightseers began to report another weird event, in addition to the glowing tomb. Many swore they had actually seen the statue on the front steps move. Even two of the cemetery gravediggers, a Mr. Todkins and a Mr. Anthony, swore they had witnessed the statue leaving her post and moving around the tomb. They claimed to follow her one night, only to see her suddenly disappear. There were also two occasions when the statue may have traveled about the graveyard. According to records, she was found both times in other parts of the cemetery. Most blamed vandals, but the legends say otherwise.

There were also stories told by people who lived in the vicinity of the cemetery. They claimed that the statue of the "Maiden" would sometimes become angry and begin pounding on the door of the crypt. This spectral pounding would create a din that could be heard for blocks. Anyone who asked about the noises would be told that it was the Maiden "trying to get in." The story was that Josie had lived by a certain rule regarding her bordello in Storyville. The rule was that no virgins would ever be allowed to enter her establishment. The stories say that she placed the statue of the Maiden on the steps of the tomb to symbolize this lifelong code of honor.

Others say that the statue is Josie herself. As a young girl, she stayed out too late, the stories say, and her father locked her out of the house. Even though she pounded on the door and pleaded with him, he would never allow her to enter again. After that, she went away and began a career that made her one of the richest women in New Orleans. Still others agreed that the statue may be Josie Arlington, but they say it symbolizes Josie as an outsider to the society circles that she always wanted to be inside of. They say that no matter hard she "knocked", the doors would never open for her.

The tradition of the flaming tomb has been kept alive for many years, although most claim the phenomena was created by a nearby streetlight that would sway in the wind. Regardless, no one has ever been able to provide an explanation for the eyewitness accounts of the "living" statue.

Taylor, Troy - Haunted New Orleans (2000)

Metairie Cemetery is located in the town of Metairie, a suburb of New Orleans. The cemetery can be found off of Interstate 10, coming into the city.

New Orleans

The cemeteries of New Orleans are much like the city itself. The graveyards are a mirror to the opulence and desecration of a mysterious and enchanting city. As one of America's most haunted cities, New Orleans has perhaps more than its share of ghosts. The cemeteries of this historic place boast not only hauntings, but strange stories as well. Perhaps the most terrifying tales center on New Orleans' most infamous graveyard, St. Louis Cemetery No. 1.

The cemetery was created because of the decay and overcrowding of the city's earlier burial grounds. St. Louis Cemetery No. 1 was officially opened in 1789. The new cemetery was a walled enclosure with its main entrance off Rampart Street. The poor were buried here in unmarked graves until the middle 1800's and as available space filled, the level of the soil began to sink. Contracts for dirt were frequently bid upon and city chain gangs shoveled it evenly throughout the graveyard, making room for more bodies. It is believed that beneath the grounds of the cemetery, there are layers of bones several feet thick.

For all but the indigent, above ground tombs were the rule. The reasons were obvious as the wet ground of Louisiana caused the graves to fill with water. The coffins would often float to the surface, despite gravediggers placing heavy stones or bricks on the lids. Such conditions made funerals a somewhat terrifying affair. Caskets were often lowered into gurgling pools of water and oozing mud. As often as not, the coffin would capsize as the water began to leak in, causing newly buried and half-decomposed cadavers to float to the surface of the grave. There are a number of different types of tombs in the cemetery, from family crypts to society tombs to the "oven vaults" that are located inside of the cemetery walls themselves. The tombs are often used and re-used over a period of years by different members of the same family. They are closely crowded together inside of this walled cemetery, creating narrow paths and cornered avenues that can become an eerie maze after darkness falls.

While the cemetery holds the tombs of many famous former citizens and notable of New Orleans, perhaps the most famous person buried anywhere in the cemetery is Marie Laveau. Despite long-running controversies as to whether or not Marie is really buried here, the tomb is the most frequently visited site in the graveyard. It has been generally accepted as her burial place and generations of curiosity-seekers and Voodoo devotees have visited the crypt. Many of them have left offerings behind that include anything from coins, to pieces of herb, beans, bones, bags, flowers, tokens and just about anything else. All of them are hoping for good luck and the blessings of the Voodoo Queen.

The actual religion of Voodoo, or "Voudon", originated from the ancient practices of Africa. Voodoo came about most likely in Santo Domingo (modern day Haiti) where slaves devoted rituals to the power of nature and the spirits of the dead. For many enslaved Africans, such spiritual traditions provided a means of emotional and spiritual resistance to the hardships of life. In time, slaves from the Caribbean were brought to New Orleans and they brought Voodoo with them.

These slaves, most of whom spoke no French, had brought with them their religions, beliefs, charms and spells from Africa and Haiti, but soon learned that they were forbidden to practice their own religions by their masters. Many of them were baptized into the Catholic Church and later, the use of these Catholic icons would play a major role in their new religion of Voodoo. These icons would take their place in the Voodoo hierarchy and be worshipped as if they were praying to the God of the Catholic Church. Many of the Catholic saints would become "stand-ins" for important Voodoo deities and if you go into a Voodoo shop today, you will see statues, candles and icons depicting various Catholic images. There are in fact, Voodoo symbols as well.

Soon after the introduction of the African slaves to New Orleans, Voodoo began to play a major part in the traditions, and fears, of the general populace. It was not long before the white colonists also began to hear of it and to feel its power. Soon, Voodoo was firmly entrenched in the culture of New Orleans. The religion was practiced by the slaves and the free blacks as well and so strong was the power held by the upper echelons of the religion that they could entice their followers to any crime, and any deed. Whether or not these priests held supernatural power or not, the subtle powers of suggestion and of secret drugs made Voodoo a force to be reckoned with.

Marie Laveau was the undisputed Queen of Voodoo in the city. During her lifetime, she was the source of hundreds of tales of terror and wonder in New Orleans. She was born on Santo Domingo in 1794. Her father was white and she was born a free woman. The first record of her in New Orleans was in 1819, when she married Jacques Paris, another free black. He died in 1826 and Marie formed a liaison with Christophe Glapion, with whom she had she bore a daughter, also named Marie, in February 1827. During her long life (she lived until 1881) she gave birth to fifteen children.

That same year, Marie embraced the power of Voodoo and became the queen of the forbidden but widely practiced culture. She was a hairdresser by trade and this allowed her access to many fashionable homes in the city. In this way, she and her daughters had access to an intelligence network that gave Marie her "psychic" powers. She knew everything that was going on in the city just by listening to her customers tell of gossip and scandals.

Marie became a legend in New Orleans. She dealt in spells and charms, for both white and black customers, and produced "gris-gris" bags to cure their ailments. The small bags would be filled with an assortment of magical items and curative roots and could be used to work both good and bad magic. She was a clever and astute businesswoman who knew how to use her beliefs, and the beliefs and fears of others, to her own advantage.

Marie died in June of 1881 but many people never realized that she was gone. Her daughter stepped in and took her place and continued her traditions for decades to follow. Today, Marie and her daughter still reign over the shadowy world of New Orleans Voodoo from the confines of St. Louis Cemetery No. 1. Both are entombed in this cemetery in two-tiered, white stone structure. Or are they?

The actual site where Marie Laveau's remains are located has been the subject of controversy for many years. Most believe the crypt in St. Louis Cemetery No. 1 holds the bodies of Marie and her daughter, Marie II, but there are many others who do not think so. You see, there is also a "Marie Laveau Tomb" in St. Louis Cemetery No. 2. There are also tales that claim Marie is buried somewhere else altogether, including Girod Street Cemetery, Louisa Street Cemetery and Holt Cemetery.

Some believe the confusion started after the body that was originally buried in the Laveau tomb was later moved. It is said that Marie was first buried in St. Louis Cemetery No. 1 but that her spirit "refused to behave". People became so scared that they refused to go near the cemetery so another priestess, Madame Legendre, and some relatives, moved Marie to Holt Cemetery. She was re-buried in an unmarked grave so that her name would not be remembered. The ghost stayed put from that point on, the story said, but her name has yet to be forgotten.

Regardless, New Orleans tradition holds that Marie is buried in St. Louis Cemetery No. 1 and literally thousands have come here in search of her crypt. The tomb looks like so many others in this cluttered cemetery, until you notice the markings and crosses that have been drawn on the stones. Apart from these marks, you will also see coins, pieces of herb, bottles of rum, beans, bones, bags, flowers, tokens and all manner of things left behind in an offering for the good luck and blessings of the Voodoo Queen.

But does Marie's spirit really rest in peace? Many believe that Marie returns to life once each year to lead the faithful in worship on St. John's Eve. It is also said that her ghost has been seen in the cemetery and is always recognizable thanks to the "tignon", the seven-knotted handkerchief that she wears. It is also said that Marie's former home at 1020 St. Ann Street is also haunted. Many claim that they have seen the spirit of Marie, and her ghostly followers, engaged in Voodoo ceremonies there.

Perhaps the most unusual sighting of Marie's spirit took place in the 1930's when a man claimed to be in a drug store near St. Louis Cemetery No. 1. He was speaking to the druggist when an old woman in a white dress and a blue tignon came and stood next to him. Suddenly, the druggist was no longer listening to him, but looking in terrible fear at the old woman instead. Then, he turned and ran to the back of the store. The man turned and looked at the old woman and she started laughing "like crazy", he said. He thought that perhaps the druggist had been frightened of this "poor crazy woman" who lived in the neighborhood. Finally, the woman looked at the man and asked if he knew her. He replied that he didn't and she laughed some more. Then, she turned and looked behind the counter. "Where the drugstore man go at", she questioned the young man, now seeming very angry. He shrugged and at that, she slapped him across the face. Moments later, she turned and ran out the door and, to his shock and surprise, vanished over the cemetery wall. Stunned, the man then stated that he "passed out cold".

When he woke up, the druggist was pouring whiskey down his throat. "You know who that was?" he asked the man but the other was still unable to talk. "That was Marie Laveau. She been dead for years and years but every once in awhile people around here see her. Son, you been slapped by the Queen of Voodoos!"

Another tale of the cemetery, and Marie Laveau, springs from the 1930's. According to the story, a drifter with no money or prospects decided to sleep in the cemetery one night. He scaled a tomb and slept fitfully for several hours before being awakened by a strange sound. Thinking that perhaps vandals or grave robbers would injure him, he decided to make his escape to the streets. As he rounded the corner of a row of crypts, he saw a terrible sight. Positioned in front of Marie Laveau's tomb was a glowing, nude woman with her body entwined by a serpent. Surrounding her were the ghostly forms of men and women, dancing in mad but silent abandon. Needless to say, the drifter fled for his life.

But is Marie Laveau the only restless ghost of St. Louis Cemetery No. 1? Many don't believe that she is because one of the most famous "vanishing hitchhiker" stories in the South is connected to this graveyard. The stories also say that in the 1930's, New Orleans taxi cabs avoided St. Louis Cemetery No. 1 whenever possible -- or at least they never stopped to pick up a young woman in white who hailed them from the graveyard's entrance!

One driver had picked up just such a young girl one night and drove her to the address that she gave him. Once they arrived, she asked him to go up and ring the bell, then inquire for the man who lived there. The man came out, but when the driver told him of the girl waiting in the cab, he immediately asked for her description. When the driver described the girl to him, the man shook his head sadly. This was obviously not the first time that a driver had appeared on his doorstep. The young girl, he explained to the taxi driver, was his wife -- but she had died many years ago and had been interred wearing her bridal gown at St. Louis Cemetery No. 1. That was when the driver suddenly realized the white gown the woman was wearing had been a wedding dress!

He raced back to the cab and jerked open the door but the woman was gone. The driver fainted away on the spot. After that, young women in white stood little chance of hailing a cab near the entrance to the graveyard. And some say they still don't stand a chance today!

Taylor, Troy - Haunted New Orleans (2000)

St. Louis Cemetery No. 1 is located at the edge of the French Quarter in New Orleans but is not safe to be in after dark. This is a dangerous area of the city, next to several housing projects, and even during the daylight hours, visitors are only encouraged to go here in groups.

Maine

Bucksport

The Bucksport Cemetery is said to be haunted by a spirit from an event that allegedly happened long ago and it is said this spirit left her mark on the tombstone of the man who condemned her to death. The tombstone is extremely hard to miss in this cemetery. It stands nearly fifteen feet high and is clearly visible from the gates to the graveyard. An inscription on the side marks this as the final resting place of Col. Jonathan Buck, who founded the city of Bucksport, and who lived between 1719 and 1795. Apparently, soon after Colonel Buck's descendants erected this monument in 1852, a strange image appeared on the stone. It seemed to be the image of a human leg and it marked the monument just below the name "Buck". Despite attempts to remove it, the mark remained vivid to anyone who came to the cemetery.

How this mark came to be on the grave of Colonel Buck is a part of the lore and legend of the area and will forever be a mystery. There are several versions of the story and all of them end with Colonel Buck being cursed for his alleged misdeeds. What is presented here is perhaps the most popular of the stories but the reader is asked to judge the veracity of this tale for himself. What we do know is that Colonel Buck was born in Massachusetts and gained his military title during the American Revolution. He moved to Maine before the war and founded the city of Bucksport around 1762.

One version of the Buck legend, the "Witch's Curse", comes from his earlier life in Massachusetts. A woman had been accused of being a witch and Colonel Buck was asked to preside over her trial. It was a quick and dirty affair that ended with the woman being found guilty and sentenced to death. The woman, whose name was Ida Black, swore to Colonel Buck before she was hanged that she would return from the grave. She vowed that her ghost would come back to dance on the grave of the man who had accused her of the crime. Colonel Buck, apparently a superstitious man, took this threat very seriously and never forgot it.

Years passed and Colonel Buck died in 1795. A half century later, the large marker was constructed for him in the cemetery. The stories say that a short time after, on the anniversary of Ida Black's death, the blood-red image of a woman's dancing leg first appeared on the grave marker. Where it had come from, no one knew. The stone was sanded and cleaned over a dozen times -- but it was no use, the image remained. Rumors started that Ida Black had fulfilled her promise after all.

According to local lore, the Buck family had the tombstone replaced two times, but the macabre blemish always appeared on the new stone. Finally, his descendants gave up and allowed the final stone to remain. The grave marker of Jonathan Buck can still be seen today, resting in the Bucksport Cemetery and still bearing either the mark of Ida Black's dancing foot -- or an unusual blemish in the stone. It all depends on the version of the story that you hear.

Taylor, Troy - Beyond the Grave (2001)

Bucksport is located on the central coast of Maine, about 20 miles south of Bangor. The Bucksport Cemetery is located on Highway 1, just outside of town.

Damariscotta

An unusual story comes from the little New England town of Damariscotta, Maine and concerns a woman named Mary Howe, a woman that many people believe was buried alive.

Mary's family had originally come to Maine after the War of 1812. Her father, Colonel Joel Howe came up from Massachusetts and settled into the sleepy little village. He brought with him his wife and his five daughters and four sons and they opened up Howe's Tavern, a popular local spot and stagecoach stop that attracted a lot of business to town.

Besides being hard working, the family also became known for being a bit on the eccentric side. Edwin's sister, Mary, was also known for being a bit strange. One day, she decided that she possessed the ability to fly. Reportedly, she climbed to the top of the stairs, spread her arms and then fell down the steps, managing to get pretty banged up and breaking an ankle. Not long after this, Mary, the rest of the Howe family and many of the townspeople, became interested in Spiritualism. The family soon began trying their hands at contacting the dead but of all the children, Mary seemed to have a real gift at spirit communication. She was able to go into trances and see and speak with ghosts in a way that no one else could.

When word of this got out, many friends and neighbors came around to see her. In time, thanks to the many travelers who passed through Howe's Tavern, word of Mary's séances spread beyond Damariscotta. Soon, people were coming from all over New England to see her performances.

Mary differed from other mediums in that when she went into a trance for her séances, she would often remain in a coma-like state long after it was over. It was said that she once stayed in a trance for several days and that she did not even breathe. Edwin Howe even stated that she gave no sign of a heartbeat. However, he did keep warm stones stacked around her body so that she would stay warm. Days after going into a trance, Mary would emerge from it and appear to be completely fine. Mary seemed to have little difficulty in communicating with the spirits and was known for avoiding generalities and for giving detailed information to the sitters who came to the séances.

In the summer of 1882, Mary slipped in a trance during a routine séance. At first, it seemed no different from the others, until more than a week went by and found her still asleep. Friends and family members began to worry and officials began to wonder if she might be dead. Edwin Howe played the situation for all that it was worth. He escorted the many hundreds of visitors through the house and gave detailed descriptions of what was happening (or rather, what wasn't happening) to Mary. The situation soon began to bother the local authorities and especially the members of the clergy.

Finally, they called in the local doctor, Dr. Robert Dixon, to examine Mary and see if she was still alive. Dr. Dixon, a family friend, faced the difficult task of examining the young girl. He admitted that she didn't look dead. Her body as warm and her limbs were pliable and although she had been lying there for a few weeks, there was no trace of rigor mortis. He even noted that there was no smell of decay. Still, as a medical man, Dr. Dixon could not ignore the fact that Mary wasn't breathing. He could also find no heartbeat. As much as he hated to say it, it was obvious that Mary had died. He issued an order to the constable and told him that it was necessary to seize Mary's body from the family and bury it.

In spite of the protests of Edwin and many other local people, the constable, the undertaker and several ministers came, prepared the body and carried it away. The undertaker set a funeral date but the day came and went, for no one would dig a grave for Mary. She was supposed to be buried in Hillside Cemetery, directly across the street from the tavern, but owner Benjamin Metcalf refused to give them a plot. Everyone hoped that if they delayed long enough, Mary would wake up and be saved from a premature grave. Officials were determined to see her buried however so they transported Mary's body to Glidden Cemetery in nearby Newcastle. They found a plot for her there but still could find no one to dig the grave. Eventually, the constable, the undertaker and one of the preachers had to dig the grave themselves.

The stories say that onlookers forced the men to open the coffin one last time before they lowered it into the hole. It was said that Mary was still warm and that her face had a lifelike color. Despite all of that, she still refused to breathe. The lid of the casket was closed and Mary was committed to the earth.

Although more than a century has passed, it remains a mystery as to whether or not Mary Howe was buried alive. Unfortunately, many believe that she was.

Mary's grave was never marked in Glidden Cemetery, in order to keep Edwin from coming there and digging her up, but that hasn't kept the stories from being told about the graveyard. For years, people avoided coming here at night. They heard stories from those who dared to wander about the grounds -- stories of cries, moans and sobs coming from below the earth. Others swear they have seen strange lights and misty figures wandering about. Is it the ghost of Mary Howe? Or perhaps it is the spirit of Edwin, still searching for the place where his sister was buried prematurely?

Taylor, Troy - Beyond the Grave (2001)

Other Haunted Maine Cemeteries

Strange sightings have taken place near the Chute Road Cemetery (Windham) of two young girls, who play at the edge of the road during the early morning hours. According to the legend, the ghostly girls fell down an old well many years ago and their bodies were never found. Their families placed markers in the cemetery regardless and the ghosts have been seen here ever since.

According to witnesses who were walking up a hill to a veteran's crypt in St. Mary's Cemetery (Salem), they were not only overwhelmed by a feeling of panic but they also spotted a grayish man watching them in the trees a short distance away. The man stood them for a few moments and then vanished before their eyes. Other witnesses have also reported glowing lights in the cemetery and always in the vicinity of this same hill.

There is a grave of a "witch" in the Old York Cemetery (York Village) and she has been haunting the cemetery since 1774. Mary Jason Miller was actually a herbalist who grew plants and created healing medicine for her neighbors and even exorcized evil spirits from their homes. Her spirit has been encountered in and around the cemetery since her death but no one has ever been frightened. In fact, her presence has even been known to push children on the swings at the playground across the road from the graveyard.

Maryland

Baltimore

Located in Baltimore is one of the most compelling cemeteries on the east coast, although many people are unaware that a portion of it even exists. It is called the Old Western Burial Ground and it holds the remains of people like Edgar Allan Poe, the son of Francis Scott Key, the grandfather of President James Buchanan, five former mayors of Baltimore and fifteen generals from the Revolutionary War and the War of 1812.

Not all of the cemetery is easy to find, for the Westminster Presbyterian Church (now Westminster Hall), was built over a large portion of the cemetery. These graves and tombs date back to a century before the church was built. Much of the cemetery, where Poe is buried, is still accessible above ground in the churchyard but a large portion of the graveyard can only be reached by way of the catacombs underneath the building. It is here where the ghosts of this eerie graveyard are said to walk. Strangely though, these restless spirits are not the most enduring mystery of the Western Burial Ground.

This famous and unsolved mystery involves a man who has been seen in the graveyard for more than fifty years. Whoever this strange figure may be, he is always described in the same way. Dressed completely in black, including a black fedora and a black scarf to hide his face, he carries a walking stick and strolls into the cemetery every year on January 19, the birth date of Edgar Allan Poe. On every occasion, he has left behind a bottle of cognac and three red roses on the gravesite of the late author. After placing these items with care, he then stands, tips his hat and walks away. The offerings always remain on the grave, although one year, they were accompanied by a note, bearing no signature, which read: "Edgar, I haven't forgotten you."

There have been many stories that claim the ghost of Edgar Allan Poe haunts his gravesite but the man in black seems to be quite tangible, although who he is remains a riddle. In addition, scholars and curiosity-seekers remain puzzled by the odd ritual he carries out and the significance of the items he leaves behind too. The roses and cognac have been brought to the cemetery every January since 1949 and yet no clue has been offered as to the origin or true meaning of the offerings.

The identity of the man has been an intriguing mystery for years. Many people, including Jeff Jerome, the curator of the nearby Edgar Allan Poe house, believe that there may be more than one person leaving the tributes. Jerome himself has seen a white-haired man while other observers have reported a man with black hair. Possibly, the second person may be the son of the man who originated the ritual. Regardless, Jerome has been quoted as saying that if he has his way, the man's identity will never be known. This is something that most Baltimore residents agree with. Jerome has received numerous telephone calls from people requesting that no attempt ever be made to approach the man.

For some time, rumors persisted that Jerome was the mysterious man in black, so in 1983, he invited 70 people to gather at the graveyard at midnight on January 19. They had a celebration in honor of the author's birthday with a glass of amontillado, a Spanish sherry featured in one of Poe's horror tales, and readings from the author's works. At about an hour past midnight, the celebrants were startled to see a man run through the cemetery in a black frock coat. He was fair-haired and carrying a walking stick and quickly disappeared around the cemetery's east wall. The roses and cognac were found on Poe's grave as usual.

Not in an effort to solve the mystery, but merely to enhance it, Jerome allowed a photographer to try and capture the elusive man on film. The photographer was backed by *LIFE* Magazine and was equipped with rented infrared night-vision photo equipment. A radio signal triggered the camera so that the photographer could remain out of sight. The picture appeared in the July 1990 issue of *LIFE* and showed the back of a heavyset man kneeling at Poe's grave. His face cannot really be seen and as it was shadowed by his black hat. No one else has ever been able to photograph the mysterious man again.

Legend has it that the ghost of Edgar Allan Poe has been seen near his grave and in the catacombs of the church. The author died mysteriously in Baltimore and thus came to be buried there. He had lived in the city years before, but had only been passing through when he perished under mysterious circumstances. At the time of his death, Poe had been on his way to New York to meet his beloved mother-in-law. He was bringing her back to Richmond, Virginia, where the author was to marry his childhood sweetheart. His first wife had perished from tuberculosis years before.

The trip came to a tragic conclusion when, four days after reaching Baltimore, Poe was found barely conscious and lying in a gutter on East Lombard Street. He was rushed to a hospital but he died a short time later.

The entire time in the hospital was spent with Poe crying and trembling and he once screamed the name "Reynolds" -- although who this could have been also remains a mystery. He died on October 7, 1849.

Some said Poe's death was caused by alcohol, others say that he was in a psychotic state and even rabies has been blamed. Other writers believe that he may have been drugged and murdered as the clothes that he wore were not his own and the walking stick he carried belonged to another man. There have been literally dozens of theories posed as to what caused Poe's death but no one will ever know for sure. Perhaps the fact that his death remains unexplained is the reason why Poe's ghost remains in the Old Western Burial Ground.

Without a doubt, while the mystery concerning Edgar Allan Poe is the most famous aspect of the Western Burial Ground, it is not the only one. The catacomb beneath the church holds secrets of its own. While restored and kept in good condition today, visitors to this place will still get an eerie chill as they walk about this gothic chamber of horrors. Graves and crypts hold the bodies of those long since deceased and yet stories of the not so distant past tell of unexplained disinterment and a strange fascination that drew a number of people to commit suicide here in the years between 1890 and 1920.

I was lucky enough to be able to visit this place a few years ago and found it to be both fascinating and spooky. While I had no supernatural encounters while roaming the catacombs and tunnels, others have not been so lucky. There are a number of stories told of visitors who have come here and who have felt icy spots that have no explanation, have felt the soft caress of unseen hands and have heard the startling whispers of voices that should not exist.

Guided tours of the subterranean cemetery are available on Sunday afternoons, but organized searches for ghosts here have been few. One outing, in August 1976, brought ten ghost hunters to the graveyard in search of the ghost of a little girl who has been reported here over the years. Robert Thompson, the leader of the group and at that time, behind a drive to restore the cemetery, stated that while the ghost hunters didn't spot the small spirit, the investigation did not come up empty. "We didn't see anything," he recalled in an interview, "but we sure heard things.... like footsteps. It scared the heck out of me is what it did".

Taylor, Troy - Beyond the Grave (2001)

The cemetery is located around and below Westminster Hall in downtown Baltimore at the corner of Fayette Street and Green Street.

Pikesville

When General Felix Agnus, the publisher of the Baltimore "American", died in the 1925, he was buried in Pikesville's Druid Ridge Cemetery, right outside of Baltimore. On his grave was placed a rather strange statue. It was a large, black mourning figure. The statue's creator (sort of), Augustus St. Gaudens, was said to have called her "Grief" but to legions of Baltimore residents, she was dubbed with a different name, "Black Aggie".

In the daylight hours, the figure was regarded as a beautiful addition to the graveyard art of the cemetery. The sculpture was copied from one of the premier artisans in Maryland at the turn-of-the-century and the statue was highly regarded -- at least until darkness fell and the legends began.

Augustus St. Gaudens was a premiere American sculptor of the late 1800's. One of his greatest pieces of work was a memorial for Marian Adams, the wife of Henry Adams. Marian, called "Clover" by her friends, had fallen into a dark depression after the death of her father in 1885. In December of that year, she committed suicide by drinking potassium. The statue was never officially named, known as the "Adams Memorial" and later as "Grief". The grave of Marian Adams became a popular site for the curious, especially as the statue was so unnerving to look at. The eerie statue of a woman covered in a shroud was such a draw to curiosity-seekers that it became the subject of an incredible piracy by a sculptor named Eduard L.A. Pausch. It would be from the original Adams design that the sculptor created his own, unauthorized copy of "Grief" in the early 1900's. The statue would later come to be known as the infamous "Black Aggie".

Within a few months of the statue being placed on Marian Adams' grave, Henry Adams reported that someone had apparently made a partial casting of the piece. He wrote to Edward Robinson in 1907 that "Even now, the head of the figure bears evident traces of some surreptitious casting, which the workmen did not even take the pains to wash off."

General Felix Agnus purchased the Pausch copy of the sculpture in 1905, perhaps after having admired the original work at the Adams grave. Why he decided to use the copy to grace his family tomb, instead of commissioning an original work of some sort, is unknown but perhaps something about the Pausch statue compelled him to own it. We will never know for sure.

Felix Agnus was born in France in 1839. At the age of only 13, he traveled around the world and at 20, fought in the army of Napoleon III against Austria and later served with General Garibaldi's forces in Italy. In 1860, he came to New York and went to work as a silver chaser and sculptor at Tiffany's. When the Civil War broke out, he enlisted as a private in the Union Army and began a war record so incredible that he was promoted to the rank of Brigadier General by age 26. He saw action in dozens of battles, including Big Bethel, Richmond, the Siege of Port Hudson and the Battle of Gaines' Mills. He was wounded more than 12 times by both bullet and saber. His friend, writer H.L. Mencken later said that Agnus "had so much lead in him that he rattled when he walked."

After a severe shoulder injury at Gaines' Mills, then Lieutenant Agnus was brought to Baltimore for treatment. There, he met Charles Carroll Fulton, the publisher of the Baltimore "American" newspaper and his daughter, Annie, who nursed Agnus back to health. Fulton had met the young officer at the Pratt Street Pier when the medical steamer docked and had taken him to his home for care and rest. When the war was over, Agnus returned to Baltimore and asked Annie to marry him. She quickly accepted. After that, Agnus continued his remarkable career, working briefly in the internal revenue office, then as Consul to Londonderry, Ireland for the United States Senate. He later retired from this position to take over for his father-in-law at the newspaper. He remained the publisher of the newspaper until his death.

In 1905, Agnus began construction of a family monument in Druid Ridge Cemetery. It was during this time that he purchased Black Aggie and then had a monument and pedestal created that would closely match the setting of the Adams Memorial in Washington. The first burial at the site was of the General's mother, who had been brought over from France.

A year later, the widow of the artist Augustus St. Gaudens sent a letter to Henry Adams to inform him of the poor reproduction that had been done of "Grief" and which was now resting in Druid Ridge. There was nothing they could do legally about the theft of the design so St.

Gauden's widow traveled to Baltimore to see the site for herself. She discovered a nearly identical statue, seated on a similar stone, but with the name "Agnus" inscribed on the base. She also noted that the stone was a nondescript gray color and not the pink granite of the original. The Baltimore site also did not have the bench and the rest of the stonework as the original Washington gravesite had.

After seeing the site, Mrs. St. Gaudens declared that General Agnus "must be a good deal of a barbarian to copy a work of art in such a way". Agnus quickly responded and claimed to be the innocent victim of unscrupulous art dealers. The artist's widow then requested that he give up the sculpture and file suit against the art dealers. Strangely, Agnus did file suit (and won a claim of over $4,500) but he refused to give up the copy of the statue.

The General's wife, Annie, died in 1922 and Agnus himself died three years later at the age of 86. He was also laid to rest at the feet of "Aggie" -- and shortly thereafter, her legend was born.

While the Agnus Monument seemed innocent enough in the daylight, those who encountered the statue in the darkness, gave her the nickname of "Black Aggie". To these people, she was a symbol of terror and her legend grew to become an occasional story in the local newspaper and of course, the private conversations of those who believed in a dark side. Where else could you find a statue whose eyes glowed red at the stroke of midnight?

The legend grew and it was said that the spirits of the dead rose from their graves to gather around her on certain nights and that living persons who returned her gaze were struck blind. Pregnant women who passed through her shadow (where strangely, grass never grew) would suffer miscarriages. A local college fraternity decided to include Black Aggie in their initiation rites. Not really believing the stories, the candidates for membership were ordered to spend the night in the cold embrace of Black Aggie. Those who remember the statue recall her large, powerful arms. The stories claimed that the local fraternity initiates had to sit on Aggie's lap and one tale purports that "she once came to life and crushed a hapless freshman in her powerful grasp." Other fraternity boys were equally as unlucky.... One night, at the stroke of midnight, the cemetery watchman heard a scream in the darkness. When he reached the Angus grave, he found a young man lying dead at the foot of the statue -- he had died of fright, or so the story goes. Just another legend that grew over the years into a ghost story? Maybe, and then again, maybe not.

One morning in 1962, a watchman discovered that one of the statue's arms had been cut off during the night. The missing arm was later found in the trunk of a sheet metal worker's car, along with a saw. He told the judge that Black Aggie had cut off her own arm in a fit of grief and had given it to him. Apparently, the judge didn't believe him and the man went to jail.

However, a number of people did believe the man's strange story and almost every night, huge groups of people gathered in Druid Ridge Cemetery. The public attention gained by the news story brought the curiosity-seekers to the grave and the strange tales kept them coming back. The lurid tales brought many listeners and the Angus grave site began to be trampled by teenagers and curiosity-seekers. Although Pikesville (where Druid Ridge is located) was fairly remote at the time, the site was visited, and vandalized, by hundreds or perhaps thousands of people over several decades. In addition to the statue's arm being stolen, hundreds of names and messages were scrawled on the statue, the granite base and the wall behind it. Today, these have been blasted away, although some evidence of the damage sadly remains.

Cemetery groundskeepers did everything they could to discourage visitors, including planting thorny shrubs around it, but they failed to keep people away. There is no indication as to why the cemetery was not better patrolled at night, but perhaps they just couldn't afford it. For every trespasser arrested, dozens of others managed to reach the site. A fence surrounds the grave of the Agnus family today, but back then, the cemetery was wide open, especially at night.

Eventually, the number of nighttime visitors and the destruction they caused became too much for the cemetery to handle. By the 1960's, it had gotten so bad that the descendants of Felix Agnus elected to donate Black Aggie to the Maryland Institute of Art Museum. However, this move never took place and the statue remained at her resting place for one more year, until 1967. On March 18, the Angus family donated Aggie to the Smithsonian Institution for display.

For many years, this donation would prove to be quite an enigma for researchers who attempted to track down the whereabouts of Black Aggie. You see, according to the Smithsonian, they didn't have her. Despite some people recalling that Aggie was displayed in the National Gallery for a brief period, officials at the Smithsonian claimed they had never displayed her at all. Conspiracy theorists "smelled a rat" and believed that perhaps she was simply placed in storage, rather than put on display -- because of her cursed past. "Maybe, just maybe," wrote a columnist for the *Baltimore Sun,* "they're not taking any chances."

The real answer would not be as strange. Somewhere along the line, the staff at the Smithsonian gave Aggie away, which explains why she does not appear in their records. They had no interest in displaying her and instead, gave her to the National Museum of American Art, where she was then put into storage and never displayed. For years, she would remain in a dusty storeroom, shrouded in cobwebs, until recently, when Black Aggie would "rise from the dead"!

In 1996, a young Baltimore area writer named Shara Terjung did a story on Black Aggie for a small newspaper. After having been long fascinated with the legends, she became determined to track down the present location of the statue. Finally, shortly after Halloween, she got a call from a contact at the General Service Administration who was able to discover where the elusive Aggie had ended up. The statue can still be seen today at the Federal Courts building in Washington, in the rear courtyard of the Dolly Madison house. The mysterious statue had finally been found.

Black Aggie may be gone from Druid Ridge Cemetery, but she's certainly not forgotten. "We still have people coming to Druid Ridge, asking for Black Aggie all the time," said one of the cemetery spokesmen in an interview. "I don't think there's a week that goes by when we don't get a call about it."

The Angus grave site is well cared for today and shows little sign of the desecration of the past. Grass grows now in the place where for many years it could not. The only lingering evidence of Black Aggie is a chipped area on the granite pedestal and a faint shadow where she once rested. Whether the Angus grave site was ever haunted or not, Black Aggie has left an indelible mark on not only Druid Ridge Cemetery but the annals of the supernatural in America as well.

Taylor, Troy - Beyond the Grave (2001)

Pikesville is a suburb of Baltimore and the cemetery is located at 7900 Park Heights

Avenue. However, the statue that has been dubbed "Black Aggie" can now be found in Washington behind the Dolly Madison house. The house is located at the corner of Madison Street and H Street Northwest.

Massachusetts

Leicester

Spider Gates is a beautiful, secluded, old Quaker cemetery in Leicester. Its actual name is Friends Cemetery (just one of the many misconceptions about the place) and it is privately owned by the Worcester-Pleasant Street Friends Meeting. The graves here date back to the 1700's and are as recent as 2000. Spider Gates is set back on its own private gated lane, Earle Street, about 800 feet from the main road. The wrought-iron gate has a spider web pattern -- hence the name.

Spider Gates has a very haunted reputation and there have been many legends created about it, spread mostly by the Internet. For one thing, it is (like Stull Cemetery in Kansa) referred to as one of the "gateways to Hell". Other stories include that a young boy committed suicide by hanging himself from a tree near the entrance gate in the 1980's; there is a strip of lawn where grass refuses to grow; strange creatures have been heard in the woods; there is raised area in the center of the burial ground (which has been dubbed "the altar") that is used for Satanic activities; there is cave on the property where a girl was murdered; there is a haunted house down a dirt road across from the gate; ghostly apparitions are seen and that voices are sometimes heard when no one is around; and that if you turn over rocks in an area outside of the cemetery wall, you will find runes etched on them. And there are others as well -- legend has it that this is a very haunted place. But how much truth is there to the stories?

As mentioned, the gates to the cemetery have not only been the source of the nickname for the place, but the interesting design may have played a part in the spreading of the stories. They are an unusual design and while described as a spider web pattern, it is actually more of a sunburst with radiating waves. The gates are located just a short distance away from the "hanging tree", a large oak that has a thin rope hanging from a fork about 15 feet from the ground. Could the rope have given rise to the rumor of the boy who killed himself? No records exist to say that this ever happened and its unlikely that the rope that remains in the tree would have been used in the suicide. Relatives or the police would have removed such a gristly reminder.

In the middle of the cemetery, on a small rise, is the raised area that has been called "the altar". It is a square earthen area that is about 20 feet across and about six inches high. At each corner is a granite post. Although this area has been referred to as an altar, this was actually where the old Quaker meeting house used to stand. The flat square was actually the footprint of the foundation. There are no runes on the stones against the side area of the cemetery wall either and the only stretch of ground where no grass grows is a trench that is filled with moss. There is also no cave within the cemetery but on the southern slope behind it is a small overhang of rock. Not far away though, the old route of Earle Street runs through a swamp and crosses a stone culvert. This spot is large enough to have hidden a body in but the problems remains that, like the suicide, there is no record of anyone being murdered here.

Further along, this same path runs up a steep hill to Mulberry Road. Strangely, it is at the bottom of the hill on Earle Street where there have been many reports of frightening encounters and ghostly sightings have taken place. Could this haunted spot have been "moved" in order to incorporate the atmospheric graveyard into the legends? Where Earle Street crosses Manville Street it becomes an even less-traveled dirt road. Supposedly, somewhere along it is a haunted abandoned house. The house in question is actually not on this path and according to those who recently purchased it and began renovating it, it's not haunted either.

So what is it about this place that attracts so many ghost hunters and which has spawned such strange tales of horror, death and the occult? Overactive imaginations or something more? As has been stated already, such tales (true or not) often get started for a reason and perhaps there is more to this place than meets the eye.

Just remember that should you plan to visit the place, it is an active burial ground and while the Quakers do allow visitors in the cemetery during the daylight hours, they do ask that you treat the location with the respect that it deserves. The Society of Friends have been both alarmed and amused by the recent interest in the site and while they do not claim to have had any supernatural experiences at the cemetery, they do respect the opinions of others. They simply ask that visitors recognize and respect the fact that it is an active cemetery and refrain from activities that include but are not limited to the use of alcohol or drugs, parties, séances, sexual activities and vandalism. If you wish to visit Spider Gates legally and without hassle, you should abide by the wishes of the Friends, and also announce your visit to the Leicester Police Department.

Boudillion, Daniel - Spider Gates Cemetery: The Eighth Gate to Hell? (2001)
Personal Interviews & Correspondence

Rehoboth

The small town of Rehoboth, Massachusetts is a quaint and historic place, located on Route 44, about forty miles southwest of Boston. It is a perfect example of a stereotypical New England town and so not surprisingly, it does boast its share of haunted places. One such spot is the Village Cemetery, which dates back to the Seventeenth Century and was a favorite locale of author H.P. Lovecraft. The place is quite ancient, yet has only gained a reputation for being haunted over the past few years.

The cemetery's resident specter has been dubbed "Old Ephraim" and he has become a leading spooky attraction in the village since the first sighting of him back in 1994. The apparition was first seen on January 17 by a couple that was visiting the cemetery. They were standing near a relative's grave in the center of the graveyard and happened to notice a man that they had not seen earlier. In fact, they were convinced that he had not been there at all just moments before. They described him as an elderly man, wearing old-fashioned, possibly eighteenth-century clothing. They also said that he had a "hooked nose and a sneering facial expression" and he was kneeling on the ground in the southwest rear corner of the cemetery. He seemed to be praying, they said, and alternating back and forth between laughing and sobbing. In less than a minute, the figure vanished.

The second reported sighting came in August of 1995 and the witnesses were Lisa and Karen Mackey, two sisters and long-time residents of Rehoboth. The two girls had no idea that the same figure had been spotted before and yet their sighting was eerily identical.

On August 20, the two women visited the cemetery to pay their respects at their mother's grave, who had been buried there since 1966. The cemetery was completely empty of other people when they arrived and they stayed about twenty minutes. Just as they were getting ready to leave, they heard a strange sound, also coming from the southwest rear corner of the burial ground. The noise was that of a human whistling and calling in a suggestive manner, like the rude sounds sometimes directed at women. Surprised, Lisa and Karen looked up and saw a strange-looking elderly man. He was staring at them and making peculiar gestures with his hands. He was visible for no more than thirty seconds and then he disappeared. The sisters quickly left the cemetery and, despite the fact that their mother is buried there, have not returned to the graveyard again.

The last (reported) sighting of "Old Ephraim" occurred in April 1996 and he was seen by a schoolteacher from nearby Taunton. She was especially shaken by the sighting, perhaps because she was in the cemetery alone that day, taking a walk for relaxation. In this case, she too saw the same man kneeling and sobbing in the southwest rear corner of the graveyard. When she saw him, she did not at first notice anything out of the ordinary. In fact, she thought that he was simply an old man, perhaps mourning for the loss of his wife. Concerned, she began to approach him and planned to try and offer him some comfort.

When she came to within a few yards of him, the man suddenly sprang to his feet and began laughing maniacally. He then turned to the teacher and called her an obscene name. Stunned, she turned away and began to walk very quickly toward her car, which was parked on the far side of the cemetery. The old man, she reported, started to follow her, laughing and yelling out a woman's name that did not belong to the witness. "Catherine, Catherine!", he cried as he stumbled after her.

Now, filled with terror, the teacher began to run toward her car. When she reached it, she turned around and saw that the old man had inexplicably reappeared in the corner of the cemetery where she had first seen him. He had somehow covered the distance in a matter of seconds. She quickly climbed into the car, started it and drove away. As she did, she now saw the man was leaning over and beating the figure of a young woman who was lying on the ground. In seconds, both figures vanished.

Taylor, Troy - Beyond the Grave (2001)

Michigan

Jackson

At a time between dusk on November 21 and dawn on November 22, the ghosts of a father and daughter are said to reunite in this secluded cemetery outside of Jackson The two spirits were the victims of a heinous crime that took place many years ago -- a crime that remains unsolved to this day.

The strange series of events began on November 21, 1883 in the small community of Jackson. A horrible mass murder took place here, claiming seven victims and creating a mystery and a haunting. The victims were Jacob Crouch, his daughter Eunice White, who was in her ninth month of pregnancy, Eunice's husband, and a man named Moses Polley, who had been visiting the Crouch family from out of town. These four people (five, including the unborn child) were all shot to death while sleeping. The crime was carried out during a terrible thunderstorm that muffled the sounds of violence from nearby farms.

Two months later, on January 2, the naked body of Susan Halcomb, Jacob's surviving daughter, was found on the floor of her bedroom. She had been force-fed poison and had died. James Fay, who had worked as a farm hand for Jacob Crouch, was also found dead shortly after. What could these people have done, seen or heard that would have committed them to their horrible deaths? No one knows...

In the years that followed the murders, several men were brought to trial for the crimes but no one was ever convicted. What really happened has never been known, and never will be known, as all of the principals and investigators in the case have long since carried the tales to their graves.

Jacob Crouch was buried in a small cemetery at the corner of Horton and Reynolds Roads, a mile away from the site of the Crouch home. Eunice and her husband lie five miles away in St. John's Cemetery in Jackson. The two burial grounds are very different. Jacob's grave is neglected and forgotten while Eunice's lies in a well-cared for cemetery that is still in operation today. The legend began many years ago that on the anniversary of the murders, Eunice's spirit would leave her grave and travel to Reynolds Cemetery, where it would reunite with the ghost of her father.

Many claim to have witnessed this over the years, including two ghost researchers in 1989, who insist they saw an ectoplasmic cloud appear in the cemetery that night. The glowing mist floated through the cemetery until it reached Jacob's grave, where it suddenly vanished.

Jackson, Michigan is in the south central part of the state, between Battle Creek and Ann Arbor. The grave of Jacob Crouch can be found in the Reynolds Cemetery, at the corner of Reynolds and Horton Road. The reunion is always said to take place at the small, older cemetery and not where Eunice is buried.

Westland

Butler Cemetery is located outside of Westland and along Henry Huff Road. It is a deserted and abandoned spot and if the stories of the local folk are to be believed, a very haunted one. The cemetery is neglected and in poor condition, overgrown with weeds and choked with grass and fallen tree limbs. A wire fence that runs around it is grown over with vines and a rusty gate is broken at the entrance. There are no structures nearby, save for a deserted house, so it is easy to imagine why this cemetery has gotten such a reputation as a haunted place. Are the stories here simply imagination at work -- or something supernatural?

A witness reported a few years ago that he encountered a woman in white crossing the road in front of the cemetery. He swerved to avoid her and she vanished right in front of his eyes. A year later, he saw this woman again and this time, she was in the graveyard itself. He claimed to see her standing next to a tall monument and nearby was another apparition. This ghost was that of a man wearing some sort of uniform. He stopped his car for a closer look and the two figures faded away. Thinking that someone might be playing a trick on him, he quickly searched the area for either people or automobiles, but found nothing.

The stories of ghosts in the cemetery still continue today and researchers have pointed out that there have been an inordinate number of auto accidents along the stretch of road near the cemetery -- perhaps these drivers were swerving to avoid a woman in white who wanders out across the road?

Westland, Michigan is located just west of Detroit. Butler Cemetery can be found on

Henry Huff Road.

Other Haunted Michigan Cemeteries

Sightings of a ghost have taken place over an area of about three miles around the Findlay Cemetery (Ada), occasionally ending up between Egypt Valley and Honey Creek. The spirit is thought to be that of a woman who was killed years ago. Her husband believed that his wife was having an affair, so he followed her one night when she thought he was asleep. He discovered her in a field near their property with another man. The husband was enraged and killed the wife and then died fighting the other man. It is now said that, late at night, especially just before the full moon, witnesses will often see the ghostly woman in a white gown near the cemetery and along the roadways, searching for her lover. Many have tried to communicate with the lost spirit but she always runs away and vanishes into the woods. Although it is said that she is most often seen haunting the field on Honeycreek Road where she died, other witnesses have reported her in nearby Seidman Park, and in nearby Findlay Cemetery, where she is thought to be buried.

Many people have reported seeing a woman in a white bridal gown in the North Bluff Cemetery (Gladstone). She is believed to be the wife of a man named Raymond Visnaw, who was murdered years ago. The spectral figure now searches for his killers and has often walked towards people, only to disappear.

The Pere Cheney Cemetery (Near Grayling) was started in the 1800's and is all that remains from a small town that died out around 1900. The cemetery has only a handful of tombstones remaining, most faded by time and weather, but there are believed to be a number of common graves here that hold victims of both a fire and a smallpox epidemic that ravaged the town. Over the years, witnesses have reported many ghostly figures here, as well as the sounds of voices and children's laughter that seems to come from nowhere. Those who come here also tell of strange failures of automobiles, radios and flashlights, as if there exists an energy here that has not been explained.

There is reported to be a "glowing tombstone" in the Harrison Cemetery (Schoolcraft). The burial ground is named for Bazel Harrison, who led the first settlers to the region. He is buried here with his wife, Martha. According to the story of the graveyard, the glowing stone can only be seen from a distance and then fades out as the witness nears the edge of the cemetery. There are no lights around the cemetery to cause this and despite tests and research, no explanation has yet been given.

Hawks Head Cemetery (Van Buren) is rumored to the final resting place of a former mistress of Al Capone, a woman named Flora. Many people have seen the apparition of a woman in a white dress here and it is believed to be her. According to the legend, she appears just moments after the sound of what seems to be a chiming clock comes from the back corner of the graveyard. No one has been able to determine what connection Flora has to the chiming clock but each time she is seen, the witnesses note that the sound announces her appearance.

Minnesota

Albin Township

In a remote area in southern Minnesota is a place called Albin Township and it is at this place where you can hear the story of Annie Mary, her strange death, premature burial and ghostly afterlife. The place where her grave once rested was on a farm, the old Twente Place, which is about eighteen miles southwest of New Ulm, Minnesota and a little West of Hanska. The owners of the farm once tended to the grave and to the strange stories that have grew up around it.

Annie Mary was the six-year-old daughter Richard and Lizzie Twente. She died, or so everyone believed in 1886, of "lung fever". Before she died, she slipped into a coma, leading everyone to believe that she was dead. In 1886, the death of a child was not uncommon and neither was her burial site, as many settlers buried their dead on their own farms.

No one knows for sure why Annie Mary's grave was first opened. Some claim that Lizzie began to have dreams in which her daughter had been buried alive. Others claim that Richard Twente's own peculiarities may have caused him to open the grave. Twente was always regarded as a strange man, although a brilliant and hardworking one. He sold trees and nursery stock from his farm and in 1918 published a book about planting fruit trees. He was also a very physically strong man who built a large, three-level barn almost single-handedly. He also built a granary that has been listed on the National Register of Historic Places with a scale, a hoist and belt system and seven storage bins.

He also did some very strange things. Once he forced his wife and daughters onto a sled and started across the prairie with no destination in mind, only turning back because they were in danger of freezing to death. People were afraid of him because of his extreme strength and the fits of anger he suffered from. On another occasion, he left his family and journeyed to Canada where he bought a parcel of land. A short time later, he wrote his wife and asked to borrow $10 to buy bread. He eventually died of a heart attack in 1920.

It is said that Richard Twente may have dug up his daughter's grave because he feared that someone may have stolen her, but whatever the reason, Annie Mary's grave was opened a short time after her death. The inside of the coffin showed signs of a struggle and scratches covered the inside of the lid. Annie Mary's fingernails were torn and bloody and her face was frozen into a mask of terror.

The grieving parents now moved Annie Mary's body to another grave site, this one located on the highest hill overlooking the farm. Twente constructed a wooden fence around her grave but found that it didn't satisfy him and soon tore it down. He then installed a four-foot high wall of stone around the grave and placed a locked iron gate at the opening. Legends soon began that the wall could not keep the girl's spirit from wandering. It is said that her restless ghost, wearing a white dress, would wander the hillside at night, attracting the attention of travelers along the nearby road. It was said that whenever the gate was open, the spirit would walk. Some years later, the stories stated that car headlights would fail as people drove past the grave site. Others claimed that cars would inexplicably stall on the nearby bridge and that before that, horses would refuse to pass that way.

The tombstone that marked Annie Mary's grave eventually was uprooted from its base by trees that Twente planted there. They grew through the walls, cracking them and causing the structure to lean. The gate also eventually disappeared, although its iron hinges remained for some time after. Many believe that Annie Mary's ghost departed because of the poor condition of her grave and the vandals who often visited there, showing their disrespect.

In 1996 though, Annie Mary's body was exhumed and was moved to a cemetery plot in northern Minnesota, where her parents were buried. The years of vandalism and desecration had taken their toll on the grave site and the marker itself had been stolen long before. The grave of Annie Mary now lives only in memory. The stone wall was demolished and the trees cut down. Ironically, Richard Twente had built the enclosure to try and protect the site but as it turned out, it caused it to stand out from the landscape, drawing attention to the grave and contributing to the eerie legends.

The removal of Annie Mary's remains marked the end of the legend, which is both for the best and a little bit sad as well. The little girl will probably be happier now, wherever she is now, and if that means the end of the ghost of Annie Mary's grave, then perhaps that is for the best.

Rest in peace.

Goodhue

The tales of a ghost in the cemetery near Holy Trinity Church, plagued the little town of Goodhue during the years of the 1920's. Do spirits still haunt the place, has the ghost faded away with time, or was the spirit simply the result of an overactive imagination?

A man named Tunis Parkin was the first to see the ghost. He was the town painter, a respected and upstanding young man, and he was walking past the graveyard one night on his way to the home of a young lady that he had been courting. As he approached the apple orchard beside the church, he froze with fear. He was being followed from the cemetery and he caught a glimpse of his pursuer -- a glowing apparition that was shrouded in mist. He walked quickly but the ghost seemed to follow. Finally, Parkin broke into a run and didn't stop until he reached the home of the town Marshall, T.W. Taylor. He hurriedly told his tale to the lawman and while Taylor expressed some doubts, he went and investigated the churchyard. But found nothing to lead him to believe the place was haunted.

In the morning, every resident of Goodhue knew about Tunis Parkin's ghost. Most mere skeptical, saying that he had been spooked by his shadow. But many were taking no chances and young ladies in town were told to not be unescorted near the churchyard after dark.

Two weeks later, another man, Thomas McNamara, had his own encounter with the ghost. He was walking home from a dance and passing the orchard when the apparition appeared and approached him. He panicked and ran from the area.

Tom Riley also met the ghost in the graveyard. He was walking along the edge of the cemetery when the pale form appeared among the tombstones. Riley ran all of the way to the main street of town, yelling that he had seen the ghost, although some claimed that it had only been s white cow owned by a local farmer. Nearly every day brought new stories and encounters with the spirit, although some of them were easily explained away as nothing but high spirits, anxiety and just plain foolishness.

Finally, S.W. Taylor decided to act. He was the man responsible for law and order in Goodhue and he planned to settle the ghost business once and for all. His plan was a simple one-- he and Tunis Parker would hide in the apple orchard and capture the ghost. Unknown to Taylor, as he and Parkin hid in the bushes, Parkin had also alerted all of his friends to the ambush and they too waited close by with all of the guns they could muster together, also waiting for the ghost to appear.

The evening was dark and quiet and Taylor and Larkin sat silently side by side in the trees. Nothing was happening and no ghost had appeared. A couple of hours had passed, and then suddenly, a terrifying scream pierced the darkness. Taylor sprang forward and grabbed the culprit -- two apple tree branches that were scraping together and causing the wailing sound whenever the wind blew. Across the orchard, the ambush party also went into action when they heard Marshall Taylor running through the trees. Thinking he was the ghost, they attacked, but luckily no shots were fired.

Finally, when dawn came, Taylor and the deputies gave up the search, finding nothing to make them believe the churchyard was haunted. Apparently, their efforts did have some effect though for the ghost was never heard from again.

Scott, Beth & Michael Norman - Haunted Heartland (1985)

Goodhue, Minnesota is located in the southeast corner of the state, not far from the Wisconsin border. The tale of the Holy Trinity Churchyard ghost is an often repeated legend of the area.

Lakefield

Located a distance south of Lakefield, Minnesota, and a short ways from the highway between Jackson and Petersburg, lies an abandoned and forgotten graveyard called the Loon Lake Cemetery. For many years, this place has been reportedly haunted by a variety of ghosts and legends that have appeared since the last burial here in 1926. The ghosts that haunt this place are not your average spirits either. They are strange and they are many -- leading many to believe that the place has more than its share.

There is no longer a road that journeys back to Loon Lake Cemetery but those who seek the place can still find it, despite swampy and treacherous ground. The only ones who still come here today are ghost hunters and curiosity-seekers, and the occasional researcher who is searching for some family history.

The cemetery is said to be haunted by the spirits of three witches who were buried there many years ago. It is said that anyone who violates their resting places will die and unnatural death. One of these three witches has been remembered as "Mary Jane", who supposedly had supernatural powers and allegedly died in 1881, when the townspeople of Petersburg cut off her head. It is also claimed that if one walks over the grave of this woman, that person will also die.

How many of these stories are true? No one really knows, but the place certainly seems conducive to a haunting in its abandoned and remote setting. At least 67 tombstones once stood in Loon Lake Cemetery, but today it is said that only about 18 remain. Do the fallen ones remain as victims to a witch's curse or the work of vandals?

Hein, Ruth - Ghostly Tales of Southwest Minnesota (1989)

The abandoned Loon Lake Cemetery lies in Jackson County, in the southwest portion of the state, just north of the Iowa border. The cemetery is south of Lakefield and west of Petersburg in a remote location.

Other Haunted Minnesota Cemeteries

Oakland Cemetery (St. Paul) is said to be haunted by the ghost of woman who wears a white, lacy dress from the early 1900's. She is said to be in her early 20's, with long brown hair and appears to be a flesh and blood person until she suddenly disappears. No one knows for sure who this apparition might be. Those who have tried to talk to her, as she appears quite life-like, state that she vanishes when approached.

The ghost of a young girl haunts the Sanborn Corners Graveyard (Lamberton) and according to the story, she was accidentally buried alive here many years ago. She now roams the burial ground at night and has also been seen and heard moaning and crying from the intersection at the bottom of the hill.

Mississippi

Mansdale

The small community of Mansdale is located about fifteen miles north of Jackson. In this small town is a gothic church, the Episcopal Chapel of the Cross, and beside it is a churchyard. It sits on a small knoll and is nearly hidden from the road by a grove of trees. This shaded cemetery is the final resting place of a man named Henry Vick, a tragic figure in Mississippi history. The graveyard is also the place where Vick's lover, Helen Johnstone, came to grieve for him in the weeks and months following his death in May 1859. Some say that she grieves here for him still....

The story of Helen Johnstone and Henry Vick began during the holiday season of 1855. Helen and her mother, Margaret Johnstone, were spending Christmas with Helen's sister, Mrs. William Britton, at Ingleside, the home that John Johnstone had built as a wedding gift for his oldest daughter. The plans for the house had been delayed by his wife's insistence that they first build a chapel though and sadly, Johnstone died before the chapel could be completed. Mrs. Johnstone went ahead with the plans however and personally supervised the building of the church. When it was consecrated in 1852, her husband's body had been moved into the small churchyard behind it.

One night, just before Christmas, the family was seated to dinner when a knock came on the front door. The servant who answered it returned to the dining room to inform Mr. Britton that a young man named Henry Vick wished to speak with him. Vick, spattered with mud, was there to ask for help in getting his carriage repaired. While servants tended to the carriage, Vick became a guest at Ingleside. He stayed for several days and while he was there, he and Helen fell deeply in love.

In fact, he had charmed the entire family and Helen's mother approved of their match. Vick came many times to the Johnstone home over the next three years. As Helen had only been sixteen when they met, her mother requested that they wait to be married. A date was eventually set for May 21, 1859 and the location would be the family's Chapel of the Cross. A reception would be held at Annandale.

A week before the wedding, Vick boarded a steamer in Vicksburg. He planned to travel to New Orleans to buy a suit for the ceremony. Soon after his arrival, he stopped in a billiard room where he had a chance meeting with James Stith, a former friend that had caused him many problems in the past. A passing insult from Stith led the two men to get into a heated argument and an altercation. Vick, in the heat of the moment, challenged the other man to a duel. Stith quickly accepted.

Hours later, when his passions had cooled, Vick regretted his hasty actions and sent a friend to try and cancel the duel. Stith refused to back down however and the illegal affair was scheduled to take place in Alabama within days. They traveled to Mobile with their seconds and assembled one morning at a place called Holly's Garden. This was to be one of the last duels ever fought in the city and the weapons were Kentucky rifles, fired from thirty paces. The duel ended with Vick being shot in the head. He fell, dead before he hit the ground.

Stith and his friend escaped back to Mobile but Vick's second, A.G. Dickinson, was delayed by an undertaker who had to take charge of his friend's body. Before he could leave Mobile, the authorities issued a warrant for his arrest. He took refuge in the home of friend who was a local physician and managed to avoid the search for a few days. Finally though, guilt-ridden over his part in Vick's death, Dickinson sent a message to the Mobile chief of police, Harry Maury, and confessed to his role in the duel. He asked that he be permitted to take his friend's body back to Vicksburg. Maury was so impressed by the man's honesty that he sent his own carriage to take Vick's body to the riverfront docks.

The body was taken to New Orleans and then loaded onto a packet going upriver. Ironically, on this same boat were the caterer, the cooks and the helpers who were on their way to Annandale for Helen and Vick's wedding dinner. Their supplies were loaded right alongside Vick's coffin.

Helen and her family buried her betrothed in the same graveyard where her father's body was put to rest. His grave was marked with a simple granite cross and small statues of his hunting dogs. Day after day, Helen sat on an iron bench near the grave and wept for her beloved fiancée. When darkness fell, some member of the family would gently lead her home, but she would return early the next morning to resume her vigil. She was said to have made her family promise that the grave space next to Vick would always remain empty. She wanted it saved for herself and wanted no one else to ever be buried there.

Months passed and Mrs. Johnstone, fearing that Helen would never recover, took her to Europe so that she would have time for her broken heart to heal. They remained away for many months and by the time they returned, Helen had recovered from her depression. She later married Reverend George Harris, but never forgot about Henry Vick. She and her husband later moved to the northern part of the state and Helen died in 1916.

The space next to Vick's grave at the Chapel of the Cross remains empty today but the ghost of Helen Johnstone still appears there to weep for her lost love. Many visitors to the secluded cemetery have told of seeing a young woman kneeling in grief beside Vick's stone cross. When they try to approach her, she looks up and then vanishes before their eyes.

Taylor, Troy - Beyond the Grave (2001)

Mansdale, Mississippi is located about fifteen miles north of Jackson.

Missouri

Joplin

Peace Church Cemetery is an old, ramshackle and mostly abandoned burial ground near Joplin. Over the years, reports have circulated about strange sounds, voices and eerie lights that have been heard and seen in the cemetery. There are also reports of a ghostly figure who has been seen lurking in the trees, peering out at passersby and then vanishing when approached. It would be safe to assume that one of the restless souls buried here does not rest in peace. And when those from the area learn just who is buried in this cemetery, in a forsaken, unmarked grave -- a likely culprit for this restless spirit emerges.

Few mass murderers have ever gone on a worse killing spree than the one 21-year-old Billy Cook started on December 30, 1950. On that day, Cook, posing as a hitchhiker, forced a motorist at gunpoint to get into the trunk of his own car and then drove away. Over the next two weeks, Cook went on a senseless rampage. He kidnapped nearly a dozen people, including a deputy sheriff, and murdered six of them in cold blood, including three children. He also attempted other killings and terrorized the southwestern border states.

Cook was a Joplin native and was in and out of trouble as a child, spending most of his formative years in reform schools. He was simply born bad, most believed, and when he was young, he had the words "Hard Luck" tattooed across the knuckles of both of his hands. Cook simply hated people -- all people -- and he decided to put those feelings into action when he kidnapped his first victim, a motorist, near Lubbock, Texas. Luckily for the driver, he was later able to force the trunk open and escape.

Far less lucky though was the family of Carl Mosser. Mosser, his wife Thelma, and their three small children were on vacation from Decatur, Illinois and on their way to New Mexico when they picked up Cook alongside the road. Many would wonder today why they would have picked up a hitchhiker with small children in the car but those were different times then and Americans had not yet been bombarded with the gruesome images of death and murder that were to come in the media and in entertainment. They had nothing to fear, they believed, and simply wanted to help out a man who was down on his luck. Cook repaid the family's kindness by pulling a gun and forcing Mosser to drive first to Carlsbad, New Mexico, then to El Paso and on to Houston. After a time, Cook shot and killed all of them and for good measure, shot the family dog too. He dumped their bodies in a place he knew well, an abandoned mine shaft near Joplin.

Eventually, the Mosser's car was found abandoned near Tulsa, Okalahoma. It was like a slaughter pen, with the upholstery ripped by bullets and blood splashed everywhere. Their bodies were soon discovered but Cook left something behind in the car -- the receipt for the handgun that he had bought. His identity was soon learned and a massive manhunt was launched.

Cook headed for California and there, he kidnapped a deputy sheriff who had almost captured him. He forced the deputy to drive him around while he bragged about executing the Mosser family. After more than 40 miles, Cook ordered the lawman to stop and forced him to lie down in a ditch with his hands tied behind his back. He told the man that he was going to put a bullet in his head and then, for some reason, climbed into the car and drove away. The officer waited for the bullet but it never came. A short time later, Cook flagged down another motorist, Robert Dewey, that he did kill. The officer would never know why he was spared.

By this time, an alarm had been raised all over the region and so Cook decided to head into Mexico. He kidnapped two men and brought them along to Santa Rosalia, about 400 miles across the border. Amazingly though, Cook was recognized by the local police chief. He simply walked up to Cook, snatched the gun from the man's belt and placed him under arrest. Cook was then rushed to the border and turned over to FBI agents.

Despite the slaying of the Mosser family, the Justice Department turned Cook over to the California courts and he was tried for the murder of Robert Dewey. Cook displayed as regret about this murder as he had the others -- in other words, none -- and he was sentenced to death. On December 12, 1952, he died in the gas chamber at San Quentin.

Billy Cook's body was later returned to Joplin and he was buried in Peace Church Cemetery in an unmarked grave. But as many believe, he does not rest here in peace.

- Personal Interviews & Correspondence (thanks to Tammy Leach)
- Nash, Jay Robert - Bloodletters and Badmen (1995)

St. Genevieve

Memorial Cemetery is one of the oldest burial grounds in St. Genevieve, the first settlement in Missouri. The cemetery is located at the end of Merchant Street and while not large, contains nearly 5,000 souls -- many of whom do not rest in peace. The cemetery was started in 1787 and became the burial place for many of the city's most prominent leaders and settlers. By the late 1880's, it had become seriously overcrowded and many complained that new graves were disturbing the graves of those who has been buried previously. The cemetery was declared a public nuisance and a health hazard in 1879 and was finally closed in 1881.

There was one last burial after that date, however. Odile Pratte Valle, wife of city leader Felix Valle, was determined to spend eternity next to her husband. He had died in 1877 and had been interred in Memorial Cemetery. Madame Valle approached the city fathers with an attractive proposal shortly after the cemetery was closed. She would donate a large tract of land for use as a cemetery if she could be buried next to her husband in the closed cemetery whenever she passed away. The proposal was accepted and she died at the age of 90, 15 years after the cemetery had been closed down. Many of the graves here are unknown and the cemetery has been largely abandoned and neglected since 1882. None of the old wooden markers remain and most of the iron French crosses have been stolen. Most of the smaller monuments have also disappeared, lost to the ravages of time and the elements. In recent years, a foundation has formed to try and protect the cemetery from further damage.

Needless to say, the years of ruin and abandonment have given birth to a number of legends about the cemetery. The most popular sprang up shortly around 1900 when rumors stated that the spirits of the dead people buried in Memorial Cemetery played a deadly game of hide-and-seek every Halloween night. It was said that anyone who ventured into the cemetery and saw this event would join the spirits before the next Halloween!

St. Genevieve is located about two hours south of St. Louis, along the Mississippi River.

St. Louis

As recounted in Chapter One of this book, both Bellefontaine and Calvary Cemeteries in St. Louis were created because of cholera epidemics that flooded the city's burial grounds in the late 1840's. They remain today as wondrous showplaces of cemetery design and fabulous artwork and are well worth a visit.

But if you do come to Bellefontaine or Calvary Cemeteries, don't come with the idea of looking for ghosts. Strangely, neither one of these graveyards boasts a single ghost story, however there is a spirited tale connected to Calvary Drive, the road that runs between the two burial grounds, connecting Broadway and West Florissant Road. The best-known ghost to haunt this road is "Hitchhike Annie", a young woman who is picked up in cars and then disappears. According to the accounts, motorists who passed along Calvary Drive (and sometimes other streets in the area) would be flagged down by a young girl in a white dress. She was usually described as being quite attractive with long brown hair and pale skin. After climbing into the car, she would sometimes claim that she had been stranded or that her car had broken down. Either way, she would ask for a ride and direct the driver to take her down the street. In every case though, just as the automobile would near the entrance to Bellefontaine Cemetery, the girl would mysteriously vanish from the vehicle! The door would never open and no warning would come to say that she was getting out. Annie would simply be gone.

The story of Annie started in the 1940's and persisted for many years, but by the early 1980's seemed to die out. If the girl has been seen in recent times, I have been unable to find anyone who has encountered her.

There is also another ghost said to haunt this road. He is the phantom is a boy who is dressed in old-fashioned clothing from the late 1800's. He is said to appear in the middle of Calvary Drive when there are cars coming, causing the vehicles to swerve and slam on their brakes to avoid hitting what they think is a flesh and blood child. When the drivers try to look for him, they always discover that he has simply vanished.

And that's not the last ghost who allegedly haunts this stretch of roadway either. Stories were also told for many years of a woman in a black mourning dress who would also cross this roadway. According to the man who passed the story on to me, who remembered it being a current tale when he was a child about two decades ago, the woman would suddenly appear in the street, much like the little boy. She looked like a real person, clad in a long, rather old-fashioned dress and wearing a hat and a veil over her face. From the description, she was apparently an almost stereotypical mourner from the Victorian era. The woman walked out into the street, or appeared suddenly in the middle of the roadway, and drivers were forced to come to sudden stops so that they wouldn't strike her. Each time though, she would vanish before their eyes.

Once again, this story made the rounds for a number of years and then seemed to fade away. What was it that made this stretch of road one of the most haunted highways in St. Louis, at least for a time? Could it have been the close proximity of the city's two most hallowed burial grounds, or something else? And what caused the stories to stop being told? Could the haunting here have ended - or could it be waiting to simply start back up again someday? Who knows? My advice though, is that if you happen to be traveling along Calvary Drive someday and you happen to see a girl in a white dress trying to flag you down for a ride - you may not want to stop and pick her up!

Haunted St. Louis by Troy Taylor (2002)

Both Bellefontaine and Calvary Cemeteries are located on West Florissant Road in North

St. Louis. The road where Hitchhike Annie and the other ghosts have been seen is Calvary Avenue, which runs between the two graveyards.

St. Louis

Jefferson Barracks is one of the oldest active military posts west of the Mississippi River. The post was founded back in 1826 and has sent men to every conflict that the United States has been involved in since that time. A major hospital was also formed here to give comfort during the Civil War and beyond. There are numerous ghost stories connected to Jefferson Barracks, including to the National Cemetery that has been established here.

Soldiers who did not survive their stay at the Jefferson Barracks hospital of the Civil War, were buried in the National Cemetery, which was established south of the post in 1863. The cemetery here did not have such an auspicious beginning though. It was originally started as a small piece of land set aside for soldiers and their families who died while stationed at Jefferson Barracks. The first person buried in the cemetery was Elizabeth Ann Lash, the 18 month-old daughter of an officer who was posted here, and her death was followed by other victims of disease, duels and violence on the frontier.

The small burial ground grew and a wooden fence was erected around it in a foolhardy attempt to keep out wild animals. But time was not kind to the post cemetery and thanks to the fact that most of the soldiers who buried friends or loved ones here were usually reassigned or moved on, there was no one to take care of the graves. Soon, the cemetery fell into a state of disrepair. As the cemetery expanded years later, the old memorials were forgotten and in many cases the identities of those buried beneath them were lost. The remains of these poor souls were re-interred with only a number or the word "unknown" carved on their headstone.

By 1862, it was obvious that more space than was currently available was going to be needed to bury the men killed during the Civil War. Major General Henry Halleck, commander of the Department of Missouri, recognized that the post cemetery at Jefferson Barracks could easily be expanded and would make an excellent choice for a national cemetery, as it was easily accessible from both land and riverboat. Based on his observations, President Abraham Lincoln expanded the "Old Post Cemetery" in 1863 and formally designated the burial ground as Jefferson Barracks National Cemetery.

The grave sites began to fill quickly as the remains of soldiers from both the North and the South began to arrive at the post for burial. In addition, men who died at the post hospitals were also buried in the cemetery. Before the war ended, more than 1,140 Confederate soldiers were buried at Jefferson Barracks and were joined by over 12,000 men who fought for the Union.

In 1867, Sylvanus Beeman was appointed as the first superintendent of the cemetery with Martin Burke installed as his assistant the following year. Under their care, the cemetery was enlarged and improved and divided into sections for the ease of identification. A short time later, other military cemeteries from the region began to turn over their dead to Jefferson Barracks.

In 1876, the first graves were moved. The remains of 470 people were taken from a place called Arsenal Island and were reburied at Jefferson Barracks. The island, which was also known as Quarantine Island, was little more than a glorified sandbar that had been created by the currents of the Mississippi River. Located just north of Arsenal Street in St. Louis, it was only a half-mile wide and three-quarters of a mile long. Arsenal Island served the city for many years as a quarantine camp, where soldiers and civilian river passengers were taken when they were suspected of carrying some sort of contagious diseases. During its years of operation, it saw cases of cholera, smallpox, yellow fever and more. Steamboats were often directed to the island if suspicious illnesses were on board and the passengers could be held in quarantine for weeks. Medical surgeons on the island inspected the passengers before allowing them into St. Louis and if they were found to be sick, forced them to live on the island until they recovered or died from their illness. Those who died were buried on the north end of the island.

The bodies from the island graveyard were moved because of the threat to the island caused by the changing channels of the river. By 1880, surveyors discovered that the island had moved nearly 4,800 feet downriver, a half mile from its position in 1862. Frequent spring flooding had already washed away many of the graves of the diseased and it was not uncommon to find human remains in the river. For that reason, the bodies were moved and their graves marked with tombstones bearing the legend "unknown".

In April 1904, the remains of 33 officers, soldiers and civilians who had been buried at Fort Bellefontaine were moved to the National Cemetery as well. These "unknown" burials, which did include the two year-old daughter of former officer and explorer Zebulon Pike, were buried on the same bluff, near the grave of Elizabeth Lash... a young child who may not rest in peace.

As with many great graveyards, the Jefferson Barracks National Cemetery has its share of ghostly stories. One of these involves a spectral child who has been seen on a bluff in the cemetery. As she has often been spotted near the grave of little Elizabeth Lash, legend holds that it is her ghost who walks here. Unfortunately, little is known about the Lash family or how the young girl actually died. She was buried in the Old Post Cemetery on August 5, 1827 and its likely that she passed away from one of the many diseases that were prevalent in the Mississippi Valley in those days. But what might make her ghost become restless?

That part of the story remains a mystery but what we do know is that employees of the cemetery and at least one soldier assigned to Jefferson Barracks have seen the ghost of a very small girl walking between the marble tombstone near Elizabeth's grave. But is it really Elizabeth Lash?

Author Dave Goodwin, who wrote an entire book on the hauntings at Jefferson Barracks, isn't so sure. He believes there may be another explanation for a toddler spirit to be wandering the cemetery. In 1900, shortly after the death of Martin Burke, who was by then the superintendent of the graveyard, a new caretaker took his place named Edward Past. Not long after filling this position, he discovered the remains of several unidentified children in the Old Post section of the cemetery. Their graves had long been hidden beneath bushes and undergrowth. While their identities and the reasons for their deaths could not be discovered, it's likely that they were the victims of some epidemic, like cholera. It's possible that one of these young spirits may be the little girl who roams the cemetery, perhaps in an attempt to somehow not be forgotten after all.

And there is another legend that has long been told of this cemetery, involving two ghosts. One of them is a Federal "Buffalo Soldier" and the other is a Confederate soldier. It has been told that the graves of these two men are located close to one another and that at certain times this black man from the north and this white man from the south both appear near their grave sites to acknowledge one another. It is said that this ghostly greeting occurs around sunset or occasionally in the morning, around dawn. The two shadowy forms rise from their graves and have been seen moving across the cemetery toward one another. When they meet, witnesses claims that they extend a hand to one another in friendship and some have surmised that they are doomed to continuously try and make peace with one another, not only for themselves but also for the fallen soldiers who are buried around them.

Goodwin, Dave - Ghosts of Jefferson Barracks (2001)

Jefferson Barracks is located on the south side of St. Louis. While the military section of the post is not open to the general public, there are museums and a state park located here as well.

Other Haunted Missouri Cemeteries

Woodlock Cemetery (Davisville) has been connected to many unexplained events over the years. Before Davisville had become little more than a post office, many of the locals spoke of the strange things they saw and heard in the graveyard. The cemetery today is accessible only by a set of stone steps that lead up a hillside but this has not stopped witnesses from coming here. Many of them have reported eerie lights and even apparitions of people and a horse walking along the top of the hill.

A ghostly woman in white who carries a cat has been reported for many years in the Doniphan Cemetery (Doniphan). According to the legend, this woman walks through the cemetery and weeps for the apparently slain animal in her arms. She is usually seen emerging from the wall of an old crypt and then walking along the back row of headstones. The story says that she lived in Doniphan in the 1920's and her cat ran out of the house one day. She chased it into the middle of the street and as she picked it up, they were both run over by a wagon and were killed.

Historic Elmwood Cemetery (Kansas City) is said to have its share of hauntings too. The cemetery was officially established in 1872 but burials began here nearly 30 years prior to that. According to witnesses, apparitions have been seen here for nearly a century. The two young female ghosts are always seen wearing white dresses and appear to be playing together. They have been reported at night and in the daytime as well, but only when skies are overcast.

New Hampshire

Some of New Hampshire's Haunted Graveyards

Pine Hill Road Cemetery (Hollis) is said to be haunted by the ghosts of a family who were buried here after being murdered in the middle 1800's. According to the legend, only one member of the family, their youngest son, survived the slaughter but the crime was never solved. After the son died many years later, he was buried beside his family in the graveyard and soon after, those who passed the site at night began to report seeing the spectral figure of a boy standing alongside the road, trying to flag down people for help.

According to witness accounts, there have been reports of strange sightings in Gilson

Road Cemetery (Nashua). The stories say that visitors who have come here after dark often tell of hearing voices coming from the back, right-hand corner of the graveyard, even though no one else is present at the time. There are also accounts of seeing "misty" people vanishing among the headstones and a black, hooded figure that has been seen on occasion.

Vale Cemetery (Wilton) is reportedly haunted by a ghost who has been dubbed the "Blue Lady". The legends say that her name was Mary and that she was buried here in the late 1800's. Eerie blue lights have been seen coming out of her grave and even on warm afternoons, the air near her gravesite is especially cold.

New Jersey

Ringwood

One of the most historic sites on the Saddle River, in New Jersey is Ringwood Manor, a majestic mansion that was built in 1807. For years there have been numerous stories told about the ghost who haunts this place, a mixed race man who has wreaked havoc for generations. This restless spirit may have been one of the notorious "Jackson Whites", a group of black, white, Indian and runaway slave descendants who settled in remote enclaves of the region as far back as the Civil War.

While this man is certainly an enigmatic ghost, the most famous specter attached to the location is undoubtedly that of Robert Erskine, who built the first house on this property in 1762. Although he may not haunt the manor house, Erskine is never far from the site of his beloved home. His ghost is usually encountered at the Ringwood Manor Cemetery, which is accessible by a dirt road from the grounds of the estate. Here, Erskine has been seen for well over a century, always appearing near his tomb.

Robert Erskine was a General in the Continental Army and was invaluable to George Washington during the War for Independence. As a surveyor, he was able to provide accurate maps that enabled troop movement and the proper positioning of the American armies during the fighting. When the war was over, Erskine settled in his home in New Jersey and began a successful surveying business. He constructed the first house at Ringwood Manor and it became a showplace in the area. He lived there for the rest of his life and when he died, he was laid to rest in the small cemetery on the grounds. Apparently though, he does not rest in peace. Some say that Erskine had too many plans and too much activity in his life to settle into oblivion in the next world. For this reason, they say that he has returned and now interacts with those who visit his burial place.

The stories say that Erskine's ghost was released from the tomb when a brick fell out of the wall and was not replaced. He has been seen in this tiny graveyard ever since. Legends say that on the darkest nights, when the moon is new and the sky is black, Robert Erskine will appear on top of his cemetery vault, swinging a lantern in one hand. Some brave visitors to the graveyard even claim that Erskine will sometimes even escort them down the shadowy road to the old bridge that takes them out of the cemetery.

One night in the early 1970's, three young men visited the Ringwood Cemetery to see if the stories of the ghost were true. The young men had driven to the cemetery and entered through the gate, quickly finding Robert Erskine's grave. They sat around for awhile talking, never really expecting to see anything, and making jokes about the validity of the story. Just as they were getting ready to give up and leave, one of the boys noticed a hazy, blue light that had appeared above Erskine's burial vault. He pointed this out to the others and they fell into a stunned silence.

Finally, summoning up their courage, they walked around the crypt and looked carefully at every corner of it, thinking that perhaps someone had rigged the light to appear. However, there was no wire or artificial light to be found -- the blue glow still remained. That was enough to convince them that they should leave. As they hurried toward their car, one of the young men looked back and saw that the light had left the crypt and was now moving after them. In a state of panic, they reached the car and fumbling with the keys, piled inside of it. Suddenly, the blue light was now directly in front of the car, hovering and thrumming with an electric glow. The driver quickly pulled away and drove off, but the light remained right next to them, slowing down and speeding up as they did. When they reached the main road though, the light vanished, as if it had never existed at all.

Taylor, Troy - Beyond the Grave (2001)

Ringwood is located on the Saddle River in northeast New Jersey and the Manor is located just outside of town. The cemetery is also located in the park and just before reaching the manor house, a left turn will reveal Farm Road The cemetery can then be reached by way of a dirt path.

Other Haunted New Jersey Cemeteries

Rose Hill Cemetery (Matawan) is a historic site that dates back to the Revolutionary War period. The windy roads and rolling terrain make this an unsettling place, especially at night, when the majority of the reported paranormal encounters take place. There have been strange tales of ghosts, weird sounds and chilling apparitions sighted on the grounds and the stories date back several decades.

It is said that on rainy night in New Jersey, the Alpine Cemetery (Perth Amboy) literally comes to life. According to the stories and legends, the ghosts here become more active when it is raining, or when these is strong humidity in the air. For some reason, the odd activity seems to feed off the dampness and moisture and it is during this time that not only are shadowy figures seen in the graveyard but witnesses have reported the sounds of running feet in the wet grass and leaves -- but there is never anyone there.

Three soldiers from the World War II era are believed to haunt St. Mary's Cemetery (Perth Amboy). People who have walked or have driven past the graveyard at night and have looked in say that it appears that three dark figures are standing near the site where the soldiers are buried. When they look again, the figures have vanished. Other witnesses say that they have often felt unusual cold spots near the grave site as well.

Laurel Grove Cemetery (Totowa) has been the scene of numerous sightings of a woman in a white bridal dress or gown. Dozens of people have reported the ghost in newspaper accounts and on radio interviews in recent years. Most of the time, she has been seen after dark as witnesses have passed the main gates. She tends to linger just inside and then vanishes out among the headstones.

New Mexico

Cimarron Area

Everyone thought that J.B. Dawson was crazy back in New Mexico of the 1880's when he started scraping coal from his farm land and using it to provide heat for his home rather than burning wood. They thought so until they tried it themselves and realized how well it worked.

Dawson, with his homestead, was just one of the ranchers with a few hundred acres that was giving trouble to the Maxwell Land Grant Company, which had purchased a huge section of land from Lucien Maxwell himself. The company had never looked into the matter of ranchers living on the land and had no idea who was squatting and who was a legal owner. However, when they saw how heavily laced with coal Dawson's land was, they immediately tried to have him evicted. Dawson fought back and claimed that he had bought the land from Maxwell, and had sealed the deal with a handshake -- which turned out to be the truth. The company still wanted him out though and while Dawson planned to settle the matter with guns, he eventually agreed to abide by a court ruling. The case was tried in 1893 and Dawson won. Along the way, he also discovered that the land parcel that he thought was just 1,000 acres, was actually more than 20,000 acres!

Dawson soon set about marketing his coal and sold the richest area to the Dawson Fuel Co. and another section for a town site. He retained about 120 acres for himself and watched as the town that was named in his honor began to grow. Much of the development was under the control of C.B. Eddy, the president of the El Paso & Northeastern Railroad, and soon plans were made to connect the town to other cities by rail line. The first mine opened in Dawson in 1901 and a sawmill was built that same year. Lumber was being produced at a steady rate and by the end of the first year, Dawson was well on its way to becoming the largest coal mining operation in New Mexico. A post office was soon established, as was a liquor store, the Southwestern Mercantile Co., a bank, church, a school and doctor's offices. By 1902, the population had already reached 600 and the town was regarded as having a "fine, stimulating climate" with "plenty of work for everyone". Dawson seemed blessed but it was doomed to suffer a series of tragedies that would bring its shadowed history to an end.

The first disaster occurred on September 14, 1903 when a fire and explosion at Mine No. 1 killed three miners. The bodies of the men were quietly buried in the new town cemetery and largely forgotten. Unfortunately, this would be only the beginning.

The year 1905 brought more business and more people to Dawson. A newspaper was established and an enormous amount of growth took place, pushing the population of the town to over 2,000 people. The mine expanded and then expanded again. About this time, the giant Phelps Dodge Corporation began to show an interest in Dawson. They ended up buying the mine company and re-organizing it as the Stag Canyon Fuel Co. and under new management, the town expanded even more with a population of 3,500. The local hotel gained a new addition and the palatial Dawson Theater was constructed at a cost of nearly $40,000.

The town's bordellos were forced to build their own addition to keep up with the arrival of single miners, most of whom were recent immigrants. Most of the single men, and those who had to make a stake before sending for their wives, lived in a part of town called Boarding House Row, an area where many of the inhabitants did not speak English. It was also an area of town that would become tragically empty in just a short time to come.

Dawson continued to grow and many of the old wood-framed buildings, like the school and the hospital, were replaced by sturdier structures made from brick. On April 6, 1913, the Dodge Phelps Corporation made plans to claim a huge section of land from the desert by building one of the largest irrigation projects in the country.

But it was during these days of prosperity and growth that the Dawson's greatest disaster occurred. On October 20, 1913, a tremendous explosion rocked Mine No. 2 and entombed 300 men, killing 263 of them. There were no warnings, no escaping gas or rumblings, only a sudden roar. Relief and disaster crews were rushed in from neighboring towns and even from as far away as Denver. In the first few hours, 22 men were accounted for and 16 were alive, which brought great hope to the rescue crews. As the days dragged on though, the bodies of the dead began to outnumber the living. The crews worked around the clock and as the rows of bodies brought to the surface grew longer, distraught wives and family members impeded the operations at the mouth of the mine. It was not until two of the rescuers themselves were killed by falling debris that the families were moved back to a safer distance.

Huge mass funerals were conducted for the victims and the tiny cemetery in Dawson overflowed, making it necessary to extend the graveyard far up the hill. Funeral services went on for weeks afterward and today, row after row of identical metal crosses still mark the graves of the men killed in the disaster.

But even after such a tragedy, life in Dawson went on. The town continued to grow and prosper and as safety measures at the mine were increased, subsequent accidents became minor and fatalities few. But then on February 25, 1923 another horrific explosion ripped through the mine and killed another 125 miners. The cemetery had to be extended once more to allow for the additional rows of graves.

In 1950, the Phelps Dodge Corporation announced that it planned to close down the mine. The mining of coal had become too costly when natural gas was so much cheaper and easier to obtain. On April 30, the mine was closed down for good and by this time, most of the inhabitants had departed. Curtainless windows looked out from vacant houses as the offices at the mine were emptied for the last time and everyone left. On June 6, the town was stripped and most of the machinery and buildings were torn down and destroyed. Only a handful of structures remained for a cattle operation and today, the scattered buildings are all that remain of the once prosperous community.

Aside from the old structures of the ghost town, only one other part of the place still exists today -- the old Dawson Cemetery. More than 350 white iron crosses mark the graves of those who perished here in the mine disasters. These silent sentinels, some with individual names and some unmarked, are reminders of the lives of the victims. And perhaps of their tragic deaths as well.

According to the legends, the dead miners of Dawson refuse to go quietly into the night, forgotten and unremembered. According to the legends of this place, eerie lights can often be seen dancing and flickering among these metal crosses in the darkness. The stories say that they are the carbide lights of the miner's helmets, still searching for rescue for the dark depths of the mine where they died.

Hauck, Dennis William - Haunted Places: The National Directory (2002)
Florin, Lambert - Ghost Towns of the Old West (1968)

New York

New York City

The Hell's Kitchen neighborhood of Manhattan is not generally thought of as one of the finest areas of the city, so most would be surprised to learn that New York governor George Clinton once resided here. In fact, an area called Clinton Court, on West 46th Street, remains as a reminder of the area's more refined past.

But this was not always such a fine area. Clinton Court may have once been the carriage house of a governor but prior to that, this whole section of the city was a potter's field -- a graveyard for the poor and for the executed. As the city started to grow, the cemetery was built over and no records show that it was ever moved, which explains why the presences here still make themselves known today.

One of the first phantoms ever reported here was a sailor who was executed for inciting a mutiny. His sentence had been carried out when the British still ruled New York and his body was tossed in a shallow grave in the potter's field. By the 1820's, after the cemetery was closed and homes began to be built on the site, this was the site of a carriage house on the estate of Governor Clinton and his family. The ghost would sometimes appear and frighten people, including the wife of a coachman, who was so startled that she stumbled and fell down a set of winding stairs to her death. The stairs still exist and the ghost of the coachman's wife is believed to still haunt them today. And she would not be the only one ...

The stories say that the children of Governor Clinton saw the ghosts here many times and the presences from the old burying ground had a habit of turning up expectedly. One afternoon while the children were playing, one of the governor's daughters was so frightened by an apparition that she fell down, struck her head and died. Her ghost is also believed to haunt the area and was seen many times by an artist who rented the downstairs apartment at Clinton Court some years ago. The ghost of a Colonial-era officer has also been spotted here on occasion.

Holzer, Hans - Where the Ghosts Are (1995)

Clinton Court can be found by entering a narrow passage at 420 West $6th Street and the building at 422 West 46th is the former carriage house. This is a private residence.

New York City

Even those who live in New York City know little about legendary Hart Island. As part of the Bronx, Hart Island rests in the waters of Long Island Sound. It is a desolate place, overgrown with weeds and stunted trees but the population of this small tract of land is made up of more than 800,000 people -- most of them nameless, forgotten and lost. And all of them quite dead. Since 1869, Hart Island has been a vast potter's field for the unclaimed dead that have piled up in the morgues of New York over the years. Labor on the island, handling the dead and digging the graves, is provided by inmates from Riker's Island, which is located just to the southwest.

The island is not really open to the public for more reasons than you might think. In addition to being a charnel house for the unclaimed and unknown, it is also the site of an abandoned missile base that was active between 1955 and 1961. The short range missiles stored here became obsolete within a few years when more advanced weapons began to be used as a last line of defense for New York, which was what this base was intended to be. The missiles were never used and the silos were sealed up and left to rust. They have long since been filled with water and have fallen into disrepair and ruin. The soldiers are gone and now only the dead remain -- but they may not be as silent or as at rest as some believe.

The occasional "official" visitor to this place must come in stages. The trip begins with a ride on a ferry that also carries a half dozen convicts and a cargo of pine boxes. Once at Hart Island, the burial detail loads the coffins onto a truck to make the trip to a long trench that has been dug to a depth of six feet. The convicts move the coffins, scratch names upon them and then shovel the dirt, as the armed guards stand nearby. The new boxes join older ones until the trench is full, with the final boxes resting just a short distance under the ground. Visits like this, which take place during the daylight hours, are largely uneventful -- but not always. One man that I had the chance to speak with told me of visiting the island as a member of the clergy. He described the place as remote and desolate, even so close to the city. One day as he was standing near a burial detail, he looked up and saw the figure of a man a short distance away near some trees. When he looked again, the man was gone. The minister still believes that he saw a ghost that day.

Much to the chagrin of city officials, the daytime visits are not the only time that Hart Island becomes habited again. It is a favorite place for teenagers from the city and from Long Island to sneak away to for a few good scares -- or to imbibe in spirits of another sort. If these adventurers are to be believed, Hart Island is a very haunted place after dark and there have long been tales of ghostly figures, strange lights and unexplained voices that are sometimes heard. This is an eerie and forbidding place and one can imagination that it would be simple to let your imagination get carried away from you here. But can all of the weird tales be attributed to alcohol and fantasy?

Jackson, Kenneth & Camilo Jose Vergara - Silent Cities (1989)
Strange New York: The Alternative Guide to New York
Personal Interviews & Correspondence

Other Haunted New York Cemeteries

The potter's field that is located at the Alms House and Poor Farm (Dewittville) dates back to the days when the farm was in use, between 1833 and 1918. No markers were used in the early days before 1869 and for that reason, many unmarked graves can be found here. The cemetery, and an old barn, on the property is believed to be haunted by those who spent their last, miserable days here and strange lights and apparitions have been seen and weird noises have been heard coming from the woods.

Strange figures have been sighted and ghostly cries have been reported at the Gootleburg Cemetery (East Aurora). Local legend has it that many of the bodies buried in the cemetery are victims of a doctor who carried out illegal abortions in town. He allegedly buried the bodies of the aborted fetuses in shallow graves on the property and when the women did not survive the crude operations, they were secretly buried here as well. Apparently, his practice was discovered when a neighborhood dog dug up one of the fetuses and brought it home one night. However, no one knows how many bodies were buried here. The story goes on to say that when the doctor was found out, he committed suicide and now his ghost haunts the place of his darkest secrets. His ghost has been reported here many times and eerily, the cries of babies can sometimes be heard in the darkness.

The Grunsey Hollow Cemetery (Frewsburg) is said to be the final resting place of a larger than normal number of children, thanks to several epidemics that swept through this area back in the 1800's. Stories say that many people have reporting glowing balls of light among the stones here and have heard the sounds of the children laughing and playing.

Forest Park Cemetery, which is also known as Pinewood and Forest Hills Cemetery (Troy) is regarded by many as one of the most haunted cemeteries in the country. Unfortunately though, little documentation exists to support this claim. The cemetery was started by a group of Troy businessmen in 1897, who purchased 200 acres of land and hired Garnet D. Baltimore, the first African-American to graduate from Rensselaer Polytechnic Institute, to design the cemetery. A dozen years later, the cemetery ran into financial problems and most of the undeveloped land was sold off. Around 1918, a group of out-of-town investors attempted to operate the cemetery under the name Forest Hills Cemetery (which explains the multiple names) but this venture also failed. Over time, the cemetery was abandoned and allowed to revert back to nature and no new burials are being carried out here. It is not open to the public today but this does not stop people from coming here. There have been many sightings of ghosts in the graveyard and unusual photos taken that have even been published in local newspapers. Some believe that the site was originally an Indian burial ground and that the spirit activity here is very turbulent and malicious. The extent of the haunting is unknown but the cemetery is (like Stull Cemetery and Spider Gates) rumored to be one of the so-called "gateways to Hell". Regardless of that silliness though, it is considered to be a very haunted place.

North Carolina

Wilmington

The shaded and tranquil surroundings of Oakdale Cemetery in Wilmington provide a peaceful illusion for the casual observer. Here, the moss-covered monuments and elaborate funeral art make the graveyard appear to be a calm and restful place. Below the surface though, restless spirits still walk here. For decades, ghost stories have been told about Oakdale Cemetery and there is much reason to believe that the dead here do not rest in peace.

The cemetery itself had dark beginnings. In the early and middle 1800's, the city of Wilmington was devastated by a number of epidemics. Yellow fever, typhoid and diphtheria all took a great toll on the population and with so much death, it soon became apparent that the local churchyards would not be able to hold the bodies of the dead. In 1852, a committee was appointed to locate a site for a new cemetery. Within two years, a parcel was chosen and sixty-five acres of land along Burnt Mill Creek were purchased for the new burial ground.

Dr. Armand J. deRosset, a prominent local physician, was chosen to serve as the first president of the cemetery board. Ironically, the first burial carried out in the new Oakdale Cemetery would be that of Dr. deRosset's own daughter, who was only six years old. The doctor was devastated by the loss and after her death, he gave up his medical practice. He was too shaken by the fact that his years of training could not save the life of his child.

Dr. deRosset would not be the only grief-stricken father to bury his child in Oakdale Cemetery and his little Annie would not be the only ghost who legends say still wanders this place. Another father was Captain Silas Martin, who buried his own daughter here a few years later.

Captain Martin was a wealthy Wilmington merchant and ship captain. In 1857, he set sail on a voyage to the Caribbean and took with him his daughter, Nancy, and his son, John. Soon after their departure, Nancy became ill and unfortunately, with no ship's doctor, there was little that could be done for her. Soon, her condition began to get worse and Captain Martin ordered the ship to the port of Cardenas, Cuba. By the time they arrived though, it was too late and Nancy had died. Captain Martin was a broken man. He could not bear to have his daughter buried on foreign soil and so far from home, nor did he want to have her buried at sea. He wanted to take his daughter home with him, but his business commitments would keep him at sea for some time to come. So, he had her placed inside of a cask of rum and then had the barrel sealed shut. In this way, Nancy's body would remain preserved until they could return to Wilmington.

Captain Martin's decision to continue his voyage turned out to be a tragic one. Several months after Nancy's death, in a terrific storm, the captain's son, John, was washed overboard and was lost. His body was never recovered. After this, the ship turned back and returned home, where Captain Martin had to break the horrible news to his wife that both of their children had died.

The distraught parents decided not to place Nancy's body in a coffin and they had her buried in the cask of liquor instead. The marker over her grave bears only the inscription "Nance", but her name and dates of birth and death appear on the family stone, just next to her brother's name, which is followed by the words "Lost at Sea".

Nancy's ghost has long been rumored to haunt this graveyard and it is not uncommon for visitors to report a forlorn young woman standing near her gravesite, the lonely echo of a life cut short.

The Civil War also left its mark on Oakdale Cemetery. There are the graves of nearly four hundred unknown Confederate soldiers here and legends say that some of these men still roam the burial ground today. In addition, Oakdale marks the final resting place of Rose O'Neal Greenhow, a spy for the Confederacy who was known in her day as "Rebel Rose". The stories say that may walk here as well.

During the height of the war, Rose was returning from England aboard a ship called the Condor. She was bringing with her over $2,000 in gold that she had earned from the publication of a book about her experiences as a spy. The gold was going to be added to the struggling coffers of the Confederacy in order to aid the war effort. As the ship neared the Carolina coasts, it ran into the Union blockade of the southern coastline and specifically the guns of the *U.S.S. Niphon*. In the pursuit that followed, the Condor ran aground and fearful of being captured by the Federal forces, Rose exited the ship in a small dinghy. The Captain begged her to stay on board, as the sea was rough and dangerous, but she insisted on trying to escape. Almost as soon as the small boat was lowered into the water, a wave crashed over it and the boat overturned. All of those aboard it were lost.

Rose Greenhow's body washed ashore a few days later and she was brought to Wilmington for burial. In tribute to her loyalty, her body was wrapped in a Confederate flag and she was buried with full military honors.

There have been many conflicting accounts about just what happened to the gold that Rose was carrying with her. Some claim that it was sewn into her clothing and others believe that it was placed in a purse and carried around her neck with a chain. All of them feel that it must have been responsible for her drowning though, although what became of it after her body was found remains a mystery. Perhaps this unsolved riddle is the reason that her ghost is still said to walk?

Local residents of the past are not the only spirits to haunt Oakdale Cemetery, for there are reports of a spectral dog as well. Many believe this ghost is that of old "Boss", who still guards the grave of his master, a riverboat captain named William A. Ellerbrook. The captain lost his life back in 1880 while fighting a fire in downtown Wilmington. According to those present, Ellerbrook's dog, Boss, stood back on the edge of the fire and then rushed fearlessly into the blaze when his master got into trouble. Those outside anxiously watched as the animal plunged into the fire and smoke but neither Ellerbrook nor Boss came back out again.

When their bodies were discovered, Captain Ellerbrook was lying face down, trapped beneath a smoldering timber. Nearby was Boss, who had been overcome by smoke while trying to pull the captain to safety. A torn piece of Ellerbrook's coat was still clamped in his jaws. It seemed appropriate to friends that the two long-time companions be laid to rest in the same coffin and so they were. On Captain Ellerbrook's monument is the sculpted image of a dog and the inscription, "Faithful Unto Death".

Preik, Brooks Newton - Haunted Wilmington (1995)

Wilmington is located on the far southern tip of North Carolina.

Other Haunted North Carolina Cemeteries

The ghost of a young woman named Claire Townsend is said to haunt the Meadowbrook Cemetery (Lumberton). The local legends say that Claire died in a horrible accident on the way to the church for her wedding. She has been seen in the cemetery since the early 1900's, always clad in a white wedding dress.

Henkelite Cemetery (Mount Pleasant) is a Confederate graveyard that is reported to be filled with the restless dead. The soldiers who were killed and buried here have been seen many times over the years and some witnesses claim that it is not uncommon to hear the sounds of marching feet tromping through the burial ground at night and even the sounds of gunfire on some occasions.

Ohio

Athens

If there is any town that might qualify as the most haunted place in Ohio, it would probably be Athens, a sleepy community in the southeastern part of the state. Besides being home to the Ohio University, it is also nestled into the Appalachian Mountains, which for centuries has been considered a region of magic and ghostly folklore. There are many stories to Athens -- and many ghosts. The ghost stories and legends here are numerous and include everything from the hauntings of an abandoned mental hospital, a myriad of haunted houses and stone angels who shed tears in local cemeteries.

For many years, Athens has been plagued, not only with tales of ghosts, but tales of cults and strange rituals also. For many, these stories are simply a part of the Appalachian folklore of the area, but for others, these stories are terrifyingly real. There have been many stories recounted in Athens about satanic groups and odd religious cults. It is believed that many such cults meet in areas that are regarded to be haunted, or are "power spots", and Athens certainly has more than its share. These cults (if they exist) have given birth to many related legends, especially in the graveyards of the surrounding area.

During the 1970's, these stories became especially widespread, perhaps corresponding with what became known as the "Hocking Hill Murders". Over a span of about eight years, a number of animals in Hocking County were mutilated and then left to die in fields and farm lots. Often the animals were discovered bleeding to death with their heads or their genitalia severed off. Although rumors were rampant about cult rituals, the authorities were reluctant to pursue this angle. The cases remained unsolved and the activity mostly died out in the 1980's.

This may have been the peak in Athens modern occult activity, but stories of local cults and ritual activities are countless and date back many years. This may be because of the huge influx of Spiritualists who came to the area many years ago. Their faith must have seemed strange to local residents and one thing is certain, many strange tales came about during their heyday in the Athens area. The area became most famous in 1852 when a local farmer named Jonathan Koons received word through a Spiritualist medium that he and all of his eight children were to be given the ability to communicate with spirits. He built a large house on top of a hill, according to directions he received from beyond, and the place became famous for its many séances and strange events.

Even outside of Mt. Nebo, there are other ghosts in Athens and a number of stories are connected to the Ohio University campus, including the Zeta Tau Alpha house, which is alleged to be haunted by an escaped slave who perished here years ago. This is not the only building on campus that is said to be haunted either. Another is Wilson Hall, which is home to the ghost of a student who died mysteriously there in the 1970's. The student died in room 428 and for years after, residents of the room claimed to hear footsteps and strange sounds and witnessed objects moving about the room on their own. The room has since been closed off and it is not given out to new students anymore.

Strangely, Wilson Hall is said to rest in the very center of one of Athens' most enduring legends. The building apparently falls in the middle of a huge pentagram that is made up by five of the area's cemeteries. The graveyards are located in the Peach Ridge area and allegedly, when the positions of each are plotted on a map, they actually do form the shape of a pentagram, the occult symbol of magic and power. The stories say that an Ohio University student once computed the actual distances to create the pentagram and found that the distance of the side actually matched up to within less than one-quarter mile of each other.

The five cemeteries are the largest ones in the area and are Simms, Hanning, Cuckler, Higgins and Zion. Of these five, Hanning and Simms are the most famous, and perhaps the most haunted. According to the stories, Simms Cemetery is said to have a rocky cliff on one side from which a tree protrudes outward. This was once used a gallows for executions and the rope scars can still be found marring the trunk. Local historians claim that John Simms, for whom the cemetery was named, may have once been the local hangman. This leads some people to believe that some of the reported ghosts of Peach Ridge many be spirits of those executed here. It is also said that John Simms himself is sometimes seen in the graveyard, perhaps still carrying out his duties from the other side.

Hanning Cemetery is another reportedly haunted spot. The ghost who has been seen here is an old man who wears a long robe. He is usually accompanied by the disembodied sounds of screams that echo into the night. There have been a couple of locally famous séances conducted at the burial ground, including one in 1969, when the heavily padlocked gate of the cemetery unlocked and opened on its own during the proceedings. During another séance in 1970, the spirit of David Tischman, a deceased Ohio University student was supposedly contacted by a group of his friends.

Another infamous graveyard in the area is Bethel Cemetery, located in nearby Troy Township. The cemetery is located near the border of Athens and Meigs County and is noted, not only for its ghost stories, but also for the strange way in which some of the graves are laid out. In most cemeteries, the graves are laid in an east-west direction to face the rising sun. At Bethel Cemetery, a whole plot of graves, that are more than one hundred years old, are inexplicably laid out in a north-south direction. Despite searches through old records, and accounts from long-time residents, no one seems to know why this section is placed differently from the rest of the graves in the cemetery.

Haines Cemetery on Lurig Road is also said to be haunted and this time by the ghost of a Civil War officer who went insane after the war. After returning home, he killed his entire family, burned down his house and then committed suicide. He and his family are buried in Haines Cemetery and his spirit still reportedly haunts the place, restlessly pacing back and forth. Those who might come face to face with him are supposed to have bad luck for years to come.

Taylor, Troy - Beyond the Grave (2001)

Athens is located on a mostly mountainous region in the southeast corner of the state. It can be reached by traveling southeast of Columbus, most of the way to the West Virginia line.

Columbus

For many years, fresh flowers have mysteriously appeared on the grave of Benjamin Allen, a soldier in the Confederate Army, who is buried in the Camp Chase Confederate Cemetery in Columbus, Ohio. The mysterious flowers have also been found on the grave of an unknown soldier here. Who leaves these offerings behind remains a mystery.

During the Civil War, Camp Chase was located on Livingston Avenue near Columbus. It was used for a variety of things during the conflict. In the early days of the war, it was a training camp and then a mustering-out point for Union soldiers but as prisoners-of-war began to tax the facilities on both side, it became a Confederate prison camp. Camp Chase was considered a pretty horrible spot, as most of the prisons were during the war. Some 2,000 prisoners died there of disease and malnutrition and so it is not surprising that the place has come to be considered as haunted. Many of these soldiers who died were buried in the prison cemetery and it is here that the famed "Lady in Gray" still walks and leaves gifts of flowers behind.

She is said to be a young woman who wears a gray traveling suit in the style of the Civil War era. She walks through the cemetery with her head bowed and appears to be weeping.

She has been observed walking directly through trees and through the iron cemetery gates.

Who this woman may be is unknown, but she is most likely the widow of one of the men who died here. Even after the war ended, many of the men who fought and died remained missing. Mass burials had taken place at the battlefields and at prisons like Camp Chase, which had created the Confederate cemetery here. Many women from the South journeyed to the northern camps in hopes of finding the resting place of their dead husbands.

The legends say that the Gray Lady was one of these widows. She came to the cemetery at some point in the years following the war, most likely around 1870. Only one burial in the graveyard, No. 46, had recorded the dead man as "Unknown" but the widow who searched the weed-choked grounds could find no grave for her husband. Sadly, the cemetery was in poor condition and the wooden markers had deteriorated and were rotting away. Many of them had already been lost. In these bitter days after the war, few in the North carried about the graves of Confederate soldiers.

The lonely widow came and went from the cemetery each day, looking for a name on a fallen grave marker that might belong to her husband. She became a familiar sight to those who lived in the area and the people who passed by often saw her walking through the cemetery in her gray dress, a wrinkled handkerchief clutched in her hand. She was soon dubbed the "Gray Lady of Camp Chase".

One day, the widow disappeared and was never seen in the graveyard again. She most likely gave up her search and went home, although someone conceived the romantic notion that she had died of a broken heart. She would not be seen again for many years and even then, it would be in a spectral form.

As the years passed, the cemetery continued to decline. The grave markers, now mostly rotted away, had fallen down and a great number had become lost. Weeds and brush overran the grounds and the place had been largely forgotten. Around 1900, a Confederate veteran named William H. Knauss took notice of the Camp Chase Cemetery. Thanks to his efforts the grounds were cleared of the tangled brush and a stone wall was built around the grounds to replace the old wooden fence. New headstones were also placed, as accurately as possible, based on the poor burial records. Knauss also organized memorial services for the dead, inviting local officials, other Confederate veterans and members of the Daughters of the Confederacy. His plans did not please everyone in the area and a number of newspaper editorials railed against him. The services brought many threats to those who attended and guards had to be posted to insure that order was kept. Over time though, the cemetery was saved and because of Knauss has been preserved for history.

Not long after the cemetery was restored, local people began to notice a strange figure walking through the cemetery day after day. Many of the older folks remembered the story of the Gray Lady who had once searched the graveyard for the burial site of her husband. Could this be the same woman after all of the years? And is so, how could she look so young? Then, passersby noticed something that gave the most hardened disbelievers a cold chill down the spine -- The Gray Lady of Camp Chase was apparently a ghost! Far too many people began to tell of seeing her walking among the new gravestones, only to suddenly vanish without a trace! The tales would go on to say that she was seen walking directly through trees and passing like a wisp of fog through the cemetery wall.

For many years, the stories have continued to be told about the Gray Lady. She still walks in Camp Chase today, they say, and many have encountered her. In the summer of 1988, during a Civil War re-enactment, many of the people present heard the sounds of a woman crying. There was no woman present but the weeping sounds were unmistakable.

Taylor, Troy - Beyond the Grave (2001)

Columbus is in Franklin County, in the central part of Ohio. The cemetery is located on Sullivant Avenue.

Marion

There is a "haunted" monument that stands in the Marion Cemetery. This sphere can be found marking the grave site of Charles Merchant and his family. The monument was built in 1887 and is a white stone column that is topped with a granite ball.

In July 1905, workmen discovered that this sphere seemed to rotate on its own accord. The ball could not have been moved without a number of workmen and a block and tackle. Perplexed, the officials at the cemetery poured concrete into the stone base and set the sphere back into position. Two months later, it was discovered to have moved again and the rough bottom patch was once again visible.

Curiosity seekers began traveling to the cemetery. One geologist theorized that the movement of the stone occurred because of unequal expansion caused by resting in the sun on one side and shade on the other. Others believed that weather might be the culprit. If moisture on the stone froze at night and then thawed in the daylight hours, the ball might shift slightly in its base as the dampness lubricated it. This theory seemed to hold up in the winter months, but what about in the summer, when the stone was also reported to move? The rotation was first noticed in July and has continued to turn ever since. And, how does the stone turn at all if was designed and fixed to stay in place? The mystery remains unsolved to this day.

Edwards, Frank - Strange World (1964)

Marion is in north central Ohio, about an hour north of Columbus.

Other Haunted Ohio Cemeteries

Woodland Cemetery (Dayton) is home to a glowing tombstone that marks the final resting place of a young girl who has been seen in the cemetery on many occasions. Strangely, she is normally seen during the daylights hours and described in a very distinctive manner, playing in the grass and skipping down pathways in the cemetery. She is said to have blond hair and is always seen with a blue sweater around her waist and Nike tennis shoes on her feet.

The old and forgotten Grove Cemetery (Troy) has not seen new burials since the late 1800's and is located in a wooded area and is rather difficult to find. Those who have come here though say that it can be a very eerie place after dark. Footsteps are often heard in the dark woods around the burial ground but are nowhere near as unsettling as the woman's screams that are sometimes heard and the moaning sounds that come from the back left corner of the graveyard. According to local legend, a woman was raped and murdered here back in the 1870's while visiting her grandfather's grave.

There is a legend concerning Stoney Creek Cemetery (Adams County) that dates back to the 1820's. The story goes that the cemetery caretaker discovered the victim of a brutal murder in the graveyard one morning, lying beneath a tree. The man had been decapitated and it was believed that his head had not been severed but rather ripped from his body and the killer had then carried it away with him. The police were unable to determine the man's identity and the case went unsolved and eventually was forgotten. Legend has it that on certain nights, the ghostly form of a headless man returns to the cemetery and can sometimes be seen under the tree where the body was found. Some believe that he is still hoping to be recognized so that his murder will someday be solved and he can rest in peace.

Oklahoma

Arapaho

A strange cemetery tale from Oklahoma dates back a number of years and involves a cemetery that is located in the town of Arapaho. It follows along the line that some ghosts are not seen, but only heard. This one in particular is said to cry out the words, "Oh no! Oh, my god! Robina has not been saved!"

When the voice was first heard, it was identified as that of a recently departed local named George Smith, a pious and religiously devout man. In 1936, his daughter was killed in an auto accident when she was only 19 years old. He never really recovered from the loss of his child and to make matters worse, the fact that she had not achieved salvation from the church haunted him until the day that he died. After Smith's death in 1972, visitors to the graveyard began to report an eerie disembodied voice coming from his gravesite. The stories quickly made the rounds and people began coming from all over to hear the words, lamenting the fact that Robina was not "right with God" when she died. Locals in the area report that the voice can still sometimes be heard today.

Witnesses vary in credibility, but even one minister claimed to hear the voice. In March of 1979, while holding a funeral service at a nearby gravesite, the pastor was startled by the sound of Smith's voice. In 1980, a couple named Cecil and Sharon Rutherford came forward with their own experience. They had been putting flowers at a grave that was located nearby when they heard a deep groan and then a bawling voice that cried that Robina had not been saved. Not knowing the ghostly tale of the cemetery, they thought someone might be playing a trick on them. They looked around but found no one else in the vicinity.

A few years ago, a geologist and part-time ghost hunter named Arthur Turcotte, attempted to find a natural explanation for the strange phenomena. He studied the gravesite and ran every test that he could possibly think of. Not only did he find no logical explanation for the voice, but he was also stunned to clearly hear it himself. The strange voice remains unexplained.

Taylor, Troy - Beyond the Grave (2001)

Arapaho is located in Custer County in western Oklahoma. The cemetery is just east of town.

Tulsa ????

The state of Oklahoma is infested with ghosts -- and legends. In gathering stories and locations from this state, I learned several years ago that if there are any stories that Oklahoma has more of than any state, it is the story of "Crybaby Bridge" (where a woman threw her baby into the river for one reason or another and on certain nights visitors can hear the sound of a baby crying) and of course, "Sparky's Graveyard". Since 1998, I have been deluged with different accounts of the cemetery and from scores of people who assure me that they can tell me the location of the "real" Sparky's Graveyard. In every case, the legend behind the site is a close variation on the same theme but the cemeteries are rarely ever in the same place.

The common location for Sparky's Graveyard is in Tulsa and while few can agree on the exact location, one popular spot is a cemetery that is located between Harvard and Yale on 91st, right in front of Jenks Middle School. Other claim that the cemetery is 20 or 30 miles west of Prattville, on a desolate road near Coyote Trail. I have also received accounts that it is in northeast Oklahoma, in Oklahoma City and even as far west as Weatherford. I will leave the location up to the reader to decide.

Not only is there a disagreement as to where Sparky's Graveyard is located, there is also a question as to who Sparky was -- or is, depending on your take on things. One thing that most can agree on is that the graveyard that he watched over was an African-American burial ground. Some claim that Sparky was a Native American caretaker for the cemetery and others claim that he is simply an Indian ghost. Regardless, he somehow ended up without his head and now his ghost still haunts the place.

Others claim (and this is the most popular version) that Sparky was an albino who cared for the cemetery. He was only ever seen at night, cleaning the cemetery and mowing the grass, and was such a spooky figure that no one would go near him. However, the cemetery was always clean and well kept and so everyone left him alone. One day, Sparky died and no one noticed until the cemetery started to become overgrown. Since that time, it has never been properly cared for and so Sparky's ghost has come back to haunt the place and to scare away trespassers and vandals. He appears suddenly, with his shockingly white skin, long white hair and glowing red eyes to drive people out of the graveyard after dark.

There are variations to the albino version of the story as well. One of them tells of a time in the 1940's when a local newspaper started a contest that dared people to enter the ghostly burial ground. A red ribbon was tied on a tombstone in the middle of the cemetery and anyone who would retrieve the ribbon at midnight and come back with it in hand, would receive a reward. Weeks went by before someone got up enough nerve to do it. A huge crowd gathered at the gate to witness the young man's daring. He went into the cemetery, minutes passed by and then hours -- finally, days and then weeks. The boy never returned and neither he nor the ribbon were ever found. Legend has it though that if you venture out to the cemetery at midnight, you will find Sparky and his assistant, with a red ribbon tied around his neck, walking through the graveyard, waiting for vandals and trespassers to appear.

So, where is Sparky's Graveyard? I have no idea. It may be in Tulsa or it may be somewhere else on the Oklahoma plains -- or even thriving in the imaginations of those who reside in this region. However, if someone tells you that they can show you the "real" Sparky's Graveyard, go along with them because this story had to have gotten started somewhere. Perhaps the next ramshackle graveyard may be the place!

Other Haunted Oklahoma Graveyards

There is a place called old Bennett Cemetery (Warner) that was allegedly started after a house fire killed all of the children in the Bennett family in the late 1800's. According to witnesses, the cemetery is alive at night with shimmering lights that appear among the tombstones and then flicker back and forth across the grounds. The stories also say that the lights sometimes come out of the cemetery and follow people to the section line, then turn around and go back into the cemetery again.

The Native American fighter Geronimo was captured and then imprisoned at Fort Sill until his death. Since that time, the Apache Cemetery (Lawton) has been believed to be haunted by his spirit. Although no apparitions have ever been seen, many who come to his grave claim to have felt his presence.

Timberidge Cemetery (Catoosa) is located about six miles east of town and is located in an area that local residents dubbed "Haunted Hollow" many years ago. According to accounts, a young Native American boy was struck and killed near the cemetery in 1989. He was riding his bicycle and had stopped to fix the chain when the car hit him. He was buried in the cemetery, apparently near the front gates. The gates that mark the entrance are located at the bottom of a hill and since 1993, motorists who are coming down the hill often claim to see a boy kneeling beside a bicycle on the side of the road. Many say that they have swerved to miss him but still others claim that they have heard the sound of striking something with the car, or feel the shudder of the impact. When they stop, nothing has ever been found, although there have been claims of finding bloody handprints on the fender of the car. Allegedly, the Catoosa police have on file a number of reports from drivers who say they struck a boy on a bicycle and even photos of minor damage to cars, but no accident victim is ever found.

Pennsylvania

Blairsville

Livermore Cemetery is a place of many legends and can be found in the small town of Livermore -- or at least it could be found there if Livermore still existed. The town was closed down in 1950 to make way for the Conemaugh River Lake, a flood control project for the Army Corps of Engineers. The town was named in honor of Alonzo Livermore, an engineer for the Pennsylvania Canal, which was the main industry for the town in its early days. Livermore was a place of considerable size and was large enough to have been incorporated as a borough in 1863. There were more than 40 homes and businesses here at one time, but all are gone now. The inhabitants have moved on and the area is now abandoned -- or is it?

Livermore has become the subject of many ghost stories, dark tales and legends over the years. Some say that if the water is clear, and the moon is just right, you can still see the tops of house and the steeple of the church out in the lake where the doomed town still stands. Many also believe that the spirits of long dead Livermore residents were disturbed when the town cemetery was relocated to higher ground just before the dam was constructed. It has been said that their ghosts are now restless and roam the forest searching for the homes and the places they once knew. Many who have come to this place, searching for these ghosts, vow never to return.

Over the years, stories of circulated about ghostly apparitions and strange sounds, like the man and his cow who have been seen walking down a path toward the old town site and the horse and carriage that travels along the road and then simply vanishes. A woman in an old fashioned dress has been seen as well and eerie voices have been known to echo out in the trees when no one living is around.

Tales of ghosts have been around for years but the most persistent and famous legend would have to be that the graveyard scenes from George A. Romero's classic "Night of the Living Dead" were filmed here at Livermore. Given that Romero is a Pittsburgh native and that the sequel "Dawn of the Dead" was filmed in the area, this is certainly possible. It would certainly be ironic that one of the classic horror films of all time was filmed in a real-life haunted cemetery, wouldn't it?

If you do come here though, be sure to obey the hours that are posted at the cemetery gate. The graveyard has been the site of repeated vandalism over the years, due to its remote location and its reputation for being haunted. There have also been occurrences of occult ritual activity also. For this reason, visitation to the cemetery is restricted and trespassing is not tolerated. If Romero's flesh-eating zombies don't get you, the cops will!

Personal Interviews & Correspondence

The former site of Livermore is located near Blairsville, which is about 35 miles east of Pittsburgh. Go four miles west of Blairsville to the intersection of routes 22 and 982. Go north from this intersection on Livermore Road for approximately three miles to the Livermore Cemetery.

Lehighton

For many years, the Lehighton Cemetery has been rumored to be haunted by the ghosts of the victims of a little-known Indian massacre that occurred in Pennsylvania in 1755. The town got its start back in 1746 when the Moravian Brethren society began converting Indians to Christianity. The Moravians organized a mission in what is now South Lehighton, and named this settlement "Gnadenhuetten", which means "huts of mercy." The mission served as an agricultural and religious school for the native Delaware Indians.

As Gnadenhutten grew and prospered, the missionaries began a new settlement along the east side of the river, now Weissport, and named it New Gnadenhutten. The Delaware Indians and the Moravians lived together peacefully in these settlements. In 1750, a great war king of the Delaware Indians, Teedyuscung, was even baptized as a Christian.

However, some members of the Delaware tribe began to resent the presence of the European settlers and the loss of their land, and joined forces with the Shawnees and Mohicans to wage war on the settlers. The Moravians decided to stay in Gnadenhutten even though they knew they were in danger. In late 1755, the mission house was attacked. Ten people died, one person was captured, and all of the buildings were burned to the ground. New Gnadenhutten settlers were warned of the attack and were able to escape to Bethlehem. The massacre slowed the settlement of Carbon County somewhat. However, when hostilities ended in 1758, settlements along the river began to thrive.

As time has passed, it has been said that the victims of the massacre have been seen, both during the day and at night, wandering around the tomb where they were buried and memorialized.

Personal Interviews & Correspondence

Lehighton is located in eastern Pennsylvania, about 18 miles north of Allentown.

Other Haunted Pennsylvania Cemeteries

Forest Lawn Cemetery (Johnstown) has been the site of a ghostly woman in white for many years. She has been seen walking through the cemetery at night by a number of reliable witnesses but no one has any idea of who she is.

There have also been a number of unusual sights reported at Palmer Cemetery (Philadelphia). There have been reports of an apparition of a woman and a young boy who have been seen walking through the burial ground, as well as shadowy figures and a woman who walks along holding a baby.

There have been a number of people who have reported seeing a ghostly woman near a grave in Haag Cemetery (Bernville). The grave monument honors George D. Fahrenbach, a Civil War veteran who lived from 1846 to 1919. However, the identity of the man's ghostly companion remains unknown.

Rhode Island

Exeter

The spirit of a vampire still lingers in Exeter, Rhode Island.

Whether or not this spirit literally remains here or not may be an unanswered question but regardless, if you ask anyone in the region of the most famous vampire in American history, you are sure to hear about Mercy Brown. Her story is told and re-told and of Rhode Island's many vampire tales, hers is the best known and perhaps even the most tragic.

The story of Mercy Brown may end in the Chestnut Hill Cemetery in 1892, but it actually started a number of years before that in 1883. The story began with an outbreak of the "White Death", as tuberculosis was often referred to in those days. With no knowledge of medicine, many people believe that diseases and plagues were caused by supernatural means. An outbreak of the white death was often thought to be a string of vampire-related murders. Several heart-breaking deaths occurred in the George Brown family in 1883 and the first of them succumbed to the mysterious ailment in the winter of that year.

George Brown was a hard-working farmer who prospered in the Exeter area. He and his wife, Mary, had raised six children and lived a comfortable but simple life. In late 1883, the first in a series of terrible events occurred on the Brown farm. Late that year, Mary Brown began to show signs of consumption. The sturdy, once healthy woman began to suffer from fainting spells and periods of weakness. Most of all, she was gripped with a harsh cough that kept her awake through the night. The disease began to ravage her body and on December 8, she slipped into unconsciousness and did not awaken.

The following spring, Mary Olive, George's oldest daughter, also came down with the dreaded illness. She began to complain of terrible dreams and of a great pressure that was crushing her chest at night, making it impossible for her to breathe. Mary Olive grew paler and weaker with each passing day and on June 6, 1884, she followed her mother to the grave.

Several years of peace followed the death of Mary Olive and during this time, Edwin Brown, George and Mary's only son, got married and bought his own farm in nearby West Wickford. Here, he hoped to make a life for himself and his new bride while he worked in a store to support his family and save money for the future. All was going well until about 1891, when Edwin began to notice the symptoms of the disease that had killed his sister and mother. He resigned from his job and following advice from friends, moved west to Colorado Springs. Here, he hoped that mineral waters and a drier climate might restore his health.

While Edwin was out west, things got worse for the family in Exeter. In January 1892, he received word that his sister Mercy had become sick and had died. He also began to realize that his health was not improving either. He came to the decision that he should return home and spend the remainder of his days with his family, friends and loved ones.

By the time he reached Rhode Island, he found his father in a dreadful and worried state. He had become convinced that the family was being preyed upon by a vampire. After much debate, it was decided that they should exhume the bodies of the other family members and see which one of them it was. How they convinced Edwin to go along with this is unknown, but a group of men went out to the cemetery during the early morning hours of March 18, 1892.

It is likely that this exhumation would have remained a secret, if not for the fact that the men sought official sanction for it from the local doctor. They approached the district medical examiner, Dr. Harold Metcalf, and asked him to come to the graveyard to examine the bodies. He discouraged them but eventually agreed to go along, realizing that he could not persuade them from what they believed was their duty. By the time that he arrived at the cemetery, the bodies of Mary Brown and her daughter, Mary Olive, had already been unearthed. Dr. Metcalf took a look at them and found them in a state of advanced decay. They were "just what might be expected from a similar examination of almost any person after the same length of time", he stated with certainty.

Mercy's body had not yet been buried. As she had died in the winter, the ground was too hard for a burial. Her body had rested for the past two months inside of a small crypt on the cemetery grounds. The coffin was placed on a small cart inside of the tomb. Once the casket was opened, Dr. Metcalf looked inside and began a quick autopsy of the corpse. What he noted, mainly decay and the marks of consumption on the lungs, did not convince him that she was a vampire. He finished the examination and quickly left.

The other men remained behind. To them, Mercy seemed relatively intact, or at least more so than she should be after two months in the grave. In addition, they were also sure that her body had moved. She had been laid to rest on her back and somehow, the corpse was now resting on her side. Could she have left the casket?

They were nearly sure that Mercy was a vampire and what happened next convinced them entirely. One of the men opened up her heart with his knife and was startled to see fresh blood come pouring out of the organ. It was quickly removed from her chest and burned in the cemetery. As it was engulfed in the flames, ashes were gathered with which to make a tonic that would hopefully cure Edwin of the disease.

Edwin consumed the macabre mixture, but it did no good and he died soon afterwards. On May 2, he too was buried in the cemetery. While tragic, all was not lost. He became the last of the Brown family to die from the mysterious "White Death". The exhumation had ended the vampire's control over the family once and for all.

Even though these events took place more than a century ago, Mercy Brown has not faded from the memory of those in Exeter. Famous Rhode Island author H.P. Lovecraft even included a thinly disguised Mercy Brown in his vampire tale *The Shunned House.* In addition, the story has appeared many times in documentaries and books about the supernatural. Gone, but not forgotten -- Mercy Brown lives on as America's most celebrated vampire.

Rondina, Christopher - Vampire Legends of Rhode Island (1997)
Bell, Michael E. - Food for the Dead (2001)
Taylor, Troy - Beyond the Grave (2001)

Exeter is located in central Rhode Island and the cemetery can be found by following signs to the Chestnut Hill Baptist Church, which lies behind Rhode Island Historical Cemetery No. 22. Mercy Brown's grave is in the center of the small cemetery.

South Carolina

Charleston

St. Phillips Church was founded in 1710 and is recalled as the first Anglican Church to be organized south of Virginia and remains today as the oldest church organization in Charleston. The church that now stands as St. Phillips was constructed in 1835 but the earlier church stood here for many years. Because of the age of the site, the cemetery that exists around it is a wonderful example of an early American churchyard. It is classic in many ways -- including the fact that it harbors at least one ghost.

After St. Phillips was completed, it was called the "most elegant religious edifice in America." Boatmen on the nearby docks came to use the church as a landmark as it was 100 feet long, 60 feet wide and 40 feet high, with a cupola that towered 50 tall and contained two bells and a clock. Charleston was a busy port in those days, shipping out loads of indigo and rice and playing host to steamers that traveled back and forth between New York and the West Indies. Although the boatmen and the dockworkers may have thought highly of the church, they did not attend services there. Most of them were slaves and were owned by the wealthy planters whose names were on the St. Phillips membership rolls.

One of the dock workers was a slave named Boney and he handled shipments of rice for his master, the owner of a large Waccamaw River plantation. Boney lived in a small house behind the master's town house on King Street and while he worked mostly during the daytime, he would often come down to the docks at night to watch the ships go out of the port. One night in 1796, Boney was on the docks, as he knew that his master was sending down two schooners of rice the following morning. He had alerted the factor, who served as the banker and stockbroker for the planter, and the two men were talking that evening about business. The factor was a friendly man, who had become wealthy from the commissions that he had made while investing the earnings of Boney's master. As the two men talked that night, the conversation eventually came around to Boney's freedom. He desired his freedom more than any slave that he had ever known but knew that he was unlikely to ever receive it. His master valued his knowledge and skills and while the planter was a kind man, Boney still longed to be free.

As the two men were taking, Boney gazed off into the distance and suddenly became alert. There appeared to be a fire burning in the steeple of St. Phillips Church. Boney ran as fast as he could and when he reached the building, he began climbing up the side of it, working his fingers into the bricks. He scaled the structure and when he reached the cupola, he saw that some of the shingles were burning on the top. He pushed himself harder, knowing that if more of the shingles caught fire, the entire church would burn. As Boney reached the top of the steeple, he burned his hands as he pulled the shingles loose and tossed them away. Then, tearing off his shirt, he smothered the smoldering flames that remained. Satisfied that the building was saved, he climbed back down to the ground. When he reached the bottom, the factor and a group stood watching. They assured him that he had saved the church from destruction.

The following morning, Boney's master accompanied the rice schooners to the Charleston docks and the factor told him what Boney had done at the church. His master was overwhelmed. He loved the church and he and his wife had been married there. He was so proud of Boney that he granted the young man his freedom. Boney hardly knew what to do with himself. He immediately went home and told his wife and children the good news and he never worked another day in his life. Most of them time, he spent down on the docks staring at the ocean or in the St. Phillips churchyard, sleeping and staring up at the steeple that had been responsible for his freedom.

Unfortunately though, Boney had loved his work. He had wanted his freedom -- desperately -- but now he was lost and unable to adjust to the fact that he was free. Slowly, his health deteriorated and Boney wasted away and he died. His master was heartbroken and he took Boney's body and laid him to rest in the slave cemetery on his plantation.

Time passed and the original church was replaced in 1835. A new steeple was added around 1848 but the bells were removed during the Civil War and were given to the Confederacy to be used in making cannon. The church was damaged during the war but managed to endure.

Since those days, sightings of a "gray man" have repeatedly occurred in the graveyard. The first recorded sighting happened in the early 1900's, when a woman was walking through the cemetery looking at the graves of the famous people who have been buried here, including several early governors, Edward Rutledge, a signer of the Declaration of Independence, John C. Calhoun and others. Just as she was about to leave, she saw someone standing out among the markers. She stepped a little closer and saw a man with his back resting against a tombstone. His gaze was intense and his eyes were locked on the church steeple. His skin and his hair were dark, she later noted, but his eyes were almost completely white. The man has been seen many other times over the years but each of the sightings are the same. Most believe that it is the spirit of Boney, still lingering here and staring up at the church that brought him the one thing that he most wanted -- and the thing that he found he never really wanted at all.

Rhyne, Nancy - Coastal Ghosts (1985)

St. Phillips Church and Cemetery is located at 142 Church Street in Charleston.

Myrtle Beach

The story of Alice Flagg is one of the most enduring tales of the region known as South Carolina's Grand Strand. Alice's story is one that is steeped in romance, tragedy, death and despair and one can hardly be surprised to know that her ghost still walks near her gravesite in All Saints Waccamaw Cemetery. The story would almost not be complete without that detail...

Alice's tale begins in 1849 when she and her family built the Hermitage Plantation house, south of Myrtle Beach at Murrell's Inlet. The head of the family was Dr. Allard Belin Flagg, Alice's brother, and he moved Alice and their mother into the house. Dr. Flagg was very protective of his sister and was angry and upset when she fell in love with a common laborer, a man he felt was beneath the station of their family. He refused to let Alice have anything to do with the man, which only caused her to want to see him more. Eventually, the two became engaged but Alice had to hide the ring on a ribbon around her neck to prevent her brother from seeing it. Unfortunately, she became ill with malaria and her brother discovered the ring. In fit of anger, he tore it from her neck and hid the ring somewhere in the house.

Alice seemed to get better for awhile and then grew even sicker. The family and the doctors they brought in to treat her realized that she was soon going to die. As she lay on her deathbed, Alice asked her brother over and over again if he would return the ring to her. Stubbornly though, he refused and finally, it was too late. Alice slipped into a coma and died without ever getting a chance to see her fiancée again -- and without ever having her ring back on her finger. She was placed in her favorite dress and laid to rest in the All Saints Waccamaw Cemetery.

But Alice has never rested in peace. Soon after her demise, her spirit returned to the Hermitage to search for the engagement ring that her brother took from her. She has been seen here many times and often, items are found to have been rummaged through in the house, as if someone had been looking for something. Her face has also been seen peering out the round window of her second-floor bedroom and reflected in the mirrors in the house.

The plantation house is not the only place where Alice's ghost has been encountered either. She has also been seen many times near her grave in the cemetery, which is marked with a wide, flat stone that lies flush with the ground. Only a single word is inscribed on it -- "Alice". For more than a century, romantic young women from all over the state have come here to place fresh flowers on her grave. They believe that by doing so, and by following a certain ritual, that their own love life will be lucky and that none of them will be doomed to endure what Alice went through. The story goes that if you leave a bouquet of flowers on Alice's grave, then walk backward around her grave 13 times, you will awaken her sleeping spirit and will have a happy life that will be filled with love.

Rhyne, Nancy - Coastal Ghosts (1985)
Personal Interviews & Correspondence

Myrtle Beach is located along the South Carolina coast and the church cemetery lies three miles west of Pawleys Island. The Hermitage remains south of town on Murrell's Inlet.

Other Haunted South Carolina Cemeteries

Bethabara Church Cemetery (Cross Hill) is the site of a glowing tombstone that reportedly lights up about three to four times each year. The accounts have it that the marker is a stone cross that is a rust color and that it rests on the grave of a Civil War veteran. For unknown reasons, the cross will glow and reportedly change colors several times before returning to normal.

The old Montrose Graveyard (Mechanicsville) is a place of many legends. According to the stories, the old Montrose church mysteriously burned down in the middle 1800's and was rebuilt and called Mount Hope Church. This church also burned down years later and while the ruins remained for some time after, they are completely gone now. However, the cemetery is still there, although it fell into such a state of disrepair by the 1940's that it was closed down and a collective marker was placed outside of it for all of the graves and stones that were lost. Then, once more according to the legends, a man came here in the 1960's with his children and murdered them. They say that to this day, the sounds of children screaming and crying come be heard coming from the burial grounds at night. The frightened wails cry for their father to not hurt them -- and are followed by silence.

West End Cemetery (Newberry) is said to be haunted by a ghost that has been dubbed the "Bride of West End". This woman in white appears within the confines of the cemetery on certain nights, standing next to her grave or roaming about. She is always seen wearing a dreary-looking bridal gown and is said to be waiting for her lover to return to her. The story states that she committed suicide on her wedding day many years ago when her fiancée left her waiting at the altar.

South Dakota

Deadwood

Deadwood, in the Dakota Territory, was sometimes referred to as the "wildest gold town in the West". It came into existence thanks to the Black Hills gold rush of 1874 to 1876. At that time, the Black Hills belonged to the American Indian tribes and trespassing and prospecting here was forbidden. However, men dubbed the "sooners" were the first to learn that gold could be found in the Hills. Scientific expeditions confirmed the presence of the precious metal and before long, packs of "sooners" were squatting illegally in the Hills area. The prospectors were forcibly removed by the authorities.

It wasn't long though before the military was having a hard time keeping the prospectors out, so the U.S. Government embarked upon another round of land cession from the Native Americans. The land was seized and the Indians were moved out once again. The prospectors moved in to take their place and slowly the Dakota rush moved northward, finally hitting Deadwood Gulch. Tents and shacks began to sprout up in the area and were quickly serviced by saloons, suppliers, opportunists and "camp girls". Soon, Deadwood was born.

The rich takings of the gold fields brought all manner of people to the area, including those who came to take the wealth from the hands of those who worked for it. Those who offered services came first, but the gamblers, the thieves and the lawbreakers soon followed them. The wide-open atmosphere of the region helped spawn the tales of adventure and the legends that still circulate around this area today. These tales were born in the saloons, the gambling parlors and the bordellos of Deadwood. Such establishments were considered the most legitimate of the town's early businesses. Then came to Deadwood a man that became a legend. His name has been permanently attached to this town and while he may have been mercilessly gunned down years ago, his spirit has never left.

James Butler Hickok, or "Wild Bill" as he came to be known, was one of the rare breed of gunfighters who never asked for fame and notoriety. All he wanted was a good card game and a steady income. On a good day, he managed both but he also went on to become one of the greatest legends of the Old West. Hickok was born on a farm in Illinois and was raised with a taste for danger, having been exposed to it throughout his life. His father, a long-time abolitionist, allowed the farm to be used as a station on the Underground Railroad. This meant a constant stream of escaped slaves from the South and a constant danger of being found out by the authorities.

During the Civil War, Hickok joined up with the Union forces and served under General John C. Fremont, a future explorer of the far western states. It was said that Hickok greatly impressed his friends and officers by showing a deadly speed and accuracy with a gun. At the Battle of Pea Ridge in March 1862, he was said to have picked off 36 Confederate soldiers in a matter of minutes.

After the war was over, Hickok settled in Springfield, Missouri and during his time here, made history. On July 20, 1866, while playing cards, Hickok quarreled with a man named Dave Tutt over a poker game, or over a woman named Susannah Moore, depending on the version of the story told. During the altercation, Tutt took Hickok's prized Waltham pocket watch and refused to give it back. The following day, Tutt strolled down the street, wearing the watch. He stood in the dusty road, about 75 feet away from where Hickok waited, leaning against a porch post.

"Don't come any closer, Dave!" Hickok warned the other man.

Tutt came no closer, but he did reach for his gun. He fired first but the shot never came close. It was said that Hickok's hand moved so fast that it blurred. He cleared leather and fired one shot. The bullet entered Tutt's chest and the man died instantly. He was dead before he hit the street. The West had just seen the first recorded showdown.

The pistol remained in Hickok's hand. He turned to where several of Tutt's friends stood watching. "Aren't you satisfied, gentlemen?" he reportedly questioned them. "Put up your shooting irons or there will be more dead men here." None of the others dared to face him. Hickok reclaimed his pocket watch from the dead man's coat and he surrendered himself to the local sheriff. He was cleared of all charges on August 5.

In September of that same year, Hickok ran for marshal of Springfield but lost the election. On that same day, a writer for "Harper's" magazine named Colonel George Ward Nichols arrived in town, looking for material for an article that he was writing about the West. He was introduced to Hickok and told the story of the gunfight. Nichols published the story, now very sensationalized, in February 1867. Later that year, a story called "Wild Bill, the Indian Slayer" appeared and caught the attention of the public, whose thirst for Western adventure was beginning to grow. It wasn't long before "Wild Bill Hickok" became a household name.

Unfortunately for Hickok though, fame didn't put food on the table. He ran for the Ellsworth County Sheriff's office in November but was defeated again. After that, he turned to scouting and worked briefly for Custer's Seventh Cavalry. In early 1868, he joined William "Buffalo Bill" Cody to supervise prisoner relocation from Fort Hays to Topeka, Kansas. He put the military behind him in February 1869.

Hickok eventually became a lawman. He was elected sheriff of Ellis County, Kansas and on the day after the election, shot to death a man named Bill Mulvey. He was determined to let the lawless element of the region know that he meant business and a month later, he killed a desperado named Jack Strawhim in Drum's Saloon. His tenure as sheriff ended in July 1870 though when he put down a disturbance of drunken soldiers, killing one and wounding another. General Sheridan was furious with the gunfighter and ordered Hickok arrested. By that time though, Hickok had already drifted out of town.

He ended up in Abilene, Kansas, following the card games and the rich pockets of the inebriated cowboys who ended up in town after months on the trail. Hickok found easy pickings for his card-playing skills. Abilene was a rough town at the time, so it's no surprise that Mayor Joseph McCoy tapped Hickok to serve as the town's sheriff. He was appointed with a salary of $150 a month, which supplemented his poker games. His first act as sheriff was to ban firearms within the city limits.

On the night of October 5, 1871, a group of about 50 cowhands began raising hell in town. A stray dog nipped the ankle of a cowboy named Phil Coe and in his intoxicated state, he shot the dog dead. Hickok, gambling at the Alamo Hotel, heard the shot and came running. He demanded to know who had the gun within the limits of Abilene and he spotted Coe with a pistol in his hand. Hickok attempted to disarm him but a fight ensued. Hickok's hat was shot from his head but Coe died with a fatal wound to the groin.

In the confusion, Hickok's friend Mike Williams rushed to help. Hickok saw only a flash of movement and thought that he was being ambushed by one of the other cowhands. He spun and fired and shot Williams dead by mistake. Hickok was so distraught over the shooting that he got drunk and ran every cowboy out of Abilene, shooting up the town in the process. At the next election, the citizens of Abilene decided that they were tired of both cattle drives and Wild Bill Hickok. They banned one and got rid of the other.

By 1872, Hickok was both famous and broke. He decided to try and cash in on his image and he launched a theater production in Niagara Falls, New York called "The Daring Buffalo Chase of the Plains". It boasted a number of western characters, Indians and even real buffalo -- but no audience. The show soon closed and Hickok sold six of the buffalo to pay train fare home for the Indians who retired from show business.

The following year, Hickok joined up with Buffalo Bill Cody for a stage show called "Scouts of the Prairie". This endeavor proved to be much more successful and Hickok stayed with the show for seven months. Although steadily working, Hickok took to drinking and one night, shot out all of the stage lights in the theater. That night's appearance was his last and Cody kicked him out of the show. As he packed up and left, Cody was heard to mutter, "I wish I had killed that son of a bitch when I had the chance years ago."

Although no one knew it, Hickok's drinking was most likely a result of the fact that he was losing his vision to glaucoma. He was having a tougher time seeing and facing down the young toughs who decided to try their hand at beating Wild Bill Hickok to the draw. He drifted across the West, sometimes narrowly avoiding being killed, playing poker and losing just enough money to stay broke. In 1874, he was in Cheyenne, Wyoming when an old flame named Agnes Lake appeared on the scene. The two of them were married on March 5, 1876 but after a short honeymoon in Cincinnati, they parted ways. Hickok was off to hunt gold in the Dakota Territory and in April 1876, rode into Deadwood.

Early in the afternoon on August 1, Hickok sat down to a game of poker at Carl Mann's No. 10 Saloon. He took his seat in the corner, with his back to the wall, just as he always did.

At some point in the game, a saddle bum named Jack McCall got into the game. The stories vary as to what passed between McCall and Hickok. Some say the gunfighter cursed McCall when he fell short on settling up and others say that he embarrassed the cowboy by giving him breakfast money when he played his last bad poker hand. Regardless, Hickok went about his business, oblivious to trouble, while McCall seethed and swore revenge.

The next day, Hickok returned to the saloon to find a game in progress between Carl Mann, Charles Rich and an ex-riverboat captain named William R. Massie. They invited Hickok to sit in and Wild Bill said that he would if Rich, who had the seat by the wall, would trade him places. Rich made a joke about it and Hickok sheepishly took a seat with his back to the door.

By late afternoon, Hickok was losing badly to Massie. Still, he held a promising hand -- two black aces, two black eights and a jack of diamonds. There was a potential here, he knew, but was unaware that danger had entered the saloon behind him. Some time around 4:15, Jack McCall had slipped into the saloon. He inched his way along the bar until he was two or three feet behind Hickok. He suddenly pulled his Colt from its holster and aimed it at Hickok's back. "Damn you, take that!" he yelled and pulled the trigger.

The bullet slammed into the back of Wild Bill's skull, exited just under his right cheekbone and struck Captain Massie's forearm, just above his left wrist. (Massie never had this slug removed and carried it with him until his death in 1910. It is now buried in Bellefontaine Cemetery in St. Louis) Hickok died without knowing what had happened to him. He fell forward onto the table and his cards, known today as the "Dead Man's Hand", slipped out of his fingers and fell to the floor.

McCall turned his pistol on the onlookers and dared them to come after him. He ran out of the rear door and cries of "Wild Bill is dead!" followed him out into the alley. Hickok's friends found the man hiding in a butcher shop less than a half-hour later. A trial was organized by the following morning, only to adjourn in the afternoon for Hickok's funeral. When the hearing when back into session, McCall claimed that Hickok had killed his brother in Hays City in 1869, but could offer no proof of this. Regardless, a jury found him not guilty, to the dismay of Hickok's friends and the prosecutor, a lawyer named May. McCall remained in Deadwood a free man, but he became nervous thanks to threats from Hickok's friends and angry local residents. May claimed that the jury had been paid off in the trial and he harassed and followed McCall everywhere. He would not rest, he vowed, until justice had been done.

Many legends have sprung up about the death of Wild Bill and some have suggested that he might have envisioned the fact that he was to soon die but if possible, planned to return to this world. A short time before that fateful day in the No.10 Saloon, Hickok posted a letter to his wife, Agnes. In it he said "Agnes Darling, if such should be we never meet again, while firing my last shot, I will gently breathe the name of my wife--- Agnes---and with wishes even for my enemies I will make the plunge and try to swim to the other shore."

Hickok was buried in Deadwood's Mount Moriah Cemetery but the local legends say that he does not rest there. Many believe that because he died unaware of what was about to happen to him, his confused and angry spirit still walks in Deadwood. In the years since 1876, a shadowy figure has frequently been reported inside of the old No. 10 Saloon, which remains a landmark in Deadwood. Others claim to have seen this figure in the doorway to the building, as if looking out and perhaps seeking someone.

Still othesr claim that his ghost walks in Mount Moriah, along with others who died so violently in this rough town. There have been many sightings of apparitions here and its possible that one of them just might be Wild Bill himself.

Taylor, Troy - No Rest for the Wicked (2001)

Deadwood is located in Lawrence County, near the Wyoming border. There are many places in town that are alleged to be haunted, including the cemetery and the saloon where Hickok was killed.

De Smet

There is perhaps no author as beloved in American history as Laura Ingalls Wilder. When she began writing her classic "Little House" books in 1932, she had no idea that she was creating fame not only for herself but for the places that she had lived as well. She wrote simply to preserve the tales of an era in history, the pioneer period that she so vividly recalled growing up in the Midwest in the 1870's and 1880's. She had no idea she was writing history when fans starting sending letters to her home on Rocky Ridge Farm in Missouri but she had created a legacy that has been embraced by people all over the world.

The town of De Smet is known as "the Little Town on the Prairie" and it provided the locale for the last several of the "Little House" books, including *By the Shores of Silver Lake, The Long Winter, Little Town on the Prairie , These Happy Golden Years, The First Four Years* and the beginning of *On the Way Home.*

The small town was named in honor of Father Pierre Jean De Smet, a Belgian Jesuit Priest, known as "The Apostle of the Indians", and was founded in 1880. It became the final home of the Ingalls family in 1879 when they moved into what has been dubbed the Surveyor's House. It was the oldest structure in town and had originally been a surveying shack for the railroad. The Ingalls spent their first winter here and rented out parts of the house as a hotel for travelers passing through the area. Charles Ingalls began a new home in 1887 and added on to it one room at a time when money allowed. It was finally completed two years later.

The Ingalls remained in De Smet for the rest of their lives and many of the family members are buried in the local cemetery, including Charles, who died in 1902, Carolina (1924), Mary (1928), Carrie (1928), Grace (1941) and an infant son of Laura and Almanzo Wilder, who died in 1889. Laura, Almanzo and daughter their daughter Rose settled in Mansfield, Missouri in 1894.

According to legend, the surveyor's house that the Ingalls first moved into is haunted to this day. The stories tell of strange events and noises as if the family knew such happiness here that they never wanted to leave. The De Smet Graveyard, where the family was laid to rest, is also reportedly haunted. Eerie will o' wisps are often spoken of here, flickering through the trees and tombstones. However, the stories say that it was haunted long before the Ingalls family was buried here. The site has a long Native American heritage and many years of ghost sightings.

Personal Interviews & Correspondence

De Smet is located on the eastern side of the state between Brookings and Huron.

Tennessee

Cleveland

Located in the southeastern Tennessee city of Cleveland is the Saint Luke's Episcopal Church, a historic chapel built in the 1870's. At the rear of the church is a marble mausoleum that, over the years, has attracted curiosity seekers from all over the region. The tomb is the burial place for the Craigmiles family, four members of which died tragically. The white surface of the stone is marred with streaks of crimson stain -- some say the dark color of blood.

John Henderson Craigmiles came to Cleveland from Georgia around 1850. He and his brother, Pleasant, operated a successful mercantile business but John soon grew restless with small town life and traveled west to the California gold fields. He soon discovered that prospecting held little appeal for him, but out west, he did make a discovery that would both change his life and create his fortune. He realized the travel and supply needs of the western territory and soon discovered that a large amount of money could be made in the shipping business. He managed to purchase a small fleet of six ships and began a shipping line between California and Panama. Not only could he trade back and forth between Central America and the West Coast, but he could also carry passengers from the eastern United States who booked passage to Panama and then on to California.

The shipping business prospered for some time, then disaster struck. Mutinous crews hijacked five of John's ships at sea and made off with the vessels and cargo. Claims from his creditors soon wiped out his fortune, but Craigmiles refused to give up. He borrowed $600 from his brother, Green, and set out to rebuild his business with the one ship that he had left. By 1857, he returned in Tennessee, once again a very wealthy man. Soon after his return, John began courting a young woman named Adelia Thompson, the daughter of local doctor, Gideon Blackburn Thompson, and on December 18, 1860, they were married.

A few months after the wedding, the Civil War began. The Secretary of State for the Confederacy, Judah P. Benjamin, recognized John's head for business and appointed him the chief commissary agent for the South. He held this position throughout the entire war and reportedly used it to great advantage. Buying cattle and speculating in cotton, he sold goods to the Confederacy at a profit and made a fortune from the war. He was also wise enough to know that paper money was of little value and only traded in gold. After the defeat of the Confederacy, when the paper money printed in Richmond turned out to be worthless, John was not ruined as many other southern businessmen were.

In August 1864, Adelia gave birth to the couple's first daughter, Nina. John soon became absolutely devoted to the little girl and along with her mother, grandparents and uncles, she became wonderfully spoiled. Perhaps no one loved the little girl more than her grandfather, Dr. Thompson. He took long walks with her in downtown Cleveland, where she was popular with the shopkeepers, and often took her on medical calls in his buggy.

It was during one of these outings that tragedy came to the Craigmiles family. The day was October 18, 1871 and Nina and her grandfather were off on a short jaunt in the buggy. No one knows how the accident happened, but somehow, Dr. Thompson steered the carriage in front of an oncoming train. He was thrown clear but Nina was instantly killed.

The whole town grieved for the little girl. John, Adelia and the entire family were crushed by the loss and could barely function during the funeral services. When it was over, John began making plans to build a church in memory of his daughter. The Episcopal congregation in town had no permanent meeting place and John felt that a new church in Nina's honor would be fitting. The ground was broken the following August and Saint Luke's was completed on October 18, 1874, the third anniversary of Nina's death.

Almost as soon as the brick and stone church was completed, the family began construction on a mausoleum for Nina's body. It was placed at the rear of the church and was built from expensive marble with walls that were four feet thick. A cross tops the marble spire of the tomb and rises more than thirty-seven feet off the ground. Inside of the tomb, six shelves were built into the walls and in the center was a marble sarcophagus, into which Nina's body was placed.

As time passed, the other members of the family followed Nina to the grave. The first to die was an infant son who was born to John and Adelia, but only lived a few hours. He was never named but his body lies in peace next to his sister.

John Craigmiles died in January 1899 from blood poisoning. Apparently, he had been walking downtown one day and slipped and fell on the icy street. An infection developed and turned into blood poisoning. He died a short time later.

Adelia, who married Charles Cross some time after John's death, was also tragically killed in September 1928. She was crossing Cleveland Street when she was struck and killed by an automobile. She was laid to rest with the other members of her family in the mausoleum.

The stories say that the bloody stains first began to appear on the Craigmiles mausoleum after Nina was interred there. With the death of each family member, the stains grew darker and more noticeable. Some of the locals began to believe that the marks were blood, coming from the stone itself, in response to the tragedies suffered by the family. To this day, the bloody-looking marks remain. What may have caused them, and why they refuse to be washed away, remains a mystery.

Taylor, Troy - Beyond the Grave (2003)

Cleveland is located in the extreme southeastern corner of Tennessee and the mausoleum can be found in the churchyard of St. Luke's Episcopal Church on Broad Street.

Surgoinsville

A well known haunted site is this area is referred to by locals as the Old White Oak. It is located in the New Providence Presbyterian Church Cemetery. Here, a huge white oak tree stands in the center of the grounds, surrounded by fallen Confederate soldiers, and even Captain George Maxwell of the Revolutionary War, a veteran of the battle of Kings Mountain in 1780. Over the years, it has been found that many of the strange encounters here occur around this grave.

Many of the encounters concern eerie lights that have been seen coming from the cemetery, strange shapes that appear in photographs and even a mysterious black dog that comes and goes without warning. The cemetery is often reported to be strangely quiet and some visitors here have heard the sounds of footsteps following them through the leaves on the ground but no one is ever there. Two witnesses even reported that on one evening, they actually saw the leaves being pressed down, as if unseen shoes were stepping on them. They became so unnerved that they fled from the cemetery.

On evening in 2002, a motorist named Joyce Summers ran out of gas on a nearby road and went up the hill towards the cemetery for assistance because she thought she saw a light burning in the church by the graveyard. As she came closer though, she saw that the light was not coming from the church windows, but rather from a tombstone in the cemetery. The stone, which bore the name "Pierce", was giving off an eerie glow and yet she saw no lights around that it could be reflecting from. The only street light nearby was not burning at the time. She later stated that she broke into a sweat and ran from the cemetery, feeling as if someone was following her. As she approached her car, she found that to her amazement, it was sitting on the road with the engine running -- even though it had been out of gas just a few minutes before. She glanced back up the hill at the cemetery and suddenly a large street light came on, which lit up the entire hilltop.

Two days later, her mother, Dorothy Pierce, passed away.

Coleman, Jerry - Strange Highways (2003)

Surgoinsville is located in the north central part of Tennessee.

Other Haunted Tennessee Cemeteries

The Old Town Cemetery (Cordova) has been the reported site for "spook lights" for many years. The cemetery is very old and graves here date back as far as the early 1800's. There is no specific legend to explain the lights, other than they are the spirits of those buried here, but they are often reported flashing and flickering in the trees. There is also an alleged glowing tombstone that is marked only as "Susan". On certain nights, witnesses say that it gives off an unearthly and unexplained shine.

One of the most famous ghosts in the south-central Tennessee area, where Jack Daniels is distilled, is said to haunt the Concord Cemetery (Tullahoma). The apparition of a spirit named Sadie Baker has been seen in this graveyard on many occasions and while most will agree that it is her ghost that haunts this place, few can agree on who Sadie was when she was alive. There are different variations of her story that say that she was either a grown woman when she died, or a little girl. There are also versions of the story that say she was anything from a witch to a prostitute. The confusion comes from the fact that a simple stone that bears only her name is marking the site believed to be her grave. No one is even sure about the exact burial either -- years ago, it was considered a test of bravery to steal her tombstone from the cemetery. More confusion comes from the legends of this place, as there are two very different apparitions that have been reported here. One of them is that of a woman and the other a little girl. Both of them are supposed to be Sadie. The woman simply roams through the cemetery and then vanishes. The little girl has been seen playing here, lost in a game of her own imagination. The identities of what may be two very different ghosts have become blurred together over time and now no one can say where one ends and the other begins.

Texas

A Collection of Texas Haunted Cemeteries

One of the strangest stories of any cemetery in Texas involves the fact that there is a allegedly an alien buried in the Masonic Cemetery (Aurora). In 1897, the *Dallas Morning News* published an article that stated that a UFO had sailed over Aurora and had crashed into a windmill that belonged to a Judge Proctor. The explosion that followed destroyed not only the windmill but a water tower and the judge's garden. The craft was supposedly made from a "strange metal" and the records on board were written in an unknown language. The pilot was killed but his remains were not human. He was buried in Aurora on April 18 -- and the story was forgotten. In 1966, it was rediscovered but generally regarded as a hoax until a strange boulder turned up in the cemetery in 1973. It had the vague outline of a circle and three arrows on it and it was thought to possibly be the alien's tombstone. Cemetery officials disagreed and stated that the grave site actually belonged to a man named Carr who had died from spotted fever in the same year as the "crash". They secured an injunction that prevented anyone from digging at the site. About that same time, metal fragments were found at the old crash site but there remains a disagreement over whether or not they have any strange qualities.

There have been many cemeteries across the west that have gone by the name of "Boot Hill" over the years and Concordia Cemetery (El Paso) is one of them. This cemetery is said to be haunted by the ghost of a Spanish lady who mourns at the grave of a particular occupant of the burial ground, the gunfighter, John Wesley Hardin. One of the most savage killers in the Old West, Hardin is credited for the shooting of at least 30 men. He spent 15 years in prison for murder and after he got out, he took a law examination and became an attorney. Three months after hanging out his shingle though, he was shot in the back. He was buried in Concordia Cemetery and his grave remains there today, outlined with red stones. A red flower is consistently placed on his grave but no one knows who the anonymous visitor might be. While likely a flesh and blood person, the stories have inevitably started that the flower is left by a ghost. Some claim that Hardin was courting a beautiful young woman when he was killed and that it is her ghost who leaves the offering after all of these years. In addition to the alleged haunting around Hardin's grave, there are always reports of the ghostly sounds of children laughing in the cemetery near a section that is filled with graves from a smallpox epidemic, as well as the sounds of horse's hooves riding through the grounds.

A young boy is said to be searching for a ride near Evergreen Cemetery (El Paso). According to local stories, many have encountered this young child during the early hours of the morning, trying to flag down cars. Many concerned motorists, who stop when they see a child out at such a strange hour of the night, pull over to the side of the road to try and help him -- only to have him vanish without a trace.

A flickering light from a long-ago lantern is still reported in the Pirtle Cemetery (Kilgore). According to the legend, Kilgore was once the home of a mother and her young son. The boy was deathly afraid of the dark and his mother did all she could to comfort him during lonely nights. In time, the boy became sick and grew weaker each day. There was nothing the doctors could do for him and the boy died. During the funeral services, the story continued. His mother remembered his fear of the dark and how he always wanted lights to be left on. She decided that she would carry a lantern to her son's grave each night so that he would never be afraid. Years later, the nightly ritual came to an end when the mother also died. The stories say that the light continues to be seen though and visitors who come to the cemetery in the evening will still see this ghostly light dancing and flickering among the gravestones here.

Maxdale Cemetery (Maxdale) is reported to be haunted -- both in the cemetery and out. The grounds themselves are said to be haunted by the apparition of a limping man who was believed to have once been the caretaker of the place. There is also a ghost story connected to the narrow iron bridge that visitors have to cross to get into the cemetery. There are in fact, two different versions of the story connected to the bridge. Legend has it that if you stop on the bridge at midnight, turn off your headlights and then turn them back on again, you will see the image of a man hanging from it. This is supposed to be the spirit of a young man who committed suicide here after he was unable to save the life of his girlfriend, who drowned in the river below. The other version of the story has it that the young man committed suicide by driving his truck off the bridge into the river. Because of this, some claim that if you stop on the bridge, then turn your headlights off and on again, you will see a phantom truck appear on the road in the rearview mirror. However, when you look behind you to see if it is really there, it will not appear to the naked eye, only in the mirror.

Baccus Cemetery (Plano) is regarded by many to be one of the most actively haunted cemeteries in North Texas. The beginnings of the cemetery can be traced back to Henry Cook, a legendary Plano settler. Cook moved to Plano, then known as Peter's Colony, in 1845. He set aside some space on his land for a cemetery, and buried his son, Daniel, there in 1847. Cook's daughter, Rachel Cook Baccus, later inherited the cemetery and deeded the burial ground to her heirs in 1878, also donating adjoining land for construction of the Baccus Christian Church Sanctuary. The cemetery was named after the church in 1915. The death roll here includes many founding members of Plano and victims of the fire that wiped out the town in the 1870's. According to area investigators, a number of people have claimed to see an apparition here in recent years. Most often, visitors report cold chills that are difficult to explain and eerie presences that come up behind them and then fade away.

The overgrown graveyard near Stinson Field (San Antonio) is believed to be haunted by the ghost of a Chinese woman -- a real-life anomaly who stood nearly seven feet tall. The woman was teased and badgered mercilessly when she was alive and in the 1930's, committed suicide. For years after her death, an unknown admirer continually placed fresh flowers on her grave but this eventually stopped after the cemetery was abandoned. The woman's ghost has been reported to hover near her gravesite ever since. Needless to say, her towering apparition is a recognizable one.

A headless ghost is said to haunt the Seguin Cemetery (Seguin) and the roadway that leads away from it. Seguin is the county seat of Guadalupe County, north of San Antonio, and was started back in the 1840's. The town was so prosperous raising livestock, peanuts, cotton and corn that it was occupied by Federal troops after the Civil War. The ghost haunts the cemetery, just three blocks from downtown, and has been seen walking down Milan Street, which leads away from it. The road curves but the ghost does not follow it and instead continues on toward the railroad tracks and disappears. Two different versions of the story say that the spirit was either a Confederate soldier who was decapitated or a railroad worker who lost his head in an accident. Either way, the restless spirit is said to be still searching for it today.

The cries of babies are sometimes reported in a cemetery that was once part of the Berechah Home (Tarrant County). The home for unwed mothers was founded by Reverend J.T. Upchurch in 1903 and was designed to minister to runaways and otherwise upstanding young women who suddenly found themselves both pregnant and homeless. Many of the girls who came here had not always received good medical care and so many of the babies born here did not survive. A cemetery was started on the property and after the home was funded and expanded in 1921, remained all too frequently in use. Many of the babies were stillborn or died soon after birth and often, their young mothers died as well. The cemetery became the final resting place for others connected to the home too but for the most part, held the graves of infants. If a mother did not name her child, the marker would be inscribed with only a number and years ago, more than 100 stones could be found in the graveyard with first names of infants and toddlers on them. In 1935, the home was closed and the land sold. It is now a public park and all that remains of the home is the cemetery. There is little to see here, as the grass has covered almost all of the stones that are not above ground -- but on certain nights there is much to hear. Witnesses claim that the sounds of crying children can still be heard coming from the darkness. It is a heartbreaking sound and one that remains with them forever.

Utah

Dixie National Forest

One of the most horrific events in Utah history occurred in September 1857 at a place called Mountain Meadows, a lush, green pasture with sparkling streams that had long been a favorite resting place for weary travelers along the Old Spanish Trail. In 1857, the meadows hosted an encampment of 138 men, women and children from Missouri and Arkansas known as the Fancher party. For reasons unknown, the encampment was attacked by a band of Mormon zealots and Indians and after a three-day siege, and a promise of surrender, the Mormons slaughtered 121 members of the party in cold blood. They spared 17 children because they were too young to remember the massacre.

Almost from the time this massacre took place, it has been seen as a blight on the history of Utah. For years, it was denied that it ever took place, then was grudgingly accepted but remains a carefully avoided subject among those of the Mormon faith. To make matter worse, rumors also ran rampant that the meadow where the massacre occurred was haunted and had been so for years. The bodies of the victims had never really been properly buried and whispers had it that their restless spirits still lingered here.

The Mountain Meadows Massacre was closely tied to the history of the small community that was located nearby called Hamblin. The town was located near the east end of the Mountain Meadows in what is now the Dixie National Forest. Although it was small, its name was destined to become known throughout the country in the years following the massacre. Sadly, it was a young town at the time, having been settled in 1856 by a small band of Mormons led by famed explorer Jacob Hamblin. It grew quickly into a number of cabins and a fort and as all of the homes in town were built on the same street, it did offer some protection from the Indians in the area. After a church and a schoolhouse were built at one end of the street and the Hamblin Co-Op store was built at the other, the street was safely closed off.

After the massacre took place, the children who were not killed were taken to Hamblin until they could be given to Mormon families to raise. Although the events were meant to be kept secret, the story soon shocked the nation and people all over the country heard of Mountain Meadows -- and of course, of Hamblin. Jacob Hamblin, for whom the town was named, had always been a peacemaker and friend to the Indians and to the travelers who passed through the area. He was completely unaware of the tragedy until after it had occurred and then was understandably devastated.

Some said that Mountain Meadows was cursed after this. The springs that once watered the meadow stopped flowing and the grass dried up and was swallowed by the desert. Sagebrush now grew where only grass had been, as though trying to hide the nameless graves. Hamblin tried to survive in spite of it disgrace and for a time, new settlers continued to arrive. A town site was surveyed and enlarged but now its days seemed numbered. Irrigation water came from Meadow Valley Creek but a series of floods in the 1890's cut deeper into the already steep wash until water could no longer be raised up into the fields. People began to leave and before long, Hamblin was a ghost town. And even at that time, rumor had it that the massacre site was haunted -- and now the ghosts of the luckless victims were said to be walking the deserted street of the town too. There is nothing left of it now. Today, a rough dirt road leaves Route 18 and winds its way to the Hamblin cemetery, which is all that remains of the town started by Jacob Hamblin.

As the years have passed, the ghostly tales have continued. The stories still say that the common grave here is haunted at the meadows, as is the cemetery in Hamblin as well. The restless ghosts of the past, both those of the Fancher party and the dead of Hamlin, refuse to rest in peace. Apparitions have been reported here, as well as glowing balls of light that flicker and wander through the tombstones of the cemetery.

Taylor, Troy - Down in the Darkness

The Mountain Meadows Massacre Site is located in the southwestern corner of Utah. Hamblin is a ghost town now -- or rather a ghost cemetery, as that is all that remains. It is located off a dirt road from Route 18, which runs through this region.

Scofield

Near the small town of Scofield was once a much larger city called Winter Quarters. The mine that was located here literally put the city on the map but a horrific disaster destroyed not only the mine, but the town itself. To this day, ghostly events still occur here, including a haunting that has plagued a local cemetery for decades.

The area near Scofield, once known as Pleasant Valley, was a welcoming place in the 1870's. There were a number of settlers who lived in the area, most of whom grazed cattle on the lush grass here. Coal was discovered in the dark canyon beyond the valley in 1875 and two years later, a small mine was opened on the western slopes of the canyon and the coal was transported out along narrow roads. The winter of 1877 came early and was very severe, stranding the miners in the coal pit and keeping them snowbound until the following February. The ordeal led the miners to name their forced camp "Winter Quarters" and this became one of the first commercial coal mines in the state.

The new town became a thriving one and one of the most impressive cities in Utah. It is hard to imagine, from the ruins that remain, just how important this town once was. The business district was said to be more than a mile long and boasted dozens of substantial stone buildings, many of them as fine as any in Salt Lake City. As the mine and the community grew, new and more efficient methods were sought to move the coal from the mines and so the Utah & Pleasant Valley Railroad was constructed, running from Springville to Winter Quarters and Scofield. It connected with the Denver & Rio Grande line in Colton, which was about 20 miles away. Its businesses included Covington's Hotel, Higney's Store and five saloons. The town actually burned and was rebuilt three times but Colton's future as a bustling city was tied directly to that of Winter Quarters. Unknown to both of them, the future was not very bright.

In 1882, the Utah Fuel Company took over the mine and town and it soon became a subsidiary of the Denver & Rio Grande Railroad. The region continued to thrive until 1900, when there were several hundred men in the mines and residents that numbered as high as 1,800. The mine was considered to be the safest in the region and according to reports, was free from the gases that plagued so many other coal operations. But that was not enough to save it from disaster....

On May 1, 1900, an errant spark touched off the fine haze of coal dust deep underground and the Winter Quarters #4 mine exploded with fury. Exactly 100 of the men were killed in an instant and another 99 died from the poisonous afterdamp, making this one of the worst coal mine disasters in history. That one moment of time left 105 widows and 270 fatherless children behind. Men from all over the area descended on the city and began to pull the mutilated bodies of the victims -- and a few survivors -- from the debris. The town's boarding houses, churches, hotels, school and barns were cleared out to receive and identify the victims. As imagined, trying to cope with the disaster stretched the town's resources to the limit. Mistakes were made when the bodies were identified and many of the men were buried under the wrong names. Grave markers were made up in such a hurry that many of the men's names were misspelled on them. When word spread, every available casket in Utah was sent to Winter Quarters. This did not prove to be enough to hold the dead though and another carload had to be sent in from Denver. Almost 150 of the slain miners were buried in the cemetery in nearby Scofield and two special funeral trains carried the rest of the victims to burial grounds in Utah and in other states.

The terrible tragedy cast a pall of sorrow over the entire town and the deaths of the miners seemed to signal the slow death of Winter Quarters. The gloom never lifted, although the mine remained in operation until 1928. The coal became suitable only for inexpensive locomotive fuel though until finally the transportation costs doomed the mine. By 1930, many houses had been moved to Scofield and Winter Quarters was abandoned. Only caved in cellars and broken foundations remain today.

Stories were told about ghosts at Winter Quarters for years. In fact, less than a year after the disaster that claimed so many lives, an article appeared in the *Utah Advocate* newspaper in January 17, 1901. It read:

"The superstitious miners, who are foreigners, have come to the conclusion that the property is haunted, inhabited by a ghost. Several of them have heard strange and unusual noises, and those favored with a keener vision than their fellow workmen have actually seen a headless man walking about the mine and according to their statements have accosted the ghost and addressed it or he.

"At other times the headless man would get aboard the coal cars to which mules and horses are worked and ride with the driver to the mouth of the tunnel when he would mysteriously vanish and again reappear in the mine. Many supposedly intelligent men have claimed this and some twenty-five or forty have thrown up their jobs in consequence.

"These same people and others have seen mysterious lights in the graveyard on the side of the hill where many victims of the explosion of May are buried.. Efforts to ferret out the cause have been fruitless though close observations have been made by reputable citizens of the camp. These lights are always followed by a death, so it is alleged by others than the miners who might be disciples of the supernatural.

"Tombstones where the light appeared have been blanketed but the light remains clear to the vision of those who watch from town."

Taylor, Troy - Down in the Darkness (2003)

Scofield is located in northern Utah, not far from Salt Lake City. The cemetery is located in town. A dirt road leads to the old site of Winter Quarters and is only accessible by foot along an old railroad bed. Ruins of the old Wasatch store still remain in town by the mine was located in the valley ahead. Visitors still claim to hear eerie sounds in the hills and I experienced ghostly happenings myself while camping in this area in 1990.

Other Haunted Utah Cemeteries

The street outside of the Ogden City Cemetery (Ogden) is reportedly haunted by a young woman named Florence, who was killed here years ago. She was sitting on the curb one night, waiting for a ride, when an out of control car came around the corner and struck her. She was killed instantly. Local legend now has it that if you come to the cemetery at night, park outside and then blink your lights three times, she will appear on the roadway, once again looking for a ride.

At the Spanish Fork Cemetery (Spanish Fork), the statue of a weeping woman is said to come to life and cry real tears. The stories say that this monument marks the grave of a woman who died after losing her only child. This statue was placed on the site and shows a woman who is crouched down with one arm extended and the other near her face. On certain nights, it is said that you can hear her in the cemetery weeping and the legend goes on to say that on these nights, the stone statue will start to cry. An examination of the statue does reveal old water markings on the stone. Coincidence?

Vermont

Woodstock

In October of 1890, a story appeared in the *Boston Transcript* newspaper about some events that allegedly took place in Woodstock, Vermont in the 1830's. The article recalled a series of events that were said to have occurred years before, a short time after a local man named Corwin passed away. He was supposed to have died of consumption and there was reason to doubt this --at first anyway. Regardless, he was buried in Cushing Cemetery, where he was laid to rest for all eternity.

Not long after the funeral, Corwin's younger brother also began wasting away. His symptoms were remarkably like his brothers and today, we would assume that he had the same disease. It wasn't long in those days though before someone suggested a more mysterious culprit behind his illness. Rumor had it that the dead Corwin was returning from the grave as a vampire. Many believed that he was feeding off his younger brother's blood, causing his health to slowly fail.

There was only one way to find out for sure and a group of men from town disinterred Corwin's body. To their horror, they soon discovered they were indeed dealing with a supernatural being. The town's doctor, and head of the Vermont Medical College, Dr. Joseph Gallup, examined the body and observed that the "vampire's heart contained its victim's blood". They removed it from the Corwin's chest and destroyed it by heating up an iron pot and cooking the organ until it was in ashes. Most of the town turned out for this macabre event, which ended with the men placing the iron pot into a deep hole in the center of the town square. A stone slab was then placed over it and the area was purified by sprinkling bull's blood over it.

Finally, they forced the ailing, but still living, Corwin brother to drink a horrible concoction that was mixed from blood and the ashes of his dead brother. It was believed this mixture would cure the man of vampirism and stop his body from wasting away. Whether or not it actually worked is anyone's guess, but this was the last report of vampires to ever come from Woodstock.

But it was not the last weird event to be connected to this story. A few years later, several men tried to discover the resting place of the Woodstock vampire. They began digging under the town common and after uncovering several feet, they heard a great roaring noise and the "smell of sulphur began to fill the cavity". Alarmed, they refilled the hole and quickly left.

Citro, Joseph A. - Passing Strange (1996)

Virginia

Fredericksburg

Fredericksburg is said to be one of the most historic cities in America and, according to many, one of the most haunted as well. One could spend weeks tracking down ghost stories and strange reports in Fredericksburg, and you would soon find that the place is a treasure trove for history buffs and supernatural enthusiasts alike. Nearly every building in town claims at least one ghost and many of them are said to have several. It is believed that most of them are spirits from the city's past, as little has changed here in years, remaining virtually the same as it was in colonial times. With that in mind, is it really a surprise that local folks often encounter the ghosts of those long dead?

One Fredericksburg haunting, the Aquia Church and adjoining graveyard, is located about twenty miles north of the city. It is high on a wooded hill that overlooks the town of Stafford and U.S. Highway 1. Since the middle 1700's, this beautiful chapel has withstood the changing force of history from the American Revolution and the War of 1812 to the Civil War. Inside, it has one of the only known triple-deck pulpits and rustic pews that have seen generations of families. These same families may have been the first to realize that there was something strange going on in the church. It soon became a tradition that no one went into the building after dark -- and none dared set foot into the adjacent churchyard.

Construction was started on the church in 1751, but in 1754, it was severely damaged in a fire, just three days before it was to be completed. It took another three years for it to be finished. The hauntings here had their beginnings during the American Revolution. For decades, visitors have reported the sound of feet running up and down stairs, heavy noises of a fierce struggle and even the apparition of a terrified young woman standing at a window.

These frightening events reportedly stem from a night in late 1770's when a woman passing nearby was set upon by thieves. She managed to escape into the darkness and came upon the church. She tried to seek shelter but found that it was empty. The church was not used during the war and in fact, its precious silver, including an old dish, chalice, cup and plates were all buried for safekeeping. After her desperate pounding on the door failed to rouse anyone, she managed to slip the lock and get inside but it was too late. The highwaymen found her hiding place and followed her into the building. Here, she was brutally attacked and killed. They dragged her body to the belfry and left her there, not knowing that it would remain hidden for years. When the skeletal remains were finally discovered, it was said that the woman's golden hair remained intact. Until the early 1900's, when a new cement floor was laid, the bloodstains where she had been slain were clearly visible.

The repeated events of that dark night are the most famous manifestations in the church but they are not the only odd things that happen here. There is another story about a prominent socialite who spent her summers in Stafford County in the 1920's and who became interested in the Aquia chapel because of the ghostly tales that she heard in the area. She decided to go and spend the night in the place, but found that she couldn't get any of the men from the vicinity to go into the chapel with her after dark. She refused to give up her plans and recruited two scientists from Washington who had a shared interest in the supernatural. After darkness fell, they entered the Aquia Church with the socialite leading the way. She had no more than walked in the door though when an unseen hand slapped her sharply across the face! The two men ran inside and searched the place but found no one there. They were unable to provide a logical explanation for what had happened. The mark remained on the woman's face for several days afterward. Could it have been the ghost of the murdered woman?

A much less angry spirit appears in a tale that was told about the church during the Civil War. The story was first told by William Fitzhugh, a Confederate soldier who stopped for rest at the church during a scouting mission. He credited the ghost here for saving the lives of he and another scout in 1863. The two young men had come to the church in search of a place to sleep. They had heard about the chapel being haunted but were too tired to care. At some point during the night, the two men were roused by what Fitzhugh described as "unmistakable footsteps at the rear of the church on some stone flagging". Then they heard someone sharply whistle the tune "The Campbells are Coming". The frightened men jumped up and struck a light, but they were in the place alone. One of them went to the door and looked out and saw a troop of Federal soldiers coming down the road. The soldiers were heading right for the church! They jumped out a window at the back of the chapel and escaped. Fitzhugh never forgot the ghost that saved his life!

Was this the same spirit who also slapped the socialite across the face? And if so, is she also the apparition that has been seen in the old churchyard? According to a former caretaker named Robert Frazier, ghosts are often seen here, flitting among the tombstones and appearing like white, blurry shapes. Frazier and his son recalled numerous sightings over the years in a past interview. Each of the sightings occurred at night and when the two Fraziers went over to see what the figures were, they vanished. Since that time, many other visitors have reported apparitions here as well.

Taylor, Troy - Beyond the Grave (2001)

Fredericksburg is in northeastern Virginia and the church and graveyard are about 20 miles north of the city in Stafford County.

Richmond

The hauntings of Hollywood Cemetery in Richmond are many but perhaps the greatest story involves the former president of the Confederacy, Jefferson Davis, and a little boy who simply died too soon.

Jefferson Davis had been born in Kentucky in 1808 and ironically had been raised just miles away from the early home of Abraham Lincoln. He attended and graduated from West Point in 1828 and was sent to the infantry. He soon fell in love with Sarah Taylor, the daughter of his commander and future president, Zachary Taylor. He left the military in 1835 with a career that was only distinguished by several blow-ups with superior officers. Davis never believed that he had the temperament to be a common soldier. He was a man suited to command and in later years, would have preferred a military command to the presidency of the Confederacy.

Davis left the army and moved to Mississippi, where he helped run the Davis plantation with his brother Joseph. The family had many slaves, but by the standards of those days, treated their slaves quite well. Their food was never rationed, they were allowed to choose their own names and the slave quarters were far above those found on most plantations of the time. However, they were still property and in Davis' eyes, rightfully his under the laws of the Constitution.

In 1835, Davis married Sarah Taylor without the blessing of her parents. Five weeks later, both of them fell ill from malaria, a disease, like yellow fever, not uncommon in the swampy regions of the south. A short time later, Sarah died at the age of 21 and became the first of many tragedies to come in Davis' life.

In 1845, Davis entered the political arena and was elected to Congress as a Democrat. That same year, he married Varina Howell, a beautiful young woman who was half his age. Davis served for one year in the House of Representatives before resigning to lead a group of Mississippi volunteers during the Mexican War. As fate would have it, he found himself with a command under Zachary Taylor, who now greeted him warmly, their differences forgotten in their shared grief over Sarah's death. Davis was wounded at the Battle of Buena Vista and gained a reputation for bravery, which he used to his advantage during the next Senate election. He handily won the seat and remained in office until 1853, when he was named war secretary by President Franklin Pierce.

In 1857, Davis reclaimed his Senate seat and became one of the most forceful advocates of southern rights, regularly threatening secession if those rights were challenged. A few years later, Davis would test the waters for a run at the White House as a Democratic candidate in 1860. At the Baltimore nomination convention, his name was placed under consideration, but

Davis never pressed the issue, knowing that he would never gain enough northern support to win an election.

Later, when the Democrat vote was split between Stephen Douglas and John Breckinridge, they were defeated. Although cautious and still hoping to compromise, Davis pushed for Mississippi's secession. He made an emotional farewell speech to the Senate on January 21, 1861 and then withdrew from his seat with four other senators. He was soon named the commander of the militia in Mississippi and also a compromise candidate for the presidency of the six states that now made up the Confederacy. He was elected on February 9 and inaugurated nine days later in Montgomery. Despite his poor health, an ongoing illness related to the malaria he had contracted years before, he still would have preferred a military command.

The years that would follow Davis' election as the President of the Confederacy would be terrible ones and they weighed heavily on Davis, just as the concerns of the north brutally wore down Abraham Lincoln. And this would not be the only sadness and despair the two men would share during the war....

The home that would serve as the "White House of the Confederacy" was located on Clay Street in Richmond and was built in 1818 by Dr. John Brockenbrough. The house was remodeled in the 1840's, again in 1857, and in 1861, was chosen to serve as the home of Jefferson Davis and his family. When the war had broken out that same year, the capital of the Confederacy was moved from Montgomery, Alabama to Richmond. The city purchased the Brockenbrough house and offered it to Davis as his residence. He declined to take the house for nothing and began renting it instead. The family remained in the house until April 1865, when Richmond was evacuated. It then served as a Union Army headquarters until 1870 and then became a public school. In 1893, the house was purchased by the Confederate Memorial Literary Society and was made into a historical museum, as it remains today.

There is every indication that the Davis family was happy living in this house, despite the pressures of the war and the agonizing hours that President Davis spent working, often until the darkest hours of the night. As time wore on, his health declined to the point that friends and associates urged him to rest and exercise. It was said that Davis' only remedy for the long hours of work was his family. He often said that they eased his mind for precious minutes every day, especially his children, whom he constantly indulged. It was said that many important meetings and consultations, with anyone from General Lee to the presidential staff, would be interrupted by the arrival of the children.

Davis' special favorite was little Joe, who turned five in April 1864. He often remarked that Joe was the hope and greatest joy in his life. Unfortunately, like President Lincoln's favorite son, Willie, that greatest joy was taken away all too soon.

On April 30, 1864, Varina Davis left the children playing while she made lunch for her husband. A short time later, Joe, and his older brother, Jeff, wandered outside and onto the balcony in back of the house. Apparently, Joe was climbing on the railing when he lost his balance and fell to the brick pavement below. The fall fractured his skull and he died a short time later.

Varina became hysterical and it was said that passersby could hear her screaming inside of the house throughout the afternoon and into the evening. President Davis was himself crushed. He sat beside his wife for more than three hours, turning away everyone who called, including a courier with an important message from General Lee. Then, he vanished into the upper floors of the house, where his footsteps could be heard, incessantly pacing back and forth.

Over the course of the next few days, cards and letters flooded the Davis home, including a heartfelt message from Abraham Lincoln, who was returning the gesture extended by Davis when his own son had died. The funeral took place a short time later and the Hollywood Cemetery in Richmond offered a free plot for the boy's burial. An immense crowd gathered at the cemetery on the day of the burial and it was reported that children from all over the city, many of them Joe's playmates, covered the grave with flowers and crosses. The children also collected $40 and bought a monument to place on the boy's burial site which read "erected by the little boys and girls of the southern capital."

The last year that Jefferson Davis spent in Richmond was one of extreme sadness and grief. The house had become a place haunted by the memories of Joe's smiling face, and his horrible death. Davis even had the balcony that the boy fell from removed from the house and destroyed. The only moment of joy the Davis' experienced in the house was the birth of Winnie Davis on June 27, 1864. She would be called the "Daughter of the Confederacy."

On Sunday, April 2, 1865, word reached Davis from General Lee. The army was evacuating the Petersburg and Richmond lines and soon the city would fall. As the Federal forces neared the city, Davis assembled his cabinet and staff and directed the removal of public archives, the treasury, and all records to Danville. Later that afternoon, Davis himself left the city on a special train. In the months and years that followed, Davis endured capture and imprisonment under often barbaric conditions. Not surprisingly, his ghost is believed to haunt old Fort Monroe where he was held.

On May 13, 1867, after two years of confinement, Jefferson Davis was released. He lived on for 24 years after the end of the Civil War, traveling extensively and writing about the "Lost Cause" and its consequences. When he died in 1889, he was buried in Metairie Cemetery in New Orleans, where he had been living. A short time later, Varina Davis had her husband exhumed and moved to Beauvoir, their family home in Mississippi. This did not prove suitable either as the estate was located on a narrow peninsula on the Gulf of Mexico. It was feared that flooding might someday destroy the site and Varina pondered what to do.

At this time, large numbers of Confederate veterans wrote to her and asked that she choose Richmond for her husband's final resting place. Here, in the city's Hollywood Cemetery, he would rest among the honored dead of those who had fought and died for the South. Varina agreed and moved Davis' body to Richmond, aboard a special train, in the Spring of 1893. The trip took several days, stopping frequently in towns across the south so that people could pay their last respects to the Confederacy's first and only president. They arrived in Richmond on May 30 and the coffin was taken to the rotunda of the capitol building, where it lay in state for a day. On May 31, a black hearse, drawn by six white horses, took the coffin to Hollywood Cemetery. It was followed by a band which played "Dixie" and passed along streets which were draped in mourning for the deceased president.

But still the legends persist that Davis does not rest quietly in his honored grave. Down through the years, numerous witnesses have reported sighting apparitions in and around the casemate where Jefferson Davis was confined at For Monroe. Most of the sightings have been of strange mists and energy masses of different shapes and forms but most believe the ghost seen here is that of Davis, perhaps reliving the trying ordeal that he suffered through. There have also been sightings at Hollywood Cemetery as well. Stories tell of a lonely man who stands along near the grave monument and then vanishes.

There are also legends surrounding the ghost of Little Joe Davis. It has been said that for more than 30 years after Jefferson Davis left Richmond, dozens of witnesses reported seeing the apparition of a little boy, who resembled Joe Davis, wandering aimlessly near the Confederate White House on Clay Street in Richmond. The boy was oblivious to passersby and was heard to walk back and forth, muttering "He's gone! He's gone!", just before vanishing in front of startled witnesses. In 1893, when the body of Jefferson Davis was returned to Richmond, and placed in Hollywood Cemetery, the body of Joe Davis was moved and placed beside his father. Strangely enough, the apparition of the little boy who cried "He's gone!" was never seen again.

Taylor, Troy - Spirits of the Civil War (1999)

Richmond is located in the east central part of Virginia and the entrance is on Cherry Street in the city.

Other Haunted Virginia Cemeteries
The old Berkeley Cemetery (Charles City) is the final resting place of the members of the original Berkeley colony and the families of plantation owners from the region. According to the stories, there is a ghost of a young Confederate drummer boy who is seen here. The red-headed young man has often been sighted softly tapping out a beat on his drum as he looks out over the James River.

The McDowell Cemetery (Fairfield) is haunted by what may be ghosts from a massacre that took place on the site many years ago. The cemetery is located at the same place where the Massacre of Balcony Downs took place in 1742. At that time, Captain John McDowell and seven of his militia men were ambushed and slaughtered by a marauding band of Indians. Since that time, reports have circulated from witnesses who have seen a man in a long overcoat walking amongst the tombstones here. There are also accounts of flickering lights that have been seen at night and the sounds of screams that occasionally echo in the darkness.

Wisconsin

A Collection of Haunted Wisconsin Cemeteries
Stories and rumors have long surrounded the Burlington Public Cemetery (Burlington) about apparitions and strange sounds that have been heard here at night. Witnesses claim to have seen human-like figures on pathways in the graveyard, have seen glowing lights and have heard the sounds of voices coming from the darkness when no one is there.

Bantley Cemetery (Canton) is a place of many local legends. Most are likely untrue but even if a fraction of them have any relevance to them, the place must be fairly overrun with ghosts. According to reports, the cemetery was once on land owned by a farmer named Bantley and many years ago, he murdered his entire family and then committed suicide by hanging himself in the barn. A portion of his land was donated as a cemetery when he died and he and his family became the first burials here. The graveyard has been haunted ever since. Apparitions have been sighted here in the daytime and at night, including one of a little girl who is found hiding in a tree just inside of the cemetery. Another local tale involves a boy who came into the cemetery one night on a dare and died of fright after getting his foot tangled on a tree root. He believed that it was a hand grabbing hold of his ankle! His ghost has also been reported here ever since as well.

Glenbeulah Cemetery (Glenbeulah) is an old graveyard from the middle 1800's with numerous family plots, unmarked graves and an iron fence surrounding it that truly conjures up the images of a haunted place. According to stories, the cemetery is haunted by the ghost of a man who hanged himself here many years ago. He now walks the grounds at midnight. There is also said to be a glowing tombstone here that illuminates at certain times of the year. The story has also circulated that the cemetery was featured on the show *Unsolved Mysteries* a few years back, and that investigators experienced ghostly activity during the filming, but I have been unable to verify this.

Another cemetery that has been rumored to be haunted for many years is Dartford Cemetery (Green Lake). Many speak of feeling as though they are being watched and followed while here and of seeing "spook lights" at night on the burial grounds. Strange noises are often heard and apparitions sighted, including those of soldiers and of an Indian. Legend has it that this Indian apparently died while he was drunk. Some friends bet him that he could not swim across the Fox River and he took the dare and drowned. There are also the ghosts of children who haunt a mausoleum on the property. The family was wiped out by an epidemic and the children were all entombed at the same time. Their laughter and cries are sometimes reported here and tradition states that if you sit down on the steps to the crypt, you will be pushed off.

Tabernacle Cemetery (Waukesha) is also alleged to be haunted. Witnesses have reported the apparition of a woman standing next to a tree in the cemetery and have also claimed to see bright flashes of light that appear throughout the tombstones and then float off into the darkness.

Wyoming

Green River

Many places become haunted after being built on top of a burial ground and the Sweetwater County Library in Green River, Wyoming is one such place. The library opened back in 1980 and has gained a reputation for being one of the spookiest locations in the state. This comes as no surprise when you learn that it was constructed on top of the city's oldest cemetery.

The graveyard was started back in the 1860's but most of the area's early citizens rested peacefully in unmarked graves until 1926. It was in that year, as so often happens with old cemeteries, that the town decided to expand and use the land where the cemetery was located. The bodies were exhumed and then moved to the site of the current graveyard. That was the intention anyway, but they soon discovered that a few of the occupants got left behind.

In the 1940's, housing for World War II veterans started being built in the area where the cemetery had been and it soon became obvious that not all of the bodies had been discovered twenty years before. Each time that a new set of bones was found, they were moved to the new graveyard, but many of the workers wondered just how many they might have missed. That question was answered (at least in part) in 1978 when the library purchased the land for a new building. As soon as the groundbreaking took place, workers made more grim discoveries in the form of eight to twelve bodies in unmarked graves.

Work was stopped at the site and city officials were summoned to try and determine the extent of the burial ground. Unfortunately, there were no records or physical clues to say just how many bodies might have been left behind. Workers from the crew started probing the area with hand shovels and discovered pieces of rotted wooden caskets, as well as bits and pieces of human bones. The bones were collected and these remains were also moved to the new cemetery.

Almost as soon as the new library was opened, staff members began experiencing some pretty strange things and unfortunately, the discovery of human remains around the building would continue. This might possibly explain why the building continued to be actively haunted.

In the spring of 1983, landscaping work was done outside the front doors and one of the contractors uncovered what was thought to be old wood. When the landscapers looked closer, they realized they were bones. Since not all of the remains could be removed without tearing up the sidewalks, only portions of the skeletons were reburied in the local cemetery. The rest of the bones remained behind. Also, in 1985, structural work was necessary on the library, as a section of it had started to sink. When the construction crews began drilling into the foundation, one said that they found a small coffin with the body of a child inside. It was said that the body was perfectly preserved, although the "flesh was like gelatin".

Not surprisingly, such grisly finds were unsettling to library staff members, who were also making some strange discoveries of their own. They were beginning to realize that many of the strange sounds and events in the building could not easily be explained away. Library director Helen Higby first heard about the events that other staff members and maintenance workers were already talking about in late summer of 1986. She later described a security gate that people have to pass through when they leave the library. If a book is not checked out properly, an alarm will sound. There was also a bypass gate for people in wheelchairs to pass through. This gate was made from wrought iron and stood a little over waist-high.

Many of the staff members spoke of other events involving electrical disturbances, like lights turning on and off by themselves. One maintenance worker turned off the lights one evening in the multi-purpose room and then returned ten minutes later to find them on again. He was the only person in the building at the time. Another maintenance worker spoke of trying to operate a vacuum cleaner one evening. He was sweeping between the stacks of books and accidentally went too far and pulled the plug from the wall. He then switched it off and went to plug it back in again at a more accessible outlet. After he plugged it back in, he walked back over to machine. Before he could switch it on though, the vacuum turned itself back on again! He immediately turned it off, unplugged it, rolled up the cord and went home for the evening.

Another maintenance worker once heard the voices of a man and woman arguing violently in the multi-purpose room. He could only catch an occasional word, but it was obvious that they were having a very heated discussion. Curious, because he had just passed through that room taking out some trash and no one had been in it, he went to the door and opened it. Immediately, the muffled voices come to an abrupt stop. He looked around but there was no one in the room and no place that anyone could have disappeared to. It turned out later that he was not the only person to hear the voices. One former assistant was so terrified that she refused to talk about them.

As most of the strange events seemed to happen in the evening, director Helen Higby rearranged schedules and made it a rule that no one worked alone. After that, little out of the ordinary was reported, either because the activity stopped or because no one was around in the evening to hear it. But had it really stopped altogether?

One night, not long after the new policy went into effect, the library's business manager came in to do some work on a holiday. As she was going to be by herself, she brought her Doberman pinscher along. After she was in her office for awhile, her dog suddenly stood up and went over to the door. He cocked his head as if someone were outside and then sat back down again. For the rest of the evening, he stared at the door, completely alert, as if someone were in the hallway that his master could not see.

Taylor, Troy - Beyond the Grave (2001)

Green River is located ten miles west of Rock Springs in southwestern Wyoming. The library is located downtown on North First Street.

Other Haunted Wyoming Cemeteries

Amidst the history of the Old West, one graveyard, the Fort Bridger Cemetery (Fort Bridger) only became haunted a few years back, in June 1987. At this time, the apparition of an elderly man in a white cowboy hat began appearing on the grounds. He followed a caretaker around the property and even seemed to help him with his duties on occasion. The worker finally recognized the man as a recently departed old gentleman whose widow still lived in town. The ghost finally left in 1988, the same month that the widow herself died. Some believe that he was simply biding his time until his wife could join him on the other side.

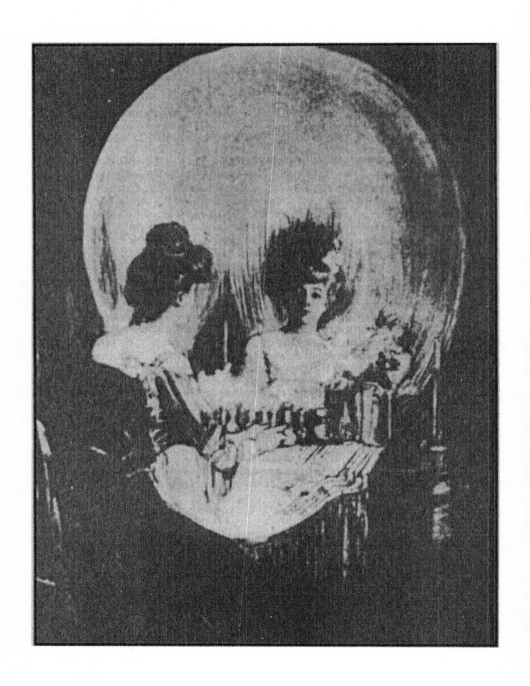

Bibliography

Many of the stories in this field guide first appeared in my book, *Beyond the Grave*, and a complete bibliography from that title is available there. I have attempted to list all of the sources for the material here after the various locations throughout the guide. Any source not listed was unintentional or may have appeared in the list of sources in *Beyond the Grave*.

I owe a special thanks to all of those who submitted stories and locations for the "field guide" section and also to author Sharon DeBartolo Carmarck, who assisted more than she could know on the research sections of the book. Her resources into genealogy were excellent. Also, thanks to Pete Haviland and Chris Moseley for assistance on the Texas sections.

See the Bibliography below for more source materials:

Abbott, Olyve Hallmark - Ghosts in the Graveyard (2002)
Adams, Norman - Dead and Buried? (1972)
Aries, Phillipe - The Hour of Our Death (1981)
Baker, Ronald - Hoosier Folk Legends (1982)
Bielski, Ursula - Chicago Haunts (1998)
Bondeson, Jan - Buried Alive (2001)
Brown, John Gary - Soul in the Stone (1994)
Buscher, David - "In the Statue's Grip" (unpublished)
Carmack, Sharon Bartolo - Your Guide to Cemetery Research (2002)
Colman, Penny - Corpse, Coffins & Crypts (1997)
Curl, James Stevens - Victorian Celebration of Death (2000)
Davies, Rodney - The Lazarus Syndrome (1998)
Edwards, Frank - Strange World (1964)
Enright, D.J. - Oxford Book of Death (1983)
Ghosts of the Prairie Magazine and Internet Website
Guiley, Rosemary Ellen - Encyclopedia of Ghosts and Spirits (2000)
Hauck, Dennis William - Haunted Places: The National Directory (1996/ 2002
Hucke, Matt & Ursula Bielski - Graveyards of Chicago (1999)
Iserson, Kenneth V. - Death to Dust (1994)
Jackson, Kenneth T. & Camilo Jose Vergara - Silent Cities (1989)
Jones, Barbara - Design for Death (1967)
May, Trevor - The Victorian Undertaker (2000)
Meyer, Richard E. - Cemeteries and Gravemarkers: Voices of American Culture (1989)
Miller, C.L. - Postmortem Collectibles (2001)
Mitford, Jessica - American Way of Death (1963)
Montgomery, Kate - "Black Angel of Oakland Cemetery" and correspondence
Murphy, Edwin - After the Funeral (1995)
Orloff, Erica & Jo Ann Baker - The Big Sleep (1998)
Robson, Ellen & Diane Halicki - Haunted Highway (1999)
Taylor, Troy - Confessions of a Ghost Hunter (2002)

Taylor, Troy - Ghost Hunter's Guidebook (2001)
Taylor, Troy - Haunted New Orleans (2000)
Taylor, Troy - Haunted Decatur Revisited (2000)
Taylor, Troy - Haunted Illinois (1999)
Taylor, LB - Ghosts of Fredericksburg (1991)
Terjung, Shara - various articles and correspondence
Ward, Frank - "An Ozark Funeral" / Ghosts of the Prairie (1997)
Wilkins, Robert - Death: A History of Man's Obsessions and Fears (1990)
Williams, Ben and Jean & John Bruce Shoemaker - The Black Hope Horror (1991)
Winer, Richard - Houses of Horror (1983)
Winer, Richard & Nancy Osborn - Haunted Houses (1979)
Winer, Richard & Nancy Osborn Ishmael - More Haunted Houses (1981)

Personal Interviews and Correspondence

ABOUT THE AUTHOR

Troy Taylor is the author of 31 books about ghosts and hauntings in America, including HAUNTED ILLINOIS, THE GHOST HUNTER'S GUIDEBOOK and many others. He is also the editor of GHOSTS OF THE PRAIRIE Magazine, about the history, hauntings & unsolved mysteries of America. A number of his articles have been published here and in other ghost-related publications.

Taylor is the president of the "American Ghost Society", a network of ghost hunters, which boasts more than 600 active members in the United States and Canada. The group collects stories of ghost sightings and haunted houses and uses investigative techniques to track down evidence of the supernatural. In addition, he also hosts a National Conference each year in conjunction with the group which usually attracts several hundred ghost enthusiasts from around the country.

Along with writing about ghosts, Taylor is also a public speaker on the subject and has spoken to well over 500 private and public groups on a variety of paranormal subjects. He has appeared in literally dozens of newspaper and magazine articles about ghosts and hauntings. He has also been fortunate enough to be interviewed hundreds of times for radio and television broadcasts about the supernatural. He has also appeared in a number of documentary films like AMERICA'S MOST HAUNTED, BEYOND HUMAN SENSES, GHOST WATERS, NIGHT VISITORS, GHOSTS OF MIDDLE AMERICA, the television series MYSTERIOUS WORLDS and in one feature film, THE ST. FRANCISVILLE EXPERIMENT.

Born and raised in Illinois, Taylor has long had an affinity for "things that go bump in the night" and published his first book HAUNTED DECATUR in 1995. For seven years, he was also the host of the popular, and award-winning, "Haunted Decatur" ghost tours of the city for which he sometimes still appears as a guest host. He also hosted tours in St. Louis, St. Charles, Missouri and currently hosts the "History & Hauntings Tours" of Alton, Illinois.

In 1996, Taylor married Amy Van Lear, the Managing Director of Whitechapel Press, and they currently reside in a restored 1850's bakery in Alton. Their first child together, Margaret Opal, was born in June 2002. She joins her half siblings, Orrin and Anastasia.

ABOUT WHITECHAPEL PRODUCTIONS PRESS

Whitechapel Productions Press is a small press publisher, specializing in books about ghosts and hauntings. Since 1993, the company has been one of America's leading publishers of supernatural books. Located in Alton, Illinois, they also produce the "Ghosts of the Prairie" Internet web page and "Ghosts of the Prairie", a print magazine that is dedicated to American hauntings and unsolved mysteries. The magazine began its original run from 1997 to 2000 but was revived as a full-cover, bi-monthly magazine in 2003. Issues are available through the website or at the Alton bookstore.

In addition to publishing books and the periodical on history and hauntings, Whitechapel Press also owns and distributes the Haunted America Catalog, which features over 500 different books about ghosts and hauntings from authors all over the United States. A complete selection of these books can be browsed in person at the "History & Hauntings Book Co." Store in Alton and on our Internet website.

Visit Whitechapel Productions Press online and browse through our selection of ghostly titles, plus get information on ghosts and hauntings, haunted history, spirit photographs, information on ghost hunting and much more.
Visit the Internet web page at:

www.historyandhauntings.com

Or visit the Haunted Book Co. in Person at:

515 East Third Street
Alton, Illinois 62002
(618)-456-1086

The Alton Bookstore is home to not only Whitechapel Press and the Haunted America Catalog but is also the home base for the acclaimed History & Hauntings Ghost Tours of the city, which are hosted by Troy Taylor. The bookstore features hundreds and hundreds of titles on ghosts, hauntings and the unexplained, as well as books on American, regional and local history, the Old West, the Civil War and much more.